FROM *God* TO US

FROM *God* TO US

HOW WE GOT OUR BIBLE

NORMAN L. GEISLER
WILLIAM E. NIX

MOODY PUBLISHERS
CHICAGO

Project editor: Jim Vincent
Interior design: Smartt Guys design
Cover design: Thinkpen design
Cover image: © 2012 Otnur Ydur / Shutterstock.com
Willaim Nix photo: Mr. Homer Thornton of Dallas, TX

Photo Credits: Plates 1–2, 7–8, 14–15, 18–21, 23, 25, 29, 32, 37 by Zev Radovan/BibleLandPictures.com; Plates 9–10, 16, 22 by Joseph Harden/Veritas Evangelical Seminary; Plate 11 by Gérard Ducher; Plate 17 by John C. Trever, Ph.D., digital image by James E. Trever; Plate 24 by William E. Nix; Plates 42, 50, 57 by Donald L. Brake Sr.; Plates 45–46, 51–56, 59 by Jim M. Bolton

Library of Congress Cataloging-in-Publication Data

Geisler, Norman L.
From God to us : how we got our Bible / Norman L. Geisler and William
E. Nix.
    p. cm.
Includes bibliographical references and index.
ISBN 978-0-8024-2882-0
1. Bible--Introductions. I. Nix, William E. II. Title.
BS475.3.G45 2012
220.1--dc23
                2012014502

To Chester Woodring Jr.
and
Charles H. Shaw
Beloved mentors in the faith

CONTENTS

PLATES

.

PART ONE

Inspiration

1

THE CHARACTER *of* THE BIBLE

THE BIBLE IS A UNIQUE BOOK. It is one of the oldest books in the world, and yet it is still the world's bestseller. It is a product of the ancient Eastern world, but it has molded the modern Western world. Tyrants have burned the Bible, and believers revere it. It is the most quoted, the most published, the most translated, and the most influential book in the history of humankind.

Just what is it that constitutes this unusual character of the Bible? How did the Bible originate? When and how did the Bible take on its present form? What is meant by the "inspiration" of the Bible? These are the questions that occupy our interest in this introductory chapter.

THE STRUCTURE OF THE BIBLE

The word *Bible* (Book) came into English by way of French from the Latin *biblia* and the Greek *biblos*. It was originally the name given to the outer coat of a papyrus reed in the eleventh century BCE. By the second century CE, Christians were using the word to describe their sacred writings.

THE TWO TESTAMENTS OF THE BIBLE

The Bible has two major parts: the Old Testament and the New Testament. The Old Testament was written and preserved by the Jewish community for a millennium or more before the time of Christ. The New Testament was composed by disciples of Christ during the first century CE.

The word *testament*, which is better translated "covenant," is taken from the Hebrew and Greek words designating a compact or agreement between two parties. In the case of the Bible, then, we have the old contract between God and His people, the Jews, and the new compact between God and Christians.

Christian scholars have stressed the unity between these two Testaments of the Bible in terms of the person of Jesus Christ who claimed to be its central theme.[1] St. Augustine said the New Testament is veiled in the Old Testament, and the Old Testament is unveiled in the New Testament. Or, as others have put it, "The New is in the Old concealed, and the Old is in the New revealed." Again, Christ is enfolded in the Old Testament but unfolded in the New. Believers before the time of Christ looked forward in expectation, whereas present-day believers see the realization of God's plan in Christ.

THE BOOKS OF THE OLD TESTAMENT

The books of our English Old Testament Bible are divided into four sections: Law, History, Poetry, and Prophecy in the following way:

BOOKS OF THE OLD TESTAMENT

The Law (Pentateuch) — 5 books		Poetry — 5 books	
1. Genesis		1. Job	
2. Exodus		2. Psalms	
3. Leviticus		3. Proverbs	
4. Numbers		4. Ecclesiastes	
5. Deuteronomy		5. Song of Solomon	
History — 12 books		**Prophecy — 17 books**	
1. Joshua		**A. Major Prophets**	**B. Minor Prophets**
2. Judges		1. Isaiah	1. Hosea
3. Ruth		2. Jeremiah	2. Joel
4. 1 Samuel		3. Lamentations	3. Amos
5. 2 Samuel		4. Ezekiel	4. Obadiah
6. 1 Kings		5. Daniel	5. Jonah
7. 2 Kings			6. Micah
8. 1 Chronicles			7. Nahum
9. 2 Chronicles			8. Habakkuk
10. Ezra			9. Zephaniah
11. Nehemiah			10. Haggai
12. Esther			11. Zechariah
			12. Malachi

---

1.   See Norman L. Geisler, *A Popular Survey of the Old Testament* (Grand Rapids: Baker, 2006), chap. 2.

THE BOOKS OF THE NEW TESTAMENT

The New Testament is also divided into four sections: Gospels, History, Epistles, and Prophecy.

BOOKS OF THE NEW TESTAMENT

Gospels	History
1. Matthew 2. Mark 3. Luke 4. John	1. Acts of the Apostles

Epistles	
1. Romans	12. Titus
2. 1 Corinthians	13. Philemon
3. 2 Corinthians	14. Hebrews
4. Galatians	15. James
5. Ephesians	16. 1 Peter
6. Philippians	17. 2 Peter
7. Colossians	18. 1 John
8. 1 Thessalonians	19. 2 John
9. 2 Thessalonians	20. 3 John
10. 1 Timothy	21. Jude
11. 2 Timothy	

Prophecy
1. Revelation

THE SECTIONS OF THE BIBLE

The fourfold division of the Old Testament is based on a topical arrangement of books stemming from the translation of the Hebrew Scriptures into Greek. This translation known as the Septuagint (LXX) was begun in the third century BCE. The Hebrew Bible does not follow this fourfold topical classification of books. Instead, a threefold division is employed, possibly based on the official position of the author. Moses, the lawgiver, has his five books listed first (Law, *Torah*); these are followed by the books of men who held the prophetic office (Prophets, *Nebhi'im*). Finally, many believe that the third section contained books by men who were believed to have had a prophetic gift but who did not hold a prophetic office (Writings, *Kethubhim*). Hence, the Hebrew Old Testament has the following structure:

THE HEBREW OLD TESTAMENT ARRANGEMENT

The Law (Torah)	The Prophets (Nebhi'im)	The Writings (Kethubhim)
1. Genesis 2. Exodus 3. Leviticus 4. Numbers 5. Deuteronomy	**A. Former Prophets** 1. Joshua 2. Judges 3. Samuel 4. Kings **B. Latter Prophets** 1. Isaiah 2. Jeremiah 3. Ezekiel 4. The Twelve	**A. Poetical Books** 1. Psalms 2. Proverbs 3. Job **B. Five Rolls (Megilloth)** 1. Song of Songs 2. Ruth 3. Lamentations 4. Esther 5. Ecclesiastes **C. Historical Books** 1. Daniel 2. Ezra–Nehemiah 3. Chronicles

SOURCE: This is the arrangement in modern Jewish editions of the Old Testament. See *TANAKH: A New Translation of THE HOLY SCRIPTURES According to the Traditional Hebrew Text*, NJV, NJPS (Philadelphia: Jewish Publication Society, 1962, 1985, 1999, 2001).

The earliest arrangement of the Jewish Bible was twofold: Law and Prophets. It is alluded to in Zechariah 7:12 and in Daniel 9:2, 6, 11, 13. It is used in the intertestamental period (2 Macc. 15:9), in the Qumran Community (Manual of Discipline 9.11), and repeatedly in the New Testament (cf. Matt. 5:17; Luke 16:31). Indeed, in Luke 24:27 the Law and Prophets are called "all the Scriptures." It is generally agreed that the earliest possible testimony to it is the prologue to the Book of Sirach, or Ecclesiasticus,[2] during the second century BCE, though it is not called "the Writings" but simply refers to "others books of our fathers" which may or may not even have been inspired books.

The reference to a third division began in the first century. Jewish historian Josephus called this section "four books [that] contain hymns to God and precepts for the conduct of human life" (*Against Apion*, 1.8). It was not until the subsequent Jewish Mishnah (*Baba Bathra*) in the fifth century CE that the current threefold division of the Jewish Old Testament with eleven books of the Writings was crystallized. Some see a hint of a threefold

---

2. The "Book of the All-Virtuous Wisdom of Jesus ben Sira" is also called the "Wisdom of Sirach" or simply "Sirach," "Ecclesiasticus," or "Siracides."

division in Jesus saying that "everything written about me in the Law of Moses and the Prophets and the Psalms must be fulfilled" (Luke 24:44). However, first of all, this is not likely since Luke had just referred to a twofold division of Law and Prophets being "all the Scriptures" (Luke 24:27). Second, he does not call it the Writings (which had eleven books). Finally, he probably singled out the Psalms here because of their messianic significance which he is stressing in this passage.

However, since the time of the Mishnah, Judaism has maintained a threefold division to date; Jerome's Latin Vulgate and subsequent Christian Bibles have followed the more topical fourfold format of the Septuagint. Combining this division with the natural and widely accepted fourfold categorization of the New Testament, the Bible may be cast into the following overall Christocentric structure:

STRUCTURE OF THE BIBLE

Old Testament	Law	Foundation for Christ
	History	Preparation for Christ
	Poetry	Aspiration for Christ
	Prophecy	Expectation of Christ
New Testament	Gospels	Manifestation of Christ
	Acts	Propagation of Christ
	Epistles	Interpretation and Application of Christ
	Revelation	Consummation in Christ

Although there is no divinely authoritative basis for viewing the Bible in an eightfold structure, the Christian insistence that the Scriptures be understood Christocentrically is firmly based on the teachings of Christ. Some five times in the New Testament, Jesus affirmed Himself to be the theme of Old Testament Scripture (Matt. 5:17; Luke 24:27, 44; John 5:39; Heb. 10:7). In view of these statements, it is natural to view the eightfold topical arrangement of Scripture in terms of its one theme—Christ.

CHAPTERS AND VERSES IN THE BIBLE

The earliest Bibles have no chapter and verse divisions (see discussion in chap. 12). These were added for convenience in quoting the Scriptures. Stephen Langton, a professor at the University of Paris and later Archbishop of Canterbury, is credited with dividing the Bible into chapters in 1227. Verses were added in 1551 and 1555 by Robert Stephanus, a Paris printer. Happily,

Jewish scholars since that time have adopted the same chapter and verse divisions for the Old Testament.

THE INSPIRATION OF THE BIBLE

The most significant characteristic of the Bible is not its formal structure but its divine inspiration. The Bible's claim to be divinely inspired must not be misunderstood. It is not poetic inspiration but divine authority that is meant when we speak of the inspiration of the Bible. The Bible is unique; it is literally "God-breathed." Now let us examine what this means.

INSPIRATION DEFINED

The word *inspiration* (Gk., *theopneustos*) is used only once in the New Testament (2 Tim. 3:16), and it refers to the Old Testament writings as being "breathed out" by God. Jesus used another phrase when He referred to the Old Testament as "every word that comes from the mouth of God" (Matt. 4:4). David said, "The Spirit of the Lord speaks by me; his word is on my tongue" (2 Sam. 23:2).

Biblical Descriptions of Inspiration

Paul wrote to Timothy, "All scripture is inspired by God and is profitable for teaching, for reproof, for correction, and for training in righteousness" (2 Tim. 3:16 RSV). That is, the Old Testament Scriptures or writings are "God-breathed" (Gk., *theopneustos*) and, therefore, authoritative for the doctrine and practice of the believer. A kindred passage in 1 Corinthians 2:13 (RSV) stresses the same point. "And we impart this," wrote Paul, "in words not taught by human wisdom but taught by the Spirit, interpreting spiritual truths to those who possess the Spirit." Words taught by the Holy Spirit are divinely inspired words.

The second great passage in the New Testament on the inspiration of the Bible is 2 Pet. 1:21 (RSV). "No prophecy ever came by the impulse of man, but men moved by the Holy Spirit spoke from God." In other words, the prophets were men whose messages did not originate with their own impulse but were "Spirit-moved." By revelation God spoke to the prophets in many ways (Heb. 1:1): angels, visions, dreams, voices, and miracles. Inspiration is the way God spoke through the prophets to others. The fact that the prophets searched their own writings to see "what person or time the

Spirit of Christ in them was indicating when he predicted the sufferings of Christ and the subsequent glories" (1 Pet. 1:11) is a further indication that their words were not ultimately self-initiated.

Combining the classical passages on inspiration, we find that the Bible is inspired in the sense that Spirit-moved men wrote God-breathed words that are divinely authoritative for Christian faith and practice. Let us now analyze these three elements of inspiration more closely.

Theological Definition of Inspiration

Properly speaking, it is only the product that is inspired, not the persons. The single time the New Testament uses the word *inspiration*, it is applied only to the writings and not to the writers. It is the Bible that is inspired and not the human authors. The writers spoke and undoubtedly wrote about many things, such as those in the mundane affairs of life, which were not divinely inspired. However, since the Holy Spirit did, as Peter said, move upon the men who produced the inspired writings, we may by extension refer to inspiration in a broader sense. This broader sense includes the total process by which Spirit-moved men uttered God-breathed and hence divinely authoritative words. It is this total process of inspiration which contains three essential elements: divine causality, prophetic agency, and written authority.

Divine Causality. God is the Prime Mover in the inspiration of the Bible. It is the divine which moved the human. God spoke to the prophets first and then through them to others. God revealed, and spokespersons of God recorded, the truths God revealed. Finally, the people of God recognized the prophetic message. That God is the ultimate source and original cause of biblical truth is the first and most fundamental factor in the doctrine of inspiration. Nevertheless, it is not the only factor.

Prophetic Agency. The prophets who wrote Scripture were not automatons. They were more than mere recording secretaries. They wrote with full intent and consciousness in the normal exercise of their own literary styles and vocabularies. The personalities of the prophets were not violated by a supernatural intrusion. The Bible which they wrote is the Word of God, but it is also the words of humans. God used their personalities to convey His propositions. The prophets and/or their amanuenses (cf. 1 Pet. 5:12) were the immediate cause of what was written, but God was the ultimate cause.

Written Authority. The final product of divine authority working through the prophetic agency is the written authority of the Bible. The Scriptures are "profitable for teaching, for reproof, for correction, and for training in righteousness" (2 Tim. 3:16). The Bible is the last word on doctrinal and ethical matters. All theological and moral disputes must be brought to the bar of the written Word. The Scriptures derive their authority from God through His prophets. Thus, it is the prophetic writings and not the writers as such which possess and retain the resultant divine authority. The prophets have died; the prophetic writings live on.

In brief, an adequate definition of inspiration must have three fundamental factors: God the Prime Mover, men of God as the secondary causes, and a divinely authoritative writing as the final result.

SOME IMPORTANT DISTINCTIONS

Inspiration Distinguished from Revelation and Illumination

Two related concepts which help to clarify by contrast what is meant by the process of inspiration are revelation and illumination. The former deals with the disclosure of truth, the latter the discovery of that truth. Revelation involves the unveiling of truth, illumination the understanding; but inspiration as such involves neither. Revelation concerns the origin and giving of truth; inspiration the reception and recording of it; illumination the subsequent apprehension and understanding of it. The inspiration which brings a written revelation to men is not in itself a guarantee that they will understand it. Illumination of the mind and heart is necessary. Revelation is an objective disclosure; illumination is the subjective understanding of it; inspiration is the means by which the revelation became an objective disclosure. Revelation is the fact of divine communication, inspiration is the means, and illumination is the gift of understanding that communication.

Inspiration of the Original, Not the Copies

The inspiration and consequent authority of the Bible does not automatically extend to every copy and translation of the Bible. Only the autographic texts themselves (or perfect copies of them) are inerrant (without error). Every other copy is inspired only insofar as it is an accurate reproduction of the original. Mistakes and changes made in copy and translation cannot claim this original inspiration. Second Kings 8:26, for example, says that Ahaziah was twenty-two years old at his coronation, whereas 2 Chronicles 22:2 (RSV) says he was forty-two years old. Both cannot be correct. Only the original and not the scribal error is authoritative. Other examples of this type can be found in present copies of the Scriptures (e.g., cf. 1 Kings 4:26 and 2 Chron. 9:25). A translation or copy, then, is authoritative only to the extent that it accurately reproduces the original text.

As we shall see later, the original text has been copied more accurately than any book from the ancient world. The mistakes in the copies are minor and do not affect any major doctrine of Scripture. Exactly how accurately the Bible has been copied will be discussed later (chap. 15) under the science of textual criticism. For now it is sufficient to note that the great doctrinal and historical content of the Bible has been transmitted down through the centuries without substantial change or loss. So, subsequent or current copies and translations of the Bible do not possess original inspiration, but they have a derived inspiration insofar as they are faithful copies of the autographs. Technically speaking, only the autographic text is actually inspired, but for all practical purposes present-day English Bibles, in that they are accurate translations of the original, are the inspired Word of God.

Since the autographs do not exist, how we know that the original text was without error? The answer is found in two Bible teachings: (1) God cannot lie (Heb. 6:18; Titus 1:2), and (2) the Bible is the written Word of God (John 10:35). Therefore, the Bible is without error. Since inspiration means the Bible was "breathed-out by God" (2 Tim. 3:16) and God cannot breath-out error, then it must be errorless. Since the Scriptures are "every word that comes from the mouth of God" (Matt. 4:4), and no error can proceed out of Him who is truth itself, it follows that the original text—which was breathed out by God—is perfect (Ps. 19:7).

The Bible claims to be an utterance of God who cannot make mistakes. And even though no originals have ever been discovered, neither has anyone ever discovered a fallible autograph that could falsify the claim for infallible autographs. What we do have are very accurately copied manuscripts that have been adequately translated into English. Hence, for all matters of doctrine and duty, today's Bible is an adequate representation of the authoritative Word of God.

But if we do not have the original texts of the Bible, then how can we know what it says? The simple answer is that it can be reconstructed accurately from the copies we have. For example, suppose a teacher read a statement from a piece of paper and asked her class to copy it down. From these copies she could reconstruct the original because where they differed would reflect the different errors that different students made. But where they agreed, they would reflect what the original said. Although it is more complicated than this, the process is called the science of textual criticism and is discussed in more detail later (see chap. 14).

Actually, even a text with errors can convey 100 percent of the truth of the original. For example, if a person received the following message (with the error in it), he would still be sure of 100 percent of the original message:

Y#U HAVE WON 20 MILLION DOLLARS.

And if they received this message (with another error in it), they would be even more sure of the original (because of the confirmation that the # should have been an "O" in the first message):

Y#U HAVE WON 20 MILLION DOLLARS.
YO# HAVE WON 20 MILLION DOLLARS.

Actually, the more errors like this, the more we would be sure of the original. For with every error, we get another confirmation of every other letter. And, as we will see, the Bible has fewer copyist errors than this illustration. Plus, in any event, even with the errors, 100 percent of the original message comes through.

Inspiration of the Teaching but Not All It Records

It is also essential to note that only what the Bible teaches is inspired and without error; not everything the Bible records is errorless. For example, the Scriptures contain the record of many evil and sinful acts, but they do not commend any of these. Instead, they condemn such evils. The Bible even records some of the lies of Satan (e.g., Gen. 3:4). It is not thereby teaching that these lies are true. The only thing that inspiration guarantees here is that this is a true record of a lie Satan actually told. The Bible records many things which it does not recommend, such as the assertion "there is no

God" (Ps. 14:1).

In summation, the Bible is an unusual book. It is composed of two testaments which contain sixty-six books claiming divine inspiration. By inspiration is meant that the original texts of the Bible were given by revelation of God and are thereby invested with absolute authority for Christian thought and life. This means that whatever is taught in the Bible is for the Christian the final court of appeal. And although we don't have the original manuscripts, we have accurate copies by which it can be reconstructed. So, even though technically only the original text was perfect and errorless, nonetheless, the Bible in our hands today is an accurate copy of it, and it conveys 100 percent of the essential truths of the original text.

2

THE NATURE *of* INSPIRATION

THE FIRST GREAT LINK in the chain of communication from God to us is inspiration. There are several theories about inspiration, some of which fall short of the biblical teaching on the subject. Our purpose in this chapter will be twofold: first, to examine these theories about inspiration, and second, to determine precisely what is implied in the teaching of the Bible as to its own inspiration.

SEVERAL THEORIES ABOUT INSPIRATION

Historically, theories about the inspiration of the Bible have varied with the essential characteristics of the three theological movements: orthodoxy, modernism, and neoorthodoxy. Although these three views are not limited to one time period only, their primary manifestation is characteristic of three successive periods in the Christian church.

For most of church history the orthodox view held sway, namely, the Bible is the Word of God. The same historical perspective is demonstrated among Baptists in *Baptists and the Bible*, which reflects the perspective of the present study.[1] With the rise of modernism many came to believe that the Bible merely contains the Word of God. Even more recently, under the influence of contemporary existentialism, neoorthodox theologians have held the Bible to be merely a fallible human witness to the Word of God (who is Christ).

1. L. Russ Bush and Tom J. Nettles, *Baptists and the Bible* (Chicago: Moody, 1980).

Orthodoxy: The Bible *Is* the Word of God

For some eighteen centuries of church history the orthodox view of inspiration prevailed.[2] With only minor dissenting voices, the great fathers of the church held firmly that the Bible is the Word of God written down. Orthodox theologians through the centuries have agreed that the Bible is verbally inspired, i.e., the written record came by God's inspiration.

However, attempts to seek an explanation as to just how the written record can be God's Word when it was obviously composed by human authors with differing styles has led to two opposing views among orthodox thinkers. On the one hand, some have held to "verbal dictation," arguing that the biblical authors wrote only what God dictated word for word. On the other hand, some have opted for the "inspired concept" theory that God only gave the thoughts which the prophets were free to put into their own words. Both of these views are contrary to the biblical description of inspiration.

Verbal dictation. A clear presentation of verbal dictation is found in John R. Rice's *Our God-Breathed Book—The Bible*.[3] While he disclaims mechanical dictation, Rice defends verbal dictation. In order to accomplish His word-for-word inspiration, Rice argues that God gave the dictation through the personality of the author. For God by His special province formed the very personalities upon which the Holy Spirit was later to call for His word-for-word dictation. Thus, argued Rice, God had prepared in advance the particular styles He desired in order to produce His exact words by using the predetermined vocabularies and styles of the different human authors. The final result, then, is a word-for-word verbal dictation of God in Holy Scripture.

Inspired concepts. On the other end of the spectrum, scholars like Jack Rogers[4] of Fuller Seminary and the late Clark Pinnock[5] argue for a more organic type of inspiration wherein God gave only the concepts and the

---

2. See John Hannah, ed., *Inerrancy and the Church* (Chicago: Moody, 1984); and Norman L. Geisler, *Systematic Theology*, vol. 1 (Grand Rapids: Baker, 2002), chaps. 17–18.

3. John R. Rice, *Our God-Breathed Book—The Bible* (Murfreesboro, Tenn.: Sword of the Lord, 1969).

4. Jack Rogers, ed. *Biblical Authority* (Waco, Tex: Word, 1978); Clark Pinnock, *The Scripture Principle*, 2nd ed. (Grand Rapids: Baker, 2006).

5. Pinnock, *The Scripture Principle*. See a critique of Pinnock's view in John D. Morrison, "Scripture as Word of God: Evangelical Assumption or Evangelical Question?" *Trinity Journal* 20, no. 2 (fall 1999): 165–190, esp. 176–181.

human authors were free to express them in their own words. God inspired only the concepts and not the particular literary expression into which each biblical author cast them.[6] God gave the thoughts to the prophets who were at liberty to put them into their own terms. In this way Rogers hoped to avoid any mechanical implications of verbal dictation and still preserve the divine origin of the Scriptures. God provided the conceptual inspiration and the men of God gave it a verbal expression characteristic of their own styles.

Modernism: The Bible *Contains* the Word of God

Along with the rise of German idealism and biblical criticism (see chap. 14), a new view of biblical inspiration evolved with theological modernism, or liberalism. In contrast to the traditional orthodox view that the Bible *is* the Word of God, the modernists contend that the Bible merely *contains* the Word of God. Certain parts of the Bible are divine and true, but other parts are clearly human and in error. They feel the Bible is a victim of its times like any other book. They say that many of the legends, myths, and false beliefs about science were incorporated into the Bible. They argue that since these are not inspired of God, they must be rejected by enlightened men as remnants of a primitive mentality unworthy of Christian belief. Only the divine truths contained within this admixture of ancient ignorance and error are truly inspired of God.

Illumination view. Some argue that the "inspired sections" of the Bible result from a kind of divine illumination wherein God granted deep religious insight to pious men. These insights were enjoyed with varying degrees of understanding and were recorded with admixtures of erroneous religious lore and scientific belief common to their day. Hence, the Bible expresses degrees of inspiration dependent on the depth of religious illumination which the author experienced.

Intuition view. On the other end of the modernistic camp are those who deny any divine element in the Bible whatsoever. To them the Bible is merely a Jewish scrapbook of legends, stories, poems, etc., with no essential historical value.[7] What others call divine inspiration is nothing but intensive

---

6.   See A. H. Strong, *Systematic Theology*, 3 vols. (Grand Rapids: Revell, 1907); also see Carl F. H. Henry, *Personal Idealism and Strong's Theology* (Wheaton, Ill.: Van Kampen, 1951); and Bush and Nettles, *Baptists and the Bible*, 265–73, 360.

7.   See Harold DeWolf, *The Case for Theology in Liberal Perspective* (Philadelphia: Westminster, 1959).

human intuition. Within this Jewish folklore known as the Bible may be found some significant examples of heightened moral and religious genius. But these spiritual insights are purely naturalistic. In no sense are they anything more than human intuition; there is no supernatural inspiration or illumination.[8]

A Divine Lure or Resonance. Some liberal process theologians, like Lewis Ford, believe that "revelation" is not supernatural but only a divine "lure," or an attempt to persuade men. As such, "God becomes the great improvisor and opportunist seeking at every turn to elicit his purpose from every situation."[9] So, "what Christian revelation reveals to man is nothing new, since such truths as it makes explicit must already be known to him implicitly in every moment of existence."[10]

Jerry Korysmeyer described "revelation" as resonance, saying, "In keeping with Whitehead's premise to start from human experience in the world, I propose as a model for revelation an analogy with the physical phenomenon of resonance." He describes this resonance as a physical phenomenon shown by a vibrating system, which responds with maximum amplitude "under the action of a force applied with a frequency that is a natural frequency of the vibrating body."[11]

Neoorthodoxy: The Bible *Witnesses* to the Word of God

At the beginning of the twentieth century, the turn of world events and the influence of the Danish father of existentialism, Søren Kierkegaard, gave rise to a new reformation within European theology. Many began to turn again to the Scriptures to hear the voice of God. Without giving up their critical views of the Bible, they began to take seriously the Bible as the locus of God's revelation to man. In a kind of new orthodoxy they affirmed that God speaks to them through the Bible; the Scriptures become the Word of God to them in a personal encounter.[12]

8. See Geisler, *Systematic Theology,* chap. 20.

9. Lewis Ford, "Biblical Recital and Process Philosophy," *Interpretation* 26, no. 2 (1972): 206.

10. Shubert Ogden, *The Reality of God and Other Essays* (San Francisco: Harper, 1963).

11. Jerry Korysmeyer, "Resonance Model for Revelation," in *Process Studies* 6 (fall 1976): 195.

12. See Donald Macpherson Baillie, *God Was in Christ* (New York: Scribners, 1948), for a view applied to neoorthodox Christology similar to John Baillie, *The Idea of Revelation in Present Thought* (N.Y.: Columbia Univ. Press), 1956. Also see Morrison, "Scripture as Word of God," 185–88.

Like the other theories on the inspiration of the Bible, neoorthodoxy developed two wings. On the more critical extreme are the demythologists, who deny any religiously significant historical or factual content in the Bible and hold only to the existential religious care beneath the myths. On the other hand, the more evangelical thinkers try to preserve much of the historical and factual data of Scripture but argue that the Bible as such is not God's revelation. Rather, God reveals Himself through the Bible in personal encounter, but not in a propositional way.

The demythological view. Rudolf Bultmann and Shubert Ogden are characteristic representatives of the demythological view.[13] They differ chiefly in that the latter sees no historical core beneath the myths of the Bible although the former sees some. Both agree that the Bible is written in the mythological language of its day, which is passé. The task of the modern Christian is to demythologize the Bible, i.e., to strip it of this legendary form and to find the existential core beneath it. Bultmann says that once the Bible is divested of these religious myths, one arrives at the real message of God's self-giving love in Christ. It is not necessary to hold to an objective, historical, and propositional revelation in order to experience this subjective and personal truth. Hence, the Bible becomes God's revelation to us when by a proper (i.e., demythological) interpretation one is confronted with absolute love as set forth in the myth of God's selfless love in Christ. Thus, the Bible in itself is no revelation at all; it is a primitive, mythological expression through which God is personally revealed when it is correctly demythologized.

A personal encounter. The other wing of neoorthodoxy, represented by men like John Baillie, Karl Barth,[14] and Emil Brunner, moves closer to the orthodox view of Scripture.[15] Acknowledging that there are some imperfections in the written record (even in the autographs), Barth nevertheless contends that the Bible is the locus of God's revelation.[16] He says that God speaks to us through the Bible; it is the vehicle of His revelation. Just as the

---

13. Rudolf Bultmann, *Kerygma and Myth: A Theological Debate* (London: Billing & Sons, 1954).

14. Baillie, *The Idea* 29-30, passim.

15. See Donald Macpherson Baillie, *God Was in Christ* for a similar view to John Baillie applied to neoorthodox Christology. Also see Morrison, "Scripture as Word of God," 185-88.

16. Karl Barth, *Church Dogmatics*, vol. 1, *Doctrine of the Word of God* (Naperville, Ill.: Allenson, 1956), 592-95.

dog hears his master's voice through the imperfect phonograph recording, so the Christian can hear God speak through errant Scripture. Brunner asserts that God's revelation is not propositional (i.e., in the words) but
always personal (in the Lord Jesus Christ).[17] The Bible as such is not a revelation but only a record of God's personal revelation to men of God in other
ages. However, when modern men encounter God through the Scriptures,
the Bible has become the Word of God to them. In contrast to the orthodox
view, the Bible is not an inspired record for the neoorthodoxy theologians.
Instead, it is an imperfect record which, nonetheless, is the unique witness to
God's revelation. When God breaks through the written record in a personal
way to speak to the reader, then the Bible at that moment *becomes* the Word
of God to him.

THE BIBLICAL TEACHING ABOUT INSPIRATION

Many objections have been leveled at the various theories of inspiration
from different viewpoints with varying degrees of legitimacy, depending on
the vantage point taken. Since the purpose of this study is to understand
the character of the Bible, the criterion here will be to evaluate all these theories in the light of what the Scriptures reveal about their own inspiration.
Let us begin with what the Bible formally teaches and then look at what is
logically implied in this teaching.

What the Bible Teaches about Its Own Inspiration

In the preceding chapter we have already examined in general the teaching
of the two great texts of the New Testament on the subject of inspiration
(2 Tim. 3:16 and 2 Pet. 1:21). The Bible claims to be a divinely authoritative book resulting from a process whereby Spirit-moved men wrote God-
breathed words. Now let us examine in detail what is meant by this claim.

Inspiration is verbal. Whatever else may be claimed about the Bible, it is
clear that the Bible claims a verbal inspiration for itself. The classical text
in 2 Timothy 3:16 declares that it is the *graphā* or writings that are inspired.
"Moses wrote down all the words of the Lord" (Ex. 24:4). Isaiah was told to
"inscribe in a book" God's everlasting message (Isa. 30:8). David confessed,
"The Spirit of the Lord speaks by me; his word is on my tongue" (2 Sam.

17. Emil Brunner, *Theology of Crisis* (New York: Scribner, 1929), 41.

23:2). It was the word of the Lord which came to the prophets hundreds of times in the Old Testament. Jeremiah was told, "diminish not a word" (Jer. 26:2 KJV).

In the New Testament Jesus and the apostles stressed the recorded revelation by the oft repeated phrase, "it is written" (see Matt. 4:4, 7, 10). The apostle Paul testified that he spoke in "words . . . taught by the Spirit" (1 Cor. 2:13). John warned not to subtract from the "words of . . . this prophecy" of his revelation (Rev. 22:19). The Scriptures (i.e., writings) of the Old Testament are continually referred to as the Word of God (cf. Matt. 5:17; 15:3, 6; John 10:35). In the famous Sermon on the Mount Jesus declared that not only the very words but even the smallest part of a Hebrew word was from God: "For truly, I say to you, till heaven and earth pass away, not an iota, not a dot, will pass from the Law until all is accomplished" (Matt. 5:18 RSV). Whatever may be theorized about the inspiration of Scripture notwithstanding, it is clear that the Bible claims for itself verbal or written authority. Its very words are said to be from God.

Inspiration is plenary. The Bible claims to be inspired in all its parts. Inspiration is plenary or full. "All scripture is given by inspiration by God" (2 Tim. 3:16 KJV). No part of Scripture is without full doctrinal authority. For the whole Old Testament, wrote Paul, "is profitable for doctrine, for reproof, for correction, for instruction in righteousness" (2 Tim. 3:16 KJV). Again, he wrote, "Whatever was written in former days was written for our instruction" (Rom. 15:4). Jesus and New Testament writers amply illustrate their belief in the full and complete inspiration of the Old Testament by quoting from every part of the Scriptures as authoritative, including some of its most disputed teachings. The creation of Adam and Eve (Matt. 19:4–6), the destruction of the world by a flood, the miracle of Jonah and the great fish (Matt. 12:39–40), and many other incidents are quoted authoritatively by Jesus (see chap. 3). No part of Sacred Writ claims less than full and complete authority. Biblical inspiration is plenary.

Of course plenary inspiration extends only to the teachings of the autographs, as has already been discussed (chap. 1). But everything the Bible teaches, whether in Old or New Testament, is fully and completely authoritative. No teaching of Scripture is without divine origin. God inspired the very written expression of all prophetic teaching. Inspiration is plenary, that is, full and complete, extending to every part.

Inspiration gives authority. Already apparent is the fact that inspiration conveys final authority of the written document. Jesus said, "Scripture cannot be broken" (John 10:35). On numerous occasions our Lord appealed to the written Word of God as final arbitrator for faith and practice. He claimed Scripture as His authority for cleansing the temple (Mark 11:17); for rebuking the tradition of the Pharisees (Matt. 15:3, 4); for settling doctrinal disputes (Matt. 22:29). Even Satan was resisted by Christ on the authority of the written Word: "It is written . . . It is written . . . It is written . . ." Jesus responded to each of Satan's temptations (Matt. 4:4, 7, 10).

On occasion Jesus would say, "Everything written . . . must be fulfilled" (e.g., Luke 24:44). But an even stronger affirmation of the final authority of Scripture is found in His pronouncement, "It is easier for heaven and earth to pass away than for one dot of the Law to become void" (Luke 16:17). The written Word is unbreakable. It comes from God and it has the authority of God invested in it.

Some Implications of the Biblical Doctrine of Inspiration

There are several things not formally presented in the doctrine of inspiration which are nonetheless clearly implied in it. Three of these will be discussed here: the equality of the New Testament with the Old, the variety of literary expression, and the inerrancy of the record.

Inspiration refers to the New Testament and the Old. Most of the passages cited above on the plenary nature of inspiration refer directly only to the Old Testament. On what basis can they be extended to the New Testament? The answer to this question is that the New Testament, like the Old, claims to be Scripture and prophetic writings, and all Scripture and prophetic writings are held to be inspired of God.

According to 2 Timothy 3:16, all Scripture is inspired. Although the explicit reference here is to the Old Testament, it is true that the New Testament is also considered Scripture. Peter, for example, classes the epistles of Paul along with the "other scriptures" of the Old Testament (2 Pet. 3:16). First Timothy 5:18, in quoting the gospel of Luke (10:7), refers to it as "Scripture." This is even more significant when one considers that neither Luke nor Paul was among the twelve apostles. Since the epistles of Paul and writings of Luke (Luke and Acts; see Acts 1:1; Luke 1:1–4) were classified as Scripture, then by direct implication the rest of the New Testament written by the apostles was also considered to be inspired Scripture. In brief, if "all Scripture is God breathed" (2 Tim. 3:16 NIV), and the New Testament is considered to be Scripture, then by clear implication the New Testament is considered to be on an equal level of authority with the Old Testament. Indeed, this is precisely how Christians since the time of the apostles have viewed the New Testament. They have regarded it as equally authoritative with the Old.

Furthermore, according to 2 Pet. 1:20–21, all prophetic writings are God-given or inspired. And since the New Testament claims to be a prophetic writing, then it follows that it too is claiming to be of equal authority with the Old Testament prophetic writings. John, for example, referred to the Book of Revelation as "the words of the prophecy of this book" (22:18). Paul claimed that the church is built upon the foundation of the New Testament apostles and prophets (Eph. 2:20; 3:5). Since the New Testament is, like the Old, a writing of God's prophets, it possesses the same authority as the Old Testament inspired Scriptures.

Inspiration includes a variety of literary sources and styles. The fact that inspiration is verbal or written does not exclude the use of literary documents and differing literary styles. The Scriptures are not dictated word for word in the usual sense of that phrase. To be sure, there were small sections of the Bible, such as the Ten Commandments, that were given through direct words from God (see Deut. 4:10), but nowhere is it either stated or implied that the Bible is a word-for-word dictation. The writers of Holy Scripture were authors and composers, not merely secretaries or stenographers.

There are several factors in the makeup of Scripture that support this contention. First, there is a marked difference in vocabulary and style from writer to writer. Compare the powerful literary expressions of Isaiah to the mournful tones of Jeremiah. Compare the complex literary construction of Hebrews to the simple style of John. The more technical language of Luke the physician is easily distinguished from the pastoral images of James.

Second, the Bible makes use of nonbiblical documents such as the Book of Jashar (Josh. 10:13), the Book of Enoch (Jude 14) and even a Greek poet (Acts 17:28). We are informed that many of the proverbs of Solomon were edited by the men of Hezekiah (Prov. 25:1). Luke acknowledges the use of many written sources of Jesus' life in the composition of his own gospel (Luke 1:1–4).

Third, the biblical authors employed a variety of literary devices not characteristic of a wooden word-for-word dictation. Much of the Scripture is poetry (for example, Job, Psalms, Proverbs). The Gospels are filled with parables. Jesus used satire (see Matt. 19:24), Paul employed an allegory (Galatians 4) and even hyperbole (Col. 1:23), and James wrote with many metaphors and similes (James 3).

Finally, the Bible uses the commonsense, everyday language of appearance as opposed to a technical or scientific language. This is not to say that it is unscientific, but that it is nonscientific. It is no more unscientific to speak of the sun standing still (Josh. 10:12) than of the sun rising (Josh. 1:15). To say the Queen of Sheba came "from the end of the earth" or the people at Pentecost came "from every nation under heaven" is not to speak with scientific exactness. The writers used common, grammatical modes of expressing their topic.

So whatever else is implied in the doctrine of inspired writings, the data of Scripture clearly indicates that it includes the usage of a variety of literary sources and styles of expression. Not everything came directly from God by dictation. And not everything was expressed in a uniform and literal way. Inspiration is to be understood historically and grammatically. It is not to be understood as a uniform, divine dictation exclusive of human sources, personalities, and varieties of expression.

Inspiration implies inerrancy. Not only is the Bible inspired, but by means of this inspiration it is inerrant, or without error.[18] Whatever God utters is the truth without error. In fact, the Scriptures claim to be the utterance, indeed the very words, of God. Whatever the Bible teaches is inerrant, since inerrancy is logically entailed in inspiration. God cannot lie (Heb. 6:18); His Word is truth (John 17:17). Hence, whatever subject the Bible speaks upon, it speaks truly. There are no historical or scientific errors in the teaching of Scripture. Everything the Bible teaches is of God and, therefore, without error.

Some wrongly claim the Bible is a human book and humans err. Hence, the Bible errs. But this does not follow, since humans do not always err. Even apart from divine inspiration, there are perfect phone books and math books—with no errors in them. How much more can there be a book inspired by God that is without errors. But how can God produce a perfect book through imperfect human authors? The answer is that God can draw a

---

18. For a more complete defense of the full inerrancy of the Bible, see our *Defending Inerrancy* (Grand Rapids: Baker, 2012).

THEORIES OF REVELATION AND INSPIRATION

View	Name	Proponents	Revelation	Errors in Originals?	Errors in Copies?	Means of Inspiration	Degree of Authority of Bible
Mechanical Dictation	Hyper-Fundamentalism	Muslims, Spiritists, Some Hyper-Fundamentalists	In Words (Individually)	None	None	By Dictation	Infallible and Inerrant
Verbal Dictation	Fundamentalism	John R. Rice	In Words (Individually)	None	Few	By supernatural molding of writer's style	Infallible and Inerrant
Verbal Inspiration	Fundamentalism Evangelicalism	B.B. Warfield F. F. Schaeffer ICBI	In Words (Wholistically)*	None	Few	Supernatural process	Infallible Not Inerrant
Conceptual Inspiration	Neo-Evangelicalism	A.H. Strong D. Beegle Jack Rogers	In Concepts (Not Words)	None theologically (or morally) Some factually	Few	Revealed ideas; Writer's own words	Usually Reliable Not Inerrant
Instrumental Revelation		C.S. Lewis	Through Words (Not in Words)	Some (in both areas)	Some	Writer's words "elevated" by God	Authoritative Not Inerrant
Personal Revelation		Karl Barth Emil Brunner John Baillie	In Acts, Events (Not Words)	Many (in both areas)	Many	Revealed Acts Writer's Record	Usually Reliable Not Inerrant
Illumination		Harold DeWolf Harry E. Fosdick	By Illumination (No Revelation)	Many (in both areas)	Many	Divine Actualization of Natural Powers	Often Reliable Not Inerrant
Intuition		Shubert Ogden	By Intuition (No Revelation)	Many (In both areas)	Largely	Purely Natural Powers	Sometimes Reliable Not Inerrant

SOURCE: Norman L. Geisler and William E. Nix, *A General Introduction to the Bible*, rev. ed. (Chicago: Moody, 1986), 190.

*Wholistically means in words as part of a whole sentence, not in isolated words individually (atomistically).

straight line with a crooked stick. God by His providence guided authors, who as humans were capable of errors, to refrain from error when writing His Book. After all, as Peter said, "No prophecy was ever produced by the will of man, but men spoke from God as they were carried along by the Holy Spirit" (2 Pet. 1:21).

It is not possible to evade the implications of factual inerrancy by claiming that the Bible has nothing to say about factual or historical matters. Much of the Bible is presented as history. The very tedious genealogies alone (cf. 1 Chron. 1–9) attest to this fact. Some of the great teachings of the Bible, such as creation, the virgin birth of Christ, the crucifixion, and the bodily resurrection clearly involve factual matters. There is no way to "spiritualize" away the factual and historical nature of these biblical truths without doing violence to an honest historical and grammatical analysis of the text.

The Bible is not a scientific textbook, but when it touches upon scientific matters in its teaching, it does so without error. The Bible is not a secular history book, but where secular and sacred history meet in its pages, the Bible speaks inerrantly. If the Bible is not correct in factual and empirical matters which are verifiable, then how could it be trusted in spiritual matters which are not subject to such tests? Or, in Jesus' words to Nicodemus, "If I have told you earthly things and you do not believe, how can you believe if I tell you heavenly things?" (John 3:12).

3

THE INSPIRATION *of* THE OLD TESTAMENT

DOES THE BIBLE REALLY CLAIM INSPIRATION FOR ITSELF or is this merely a claim that believers have made for the Bible? More specifically, do each of the sections and books of the Bible claim to be inspired? These are the questions before us in the next two chapters. First, let us examine the claim for inspiration in the Old Testament.

THE OLD TESTAMENT CLAIM FOR INSPIRATION

The general claim for inspiration in the Old Testament is based on the fact that it presented itself to and was received by the people of God as a prophetic utterance (2 Pet. 1:20–21). Books written by God's prophets were preserved in a holy place. Moses placed his law by the ark of God (Deut. 10:2). Later it was preserved in the tabernacle for teaching future generations (Deut. 6:2). Each prophet after Moses added his inspired writings to this collection. In fact, the key to the inspiration of the Old Testament is the prophetic function of its writers.

The Old Testament as a Prophetic Writing

A prophet was the mouthpiece of God. His function is clarified by the various descriptions given him. He was called a man of God (1 Kings 12:22), revealing that he was chosen of God; a servant of the Lord (1 Kings 14:18), indicating his occupation; a messenger of the Lord (Isa. 42:19), designating his mission for God; a seer or beholder (Isa. 30:10), revealing apocalyptic source of his truth; a man of the Spirit (Hos. 9:7), showing by whose promptings he spoke; a watchman (Ezek. 3:17), manifesting his alertness to do the work of God. By far and away, the most common expression was "prophet," or spokesman for God.

By his very calling, a prophet was one who felt as did Amos, "The Lord God has spoken; who can but prophesy?" (Amos 3:8); or, as another prophet who said, "I could not go beyond the command of the LORD my God to do less or more" (Num. 22:18). As Aaron was a prophet or mouthpiece for Moses (Ex. 7:1), speaking "all the words that the LORD had spoken to Moses" (Ex. 4:30), even so God's prophets were to speak only what He commanded them. God said of His prophet, "I will put my words in his mouth, and he shall speak to them all that I command him" (Deut. 18:18). Further, "You shall not add to the word that I command you, nor take from it" (Deut. 4:2). In summation, a prophet was one who declared what God had disclosed to him.

False prophets were detected by their false prophecies and by the lack of miraculous confirmation. Deuteronomy declares, "When a prophet speaks in the name of the LORD, if the word does not come to pass or come true, that is a word that the LORD has not spoken" (18:22). Whenever there was any other question of contest or confirmation, God designated His own by miracles. The earth opened up and swallowed Korah and those with him who contested Moses' call (Num. 26:10). Elijah was vindicated over the prophets of Baal by fire from heaven (1 Kings 18:38). Even the Egyptian magicians finally conceded of Moses' miracles, "This is the finger of God" (Ex. 8:19).

It is clear from the function of a prophet of God that what he uttered was the word of God. It remains for us to see that the Old Testament Scriptures were considered to be prophetic utterances. There are several ways to determine this.

Prophetic utterances were written. Many prophetic utterances were given orally, but we are concerned here with the fact that some of them were written and that the written words were considered to be the prophetic utterance of God. There is no question that Moses' written words were considered as divinely authoritative. "This Book of the Law shall not depart from your mouth" (Josh. 1:8), the children of Israel were exhorted. Joshua, his successor, also wrote words "in the Book of the Law of God" (Josh. 24:26). When the king burned Jeremiah's first written message to him, the Lord ordered the prophet to "take another scroll and write on it all the former words that were in the first scroll" (Jer. 36:28). Isaiah the prophet was commanded, "Take a large tablet and write on it" (Isa. 8:1). Similarly, Habakkuk was told by God, "Write the vision; make it plain upon tablets, so he may run who reads it" (Hab. 2:2).

Later prophets used the writings of prophets before them as the written Word of God. Daniel knew from the prophecy of Jeremiah that the Babylonian exile of his people was ending. He wrote, "I, Daniel, perceived in the books the number of years that, according to the word of the LORD to Jeremiah the prophet, must pass" (Dan. 9:2).

The Old Testament writers were prophets. All the traditional authors of the Old Testament are designated prophet by either title or function. Not all of them were prophets by training, but all possessed a prophetic gift. Amos confessed, "I was no prophet, nor a prophet's son . . . and the LORD said to me, 'Go, prophesy to my people Israel'" (Amos 7:14–15). David, credited with writing almost half of the Psalms, was a king by occupation. Nevertheless, he testified, "The Spirit of the Lord speaks by me; his word is on my tongue" (2 Sam. 23:2). The New Testament plainly calls him a prophet (Acts 2:30). Likewise, King Solomon, the traditional author of Song of Solomon, Proverbs, and Ecclesiastes, received visions from the Lord (1 Kings 11:9). According to Numbers 12:6, a vision was God's way of designating to His people those who were His prophets. Although Daniel was a statesman, he was called Daniel the prophet by Jesus (Matt. 24:15).

Moses, the great lawgiver and deliverer of Israel, is called a prophet (Deut. 18:15; Hos. 12:13). As the successor of Moses, Joshua was considered a prophet of God (Deut. 34:9–10). Samuel, Nathan, and Gad were all writing prophets (1 Chron. 29:29), as were Isaiah, Jeremiah, Ezekiel, and the twelve minor prophets.

An official register of prophetic writings was kept. Evidence indicates no nonprophetic writing was preserved with the sacred collection which was started with the Mosaic Law. And it appears that there was a continuity of prophets, each adding his book to his prophetic predecessors. Moses put his books by the ark. Joshua is said to have added his to the collection (Josh. 24:26). Following him, Samuel added his words to the collection when "he wrote them in a book and laid it up before the Lord" (1 Sam. 10:25).

This is supported by the "colophon principle" which affirmed that

"Each book completes the preceding and links the prophetic history together. Ruth was originally appended to Judges. . . . Likewise, the last chapter of Kings parallels the material of Jeremiah 52, 39, 40, and 41. Similarly, the book of Chronicles ends with the same two verses that the Ezra–Nehemiah unit begins."[1]

Samuel founded a school of the prophets (1 Sam. 19:20) that later had students who were called the "sons of the prophets" (2 Kings 2:3). There is ample testimony in the books of Chronicles that histories were kept by the prophets. David's history was written by the prophets Samuel, Nathan, and Gad (1 Chron. 29:29). The history of Solomon was recorded by Nathan, Ahijah, and Iddo (2 Chron. 9:29). This was also the case with the histories of Rehoboam, Jehoshaphat, Hezekiah, Manasseh, and other kings (see 2 Chron. 9:29; 12:15; 13:22; 20:34; 33:19; 35:27).

By the time of the Babylonian exile in the sixth century BCE, Daniel referred to the collection of prophetic writings as "books" (Dan. 9:2). According to Ezekiel (13:9), there was an official register of the true prophets of God. Anyone who uttered false prophecies was excluded from the official roll. Only the true prophet of God was officially recognized and only the writings of these prophets were kept among the inspired books. From the earliest known times, all thirty-nine books of the Old Testament constituted these prophetic writings. More will be said about this later (see chaps. 7 and 8).

Specific Claims for Inspiration within the Old Testament

The inspiration of the Old Testament does not rest merely on a general analysis of it as a prophetic writing. There are numerous specific claims within the individual books as to their divine origin. Let us examine the claims according to the currently recognized categorization of the Hebrew Old Testament into law, prophets, and writings.

Inspiration of the law of Moses. According to Exodus 20:1: "God spoke all these words." That God spoke to Moses is repeated dozens of times in Leviticus (e.g., 1:1; 8:9; 11:1). Numbers repeatedly records, "The LORD spoke to Moses" (e.g., 1:1; 2:1; 4:1). Deuteronomy adds, "Moses spoke to the people of Israel according to all that the LORD had given him in commandment to them" (1:3).

---

1. R. Laird Harris, *Inspiration and Canonicity of the Bible* (Grand Rapids: Zondervan, 1957), 166.

The rest of the Old Testament in one accord declares the Mosaic books as given by God. Joshua immediately imposed the books of the law on the people of Israel (1:8). Judges refers to the Mosaic writings as the "commandments of the LORD" (3:4). Samuel acknowledged that God had appointed Moses (1 Sam. 12:6, 8). In Chronicles his writings are spoken of as the "Book of the Law of the LORD given through Moses" (2 Chron. 34:14). Daniel refers to the curse written in the law of Moses as "His [God's] words which he spoke against us" (Dan. 9:12). Even in Ezra and Nehemiah there is recognition of the law of God given to Moses (Ezra 6:18; Neh. 13:1). That the books of Moses were divinely given is the unanimous consent of the Old Testament.

Inspiration of the prophets. According to present Jewish division of the Old Testament, the books of the prophets include the former prophets (Joshua, Judges, Samuels, and Kings) and the latter prophets (Isaiah, Jeremiah, Ezekiel, and the twelve minor prophets). These books also claim divine authority. "Joshua wrote these words in the Book of the Law of God" (Josh. 24:26). God spoke to men in Judges (1:1, 2; 6:25) and 1 Samuel (3:11) who spoke and wrote to all Israel (1 Samuel 4:1; cf. 1 Chron. 29:29). The latter prophets abound in claims of divine inspiration. The familiar "Thus says the LORD" with which they introduce their message occurs hundreds of times. From Isaiah to Malachi the reader is bombarded with divine authority.

Chronologically the Old Testament ends with this section known as the Prophets, and there is no subsequent Old Testament testimony to their inspiration. However, there are references within the Prophets to other prophetic writers who composed their books at an earlier time. Daniel considered Jeremiah's book inspired (Dan. 9:2). Ezra recognized the divine authority of Jeremiah (Ezra 1:1) as well as that of Haggai and Zechariah (Ezra 5:1). In a very important passage Zechariah refers to the divine inspiration of Moses and the prophets who preceded him, calling their works "the law and the words that the LORD of hosts had sent by his Spirit through the former prophets" (7:12). These passages leave little doubt that the books contained in the section of the Jewish Scriptures known as the Prophets bear the claim of divine inspiration.

Inspiration of the writings. The original Old Testament probably had only two basic divisions, the Law and the Prophets (see chap. 7). This last section was later divided into the Prophets and the Writings. Perhaps this is based on the official position of the author as to whether he was a prophet by occupation or simply by gift. Those falling into the latter category were put in the section called Writings. Psalms, the first book in this collection, was written largely by David who claimed that his psalms were Spirit-given to the very words (2 Sam. 23:2). Song of Solomon, Proverbs, and Ecclesiastes have been traditionally ascribed to Solomon as the record of God-given wisdom (see 1 Kings 3:9–10) and dreams from God (1 Kings 3:5, 15). Proverbs contains specific claims to divine authority. Ecclesiastes (12:13) and Job (chap. 38) both end as an authoritative teaching. Daniel's book is based on a series of visions and dreams from God (Dan. 2:19; 8:1; etc.).

Several books have no explicit claim to divine inspiration, such as Ruth, Esther, Song of Solomon, Lamentations, Ezra–Nehemiah, and Chronicles. If Ruth was written by the prophet Samuel as a part of Judges, then it would come under the general claim of a prophetic writing. By the same token, Lamentations, the work of Jeremiah, is prophetic. The Song has already been noted as a work of the God-given wisdom of Solomon. Jewish tradition ascribes Chronicles, Ezra, and Nehemiah to Ezra the priest and to Nehemiah who functioned with prophetic authority in the repatriation of Israel from the Babylonian captivity (cf. Ezra 10 and Neh. 13). The author of Esther is not stated, perhaps to preserve his anonymity in the hostile Persian setting. The point of view in Esther is notably Jewish, and the book provides the written authority for the celebration of the Jewish feast of Purim. This amounts to an implicit claim to divine authority.

In summary then, virtually every book of the Old Testament offers some claim to divine inspiration. Sometimes it is the implied authority, but it is usually the explicit claim of "thus says the Lord." From beginning to end the inspiration of the Old Testament is solidly built on numerous passages, all of which declare their divine origin.

NEW TESTAMENT SUPPORT FOR THE OLD TESTAMENT CLAIM OF INSPIRATION

There are three lines of approach in examining the New Testament teaching on the inspiration of the Old Testament. There are the passages which refer to the divine authority of the Old Testament as a whole. Also there are the references to the inspiration of given sections of the Old Testament. Finally, there are authoritative quotes of specific books in the Jewish canon.

New Testament References to the Inspiration
of the Whole Old Testament

The New Testament recognizes the inspiration of the Old Testament in many ways. Sometimes it uses such expressions as "Scripture," "the Word of God," "the law," "the law and the prophets," "the Prophets," and "the oracles of God."

The Scriptures is by far the most common title used in the New Testament for the Old. According to Paul, "All [Old Testament] scripture is inspired by God" (2 Tim. 3:16 RSV). Jesus said, "The scripture cannot be broken" (John 10:35 KJV). Often the New Testament uses the plural, Scriptures, to denote the authoritative collection of Jewish writings. Jesus responded to the Pharisees, "Have you never read in the Scriptures?" (Matt. 21:42), or "You are wrong, because you know neither the Scriptures nor the power of God" (Matt. 22:29). The apostle Paul "reasoned with them out of the scriptures" (Acts 17:2 KJV) and the Bereans "searched the scriptures daily" (Acts 17:11 KJV). In these and numerous other references, the New Testament acknowledges the whole of the Old Testament canon as divinely inspired writings.

The Word of God is a less common but perhaps more forceful description of the Old Testament's inspiration. In Mark 7:13 Jesus charged that the Pharisees made "void the word of God" through their traditions. John 10:35 uses the phrase "the word of God" as synonymous to "Scripture." There are numerous other references to "the word of God," but not all of them clearly identify with the Old Testament. Paul argued, "not as though the word of God has failed" (Rom. 9:6). In another place he speaks of his refusal to tamper with the word of God (2 Cor. 4:2). The writer of Hebrews states that "the word of God is living and active" (Heb. 4:12). Peter's statement that "to him [i.e., Christ] all the prophets bear witness" (Acts 10:43) could scarcely be limited to less than the whole Old Testament in view of Luke 24:27, 44. The passages which do clearly identify the whole Old Testament as the Word of God leave no doubt as to the assertion of divine inspiration.

The law is often a shortened form for the Law of Moses, and denotes just the first five books of Jewish Scripture. On some occasions, however, the *law* describes the whole Old Testament. John 10:34 is probably a case in point. Since the quote is from Psalm 82:6, it is clear that the law of Moses is not intended. Because "law" is used here in connection with both "scripture" and "the Word of God," that would indicate the whole Old Testament is in view. In John 12:34, the people mention "the Law," although elsewhere Jesus calls it "their Law" (John 15:25), and in Acts Paul identifies it as "the law of the Jews" (Acts 25:8). Paul introduced a quotation of the Old Testament with the phrase "in the Law it is written" (1 Cor. 14:21). In His famous Sermon on the Mount Jesus used the term "law" as synonymous with "the Law and the Prophets," a phrase which we shall see clearly refers to the divinely inspired documents of the Old Testament (Matt. 5:18).

The law and the prophets or "Moses and the prophets" is the second most common title of the Jewish Scriptures. These designations occur a dozen times in the New Testament. Jesus used the phrase twice in His famous sermon (Matt. 5:17 RSV; 7:12), claiming He came to fulfill "the law and the prophets" and that they would never pass away. Luke 16:16 presents "the Law and the Prophets" as all the divine revelation up to the time of John the Baptist. In his defense before Felix, Paul proclaimed the "Law and . . . the Prophets" to be the whole counsel of God which he as a devout Jew had practiced from his youth (Acts 24:14). It was "the Law and the Prophets" that was read in the synagogues (Acts 13:15) and of which the Golden Rule was considered the moral summation (Matt. 7:12).

The prophets occasionally referred to all of the Old Testament. Since the whole Old Testament is a prophetic utterance it is not surprising that it is sometimes called "the prophets." That it is sometimes called "Scriptures of the prophets" indicates that a group of books is intended (Matt. 26:56). The all-inclusive "everything that is written about the Son of man" would seem to point to the whole Old Testament (Luke 18:31). Indeed, the title "prophets" is used in parallel with the phrase "Moses and all the prophets" (Luke 24:25, 27); and it clearly refers to the entire Old Testament.

The oracles of God is no doubt intended to convey this notion. It appears twice, and refers to the Old Testament Scriptures. Paul said that the Jewish people were "entrusted with the oracles of God" (Rom. 3:2). Elsewhere, the need for someone to teach "the basic principles of the oracles of God" is stated (Heb. 5:12). The written word of the Old Testament is God's Word.

It is written or similar phrases are used on more than ninety occasions in the New Testament. Most of these statements introduce specific quotations, but some have a more general application to the Old Testament as a whole. Examples of this latter usage include the following: "How is it written of the Son of Man, that he should suffer many things and be treated with contempt?" (Mark 9:12; cf. 14:21). This is a summary of the general teaching about Christ's death in the Old Testament rather than a specific quotation from it. An even more definitive reference is Luke 18:31: "Everything that is written about the Son of Man by the prophets will be accomplished." Along with others like "these are days of vengeance, to fulfill all that is written" (Luke 21:22), there is sufficient support for the thesis that writings of the Old Testament as a whole were considered divinely inspired. They were predictive of Christ and were under divine necessity of fulfillment.

That it might be fulfilled is an expression frequently used with reference to the Old Testament in general. Jesus indicated that the law, prophets, and Psalms "must be fulfilled" (Luke 24:44). On another occasion He said, "I have not come to abolish [the Law or the Prophets] . . . but to fulfill them" (Matt. 5:17). This formula introduces a specific quotation from or reference to the Old Testament over thirty times. It always indicates the prophetic nature of Scripture as given by God, and of necessity it must be fulfilled.

New Testament References to Specific Sections of the Old Testament

A second indication in the New Testament that the Old Testament was considered divinely inspired is the references to the authority of given sections of the Hebrew Scriptures (viz., the Law, the Prophets, and the Writings).

The law and the prophets, as was indicated above, refers to a twofold division of the Old Testament and occurs about a dozen times in the New Testament. It indicates all the inspired writings from Moses to Jesus (Luke 16:16), which are considered to be the imperishable word of God (Matt. 5:18). Indeed, Jesus speaks of Law and Prophets being "all the Scriptures" (Luke 24:27). Besides the combined references there are some which treat the law and the prophets separately.

The Law usually designates the first five books of the Old Testament, as in Matt. 12:5. Sometimes it is called "the law of Moses" (Acts 13:39; Heb. 10:28). On other occasions these books are simply entitled "Moses" (2 Cor. 3:15), "the book of Moses" (Mark 12:26), or "the Book of the Law" (Gal. 3:10). In each case there is an appeal to the divine authority of Mosaic teaching. The whole Pentateuch of Moses was held to be from God.

The Prophets usually identifies the second half of Old Testament Scripture (see John 1:45; Luke 18:31). The phrases "the Scriptures of the prophets"

(Matt. 26:56) and "the book of the prophets" (Acts 7:42) are also used. It is not always clear that these titles refer only to the books written subsequent to Moses, although sometimes they do, as the separation of the two titles reveals. As far as the title "prophets" is concerned, its very meaning as a spokesman for God indicates the divine inspiration of the books so entitled (2 Pet. 1:20–21).

The Writings is not a term used in the New Testament. This is a nonbiblical description that divides the prophetic writings into two sections: those which were written by professional prophets ("the Prophets") and those writings which were not ("the Writings"). There is only one allusion in the New Testament to a possible threefold division of the Old Testament. Jesus spoke of "the Law of Moses and the Prophets and the Psalms" (Luke 24:44). It is not clear here whether He is singling out the book of Psalms, because of its special messianic significance, or as part of "Moses and the Prophets" to which He referred earlier in the chapter (v. 27). Whatever the case, the messianic and prophetic nature of this supposed third division of the Old Testament marks it clearly as inspired of God. And if there are only two sections to the original Old Testament canon (as we will argue in chap. 7), then the remainder of the inspired Scriptures have already been treated under the designation "the prophets."

New Testament References to Specific Books of the Old Testament

Of the twenty-two books in the Jewish canon referred to by Josephus (*Against Apion* 1.8), some eighteen are cited as authoritative by the New Testament. No citations of Judges, Chronicles, Esther, or the Song of Solomon are to be found, although there are references to events in Judges (Heb. 11:32) and Chronicles (Matt. 23:35; 2 Chron. 24:20–22). Allusion to the Song of Solomon 4:15 may be found in Jesus' reference to "living water" (John 4:10), but this would not be a support of the book's authority. Likewise, the possible reference to the Feast of Purim from Esther 9 in John 5:1, or the similarity of Revelation 11:10 to Esther 9:22, would fall short of a support of the inspiration of Esther. The divine authority of the book of Esther is adequately attested elsewhere (see chap. 8) but not by New Testament quotations.

Virtually all the eighteen remaining books of the Hebrew canon are cited with authority in the New Testament. The creation of man in Genesis 1:27 is quoted by Jesus in Matthew 19:4–5. The fifth commandment of

Exodus (20:12) is cited as Scripture in Ephesians 6:1. The law for a leper's cleansing from Leviticus 14:2–32 is referred to in Matthew 8:4. Numbers is not quoted as such, but 1 Corinthians refers to events recorded in the book as written for Christian admonition (1 Cor. 10:11). Numbers 12:7 records Moses' faithfulness and is cited authoritatively in Hebrews 3:5. Deuteronomy is one of the most quoted books in the Old Testament. Jesus quoted it twice in His temptation (Matt. 4:4 and 4:7; cf. Deut. 8:3 and 6:16).

Joshua received the promise from God, "I will not leave you or forsake you" (Josh. 1:5) and is quoted in Hebrews 13:5. Jesus cited the incident from 1 Samuel 21:1–6 of David eating bread from the tabernacle as the authority for his activity on the Sabbath. God's reply to Elijah from 1 Kings 19:18 is quoted in Romans 11:4. Ezra–Nehemiah is probably quoted in John 6:31 (cf. Neh. 9:15), although God's provision to Israel of "bread from heaven" is also referred to elsewhere (Pss. 78:24; 105:40).

The book of Job (5:12) is distinctly quoted as authoritative by Paul, "It is written, 'He catches the wise in their craftiness' " (1 Cor. 3:19). Psalms is another of the most-quoted Old Testament books. It was a favorite of Jesus. Compare Matthew 21:42, "The stone that the builders rejected has become the cornerstone," with Psalm 118:22. Peter quoted from Psalm 110 in his sermon at Pentecost (Acts 2:34–35). Hebrews abounds in references to the Psalms; the first chapter quotes Psalms 2, 104, 45, and 102. Proverbs 3:34, "Toward the scorners he is scornful, but to the humble he gives favor" is clearly quoted in James 4:6.

There is no verbatim quotation of Ecclesiastes, but some passages seem to be doctrinally dependable. Thus, Paul's statement "Whatever a man sows, that he will also reap" (Gal. 6:7) resembles Ecclesiastes 11:1. The challenge to avoid youthful lust (2 Tim. 2:22) reflects Ecclesiastes 11:10. That death is divinely appointed (Heb. 9:27; cf. Eccl. 3:2); that the love of money is the source of all kinds of evil (1 Tim. 6:10; cf. Eccl. 5:10); and that we should not be wordy in prayer (Matt. 6:7; cf. Eccl. 5:2) are also examples.

Isaiah is another of the Old Testament books frequently quoted in the New Testament. John the Baptist, in Matthew 3:3, introduced Jesus with a quotation from Isaiah 40:3. In His hometown synagogue Jesus read from Isaiah 61:1–2: "The Spirit of the Lord is upon me . . ." (cf. Luke 4:18–19). Paul frequently quoted from Isaiah (cf. Rom. 9:27; Acts 28:25–28). Jeremiah 31:15 is quoted in Matthew 2:17–18, and Jeremiah's new covenant (chap. 31) is cited twice in Hebrews (8:8; 10:16). Lamentations, which is appended to Jeremiah in the twenty-two books of the Hebrew Bible, is alluded to in Matthew 27:30 (cf. Lam. 3:30). Ezekiel is cited on several occasions in the New Testament, although none is a word-for-word quotation. Jesus' teaching on the new birth (John 3:5) may come from Ezekiel 36:25–26. Romans 6:23 states "the wages of sin is death," which reflects Ezekiel 18:20: "The soul who sins shall die." John's use of the four living creatures (Rev. 4:7) is clearly taken from Ezekiel 1:10. Daniel is identified by name in our Lord's Mount Olivet discourse (Matt. 24:15; cf. Dan. 9:27; 11:31), and Matthew 26:64 encompasses Daniel 7:13.

The twelve minor prophets were grouped together in the Hebrew Old Testament. There are many quotations from this group of writings. Habakkuk's famous, "The righteous shall live by his faith" (Hab. 2:4), is cited three times in the New Testament (Rom. 1:17; Gal. 3:11; Heb. 10:38). Matthew 2:15 quotes Hosea 11:1: "Out of Egypt I called my son."

This leaves only Judges–Ruth, Chronicles, Esther, and Song of Solomon that are not clearly cited by the New Testament. However, Judges–Ruth provides historical events that the New Testament refers to as authentic (Heb. 11:32), and Chronicles is probably intended by Jesus' reference to the blood of Zechariah (Matt. 23:35). Thus only Esther and Song of Solomon lack explicit reference in the New Testament, no doubt because the New Testament writers had no occasion to cite them. Esther is the basis for the Jewish feast of Purim, and Song of Solomon was read at the great Feast of the Passover, which reflects its esteem by the Jewish community.

The New Testament substantiates the claim of inspiration for the whole Old Testament, all of its sections, and almost every one of its books in particular. In addition to this, there is direct and authoritative reference to many of the great persons and events of the Old Testament, including the creation of Adam and Eve (Matt. 19:4), the flood of Noah's time (Luke 17:27), the miraculous call of Moses (Luke 20:37), supernatural provision for Israel in the wilderness (John 3:14; 6:49), the miracles of Elijah (Luke 4:24–25), and Jonah in the belly of the great fish (Matt. 12:41).

Jesus and the Old Testament

A survey of the Gospels reveals what Jesus taught about the Old Testament.[2] In brief, He declared that:

1. *It is divinely authoritative.* Jesus said, "It is written: 'Man shall not live by bread alone, but by every word that comes from the mouth of God.' . . . Again it is written: 'You shall not put the Lord your God to the test.' Be gone, Satan! For it is written, 'You shall worship the Lord your God and him only shall you serve' " (Matt. 4:4, 7, 10).

2. *It is imperishable.* "Do not think that I have come to abolish the Law or the Prophets; I have not come to abolish them but to fulfill them. For truly I say to you, until heaven and earth pass away not an iota, not a dot, will pass from the Law until all is accomplished" (Matt. 5:17–18).

3. *It is infallible.* "If he called them gods, to whom the word of God came— and Scripture cannot be broken . . ." (John 10:35). That is, it is literally unbreakable.

4. *It is inerrant.* (without error) Jesus replied to the Sadducees: "You are wrong, because you know neither the Scriptures nor the power of God" (Matt. 22:29). "Your Word is truth" (John 17:17). "The Law of the LORD is perfect" (Ps. 19:7), that is, "without blemish" (Heb. *Tawmeem*; also used of the Passover Lamb in Ex. 12:5).

5. *It is historically reliable.* Jesus affirmed as historically reliable some of the most disputed passages in the Old Testament regarding Adam and Eve, Noah, and Jonah. At one point He told the scribes and Pharisees, "For as Jonah was three days and three nights in the belly of the great fish, so will the Son of Man be three days and three nights in the heart of the earth" (Matt. 12:40). Later Jesus spoke privately to the disciples, making clear the flood was a historical event: "As were the days of Noah, so will be the coming of the Son of Man. For as in those days before the flood they were eating and drinking, marrying and giving in marriage, until the day Noah entered the ark" (Matt. 24:37–38).

6. *It is scientifically accurate.* "He answered, 'Have you not read that he who created them from the beginning made them male and female . . . ?' " (Matt. 19:4–5). Even an agnostic astronomer said, "The scientist's pursuit of the past ends in the moment of creation. This is an exceedingly

2. See John Wenham, *Christ and the Bible* (Downers Grove, Ill.: InterVarsity, 1973).

strange development, unexpected by all but theologians. They have always accepted the word of the Bible: 'In the beginning God created the heaven and the earth.' "[3]

7. **It has ultimate supremacy.** Jesus answered, "And why do you break the commandment of God for the sake of your tradition?... So for the sake of your tradition you have made void the word of God" (Matt. 15:3, 6). No matter how high the human tradition (teaching) may be, the Word of God has ultimate authority over it.

AFFIRMATION OR ACCOMMODATION?

Regardless of the volume and authoritative nature of New Testament citations, some have suggested that Jesus and the apostles were not really affirming the inspiration and authenticity of the Old Testament. Rather, they assert, the New Testament writers were accommodating themselves to the accepted Jewish beliefs of the day. This suggestion is subtle but not substantial. It does not square with the facts of Scripture nor with the claims of Christ. The most numerous and emphatic references to the inspiration and authenticity of the Old Testament are from the lips of Jesus, who showed no tendency toward accommodation. Chasing the money changers from the temple (John 2:15), denouncing "blind guides" (Matt. 23:16) and "false prophets" (Matt. 7:15), and rebuking leading teachers (John 3:10) are scarcely evidences of accommodation.

In fact, Jesus clearly rebuked those who held to traditions rather than to the Word of God (cf. Matt. 15:1–6). Six times in a single chapter (Matthew 5), Jesus contrasted the truth about the Scripture with false beliefs that had grown up about it when He charged, "It was said" (not "it is written") ... "but I say to you." Jesus did not hesitate to assert, "You are wrong" (cf. Matt. 22:29), when men erred. And when they understood the truth, He would encourage them by saying, "You have answered correctly" (Luke 10:28).

Jesus' teaching on the divine authority of the Old Testament is so unconditional and so uncompromising that one cannot reject it without rejecting His words. If one does not accept the authority of the Old Testament as Scripture, then he impugns the integrity of the Savior. Whatever else may be said about the inspiration of the Old Testament, this much is

---

3.   Robert Jastrow, *God and the Astronomers* (New York: W.W. Norton, 1978), 115.

clear: The Old Testament claimed inspiration for itself, and the New Testament overwhelmingly confirms that claim.

AFFIRMATION OR LIMITATION?

Others claim that Jesus was limited in His knowledge as a man and, hence, His opinion on the origin and nature of the Old Testament was subject to error like any other human being of His time. His teaching was purely doctrinal and spiritual but not historical and critical. Some critics have argued that in the incarnation Jesus "emptied Himself" of omniscience. He Himself said that He was ignorant of the time of His second coming (Mark 13:32). Nor did He know whether there were figs on the tree (Mark 11:13). Luke said that Jesus "increased in wisdom" (Luke 2:52) as other humans do, and He asked many questions that revealed His ignorance of the answers (Mark 5:9, 30; 6:38; John 14:9). This being the case, perhaps Jesus was ignorant of the true origin and nature of the Old Testament and of the historical truth of events in it.

If true, this "Limitation Theory" is damaging to the case for the authority of the Old Testament from the teachings of Jesus. So let us examine the evidence carefully.

First, it seems necessary to grant that Jesus was indeed ignorant of many things as a man. Of course, as God, Jesus was infinite in knowledge and knew all things (Ps. 147:5). But Christ has two natures: one infinite or unlimited in knowledge, and the other finite or limited in knowledge. Could it be that Jesus did not really err in what He taught about the Old Testament but that He simply was so limited as a human being that His knowledge and authority did not extend into those areas? A careful look at the evidence gives a clearly negative answer to this question.

Jesus often had a supernormal knowledge. Even though Jesus as a man was finite and limited in His knowledge, nevertheless, even in His human state Christ possessed supernormal, if not supernatural, knowledge of many things. He saw Nathanael under the fig tree, although he was not within normal visual distance (John 1:48). Jesus amazed the woman of Samaria with the information He knew about her private life (John 4:17–18). Jesus knew who would betray Him in advance (John 6:64) and "all that would happen to him" in Jerusalem (John 18:4). He knew about Lazarus's death before He was told (John 11:14) and of His crucifixion and resurrection before they occurred (Mark 8:31; 9:31). Jesus had superhuman knowledge of the location of fish (Luke 5:4).[4] So, whatever natural limitations to His knowledge there were, it is clear that at times His knowledge far exceeded what other normal men possessed.

Jesus possessed complete and final authority for whatever He taught. Christ claimed that whatever He taught came from God with absolute and final authority. Jesus believed and proclaimed that "all things have been delivered to me by my Father" (Matt 11:27 RSV). He claimed, "Heaven and earth will pass away, but my word will not pass away" (Matt. 24:35). When Jesus commissioned His disciples He claimed, "All authority in heaven and on earth has been given to me. Go therefore and make disciples . . . teaching them to observe all that I have commanded you" (Matt. 28:18–20). Elsewhere Jesus claimed that the very destiny of men hinged on His words (Matt. 7:24–26) and that His words would judge men in the last day (John 12:48). The emphatic "truly, truly" is found some twenty-five times in John alone, and in Matthew (5:18) He declared, "Not an iota, not a dot, will pass from the Law," which He came to fulfill. Jesus then placed His own words on a par with the law (Matt. 5:18, 21ff.). Jesus claimed that His words bring eternal life (John 5:24) and vowed that all His teaching came from the Father (John 8:26–28). Furthermore, despite the fact that He was a man on earth, Christ accepted the acclaims of deity and allowed men to worship Him on many occasions (cf. Matt. 28:18; John 9:38).

So, while Jesus was limited in that, as a human, He did not know everything, nonetheless, He was not errant in either knowledge or authority on what He did teach. And He did teach repeatedly and emphatically (see above) that the Old Testament is the divinely inspired and completely authoritative Word of God in whatever it teaches. Hence, while Jesus was limited in areas on which He did not teach (like the time of His second coming), nonetheless, He was not limited in either truth or authority on what He did teach.

So, despite the necessary limitations involved in a human incarnation (Phil. 2:5–6), there is no error or misunderstanding in whatever Christ taught. Whatever limits there were in the extent of Jesus' knowledge, there were no limits to the truthfulness of His teachings. Just as Jesus was fully

---

4. Since all that Jesus taught came from the Father (John 8:26–28), it is possible that this occasional supernormal knowledge came to Christ by revelation from God.

human and yet His moral character was without flaw (Heb. 4:15), likewise He was finite in human knowledge and yet without factual error in His teaching (John 8:40, 46).

Summary and Conclusion

The Old Testament claims for itself to be the divinely inspired and authoritative Word of God. The New Testament claims the same for the Old Testament. Further, Jesus Himself taught that the Old Testament came from God. He affirmed that it is imperishable, infallible, historically reliable, scientifically accurate, and ultimately divinely authoritative. So, if Jesus is the Son of God, then the Old Testament must be the Word of God.

THE INSPIRATION *of* THE NEW TESTAMENT

THE APOSTLES AND PROPHETS OF THE NEW TESTAMENT did not hesitate to classify their writings as inspired along with the Old Testament. Their books were revered, collected, and circulated in the early church as sacred Scripture. What Jesus claimed about the Old Testament inspiration He also promised His disciples for the New. Let us examine this promise of inspiration and its fulfillment in the pages of the New Testament.

THE NEW TESTAMENT CLAIM OF INSPIRATION

There are two basic movements in understanding the New Testament claims about its own inspiration. First is the promise of Christ that the Holy Spirit would guide them in the teaching of His truth as the foundation of the church. Then there is the acclaimed fulfillment of this in the apostolic teaching and in writing of the New Testament.

The Promise of Christ about Inspiration

Jesus did not write any books. He did, however, commend the authority of the Old Testament (see chap. 3) and promised to inspire the New. On several occasions Jesus promised divine authority for the apostolic witness about Himself.

The commission of the twelve. When Jesus first sent out His disciples to preach the kingdom of heaven (Matt. 10:7), He promised them the direction of the Holy Spirit. "For what you are to say will be given to you in that hour. For it is not you who speak, but the Spirit of your Father speaking through you" (Matt. 10:19–20; cf. Luke 12:11–12). Their proclamations for Christ were prompted by the Spirit of God.

The sending of the seventy. The promise of divine unction was not limited to the twelve. When Jesus sent out the seventy to preach "the kingdom of God" (Luke 10:9) He told them, "the one who hears you hears me, and he who rejects you rejects me" (Luke 10:16). They returned acknowledging the authority of God on their ministry even over Satan (Luke 10:17–19).

The Mount Olivet discourse. In His sermon on the Mount of Olives, Jesus reaffirmed His original promise to the disciples. "Do not be anxious beforehand, what you are to say," He exhorted them. "But say whatever is given you in that hour, for it is not you who speak, but the Holy Spirit" (Mark 13:11). Their words were to come from God by the Spirit and not merely from themselves.

The Last Supper teachings. The promise of the guidance of the Holy Spirit was more clearly defined at the Last Supper. Jesus promised them, "But the Helper, the Holy Spirit, whom the Father will send in my name, he will teach you all things, and bring to your remembrance all that I have said to you" (John 14:26). Here is the key to why Jesus did not write His teachings. The Spirit would quicken the memories of those who heard Him; they would be Spirit-directed in all that Christ had taught them. For, "When the Spirit of truth comes, he will guide you into all the truth" (John 16:13). "All truth" or "all things" Christ taught would be Spirit-guided. Apostolic teaching would be inspired of God's Spirit.

The Great Commission. When Jesus at last commissioned His disciples to "make disciples of all nations . . . teaching them to observe all I have commanded you" (Matt. 28:19–20), it was with the promise that they had all authority in heaven and earth to do so. Whatever they taught would be invested with the authority of God. Their words would be God's Word.

The Promise of Christ Claimed by the Disciples

The followers of Christ did not forget His promise. They claimed for their teaching precisely what Jesus promised, the authority of God. This they did in several distinct ways: by claiming to continue Christ's teaching ministry, by claiming equality with the Old Testament, and by making specific claims in their writings for divine authority.

The claim to be continuing Christ's teaching. Luke claims to give an accurate account of what "Jesus began to do and teach" in his gospel. He implies that Acts records what Jesus continued to do and teach through the apostles (Acts 1:1; cf. Luke 1:3–4). Indeed, the first church is said to have been characterized by devotion to "the apostles' teaching" (Acts 2:42). Even the teachings of Paul, based as they were on direct revelations from God (Gal. 1:11–12), were subjected to apostolic approval (Acts 15). The New Testament church itself is said to be "built on the foundation of the apostles and [New Testament] prophets" (Eph. 2:20; 3:5; cf. Col. 1:26).

Whereas it is true that the oral pronouncements of the living apostles were as authoritative as their written ones (2 Thess. 2:15), it is also true that the books of the New Testament are the only authentic record of apostolic teaching that we have today. The qualification that a member of the twelve apostles must be an eyewitness of the ministry and resurrection of Christ (Acts 1:21–22) eliminates any succession of apostles beyond the first century. In fact, when the apostle James died (Acts 12:2) he was not replaced with another apostle. Rather, the apostles "appointed elders for them in every church" (Acts 14:23). And the fact that no authentic apostolic teaching exists which is not found in the New Testament limits all that the apostles taught to the twenty-seven books of the New Testament. Along with the Old Testament, these books alone are considered inspired or divinely authoritative because only these have been found to be truly apostolic or prophetic (see chap. 10).

In brief, Christ promised that all apostolic teaching would be Spirit-directed. The New Testament books are the only authentic record we have of apostolic teaching. Hence, the New Testament alone can lay claim to be an authoritative record of Christ's teachings.

Comparison of the New Testament to the Old. The promise of Christ to inspire the teachings of the apostles and the fulfillment of that promise in the writings of the New Testament is not the only indication of its inspiration. Another indication is its direct comparison to the Old Testament. Paul distinctly recognized the inspiration of the Old Testament (2 Tim. 3:16) by calling it "scripture." Peter classed Paul's epistles right along with "the other Scriptures" (2 Pet. 3:16), and Paul quotes Luke's gospel, calling it "Scripture" (1 Tim. 5:18, quoting Luke 10:7). Indeed, elsewhere the apostle gives his own writings equal authority with "Scripture" (1 Tim. 4:11, 13).

The book of Hebrews declares that the God who spoke of old through prophets has "in these last days" spoken to us about salvation through His Son (Heb. 1:2). The author goes on to say, "It was declared at first by the Lord, and it was attested to us by those [apostles] who heard" (Heb. 2:3). The apostles were the channel of God's truth in the New Testament just as the prophets were in the Old. It is not strange, then, to observe that the apostolic books should be placed on the same authoritative level as the inspired books of the Old Testament. Both are prophetic.

As a matter of fact, Peter wrote that prophetic writings came by divine inspiration (2 Pet. 1:21), and New Testament writings distinctly claim to be prophetic. John calls his book a "prophecy" and classes himself among the prophets (Rev. 22:18–19). New Testament prophets are listed along with the apostles as the foundation of the church (Eph. 2:20). Paul probably includes his own writings when he speaks of "the revelation of the mystery that was kept secret for long ages but has now been disclosed and through the prophetic writings has been made known to all nations" (Rom. 16:25–26). He claimed in Ephesians 3:3–5 that "the mystery was made known to me by revelation . . . which was not made known to the sons of men in other generations as it has now [in New Testament times] been revealed to His holy apostles and [New Testament] prophets by the Spirit" (cf. Eph. 2:20). So the prophetic writings of the New Testament reveal the mystery of Christ who was predicted in the prophetic writings of the Old Testament. Like the Old, the New Testament is a prophetic utterance of God.

Direct claims for inspiration in New Testament books. Within the books of the New Testament are numerous indications of their divine authority. These are both explicit and implicit. The Gospels present themselves as authoritative accounts of the fulfillment of Old Testament prophecies about Christ (cf. Matt. 1:22; 2:15, 17; Mark 1:2). Luke wrote in order that the reader could know the truth about Christ, which was delivered to us by "those who from the beginning were eyewitnesses and ministers of the word [of God]" (Luke 1:1). John recorded his words that men "may believe that Jesus is the Christ, the Son of God, and that believing . . . may have life in his name" (John 20:31). He adds that "his testimony is true" (John 21:24).

The Acts of the Apostles, also written by Luke, presents itself as an authoritative account of what Jesus continued to do and teach through the apostles (Acts 1:1). This too was seen as a fulfillment of Old Testament prophecy (cf. Acts 2 and Joel 2). Since Paul quoted Luke's gospel as "Scripture" (1 Tim. 5:18), it is evident that both he and Luke considered continuation of that account in Acts to be divinely authoritative as well.

Each of Paul's epistles, Romans through Philemon, lays claim to inspiration. In Romans Paul establishes his divine call to apostleship (Rom. 1:1–3). He concludes this letter with a claim that it is a prophetic writing (Rom. 16:26). The apostle completes 1 Corinthians saying, "What I am writing to you is a command of the Lord" (1 Cor. 14:37 RSV). He introduces 2 Corinthians by repeating the claim to apostleship (2 Cor. 1:1–2). In that letter he defends his apostleship more completely than anywhere else in the New Testament (2 Cor. 10–13). Galatians offers the strongest defense of Paul's divine credentials. Speaking of the revelation of the gospel of grace to him, he wrote, "I did not receive it from man, nor was I taught it, but it came through a revelation of Jesus Christ" (Gal. 1:12 RSV). In Ephesians he further declares, "The mystery was made known to me by revelation" (Eph. 3:3). Philippians twice admonishes the believers to follow the apostolic pattern of life (Phil. 3:17; 4:9). In Colossians, like Ephesians, Paul argues that his apostolic office came directly from God "to make the word of God fully known" (Col. 1:25). First Thessalonians concludes with the admonition, "I adjure you by the Lord that this letter be read to all the brethren" (1 Thess. 5:27 RSV). Earlier he had reminded them it was "the word of God which you heard from us" (1 Thess. 2:13). Second Thessalonians also concludes with an exhortation: "If anyone does obey what we say in this letter, take note of that person, and have nothing to do with him, that he may be ashamed" (2 Thess. 3:14).

About the message of 1 Timothy, the apostle wrote, "Command and teach these things. . . . Until I come, devote yourself to the public reading of Scripture, to exhortation, to teaching" (1 Tim. 4:11, 13). Here Paul places his own epistle on par with the Old Testament. Both were to be read in the churches with binding authority (cf. Col. 4:16). Second Timothy contains the classical passage on inspiration (2 Tim. 3:16), as well as the exhortations to "follow the pattern of the sound words" received from Paul (2 Tim. 1:13). "I charge you," he wrote, "preach the word" (2 Tim. 4:1–2). Likewise, Paul commanded Titus, "Declare these things; exhort and rebuke with all authority" (Titus 2:15). Although the tone in Philemon is intercessory, Paul makes it clear that he could command what is requested in love (Philem. 8–9).

Hebrews 2:3–4 makes it evident that this book—whoever wrote it—is based on the authority of God through the apostles and eyewitnesses of Christ. Its readers are told to remember their leaders, those "who spoke to you the word of God" (Heb. 13:7). The writer then adds, "I appeal to you, brothers, bear with my word of exhortation" (Heb. 13:22). James, the brother of our Lord (Gal. 1:19) and leader of the Jerusalem church (Acts 15:13), writes with apostolic authority "to the twelve tribes in the Dispersion" (James 1:1). First Peter claims to be from "Peter, an apostle of Jesus Christ" (1 Pet. 1:1), and contains typical apostolic exhortations (1 Pet. 5:1, 12). Second Peter comes from "Simon Peter, a servant and apostle of Jesus Christ" (2 Pet. 1:11) and reminds the readers that "the commandment of the Lord and Savior through your apostles" are of the same authority with the predictions of the prophets in the Old Testament (2 Pet. 3:2). First John comes from one who has "heard, . . . seen with our eyes, . . . looked upon . . . and touched with our hands" Christ (1 John 1:1). In this book John presents the test for truth and error (1 John 4:1–2), designates the apostolic community as from God (1 John 2:20), and writes to confirm the faith of true believers (1 John 5:13). The books of 2 John and 3 John came from the same apostle with the same authority (cf. 2 John 5, 7; 3 John 9, 12). Jude writes a record of "our common salvation" in defense of "the faith which was once for all delivered to the saints" (Jude 3).

"The revelation of Jesus Christ, which God gave" (Rev. 1:1) describes the origin of the last book in the New Testament. "I was in the Spirit on the Lord's day," wrote John, "and I heard behind me a loud voice like a trumpet saying, 'Write what you see in a book and send it to the seven churches'" (Rev. 1:10–11). No book in the Bible contains a more explicit claim to divine inspiration than the Revelation. The warning not to tamper with its words is placed under a threat of divine judgment, which is the strongest such threat in Scripture. It is an appropriate conclusion to the claim that the entire New Testament is the inspired Word of God, on a par with the sacred writings of the Old Testament.

SUPPORTING CLAIM FOR THE INSPIRATION OF THE NEW TESTAMENT

There are two lines of evidence that indicate support of the New Testament claim of divine inspiration. One is within the New Testament itself, and the other begins with church fathers who followed the apostles.

Supporting Claim for Inspiration within the New Testament

The first-century church was not naive in its acceptance of inspired writings. Jesus had warned of false prophets and deceivers coming in His name (Matt. 7:15; 24:10–11). Paul exhorted the Thessalonians not to accept erroneous teaching from any letter pretending to be from him (2 Thess. 2:2). John urged the believers, "Beloved, do not believe every spirit, but test the spirits to see whether they are from God" (1 John 4:1). There were incorrect and false teachings about Christ circulating in the first century (cf. Luke 1:1–4). Hence, the New Testament church had to be discriminating from the very beginning. Any books received without apostolic signature (2 Thess. 3:17) were to be refused. The fact that books were read, quoted, collected, and circulated within the New Testament church gives assurance that they were received as prophetic or divinely inspired from the very beginning.

Public reading of New Testament books. It was a Jewish custom to read the Scriptures on the Sabbath (cf. Luke 4:16). The church continued this practice on the Lord's Day. Paul urged Timothy to "attend to the public reading of scripture" (1 Tim. 4:13 RSV). In the Colossian epistle Paul wrote, "And when this letter has been read among you, have it also read in the church of the Laodiceans; and see that you read also the letter from Laodicea" (Col. 4:16). The public reading of these letters as Scripture in the churches verified their initial acceptance as divine authority by the New Testament church.

Circulation of New Testament books. The Colossian passage cited above reveals another very important fact. The books written to one church were intended to be of value for other churches, and they were circulated in order to accomplish this purpose. Perhaps this procedure of trading inspired books led to the earliest copies of the New Testament. One thing indicated by this circulation is that churches other than the one addressed in the epistle recognized and read as Holy Scripture the various letters.

Collection of New Testament books. Not only were New Testament books read and circulated in the churches, but Peter informs us that they were collected as well. Peter apparently possessed a collection of Paul's letters which he plainly classed with the inspired writings of the Old Testament. He wrote, "So also our beloved brother Paul wrote to you according to the wisdom given him, speaking of this as he does in all his letters . . . which the ignorant and unstable twist to their own destruction, as they do the other scriptures" (2 Pet. 3:15–16 RSV). These books were read, circulated, and collected by the

New Testament church along with the canon of the Old Testament, and without question they were considered inspired writings.

Quotation of New Testament books. The books of the Old Testament were written over a much longer time span than the New. Hence, there is more quotation of earlier prophets by later ones in the Old Testament. Nevertheless, the fact that quotations from earlier New Testament books are found in later ones reveals that these books were considered inspired writings by their contemporaries. In 1 Timothy 5:18 Paul quoted Luke's gospel as Scripture: "The laborer deserves his wages" (cf. Luke 10:7). Jude clearly cites 2 Pet. 3:2–3, saying, "But you must remember, beloved, the predictions of the apostles of our Lord Jesus Christ. They said to you, 'In the last time there will be scoffers, following their own ungodly passions' " (Jude 17–18). Luke refers to his previous book (Acts 1:1) and John alludes to his own gospel (1 John 1:1). Paul mentions another letter he wrote to the Corinthians (1 Cor. 5:9); see discussion on p. 155.

While some of these examples provide no formal quotations, they do help illustrate the fact that within the New Testament itself there is recognition of one inspired writing by another. And the total process of reading, circulating, collecting, and quoting of New Testament books in New Testament times amply illustrates the recognition of their claim of divine inspiration.

Supporting Claim for Inspiration within the Early Church

Every one of the New Testament writers is quoted with divine authority by an apostolic father. These leaders of the church lived within a generation or two of the close of the New Testament (i.e., before 150 CE). In effect they provide an unbroken continuity to the New Testament claim of inspiration from apostolic time into the early church, and for that matter down through the centuries following.

The earliest church fathers. The earliest writings in Christendom contain numerous references to New Testament Scripture. Many of these citations have the same authoritative designations as those used when the New Testament quotes the Old. The *Epistle of Pseudo-Barnabas* (ca. 70–130), a work falsely ascribed to Paul's associate, cites Matthew 26:31 as what "God saith" (5:12). Later it calls Matthew 22:14 "scripture" (4:14). Clement of Rome, in his *Epistle to the Corinthians* (ca. 95–97), calls the Synoptic Gospels (Matthew,

Mark, Luke) "Scripture." He also employs the phrases "God saith" and "it is written" to designate passages from the New Testament (cf. chaps. 36 and 46). Ignatius of Antioch (d. ca. 110) wrote seven epistles in which he made numerous citations from the New Testament Scriptures.

Polycarp (ca. 110–135), a disciple of the apostle John, included many quotations from New Testament books in his *Epistle to the Philippians.* Sometimes he introduced them with expressions like "the Scriptures saith" (cf. chap. 12). The so-called *Shepherd of Hermas* (ca. 115–140) was written in the apocalyptic style (visions) of the book of Revelation and contains numerous references to the New Testament. *The Didache* (ca. 100–120), or *Teaching of the Twelve,* as it is sometimes called, records many loose quotations of the New Testament. Papias (ca. 130–140) includes the New Testament in a book entitled *Exposition of the Oracles of the Lord,* the same phrase used to denote the Old Testament in Romans 3:2. The so-called *Epistle to Diognetus* (ca. 150) makes many allusions to the New Testament without title.

What is apparent in the use of the New Testament by the apostolic fathers is this: the New Testament, like the Old, was considered a divinely inspired book. Often the quotations are loose and usually undesignated as to source. But anyone reading the Fathers cannot fail to see that the works of the New Testament apostles were given the same high esteem as the inspired books of the Old Testament.

Later church fathers. From the latter part of the second century there is a continuing support for the claim of New Testament inspiration. Justin Martyr (d. 165) regarded the Gospels as "the voice of God" (Apology 1.65). "We must not suppose," he wrote, "that the language proceeds from men who were inspired, but from the Divine Word which moves them" (1.36). Tatian (ca. 110–180), a disciple of Justin, quotes John 1:5 as "scripture" in chapter 13 of his Apology. Irenaeus (ca. 130–202) in his *Against Heresies* wrote, "For the Lord of all gave the power of the Gospel to his apostles, through whom we have come to know the truth. . . . This Gospel they preached. Afterwards, by the will of God, they handed it down to us in the Scriptures, to be 'the pillar and ground' of our faith" (5.67).

Clement of Alexandria (ca. 150–215) classes both Testaments as equally divine authority saying, "The Scriptures . . . in the Law, in the Prophets, and besides by the blessed Gospel . . . are valid from their omnipotent authority" (Stromata 2. 408–9). Tertullian (ca. 160–220) maintained that the four gospels "are reared on the certain basis of Apostolical authority, and so are inspired in a far different sense from the writings of the spiritual Christian."[1]

Hippolytus (ca. 170–236), a disciple of Irenaeus, offers one of the most definitive statements on inspiration in the early Fathers. In *De Antichristo*, speaking of the New Testament writers, he affirmed,

> These blessed men . . . having been perfected by the Spirit of prophecy are worthily honored by the Word Himself, were brought to an inner harmony, . . . like instruments, and having the Word within them, as it were, to strike the notes . . . by Him they were moved, and announced that which God wished. For they did not speak of their own power; . . . they spake that which was [revealed] to them alone by God.[2]

Origen (ca. 185–254), teacher in Alexandria, also affirmed the inspiration of Scriptures.[3] He held that the "Spirit inspired each one of the saints, whether prophets or apostles; and there was not one Spirit in the men of the old dispensation, and another in those who were inspired at the advent of Christ" (from *De Principiis*). For in its entirety, "the Scriptures were written by the Spirit" (16:6). The bishop Cyprian (ca. 200–258) clearly affirmed the inspiration of the New Testament, declaring it to be "Divine Scripture" given by the Holy Spirit. Eusebius of Caesarea (ca. 265–340), noted as a church historian, expounded and catalogued the inspired books of both testaments in his *Ecclesiastical History*. Athanasius of Alexandria (ca. 295–373), known as the "father of orthodoxy" because of his defense of the deity of Christ against Arius, was the first to use the word *canon* of the New Testament books.

Cyril of Jerusalem (ca. 315–386) speaks of "the divinely inspired Scriptures of both the Old and the New Testaments." After listing the twenty-two books of the Hebrew Scriptures and twenty-six of the New Testament (all but Revelation), he adds, "Learn also diligently, and from the Church, what

---

1. Brooke Foss Westcott, *An Introduction to the Study of the Gospels* (New York: Macmillan, 1902), 421.

2. Quoted in Westcott, *An Introduction to the Study*, 418–19; Westcott's brackets.

3. Origen, however, did allegorize away some of the literal affirmations of the Bible (like Adam and Eve and the physical resurrection of Christ), thus denying the literal truth of these passages.

are the books of the Old Testament, and what are those of the New. And, pray, read none of the apocryphal writings" (*Of the Divine Scriptures*).

It is unnecessary to proceed further. It will suffice at this point to note that the orthodox doctrine of the inspiration of the New Testament continued down through the Middle Ages into the Reformation and on into the modern period of church history. Louis Gaussen has the situation well summarized as he writes,

> With the single exception of Theodore of Mopsuestia [ca. 400], it has been found impossible to produce, in the long course of the EIGHT FIRST CENTURIES OF CHRISTIANITY, a single doctor who has disowned the plenary inspiration of the Scriptures, unless it be in the bosom of the most violent heresies that have tormented the Christian Church.[4]

In summary then, the inspiration of the New Testament is based on the promise of Christ that His disciples would be directed by the Spirit in their teachings about Him. His disciples claimed this promise, and there is clear indication that the writers of the New Testament themselves, as well as their contemporaries, recognized it as accomplished. They believed that the New Testament was divinely inspired, and from the time of the very earliest Christian records on, there has been an almost unanimous support for the inspiration of the New Testament along with the Old.

---

4. L. Gaussen, *Theopneustia: The Plenary Inspiration of the Holy Scriptures*, trans. David Scott (Chicago: BICA, n.d.), 139–40.

5

THE EVIDENCES *for the* INSPIRATION *of* THE BIBLE

THROUGH THE CENTURIES Christians have been called upon to give a reason or defense for their faith (1 Pet. 3:15). Since the Scriptures lie at the very foundation of their faith in Christ, it has been incumbent upon Christian apologists to provide evidence for the inspiration of the Bible. It is one thing to *claim* divine inspiration for the Bible and quite another to provide evidence to *confirm* that claim. Before examining the supporting evidence for the inspiration of Scripture, let us summarize precisely what it is that inspiration claims.

A SUMMARY OF THE CLAIM FOR THE INSPIRATION OF THE BIBLE

The inspiration of the Bible is not to be confused with a poetic inspiration. Inspiration as applied to the Bible refers to the God-given authority of its teachings for the thought and life of the believer.

Biblical Description of Inspiration

The word *inspiration* means "God-breathed," and it refers to the process by which the Scriptures or writings were invested with divine authority for doctrine and practice (2 Tim. 3:16–17). It is the writings that are said to be inspired. The writers, however, were Spirit-moved to record their messages. Hence, when viewed as a total process, inspiration is what occurs when Spirit-moved writers record God-breathed writings. Three elements are contained in this total process of inspiration: the divine causality, the prophetic agency, and the resultant written authority (see chaps. 1 and 2).

The Three Elements in Inspiration

The first element in inspiration is *God's causality.* God is the Prime Mover by whose promptings the prophets were led to write. The ultimate origin of inspired writings is the desire of the Divine to communicate with man. The second factor is the *prophetic agency.* The Word of God comes through men of God. God employs the instrumentality of human personality to convey His message. Finally, the written prophetic utterance is invested with *divine authority.* The prophet's words are God's Word.

The Characteristics of an Inspired Writing

The first characteristic of inspiration is implied in the fact that it is an inspired writing; namely, it is verbal. The very words of the prophets were God-given, not by dictation but by the Spirit-directed employment of the prophet's own vocabulary and style.

Inspiration also claims to be plenary (full). No part of Scripture is without divine inspiration. Paul wrote, "All scripture is inspired by God" (2 Tim. 3:16 NASB).

In addition, inspiration implies the inerrancy of the teaching of the original documents (called autographs). Whatever God utters is true and without error, and the Bible is said to be an utterance of God.

Finally, inspiration results in the divine authority of the Scriptures. The teaching of Scripture is binding on the believer for faith and practice.

Inspiration is not something merely attributed to the Bible by Christians; it is something the Bible claims for itself. There are literally hundreds of references within the Bible about its divine origin (see chaps. 3 and 4). But to claim is not to prove. Hence, we turn to the proposed evidence for the Bible's claim to be the Word of God.

SUPPORT FOR THE BIBLICAL CLAIM TO DIVINE INSPIRATION

The argument for the divine origin of the Bible can be stated simply: (1) The Bible claims to be the Word of God; (2) the Bible proves to be the Word of God. Since the claim for divine inspiration was covered previously, we will explore the credentials for this claim in this chapter. The discipline that covers this is called *apologetics.*

An Apologetic for Apologetics

Not all Christians believe in apologetics. So, we must first give a defense for giving a defense for the faith. Two points will suffice here. First, the Bible commands it, and second, reason demands it.

The Bible commands apologetics. Defenders of the Christian faith have responded to this challenge in different ways. Some have transformed Christianity into a rational system, others have insisted it must be accepted by faith alone. But the great mass of informed Christians through the centuries have avoided either rationalism or fideism. Claiming neither absolute finality nor complete skepticism, Christian apologists have given "a reason for the hope that is in [them]" (1 Pet. 3:15) and have taken heed to the exhortation to "contend for the faith" (Jude 3). Paul added, "I am put here for the defense of the gospel" (Phil. 1:16), and "Know how you ought to answer each person" (Col. 4:6). He set the example with the unbelieving Jews when he "reasoned with them from the Scriptures, explaining and proving that it was necessary for the Christ to suffer and to rise from the dead" (Acts 17:2–3). Later, he did the same with the Greeks, citing from some of their own philosophers, and "some men joined him and believed, among whom also were Dionysius the Areopagite and a woman named Damaris and others with them" (Acts 17:34).

Reason demands apologetics. Reason demands that not all views can be true. Opposite claims cannot both be true. But there are opposing religious systems which all claim their Holy Book is the Word of God. For example, Jews, Christians, and Muslims all claim their Holy Book is the complete Word of God to mankind. But the Bible, Torah, and Book of Mormon cannot all be the Word of God since they teach opposing views. For example, the Qur'an teaches there is only one Person in God, and Christianity insists there are three Persons in the One God: Father, Son, and Holy Spirit. Jews believe, based on the Torah, that Jesus is not the Messiah, but Christians claim that He is. Both can't be true, and so on.

Some Christians claim that the Bible needs no proof; it is the self-authenticating Word of God. They insist that the Bible, like a lion, does not need to be defended; it simply needs to be let loose. However, reason demands that this cannot be so. For no Christian would accept a Muslim claim that "the Qur'an does not need to be defended; it simply needs to be expounded." Likewise, the Mormon claim that the Book of Mormon must be true, since they have the witness of the Holy Spirit that it is the Word of God, would not be accepted by Jews, Christians, or Muslims. A subjective feeling is not enough; there must be some objective evidence to adjudicate the matter.

Objective Evidence that the Bible Is the Word of God

The evidence that the Bible, and the Bible alone, is the Word of God is very strong. The complete argument has several steps. These have been detailed elsewhere.[1]

Here we will only sketch the overall argument and stress a few key points:

1. Truth can be known.
2. The opposite of true is false.
3. It is true that a theistic God exists.
4. If God exists, then miracles are possible.
5. Miracles can be used to confirm a message from God.
6. The New Testament is historically reliable.
7. In the New Testament Jesus claimed to be God in human flesh.
8. Many miracles confirmed Jesus' claim to be God.
9. Therefore, Jesus is God.
10. But whatever Jesus (who is God) teaches is true.
11. Jesus taught that the Bible is the Word of God.
12. Therefore, the Bible is the Word of God (and whatever is opposed to it is false).

Now let's fill the premises with some content, stressing the crucial points. This will be necessary to get the full impact of the argument for the divine inspiration of Holy Scripture.

1. Truth can be known. Truth is what corresponds to the facts (i.e., to reality). This is undeniable, since the claim "Truth does not correspond to the facts" contains the implicit claim that this statement corresponds to the facts.

Further, that truth can be known is undeniable, for the claim "Truth

1. See N. L. Geisler, *Christian Apologetics*, rev. ed. (Grand Rapids: Baker, 2012) or Norman L. Geisler and Frank Turek, *I Don't Have Enough Faith to Be an Atheist* (Wheaton, Ill.: Crossway, 2004).

cannot be known" is a truth which claims to be known. The claim that we can know that we cannot know truth is self-defeating.

2. The opposite of true is false. This too is an undeniable truth. For the denial of it, namely, that "the opposite of true is not false," has the implicit claim that it is true and the opposite of it is false. This is called the Law of Non-Contradiction. The famous philosopher Avicenna said anyone who is not convinced of it should be beaten and burned until he admits that to be beaten is not the same as not to be beaten, and to be burned is not the same as not to be burned. The truth is that everyone really believes in this law in all of his or her thoughts and actions.

3. It is true that a theistic God exists. This topic is too big for a small space here, and we have treated it more extensively elsewhere.[2] Only two things need to be said now: (a) If God does not exist, then obviously the Bible, however unique it may be, cannot be the Word of God. For unless there is a God, He cannot have a Word; (b) If God exists, then there can be a Word of God. So, for someone to disprove the Bible is the Word of God, he would have to disprove that God exists. But despite all the objections to God's existence, no one has proven his nonexistence, as even most atheists will admit.

4. If God exists, then miracles are possible. As C. S. Lewis put it, "But if we admit God, must we admit miracles? Indeed, indeed, you have no security against it. That is the bargain."[3] Thus, to disprove the possibility of miracles one would have to disprove the existence of God, which no one has succeeded in doing.[4] Certainly, if God can create the world from nothing (Gen. 1:1; John 1:3; 2 Cor. 4:6), any lesser miracles are no problem. In short, if there is a God who can act (in creation), then there can be acts of God in creation.

5. Miracles can be used to confirm a message from God. But if God exists, and miracles are possible, then they can confirm a message from God. As Nicodemus put it to Jesus, "Rabbi, we know that you are a teacher come from God, for no one can do these signs that you do unless God is with him" (John 3:2). The writer of Hebrews said of salvation, "It was declared at first by the Lord, and it was attested to us by those who heard, while God also bore witness by signs and wonders and various miracles and by gifts of

2. See Geisler, *Christian Apologetics*, chaps. 14 and 15.

3. C. S. Lewis, *Miracles* (New York: Macmillan, 1947), 109.

4. See Geisler, *Christian Apologetics*, chap. 14.

the Holy Spirit distributed according to his will" (Heb. 2:3-4). When Moses (Ex. 4) and Elijah (1 Kings 18) were challenged, they performed miracles to confirm they were prophets of God.[5]

6. The New Testament is historically reliable. There is more evidence for the reliability of the New Testament than for any other book from antiquity—for it has more, earlier, and better manuscripts than for any other book from antiquity (see chap. 12). There are nearly 6,000 Greek manuscripts and some 19,000 manuscripts from early translations of the Bible, totaling 25,000 manuscripts. Most other ancient books survive on the basis of ten to twenty manuscripts, Homer's *Iliad* being the exception with 643 manuscripts. Furthermore, the gap between the time of composition and earliest manuscript is about a thousand years for most other ancient books, while it is a little over a hundred years for the first copy of a gospel. What is more, the New Testament is copied with a higher degree of accuracy than other books from antiquity, retaining all the essential truths of the original in the copies (see chap. 12).

In addition to the New Testament writings being reliable, there is more, earlier, and better evidence that the New Testament writers were reliable than for any other book of their time. For there were eight or nine writers (depending on whether Paul wrote Hebrews) of twenty-seven books of the New Testament based on eyewitness testimony. Nothing like this exists for any other book from the ancient world. Further, there is historical, archaeological, legal, and secular support for the accuracy of their writings. One New Testament writer, Luke, had nearly one hundred details in his writings verified historically, without making a single demonstrable error![6] He is one of the most accurate writers from antiquity, and his two books alone, Luke and Acts, support the historicity of Christ and His immediate disciples.[7]

7. In the New Testament Jesus claimed to be God in human flesh. When one examines the central claims of the central figure in the historically reliable New Testament, he discovers that in numerous ways Jesus claimed to be God in human flesh, as did His disciples claim that He was God. Jesus claimed to be God in many ways, as follows.

5. For further discussion of all these points 1–5 see Geisler, *Christian Apologetics*.

6. See Colin Hemer, *The Book of Acts in the Setting of Hellenic History* (Winona Lake, Ind.: Eisenbrauns, 1990).

7. For further details on the historicity of the New Testament, see Norman L. Geisler and Joseph Holden, *The Popular Handbook of Biblical Archaeology* (Eugene, Oreg.: Harvest House, 2012), chaps. 1–4.

Jesus Claimed to Be Yahweh. "Yahweh" is the spelling given to the tetragrammaton or designation for God (i.e., YHWH, יהוה) in the Old Testament. Unlike the word "adonai" (usually translated "lord") which sometimes refers to men (cf. Gen. 18:12) and other times to God, the word LORD (*Yahweh*) always refers to God. For example, "God spoke to Moses and said to him, 'I am the LORD. I appeared to Abraham, to Isaac, and to Jacob, as God Almighty, but by my name the LORD [Yahweh] I did not make myself known to them'" (Ex. 6:2, 3). So sacred was this name, YHWH, יהוה, that devout Jews would not even pronounce it. Many take the word to mean "underused existence" or "He who is" from the "I AM" of Exodus 3:14. Everything else is an idol or false god. Nothing else was to be worshiped or served, nor were sacrifices to be made to them (Ex. 20:5). Yahweh was a "jealous God" and would not share either His name or His glory with another. Thus God declared through the prophet Isaiah, "I am the first and I am the last; besides me there is no god . . . I am the Lord; that is my name; my glory I give to no other, nor my praise to carved idols" (Isa. 44:6; 42:8; cf. 48:11).

Perhaps the strongest and most direct claim of Jesus to be Yahweh occurs in John 8:59, where He said to the Jews, "Truly, truly, I say to you, before Abraham was, I am." The Jews' reaction left no doubt as to how they understood His claim. They knew He had claimed not only preexistence before Abraham but also equality with God. They promptly picked up stones to stone Him (cf. John 8:59 and 10:31–33). Jesus clearly claimed to be the "I AM" of Exodus 3:14 which refers to Yahweh alone. The claim was either blasphemy or else an indication of deity. Jesus left no doubt as to which interpretation He wished them to take. His claim to be "I am" is repeated in Mark 14:62 and in John 18:5–6. In the latter case the effect on those around Christ was dramatic: "They drew back and fell to the ground."

Jesus also claimed to be many things the Old Testament affirms belong only to Yahweh. He said, "I am the good shepherd" (John 10:11), but the Old Testament declared, "The LORD [Yahweh, יהוה] is my shepherd" (Ps. 23:1). Jesus claimed to be judge of all men and nations (John 5:27ff. and Matt. 25:31ff.) but Joel, quoting the Lord, wrote: "for there I will sit to judge all the surrounding nations" (Joel 3:12). Jesus said, "I am the light of the world" (John 8:12), whereas Isaiah says, "The LORD [Yahweh, יהוה] will be your everlasting light, and your God will be your glory" (60:19). Jesus claimed in prayer before the Father to share His eternal glory, saying, "Father, glorify thou me in thy own presence with the glory which I had with thee before the world was made" (John 17:ff KJV). But Isaiah quoted Yahweh vowing, "My glory will I not give to another" (42:8 KJV). Jesus spoke of Himself as the coming "bridegroom" (Matt. 25:1), which is exactly how Yahweh is depicted in the Old Testament (cf. Isa. 62:5; Hos. 2:16). In the book of Revelation Jesus is quoted by John as saying, "I am the first and the last" (1:17), which are precisely the words Yahweh used to declare that there was no other God besides Himself (Isa. 44:6). The Old Testament declares that "the LORD [Yahweh, יהוה] is my light" (Ps. 27:1), but Jesus said, "I am the light of the world" (John 8:12).

Jesus Claimed to Be Equal with God. On numerous occasions Jesus claimed equality with God in other ways than assuming the titles of deity. Jesus said to the scribes, "That you may know that the Son of Man has authority on earth to forgive sins"—He said to the paralytic—"I say to you rise, take up your pallet and go home" (Mark 2:10, 11 RSV). Jesus had just said to him, "My son, your sins are forgiven" (v. 5), to which the outraged scribes retorted, "Why does this man speak like that? He is blaspheming! Who can forgive sins but God alone?" (v. 7). Jesus' claim to be able to forgive sins, the scribes' understanding of that claim, and Jesus' healing of the man are all evidence of His authority, and make it clear that Jesus was claiming a power that God alone possessed (cf. Jer. 31:34).

Jesus also claimed another power that God alone possessed, namely, the power to raise and judge the dead (in John 5:25, 29). He asserted, "For as the Father raises the dead and gives them life, so also the Son gives life to whom he will" (v. 21). According to the Old Testament, however, God alone is the giver of life (1 Sam. 2:6; Deut. 32:39) and can raise men from the dead (Ps. 2:7). Hence, in the face of orthodox Jewish belief that God alone could resurrect the dead, Jesus not only boldly proclaimed His ability to bring the dead back but also His right to judge them. The Scriptures, however, reserved for Yahweh the right to judge men (Joel 3:12; Deut. 32:35). In this same category, Jesus exhorted His disciples, "Believe in God; believe also in me" (John 14:1). The Jews knew well that no man should claim honor and equality with God. They wanted to kill Jesus (John 5:18) and ripped their garments (Mark 14:63–64) because they believed this was blasphemous.

Jesus Claimed to Be the Messiah-God. The Old Testament foreshadowing of the Messiah also pointed to His deity. Hence, when Jesus claimed to fulfill the Old Testament messianic predictions He thereby also claimed the deity attributed to the Messiah in those passages. For example, the famous Christmas text from Isaiah speaks of the Messiah as the "Mighty God" (9:6). The psalmist wrote of the Messiah, "Thy throne, O God, is forever and ever" (from 45:6 KJV, quoted in Heb. 1:8). Psalm 110:1 relates a conversation between the Father and the Son: "The LORD [Yahweh, יהוה] said to my LORD [Heb. *Adonai*], sit at my right hand." Jesus applied this passage to Himself in Matthew 22:43–44.

The great messianic passage from Daniel 7:13, quoted by Jesus at His trial before the high priest, is a text implying the deity of the Messiah. When Jesus quoted this passage to the high priest who demanded that Jesus declare whether or not He was deity, the high priest left no doubt as to how he interpreted Jesus' claim to be the Christ. "Jesus said, 'I am, and you will see the Son of Man seated at the right hand of Power, and coming with the clouds of heaven.' And the high priest tore his garments and said, 'What further witnesses do we need? You have heard his blasphemy' " (Mark 14:62–64).

Also, the Samaritan woman said to Jesus, "I know that Messiah is coming (he who is called Christ). When he comes, he will tell us all things." Jesus said clearly, "I who speak to you am he" (John 4:25–26). This was a clear claim to be the Jewish Messiah whom the Old Testament declared to be God.

In short, the Old Testament not only predicted the Messiah but also proclaimed Him to be God. And when Jesus claimed to be a fulfillment of the Old Testament messianic passages (cf. Luke 24:27, 44; Matt. 26:54), He laid claim to possessing the deity these passages ascribed to the Messiah. Jesus removed all doubts of His intentions by His answer before the high priest at His trial.

Jesus Accepted Worship on Numerous Occasions. The Old Testament forbids worship of anyone but God (Ex. 20:1–4; Deut. 5:6–9). In the Bible men were not to accept worship (see Acts 14:15) and even angels refused to be worshiped (Rev. 22:8–9). And yet Jesus received worship on at least nine occasions without rebuking a single one of His worshipers. Those worshiping included a healed leper (Matt. 8:2), a ruler who knelt before Him with his petition (Matt. 9:18), and the stunned disciples who had watched Him still a storm (Matt. 14:33). Among others who worshiped were a Canaanite woman (Matt. 15:25), the demoniac of the Gerasenes (Mark 5:6), and a blind man whom Jesus healed (John 9:38).

Not to rebuke these people who knelt before Him, prayed to Him, and worshiped Him would be not only utterly pretentious but blasphemous, unless Jesus considered Himself to be God. The repetition and the context necessitate the conclusion that Jesus not only accepted but sometimes even elicited worship from the disciples, as He did from Thomas who cried out, "My Lord and my God!" (John 20:28).

Jesus Blessed Those Who Called Him God. On one occasion Jesus pronounced a blessing on those who recognized His deity. When Peter confessed, "You are the Christ, the Son of the living God," Jesus answered, "Blessed are you, Simon Bar-Jonah! For flesh and blood has not revealed this to you, but my Father who is in heaven" (Matt. 16:16–17). Also, at the climax of the gospel of John, when even Jesus' most doubtful disciple exclaimed of Him, "My Lord and my God," Jesus accepted his acclamation without rebuke, saying, "Have you believed because you have seen me? Blessed are those who have not seen and yet have believed" (John 20:28–29).

Jesus Requested That People Pray in His Name. Jesus not only asked people to believe in Him (John 14:1) and to obey His commandments (John 14:15), but He asked them to pray in His name. "Whatever you ask in my name, I will do it," He said. Again, "If you ask anything in my name, I will do it" (John 14:14 RSV). Later, Jesus added, "If you abide in me, and my words abide in you, ask whatever you wish, and it will be done for you" (John 15:7). Indeed, Jesus insisted that "no one comes to the Father except through me" (John 14:6). It is interesting to note in this regard that not only did the disciples of Christ pray in Christ's name (1 Cor. 5:4) but they also prayed to Christ (Acts 7:59). There is no doubt that both Jesus intended and His disciples understood it was Jesus' name that was to be invoked both before God and as God's in prayer. But prayer is a form of worship, and the Bible forbids worshiping anyone but God. Indeed, Jesus declared, "You shall worship the Lord your God and him only shall you serve" (Matt. 4:10).

Throughout Jesus' claims, several important points emerge. First, there is no question that Jesus often accepted and sometimes even encouraged the appellations and attitudes appropriate only for God. Second, Jesus Himself unquestionably affirmed by words and actions these characteristics and prerogatives appropriate only to deity. Third, the reaction of those around Him manifests that they too understood Him to be claiming deity. The disciples responded with "You are the Christ, the Son of the living God" (Matt.

16:16) or "My Lord and my God" (John 20:28). Unbelievers exclaimed, "Why does this man speak like that? He is blaspheming!" (Mark 2:7). Whatever one may think about the truth or falsity of Christ's claims, it should be clear to the unbiased observer of the New Testament record that Jesus claimed to be equal to and identical with the Yahweh of the Old Testament.

The Cumulative Case. The sum total of all the evidence for Christ's claim to be God is overwhelming. No human being of any other major religion ever made such claims. Further, Jesus' immediate followers accepted this claim (John 1:1; 20:28; Matt. 16:16–18; Col. 2:9) and worshiped Him as God (see above). Even non-Christian writers recognized this. Pliny the Younger (112 CE) wrote of the early Christians: "They sang in alternate verses a hymn to Christ, as to god" (*Letters*, 10:96).

8. Many miracles confirmed Jesus' claim to be God. Not only did Jesus claim to be God, but He was confirmed by special acts of God (miracles) to be God. The same historically reliable documents that inform us of Jesus' claims to deity also give us His credentials to deity—miracles.

Jesus offered miracles as a proof of His deity on several occasions. He said to the scribes, "But that you may know that the Son of Man has authority on earth to forgive sins"—He said to the paralytic—"I say to you, rise, pick up your bed, and go home" (Mark 2:10–11). When asked whether He was the Messiah by John the Baptist's followers, Jesus replied: "Go and tell John what you hear and see: the blind receive their sight and the lame walk, lepers are cleansed and the deaf hear, and the dead are raised up" (Matt. 11:4–5). Likewise when the scribes and Pharisees asked for a miracle, He offered His coming resurrection as proof (Matt. 12:38–40).

To say nothing of the supernatural fulfilled prophecy or His resurrection (see below), there are some thirty-five miracles of Jesus recorded in the Gospels, many of them including multiple healings. These miracles include healing incurable diseases (John 9), walking on water (John 6), multiplying loaves (John 6), turning water into wine (John 2), and raising the dead (John 11).

These are unprecedented and unparalleled supernatural acts. There are no comparable cases of multiple, contemporary, eyewitnesses-based testimonies of anyone else in history doing miraculous events in confirmation of his truth claim. Buddhism, Taoism, Confucianism, and Hinduism are non-theistic religions, and in a non-theistic world no miracles are possible. Only where there is a theistic God who created the world, is beyond the world, and who can intervene in the natural world, are miracles possible. Islam is the only other major world religion where this would be possible, and Muhammad, knowing Jesus and the prophets before Him had done miracles, refused to do miracles himself (Súra 3:181–184)[8] as Jesus did. It was not until 150 years later that apocryphal miracle stories began to emerge, but there are no verified contemporary eyewitness-based documents of any miracle Muhammad performed. The miracles of Jesus are unique.

9. *Therefore, Jesus is God.* This is simply the logical conclusion from premises 1 through 8. For if God exists, miracles are possible. And if the New Testament documents are historically reliable, then Jesus claimed to be God and proved it by a set of unprecedented and unparalleled miracles. Hence, Jesus is God in human flesh.

10. *But whatever Jesus (who is God) teaches is true.* If a theistic God exists, then He is by His very nature morally perfect and cannot deceive (Heb. 6:18; Titus 1:2). And a theistic God is by His nature all-knowing and cannot make a mistake (Ps. 147:5; Rom. 11:33). Hence, whatever God affirms is true, and is by its very nature true. Therefore, Jesus, being God, cannot affirm a falsehood. So, whatever Jesus teaches must be true.

11. *Jesus taught that the Bible is the Word of God.* As indicated in the previous chapter, Jesus affirmed the Old Testament is the Word of God and promised the divine authority to the apostles who, with their authorized associates, wrote the New Testament.

Jesus affirmed the Bible is divinely authoritative (Matt. 4:4, 7, 10), imperishable (Matt. 5:17), infallible (John 10:35), historically reliable (Matt. 12:38–40), scientifically accurate (Matt. 19:4–6), factually inerrant (Matt. 22:29; John 17:17), and has ultimate supremacy (Matt. 15:3–5). Further, we saw (in chap. 4) that Jesus was neither accommodating nor limited in His affirmations about Scripture. He proclaimed that "all things have been delivered to me by my Father" (Matt. 11:27 RSV) and that "Heaven and earth will pass away, but my words will not pass away" (Matt. 24:35). Thus, what He affirmed, He affirmed with "all authority in heaven and on earth" (Matt. 28:18).

So, if Jesus is the Son of God, then the Old Testament must be the Word

---

8. Abdullah Yusuf Ali, *The Qur'an: Text, Translation and Commentary* (Elmhurst, N.Y.: Tahrike Tarsile Qur'an, Inc. U.S. Edition, 2005), 170–71.

of God. But Jesus promised (in John 14:26; 16:13) that the New Testament would be the Word of God as well (see chap. 4). Hence, both the Old and New Testaments comprise the Word of God.

12. Therefore, the Bible is the Word of God (and whatever is opposed to it is false). The Law of Non-Contradiction dictates that the opposite of true is false (#2 above). Hence, if everything the Bible teaches is true, then everything in any other religion that is opposed to what the Bible teaches is false. For example, since the Bible teaches that there are three Persons in the Godhead (Matt. 3:16–17; 28:18–20; 2 Cor. 13:14), then Islam is false when it claims there is only one Person in God. And since the New Testament affirms that Jesus is the Messiah (John 4:25–26; Mark 14:61–63), then Judaism is false when it says He is not. Thus, when Buddhism, Hinduism, Taoism, and Confucianism deny there is a theistic God, miracles, and that Christ is the Son of God (John 1:1; Matt. 16:16–18) and the only way to God (John 14:6; Acts 4:12; 1 Tim. 2:5), then those religions are wrong.

This does not mean there are no truths in other religions. There are. For example, Confucius had the negative Golden Rule which said, "Don't do to others what you would not have them do to you." This is not incompatible with Jesus' positive Golden Rule, which affirms, "Whatever you wish that others would do to you, do also to them" (Matt. 7:12). There are many other positive moral values in other religions that are similar to those in the Ten Commandments. C. S. Lewis listed them in an appendix to his book *The Abolition of Man*. It simply means that if the Bible is the Word of God, then anything that opposes its teachings is false.

Other Evidence That the Bible Is the Word of God

The evidence from the authority of Jesus as the Son of God is not the only evidence for the Bible's divine origin. But most of the other evidence is not stand-alone evidence. At best, it is only supporting evidence. The resurrection of Christ and fulfilled prophecy are exceptions to this.

Evidence from the resurrection of Christ. Once we grant that God exists and miracles are possible and the New Testament documents are historically reliable, the argument from the resurrection of Christ is a powerful argument for the deity of Christ and, thereby, for the divine authority of Scripture. For Jesus repeatedly predicted that He would rise again (John 2:18–22; Matt. 12:40; 17:22–23). And these same historically reliable documents demonstrate that Jesus did really die. Crucifixion assures death, as did the Roman soldiers who were professional executioners. Numerous witnesses, both friend and foe, saw Him die. The spear to His side with the blood and water assured His death. His death cry was heard by those who stood by. And Pilate made sure Jesus was dead before he gave the body for burial.

On top of all this, modern medical authorities have confirmed that Jesus actually died. *The Journal of the American Medical Association* said that "the spear, thrust between his right rib, probably perforated not only the right lung but also the pericardium and heart and thereby ensured his death. Accordingly, interpretations based on the assumption that Jesus did not die on the cross appear to be at odds with modern medical knowledge."[9]

The same historically reliable New Testament documents also reveal that Jesus actually rose from the dead bodily (cf. Matthew 28; Mark 16; Luke 24; John 20–21; 1 Cor. 15). Indeed, not only did He leave an empty grave and grave clothes behind, but He appeared in the same physical body with the crucifixion scars (Luke 24:39; John 20:27–28) to over five hundred people (1 Cor. 15:6) on twelve different occasions during a forty-day period (Acts 1:3). During those forty days people saw, heard, and touched Him; some ate with Him; and all were transformed by Him. His followers became the world's greatest missionary society overnight! If this does not confirm His claim to deity, then it is difficult to see what would. And if He is God and claims that the Bible is the Word of God, then the Bible must be the Word of God.

Evidence from prophecy. Another forceful external testimony to the inspiration of Scripture is the fact of fulfilled prophecy. According to Deuteronomy 18, a prophet was false if he made predictions that were not fulfilled. Only God can accurately and infallibly predict the future (Isa. 41:23; 46:10). Although there are hundreds of predictions in the Bible, nearly all have been fulfilled. Others await fulfillment when Christ returns. Dozens and dozens of biblical predictions made hundreds of years in advance were fulfilled during Christ's first advent. The time, city (Mic. 5:2), and nature (Isa. 7:14) of Christ's birth, death (Isa. 53), and resurrection (Ps. 2, 16), and even the date (Dan. 9) were all made hundreds of years in advance, even granting the

9. *The Journal of the American Medical Association*, 21 March (1986), 1463.

critics' late dates for the Old Testament. By stark contrast psychic predictions made even a year in advance often fail. Sometimes they are even 90 percent wrong.[10]

Other biblical prophecies, such as the increase of education and communication in the latter day (Dan. 12:4), the repatriation of Israel, and the rebuilding of Palestine (Isa. 11:11; 61:4) are being fulfilled today. Likewise, predictions about the doom of Edom (Jer. 49) and Tyre (Ezek. 26), the closing of the Golden Gate (Ezek. 44), and the unfolding of world kingdoms (Dan. 2, 7) have been fulfilled. Indeed, Barton Payne's *Encyclopedia of Biblical Prophecy* lists 1817 predictions in the Bible, and to date none have failed.[11] There are other books which claim divine inspiration, such as the Qur'an, but it does not contain predictive elements such as the Bible has.[12] Only the Bible does, and this too is an indication of its divine origin.[13]

Evidence from the testimony of the Holy Spirit. Some have offered the witness of the Holy Spirit as proof the Bible is inspired. The Spirit of God confirms the Word of God to the children of God. The inner witness of God in the heart of the believer as he reads the Bible is evidence of its divine origin. Herman Ridderbos claimed that the authority of the Bible was based "primarily upon the evidences of Scripture itself and upon the internal witness of the Holy Spirit in the hearts of believers."[14] The Holy Spirit not only bears witness to the believer that he is a child of God (Rom. 8:16) but also that the Bible is the Word of God (1 John 5:9–10). The same Spirit who communicated the truth of God also confirms to the believer that the Bible is the Word of God.

As convincing as this subjective witness is to believers, as such it is insufficient as distinguishing evidence to outsiders. Mormons have a similar experience after reading the Book of Mormon and praying the prayer in Moroni chapter 10 about receiving the witness of the Spirit. Many Muslims

---

10. See Andre Kole, *Miracle or Magic?* (Eugene, Oreg.: Harvest House, 1984).

11. See Norman L. Geisler, "Prophecy as Proof of the Bible," in *Baker Encyclopedia of Christian Apologetics* (Grand Rapids: Baker, 1999).

12. See Norman L. Geisler and Abdul Saleeb, *Answering Islam*, rev. ed. (Grand Rapids: Baker, 2002), chap. 9.

13. Of course, this argument also assumes there is a theistic God since there cannot be supernatural predictions unless there is a supernatural Being who can make them.

14. Herman Ridderbos, "The Canon of the New Testament," Carl Henry, ed., *Revelation and the Bible: Contemporary Evangelical Thought* (Grand Rapids: Baker, 1958), 190.

claim the same about the Qur'an. And Jewish believers can be convinced in the same way about the Torah being the complete Word of God. In short, at best this argument has no value in determining whose subjective experience is right. For the many subjective experiences are equally convincing to the subjects who believe in these Holy Books; but these books have mutually conflicting truth claims.

Evidence from the transforming ability of the Bible. Another internal evidence offered as proof of the Bible's inspiration is its ability to convert the unbeliever and to build up the believer in the faith. Hebrews says, "The word of God is living and active, sharper than any two-edged sword" (4:12). Untold thousands have experienced this power. Drug addicts have been cured by it; derelicts have been transformed; hate has been turned to love by reading it. Believers grow by studying it (1 Pet. 2:2). The sorrowing are comforted, the sinners are rebuked, and the negligent are exhorted by the Scriptures. God's Word possesses the dynamic, transforming power of God. God vindicates the Bible's authority by its evangelistic and edifying powers.

While conversion experiences are real to those who have them and Christian conversion stories seem unique, nonetheless, there are problems with using this alone as a proof for the truth of Christianity for several reasons. First, there are similar conversion stories in other religions associated with truth claims that are opposed to Christianity. And it is difficult in practice to distinguish a true conversion from a false one. Second, William James, in his classic book, *Varieties of Religious Experience*,[15] made a convincing case that all conversion experiences in whatever religion follow a similar pattern. And while Jonathan Edwards provided a challenging analysis for the uniqueness of a Christian conversion (in *Religious Affections*, 1746), it must be admitted that his argument is a lot more convincing to a Christian than to a non-Christian. The bottom line is that, at best, this may be a supplementary argument for the truth of the Bible, but as a stand-alone reason it leaves something to be desired.

Evidence from the unity of the Bible. Unlike the previous argument, this is not a subjective or experiential one. The argument from the unity of the Bible moves in this right direction. It begins with the facts that the Bible is

---

15. William James, *Varieties of Religious Experience* (1902; repr., New York: New American Library of World Literature, 1958), Lectures 9 and 10.

composed of sixty-six books, written over a period of some fifteen hundred years by nearly forty authors in several languages containing hundreds of topics, yet the Bible possesses an amazing unity of theme—Jesus Christ. One problem—sin—and one solution—the Savior—unify its pages from Genesis to Revelation.

Compared to a medical manual written amid such variety, the Bible shows marked evidence of divine unity. This is an especially valid point in view of the fact that no one person or group of men put the Bible together. Books were added as they were written by the prophets. They were then collected simply because they were considered inspired. It is only later reflection, both by the prophets themselves (e.g., 1 Pet. 1:10–11) and later generations, which has discovered that the Bible is really one book whose "chapters" were written by men who had no explicit knowledge of the overall structure. Their role could be compared to that of different men writing chapters of a novel for which none of them have even an overall outline. Whatever unity the book has must come from beyond them.

However, as unique as this may seem to believers, the unity of the Bible argument by no means constitutes indisputable evidence of inspiration. There are several reasons for this. First, since the Bible grew gradually, book by book, over the years, it makes sense that the succeeding canonizers would not accept any book that contradicted the message of a preceding one. Thus, its unity may be explained on less than a supernatural cause. Second, critics are quick to point out all of the conflicts in the Bible that seem to manifest a lack of unity. And even apart from the numerous alleged contradictions, there is a clear contrast between the Old and New Testaments, which Judaism sees as such a distinctive disunity that they reject the later Testament. In short, at best the argument from the unity of the Bible is supplementary. It is not a powerful stand-alone reason for accepting the inspiration of the Bible.

Evidence from archaeology. Some overzealous proponents of the view have exclaimed that "every time a spade is turned in the soil of the Holy Land a skeptic is converted!" Even less enthusiastic proponents view archaeology as only indirectly supportive of biblical inspiration. It is true, as some have pointed out, that no archaeological finding has ever refuted a biblical truth. And it is true, as Donald J. Wiseman wrote, "The geography of Bible lands and visible remains from antiquity were gradually recorded until today more than 25,000 sites within this region and dating to Old Testament times, in their broadest sense, have been located."[16]

Yet it is also true that much of the earlier criticism of the Bible has been overturned by archaeological discoveries that have demonstrated the existence of writing in Moses' day, the history and chronology of the kings of Israel, and even the existence of the Hittites, a people once known only from the Bible. Indeed, the Bible is the most archaeologically confirmed book in the world.[17]

It is also true that the discovery of the Dead Sea Scrolls (DSS) and the Discoveries in the Judean Desert (DJD) support the accuracy of the Old Testament manuscripts (see chap. 12). Further, the discovery of early New Testament manuscripts has bolstered belief in the accuracy of the New Testament text. Moreover, many biblical sites have been found that support the ancient existence of these places in the Bible. It is also true that growing confidence in the historical reliability of the Bible can encourage belief in its spiritual message as well, but there is no direct connection. Jesus said, "If I have told you earthly things and you do not believe, how can you believe if I tell you heavenly things?" (John 3:12). However, the connection is not a logical or direct one; it is indirect and inferential. At best, archaeology supports the historicity of the biblical text, but that in and of itself does not prove its divine authority.

Evidence from the influence of the Bible. No book has been more widely disseminated and has more broadly influenced the course of world events than the Bible. The Bible has been translated into more languages, has been published in more copies, has influenced more thought, inspired more art, and motivated more discoveries than any other book. The Bible has been translated into over one thousand languages representing more than 90 percent of the world's population. It has been published in some billions of copies. There are no close seconds in the all-time bestseller list.

The influence of the Bible and its teaching in the Western world is clear for all who study history. And the influential role of the West in the course of world events is equally clear. Similar influence may be seen in vast regions of the Eastern world, where the Orthodox churches gave witness to the

---

16. Donald J. Wiseman, "Archaeological Confirmation of the Old Testament," in Henry, *Revelation and the Bible*, 301–2.

17. See Geisler and Holden, *The Popular Handbook of Biblical Archaeology*.

influence of the Bible in history, culture, the arts, and literature. Civilization has been influenced more by the Judeo-Christian Scriptures than by any other book or combination of books in the world. Indeed, no great moral or religious work in the world exceeds the depth of morality in the principle of Christian love, and none has a more lofty spiritual concept than the biblical view of God. The Bible presents the highest ideals known to men which have molded civilization.

This argument in and of itself does not prove the divine origin of the Bible, but it is a confirmation of it. This is what one would expect out of a book God inspired. However, a book that has this influence is not a necessary proof it is the Word of God. The Bible's wide success could be an accident of history or the result of a political victory. So, this evidence as such is confirmatory but insufficient in itself.

Evidence from the apparent indestructibility of the Bible. Despite its importance (or maybe because of it), the Bible has suffered more vicious attacks than would be expected to be made on such a book. But the Bible has withstood all its attackers. Diocletian attempted to exterminate it (ca. 303 CE), and yet it is the most widely published book in the world today. Biblical critics once regarded much of it as mythological, but archaeology has established it as historical. Antagonists have attacked its teaching as primitive, but moralists urge that its teaching on love be applied to modern society. Skeptics have cast doubt on its authenticity, and yet more men are convinced of its truth today than ever. Attacks continue to arise from science, psychology, and political movements, but the Bible remains undaunted. Like the wall four feet high and four feet wide, blowing at it seems to accomplish nothing. The Bible remains just as strong after the attack. Jesus said, "Heaven and earth will pass away, but my words will not pass away" (Mark 13:31).

Again, this is what one would expect of a divine book, but the Bible's durability could be an accident of history or a result of a dominant political perspective. So, at best, this evidence does not prove, but merely supports, the Bible's claim to be the Word of God.

EVIDENCE THAT DEMANDS A VERDICT

Do these arguments prove that the Bible is inspired? No, these are not proofs with rationally inescapable conclusions. Even an amateur philosopher can devise ways to avoid the logic of the arguments. And even if they did prove the inspiration of the Bible, it would not necessarily follow that they would persuade it to the satisfaction of all. Rather, they are evidences, testimonies, or witnesses. As witnesses, they must be cross-examined and evaluated as a whole. Then, in the jury room of one's own soul a decision must be made—a decision which is not based on rationally inescapable proofs but on evidence that is "beyond reasonable doubt."

So, what we have is evidence that demands a verdict. Were we part of a jury called upon for a verdict, based on a comprehensive examination of the claim and alleged credentials of the Bible to be inspired, we would be compelled to vote that the Bible is not guilty of the critics' charge that it is not the Word of God which it claims to be. The reader too must decide. For those who are yet undecided, one is reminded of the words of Peter: "Lord, to whom shall we go? You have the words of eternal life" (John 6:68). In other words, if the Bible—with its clear-cut claim to be inspired, with its incomparable characteristics and multiple credentials—is not inspired, then to what else can we turn? It has the words of eternal life.

PART TWO

Canonization

THE CHARACTERISTICS
of CANONICITY

WHICH BOOKS BELONG IN THE BIBLE? What about the so-called missing books? How did the Bible come to have sixty-six books? These are the kinds of questions covered in the next few chapters.

This subject is called canonicity. It is the second great link in the chain from God to us. Inspiration is the means by which the Bible received its *authority*; canonization is the process by which the Bible received its *acceptance*. It is one thing for prophets to receive a message from God but another for that message to be recognized by the people of God. Canonicity is the study that treats the recognition and collection of the books given by God's inspiration.

DEFINITION OF CANONICITY

The word *canon* is derived from the Greek *kanon* (a rod, ruler), which in turn comes from the Hebrew *kaneh*, an Old Testament word meaning "measuring rod" (cf. Ezek. 40:3). Even in pre-Christian usage the word was broadened to indicate a standard or norm other than a literal rod or rules. The New Testament employs the term in its figurative sense to indicate a rule for conduct (Gal. 6:16).

Early Christian Usage of the Word *Canon*

In early Christian usage the word *canon* came to mean the "rule of faith" or the normative writings (i.e., the authoritative Scriptures). The word *canon* was applied to the Bible in both active and passive senses. In the active sense, the Bible is the canon by which all else is to be judged. In the passive sense, canon meant the rule or standard by which a writing was judged to be inspired or authoritative. This double usage causes some confusion that we will attempt to clarify. First, let us look at what is meant by a canon of Scripture in the active sense. Then we will look at its meaning in the passive sense.

Some Synonyms of Canonicity

The existence of a canon or collection of authoritative writings antedates the use of the term *canon*. The Jewish community collected and preserved their Holy Scriptures from the time of Moses.

Sacred Scriptures. One of the earliest concepts of a canon was that of sacred writings. That the writings of Moses were considered sacred is indicated by the holy place in which they were stored: "Take this Book of the law and put it by the side of the ark of the covenant of the LORD" (Deut. 31:26). After the temple was built, "the Book of the Law" was found [preserved] "in the house of the LORD" (2 Kings 22:8). The special accord granted to these select books alone indicates that they were considered to be canonical or sacred writings.

Authoritative writings. The divine authority of Scripture is another designation of its canonicity. The authority of the Mosaic writings was impressed on Joshua and Israel (Josh. 1:8). Each king of Israel was exhorted to "write for himself in a book a copy of this law, . . . and he shall read in it all the days of his life, that he may learn to fear the LORD his God" (Deut. 17:18–19). Since the books came from God they were invested with His authority. As authoritative writings they were canonical or normative for the Jewish believer.

Books that defile the hands. In the teaching tradition of Israel there arose the concept of books so holy or sacred that those who used them had "defiled their hands." The Talmud says, "The Gospel and the books of the heretics do not make the hands unclean; the books of Ben Sira and whatever books have been written since his time are not canonical" (Tosefta Yadaim 3:5). The books of the Hebrew Old Testament, by contrast, do make the hands unclean because they are sacred. Hence, only those books which demand that the user undergo a special ceremonial cleansing were regarded as canonical.

Prophetic books. As previously discussed (chap. 3), a book qualified as inspired only if it had been written by a prophetic spokesman of God. The works of false prophets were rejected and not collected in a holy place. In fact, according to Josephus (Contra Apion 1:8), only those books that were composed during the prophetic period from Moses to Artaxerxes (fourth century BCE) could be canonical. He wrote, "From Artaxerxes until our time everything has been recorded, but has not been deemed worthy of like credit with what preceded, because the exact succession of the prophets ceased." Only the books from Moses to Malachi were canonical since only these were written by men in the prophetic succession. During the period from Artaxerxes (fourth century BCE) to Josephus (first century CE) there was no prophetic succession; hence, it was not part of the prophetic period. The Talmud makes the same claim, saying, "Up to this point [fourth century BCE] the prophets prophesied through the Holy Spirit; from this time onward incline thine ear and listen to the sayings of the wise" (Seder Olam Rabba 30). It adds, "With the death of Hagai, Zechariah and Malachai the latter prophets, the Holy Spirit ceased out of Israel" (Tos. Sotah 13:2). In order to be canonical, then, an Old Testament book must come from the prophetic succession during the prophetic period which ended with Malachi (ca. 400 BCE).

DETERMINATION OF CANONICITY

The confusion between the active and passive senses of the word *canon* occasioned some ambiguity in the issue of what determines the canonicity of a book. Hence, several incorrect views of canonicity arose.

Some Inadequate Views on What Determines Canonicity

Several views of what determines the canonicity of a writing have been suggested. All these theories are inadequate in their notions of what determines the canonicity of a book. Let us examine them briefly.

The view that age determines canonicity. The theory that the canonicity of a book is determined by its antiquity, that it came to be venerated because of its age, misses the mark for two reasons. First, many very old books, such as the Book of the Wars of the Lord (Num. 21:14) and the Book of Jashar (Josh. 10:13), were not accepted into the canon. Further, the evidence is that books were received into the canon immediately, not after they had aged. Such quick acceptance was true of the books of Moses (Deut. 31:24–26), of

Jeremiah (Dan. 9:2), and the New Testament writings of Paul (2 Pet. 3:16).

The view that Hebrew language determines canonicity. Also insufficient is the view that those books written in the "sacred" language of the Hebrews were considered sacred books and those not written in Hebrew were not put in the canon. The fact is not all books written in Hebrew were accepted, as some of the rejected Hebrew Apocryphal books as well as other earlier non-biblical writings indicate (see Josh. 10:13). In addition, there are sections of books that were accepted into the canon that were not written in Hebrew (Dan. 2:4b–7:28 and Ezra 4:8–6:18; 7:12–26 are in Aramaic).

The view that agreement with the Torah determines canonicity. Another inadequate view is that a book's canonicity was determined by whether it agreed with the Torah (Law of Moses). Clearly those books known to contradict the Torah would be rejected, since it was believed that God would not contradict Himself in subsequent revelations. But this theory misses two important points. First, it was not the Torah that determined the canonicity of everything after it. Rather, the same factor determining the canonicity of the Torah determined the canonicity of all Scripture; namely, the fact that all of them were divinely inspired.

In other words, the view that agreement with the Torah determines canonicity is inadequate because it does not explain what determined the canonicity of the Torah. Second, the theory is too broad. Many other books that agreed with the Torah were not accepted as inspired. The Jewish fathers believed their Talmud and Midrash agreed with the Torah but never pronounced them canonical. The same is true of many Christian writings associated with the New Testament.

The view that religious value determines canonicity. Still another suggestion is that the religious value of a book determined its position in the canon. St. Augustine mistakenly used this reason to justify accepting the Apocryphal books in the canon: because they contain "the extreme and wonderful sufferings of certain martyrs."[1] Here again the cart is before the horse. It is axiomatic to say that a book without some kind of spiritual value would be rejected from the canon. But it is also true that not every book with spiritual value is automatically canonical, as a wealth of both Jewish and Christian literature, including the Apocrypha, demonstrates. The important thing,

1. St. Augustine, *The City of God*, Book 18, chap. 36.

however, is that this theory confuses cause and effect. It is not religious value that determines canonicity; it is canonicity that determines the religious value. More precisely, it is not the value of a book that determines its divine authority; it is the divine authority that determines its value.

The view that church authority determines canonicity. St. Augustine alludes to another growing view in his time, namely, that the authority of the church determines which books are canonical. He refers to books "not in the Holy Scriptures which are called canonical, but in others, among which are also the books of Maccabees. These are held as canonical, not by the Jews, but by the Church."[2] In fact, much later on the basis of the alleged authority of the Roman Catholic Church, the Apocryphal books were retroactively and infallibly canonized at the Council of Trent (1546 CE), even though, as Augustine recognized, they were "not held as canonical . . . by the Jews, but by the Church."[3] As will be shown below, this confuses the role of the Christian church, which is not to determine which books are in the canon but to discover which books God determined should be in the canon, namely, those that He had inspired. The church is not the master of the canon but the servant. The church does not regulate the canon, but simply recognizes it.[4]

The view that Christian usage determines canonicity. Once St. Augustine, who has been called "the Medieval Monolith," had mistakenly accepted the Old Testament Jewish Apocrypha as part of the Christian canon, it became more acceptable to use these book in readings, sermons, and books (see discussions in chapters 8 and 18). Subsequently, then, others appealed to their Christian usage as an indication of their inspiration. However, this is mistaken for two reasons. First, being Jewish books rejected by the Jewish community as not canonical, they should not have been put there by Christians in the first place. Second, if Christian usage determines canonicity, Thomas à Kempis's *Imitation of Christ* and John Bunyan's *Pilgrim's Progress* would be in the canon, while 1 Chronicles and 3 John should not be there since they are not read or cited nearly as much.

---

2. Ibid.

3. Ibid.

4. See Norman L. Geisler and Ralph MacKenzie, *Roman Catholics and Evangelicals* (Grand Rapids: Baker, 1995), chap. 9.

Canonicity Is Determined by Inspiration

The books of the Bible are not considered God-given because they are found to have value in them; they are valuable because they are given of God—the source of all value. As Professor Herman Ridderbos put it, "The question, to what does the Canon owe its position of authority, can by the church be answered in only one way: It derives this from God."[5] And the process by which God gives His revelation is called inspiration. It is the inspiration of a book which determines its canonicity. God gives the divine authority to a book and men of God receive it. God reveals and His people recognize what He reveals. Canonicity is determined by God and discovered by man.

Once the book is recognized by the people of God to be the Word of God, then the Bible becomes the active "canon" or rule by which all else is to be measured because it possesses God-given authority. Whatever rules (canons) may be used by the church to discover precisely which books have this canonical or normative authority should not be said to "determine" their canonicity. To speak of the people of God, by whatever rules of recognition, as "determining" which books are divinely authoritative confuses the issue. Only God can give divine authority and, hence, canonicity to a book.

The primary notion of the word *canon* as applied to Scripture is the active sense, i.e., that the Bible is the ruling norm of faith. The secondary notion, that a book is judged by certain canons and receives recognition as inspired (the passive sense), should not be confused with the divine determination of canonicity. Only inspiration determines the authority of a book to be canonical or normative.

THE DISCOVERY OF CANONICITY

The people of God have played a crucial role in the process of canonization through the centuries, albeit not a determinative one. Upon the believing community lay the task of discriminating and deciding which books were from God. In order to fulfill this role they had to look for certain earmarks of divine authority. How would one recognize an inspired book if he saw it? What are the characteristics that distinguish a divine declaration from a purely human one? Several criteria were involved in this recognition process.

5. Herman Ridderbos, "The Canon of the New Testament," Carl Henry, ed. *Revelation and the Bible: Contemporary Evangelical Thought* (Grand Rapids: Baker, 1958), 190.

The Principles for Discovering Canonicity

False books and false writings were not scarce (see chaps. 8 and 10). Their ever-present threat made it necessary for the people of God to carefully review their sacred collection. Even books accepted by other believers or in earlier days were subsequently brought into question by the church. Operating in the whole process are discernible some five basic criteria: (1) Was it written by a prophet of God? (2) Did the writer have credentials from God? (3) Did it tell the truth about God, man, etc.? (4) Did it possess the life-transforming power of God? (5) Was it received or accepted by the people of God for whom it was originally written?

1. Was it written by a prophet of God? As indicated earlier (chaps. 3 and 4), each book in the Bible bears the claim of divine authority, either explicitly or implicitly. Often the explicit "thus says the Lord" is present. Sometimes the tone and exhortations reveal its divine origin. Always there is divine pronouncement. In the more didactic (teaching) literature there is divine pronouncement about what believers should do. In the historical books the exhortations are more implied and the authoritative pronouncements are more about what God has done in the history of His people (which is "His story"). If a book lacked the authority of God, it was not considered canonical and was rejected from the canon.

Let us illustrate this principle of authority as it relates to the canon. The books of the prophets were easily recognized by this principle of authority. The repeated, "And the Lord said unto me," or "The word of the Lord came unto me," provides abundant evidence of their claim to divine authority. Some books lacked the claim to be divine and were thereby rejected as noncanonical. Perhaps this was the case with the Book of the Wars of the Lord and the Book of Jashar. Still other books were questioned and challenged as to their divine authority but finally accepted into the canon, such as Esther. Not until it was obvious to all that the protection and therefore the pronouncements of God on His people were unquestionably present in Esther was this book accorded a permanent place in the Jewish canon. Indeed, the very fact some canonical books were called into question provides assurance that the believers were discriminating. Unless they were convinced of the divine authority of the book, it was rejected.

2. Did the writer have credentials from God? The Bible came through Spirit-moved spokespersons known as prophets (2 Pet. 1:20–21). The Word of God is given to His people only through His prophets. Every biblical author had a prophetic gift or function, even if he was not a prophet by occupation (Heb. 1:1). Later there was a "school of the prophets" (1 Sam. 19:20) and "sons of the prophets" (i.e., disciples). There was even a "register" of prophets (Ezek. 13:9). Some prophets made predictions that came to pass. Other had supernatural confirmation, as did Moses (Ex. 4), Elijah (1 Kings 18), Jesus (Acts 2:22), and Paul (2 Cor. 12:12). Hebrews speaks of salvation being "declared at first by the Lord, and it was attested to us by those who heard, while God also bore witness by signs and wonders and various miracles and by gifts of the Holy Spirit distributed according to his will" (Heb. 2:3–4).

Paul argued in Galatians that his book should be accepted because he was an apostle "not from men nor through man, but through Jesus Christ and God the Father" (Gal. 1:1). His book was to be accepted because it was apostolic—it was from a God-appointed spokesman or prophet. Books were to be rejected if they did not come from prophets of God, as is evident from Paul's warnings not to accept a book from someone falsely claiming to be an apostle (2 Thess. 2:2) and from the warning in 2 Corinthians about false prophets (11:13). John's warnings about false messiahs and trying the spirits would fall into the same category (1 John 2:18–19; and 4:1–3). It was because of this prophetic principle that 2 Peter was disputed by some in the early church. Until the Fathers were convinced that it was not a forgery but that it really came from Peter the apostle as it claimed (1:1), it was not accorded a permanent place in the Christian canon.

3. Did it tell the truth about God, man, etc.? Another hallmark of inspiration is authenticity. Any book with factual or doctrinal errors (judged by previous revelations) could not be inspired of God. God cannot lie; His word must be true and consistent.

In view of this principle, the Bereans accepted Paul's teachings and searched the Scriptures to see whether or not what Paul taught them was really in accord with God's revelation in the Old Testament (Acts 17:11). Simple agreement with previous revelation would not ipso facto make a teaching inspired. But contradiction of a previous revelation would clearly indicate that a teaching was not inspired.

Many of the Apocryphal books were rejected because of the principle of authenticity. Their historical anomalies and theological heresies made it impossible to accept them as from God despite their authoritative format. They could not be from God and contain error at the same time.

Some canonical books were questioned on the basis of this same principle. They asked: Could the letter of James be inspired if it contradicted Paul's teaching on justification by faith and not by works? Until their essential compatibility was seen, James was questioned by some. Others questioned Jude because of its citation of inauthentic pseudepigraphal books (vv. 9, 14). Once it was understood that Jude's quotations granted no more authority to those books than Paul's quotes from the non-Christian poets (see also Acts 17:28 and Titus 1:12), then there remained no reason to reject Jude.

4. Did it possess the life-transforming power of God? A fourth test for canonicity, at times less explicit than some of the others, was the life-transforming ability of the writing: "The word of God is living and active" (Heb. 4:12). As a result it can be used "for teaching, for reproof, for correction, and for training in righteousness" (2 Tim. 3:16–17).

The apostle Paul revealed that the dynamic ability of inspired writings was involved in the acceptance of all Scripture as 2 Timothy 3:16–17 indicates. He said to Timothy, "The holy scriptures . . . are able to make thee wise unto salvation" (v. 15 KJV). Elsewhere, Peter speaks of the edifying and evangelizing power of the Word (1 Pet. 1:23; 2:2). Other messages and books were rejected because they held out false hope (1 Kings 22:6–8) or rang a false alarm (2 Thess. 2:2). Thus, they were not conducive to building up the believer in the truth of Christ. Jesus said, "You will know the truth, and the truth will set you free" (John 8:32). False teaching never liberates; only the truth has emancipating power.

Some biblical books, such as Song of Solomon and Ecclesiastes, were questioned because they were thought by some to lack this dynamic edifying power. Once they were convinced that the Song was not sensual but deeply spiritual and that Ecclesiastes was not skeptical and pessimistic but positive and edifying (e.g., 12:9–10), then there remained little doubt as to their canonicity.

5. Was it received or accepted by the people of God for whom it was written? The final trademark of an authoritative writing is its recognition by the people of God to whom it was initially given. God's Word given through His prophet and with His truth must be recognized by His people. Later generations of believers sought to verify this fact. For if the book was received, collected, and used as God's Word by those to whom it was originally given, then its canonicity was established. Limits in communication and transportation in ancient times sometimes mandated additional time and effort on the part of later church fathers to determine this recognition. For this reason the full and final recognition by the whole church of the sixty-six books of the canon took many, many years (see chap. 9).

The books of Moses were immediately accepted by the people of God. They were collected, quoted, preserved, and even imposed on future generations (see chap. 3). Paul's epistles were immediately received by the churches to whom they were addressed (1 Thess. 2:13) and even by other apostles (2 Pet. 3:16). Some writings were immediately rejected by the people of God as lacking divine authority (2 Thess. 2:2). False prophets (Matt. 7:21–23) and lying spirits were to be tested and rejected (1 John 4:1–3), as indicated in many instances within the Bible itself (cf. Jer. 5:2; 14:14). This principle of acceptance led some to question for a time certain biblical books such as 2 and 3 John. Their private nature and limited circulation being what it was, it is understandable that there would be some reluctance to accept them until they were assured that the books were received by the first-century people of God as from the apostle John.

It is hardly necessary to add that not everyone gave even initial recognition to a prophet's message. But God vindicated His prophets against those who rejected them (e.g., 1 Kings 22:1–38) and, when challenged, He designated who His true prophets were. When the authority of Moses was challenged by Korah and others, the earth opened and swallowed them up. "So they and all that belonged to them went down alive into Sheol, and the earth closed over them and they perished from the midst of the assembly" (Num. 16:33). The role of the people of God was decisive in the recognition of the Word of God. God determined the authority of the books of the canon, but the people of God were called upon to discover which books were authoritative and which were not. To assist them in this discovery were these five tests of canonicity.

The Procedure for Discovering Canonicity

We should not imagine a committee of church fathers with a large pile of books and these five guiding principles before them when we speak of the process of canonization. No ecumenical committee was commissioned to canonize the Bible. *The DaVinci Code,* the bestseller by Dan Brown, is wrong when it charges Constantine with determining the canon of the New Testament. His church Council of Nicaea (325 CE) did not even discuss the matter, and their vote was on the deity of Christ, not on the canon. Furthermore, it was not a close vote (as *The DaVinci Code* asserts). It was 316 in favor and only 2 against.

The process was far more natural and dynamic. The actual historical development of the Old and New Testament canons will be discussed later (in chaps. 7 and 9). What is to be noted here is how the five rules for canonicity were used in the process of discovering which books were inspired of God and therefore canonical.

Some principles are only implicit in the process. Although all five characteristics are present in each inspired writing, not all of the rules of recognition are apparent in the decision on each canonical book. It was not always immediately obvious to the early people of God that some historical books were "dynamic." More obvious to them was the fact that certain books were "prophetic," "recognized," and "accepted" (e.g., cited by other Fathers as inspired). One can easily see how the implied "thus says the Lord" played a most significant role in the discovery of the canonical books that reveal God's overall redemptive plan. Nevertheless, the reverse is sometimes true; namely, the power and authority of the book are more apparent than its authorship (e.g., Hebrews). In any event, all five characteristics were involved in discovering each canonical book, although some were used only implicitly.

Some principles operate as a negative test. Some of the rules for recognition operate more negatively than others. For instance, the principle of authenticity would more readily eliminate noncanonical books than indicate which books are canonical. There are no false teachings that are canonical, but there are many true writings that are not inspired. Likewise, many books which edify or have a dynamic are not canonic, even though no canonical book is without significance in the saving plan of God.

Similarly, a book may claim to be authoritative without being inspired, as many of the apocryphal writings indicate, but no book can be canonical unless it really is authoritative. In other words, if the book lacks authority it cannot be from God. But the simple fact that a book claims authority does not make it ipso facto inspired. The principle of acceptance has a primarily negative function. Even the fact that a book is received by some of the people of God is not a proof of inspiration. In later generations some Christians, not thoroughly informed about the acceptance or rejection by the people of God to whom it was originally addressed, gave local and temporal recognition to books that are not canonical (e.g., some Apocryphal books; see chaps. 8 and 10). Simply because a book was received somewhere by some believers is far from proof of its inspiration. The initial reception by the people of God who were in the best position to test the prophetic authority of the book is crucial. Because transportation and communication were slow, it took some time for all segments of subsequent generations to be fully informed about the original circumstances. Thus, the people's acceptance is important but supportive in nature.

The most essential principle is propheticy. Beneath the whole process of recognition lay one fundamental principle—the prophetic nature of the book. If a book were written by an accredited prophet of God, claiming to give an authoritative pronouncement from God, then there was no need to ask the other questions. Of course the people of God recognized the book as powerful and true when it was given to them by a prophet of God. When there were no directly available confirmations of the prophet's call (as there often were, cf. Ex. 4:1–9), then the authenticity, dynamic ability, and reception of a book by the original believing community would be essential to its later recognition. On the other hand, simply establishing the book as prophetic was sufficient in itself to confirm the canonicity of the book.

This test applies to the New Testament as well as the Old. For the church was "built on the foundation of the apostles and prophets" (Eph. 2:20). Every writer of the New Testament was either an apostle or a prophet (spokesperson) of God. Indeed, John the apostle was called a prophet and his last book a "prophecy" (Rev. 22:7, 18).

The question as to whether inauthenticity would disconfirm a prophetic book is misdirected. No book given by God can be false. If a book claiming to be prophetic seems to have indisputable falsehood, then the prophetic credentials must be reexamined. God cannot lie. In this way the other four principles serve as a check on the prophetic character of the books of the canon.

THE DEVELOPMENT *of the* OLD TESTAMENT CANON

THE HISTORY OF THE CANONIZATION OF THE BIBLE is a fascinating story. It is a book written and collected over almost two millennia without a contributing author being aware of how his "chapter" would fit into the overall plan. Each prophetic contribution was offered to the people of God simply on the basis that God had spoken to them through the prophet.

Just how that message was to fit into an overall story was unknown to the prophet and even to the believers who first recognized it. Only the reflective consciousness of later Christians was able to perceive that the providential hand of God which moved each individual writer was also moving through them to produce an overall redemptive story of which God alone was the author. Neither the prophets who composed the books nor the people of God who collected them were consciously constructing the overall unity in which each book was to play a part (see "unity" of the Bible in chap. 5).

SOME PRELIMINARY DISTINCTIONS

God inspired the books, the original people of God recognized and collected them, and later believers categorized the canonical books according to the overall unity they perceived in them. This in brief is the story of the canonization of the Bible. Let us explicate some of the more important distinctions implied in this process.

The Three Basic Steps in the Process of Canonization

There are three basic steps toward canonization: inspiration by God, recognition by the spokespersons of God, and collection and preservation by the people of God. A brief look at each of them will indicate that the first step in the canonization of the Bible (inspiration) was God's; the next two (recognition and preservation) were committed by God to His people under His providential hand.

Inspiration by God. God took the first step in canonization when He inspired the writings. Thus, the most fundamental reason why there are thirty-nine books in the Old Testament is that only that many books were inspired by God. It is evident that the people of God could not recognize the divine authority of a book if it did not possess any.

Recognition by the spokespersons of God. Once God determined the canonicity of a book, the people of God discovered what books they were. God authorized a writing; spokespersons of God recognized it. This recognition was given immediately by the community to which it was addressed. After the book was copied and circulated with credentials to the whole Christian community, the church universal recognized the book as canonical.

The writings of Moses were accepted in his day (Ex. 24:3), as were those of Joshua (Josh. 24:26), Samuel (1 Sam. 10:25), and Jeremiah (Dan. 9:2). As noted earlier (see chap. 3), this recognition is further confirmed by New Testament writers (Matt. 19:7; Mark 7:10; Luke 20:28) as well as by Jesus Himself (Luke 24:27, 44).

Collection and preservation by the people of God. The Word of God was treasured by His people. For example, the people preserved the writings of Moses by the ark (Deut. 31:26). Samuel's words were put "in a book and laid . . . before the LORD" (1 Sam. 10:25). In Josiah's day the Law of Moses was preserved in the temple (2 Kings 23:24). Daniel had a collection of "the books" in which were found "the law of Moses" and "the prophets" (Dan. 9:2, 6, 13). Ezra possessed copies of the law of Moses and the prophets (Neh. 9:14, 26–30). New Testament believers possessed the whole of the Old Testament "Scripture[s]" (2 Tim. 3:16), both law and prophets (Matt. 5:17).

The Difference between Canonical and Other Religious Literature

Not all Jewish religious literature was considered canonical by the believing community. Some of the earlier books, such as the Book of the Wars of the

Lord (Num. 21:14), the Book of Jashar (Josh. 10:13), and others (see 1 Kings 11:41), held religious significance. Similarly, the books of the Jewish Apocrypha, written after the close of the Old Testament period (ca. 400 BCE), have a definite religious significance but were never considered canonical by official Judaism (see chap. 8). The crucial difference between canonical and noncanonical literature is that the former is normative (authoritative) and the latter is not. Inspired books have divine binding authority on the believer; noninspired books may have some value for devotion and edification, but they are not to be used to define or delimit any doctrine. Canonical books provide the truth criteria by which all noncanonical books are to be judged. No article of faith may be based on any noncanonical work, regardless of its religious value.

The divinely inspired and authoritative books are the sole basis for doctrine and practice. Whatever complementary support canonical truth derives from other books, it in no way lends canonical value to those books. The support is purely historical and has no authoritative theological value. The truth of inspired Scripture alone is the canon or foundation of the truths of faith.

The Difference between Canonization and Categorization of Biblical Books

The failure to distinguish between the sections into which the Hebrew Old Testament has been divided (Law, Prophets, and Writings) and the stages or periods in which the collection developed has caused a great deal of confusion. For years the standard critical theory has held that the Hebrew Scriptures were canonized by sections, following the alleged dates of their composition, into Law (ca. 400 BCE), Prophets (ca. 200 BCE), and Writings (ca. 100 CE). This theory is built on the mistaken notion that the threefold categorization of the Old Testament represents its stages of canonization. As we shall see shortly, there is no direct connection between these three categories and the crucial events of canonization. The books of the Jewish Scriptures have been rearranged since their composition. Some of them, from the writings especially, were clearly written and accepted by the Jewish community centuries before the date ascribed to them by critical theorists.

PROGRESSIVE COLLECTION OF OLD TESTAMENT BOOKS

The first and most basic fact about the process of Old Testament canonization is that it is not threefold but at most twofold. The earliest and most repeated descriptions of the canon refer to it as "Moses and the prophets," the "prophets," or simply "the books." Nowhere in Scripture or in the extrabiblical literature into the early Christian period is there any proof of a so-called third canonical stage comprised of writings that were written and collected after the time of the law and prophets. As far as canonicity is concerned, the so-called writings were always a part of the canonical section commonly called the prophets.

Evidence of a Twofold Canon

The Old Testament canon was one book generally put together gradually and progressive as the books were written. This was in two major states: The books of Moses (the great Lawgiver) and then all the prophets after him. So canonization was a twofold and two-step process.

The later threefold classification has no direct correlation with the earlier canonization. The exact reasons for later dividing "the prophets" into two sections called "Prophets" and "Writings" is uncertain.

Some Theories. Some suggest that it was based on a distinction between those who were prophets by office (the prophets) and those who were prophets only by gift. However, this might explain how Daniel (who was not a prophet by office) got into the Writings section, but it would not necesarily explain how Amos, who was "no prophet, nor a prophet's son" (Amos 7:14), got in the Prophets section.

Others claim that the Writings section came later and so is classified later. But this is contrary to all the evidence above that Daniel and Chronicles were in the Prophets section in Josephus (first century CE) and don't appear in the Writings section until the fourth century CE). Nor does it explain how the books in the later Writings section were cited in the New Testament as part of the Prophets in a twofold division of the Old Testament.

Still others hypothesize about a later liturgical or festal reason for listing these books in the Writings section. The truth is that we do not know for sure. But there are some things we do know.

Some Important Facts. The threefold classification arose no earlier than the second century BCE and for most of its early history it did not have the same books in it that appeared in the fourth century CE. The first known reference is in the "Prologue" to the Apocryphal book of Sirach (ca. 132 BCE), which speaks of "the law and the prophets and the other books of our fathers" read by his grandfather (ca. 200 BCE). However, several things should be noted. First, it is not called the "Writings" which is the name given to the third section of the Hebrew Bible much later in the Jewish Talmud (fifth century CE). Second, it does not designate which books are in this collection. Third, we are not even sure the writer considered these books to be canonical.

Around the time of Christ, the Jewish philosopher Philo made a threefold distinction in the Old Testament speaking of the "[1] laws and [2] oracles delivered through the mouth of prophets, and [3] psalms and anything else which fosters and perfects knowledge and piety" (De Vita Contemplativa 3. 25). This is similar to Josephus's view (see below) of a third section of the Hebrew canon. But here again, we are not told how many or which books are in this section. And there is no reason to believe it is identical to the eleven books later placed in the Hebrew Scripture by the Talmudic scholars.

Jesus is alleged to have alluded to a threefold division when He spoke of "the law of Moses and the Prophets and the Psalms" (Luke 24:44). However, He had just referred to "Moses and all the prophets" as "all the Scriptures" (Luke 24:27). So, it is unlikely that He is contradicting that here. Since Jesus is centering on the messianic content of the Old Testament here (cf. Luke 24:27, 44), it is more likely that He is singling out the Psalms for their messianic significance.

In the first century the Jewish historian Josephus referred to the twenty-two books of Hebrew Scripture, "five belonging to Moses . . . the prophets . . . in thirteen books. The remaining four books [apparently Job, Psalms, Proverbs, and Ecclesiastes] containing hymns of God, and the precepts for the conduct of human life" (*Against Apion* I. 8).

By the fifth century CE the Jewish Talmud (Baba Bathra) listed eleven books in a third section called "the Writings" (Kethubhim): *Poetical Books:* (1) Psalms, (2) Proverbs, (3) Job; *Five Rolls* (Megilloth), (4) Song of Songs, (5) Ruth, (6) Lamentations, (7) Esther, (8) Ecclesiastes; Historical Books, (9) Daniel, (10) Ezra–Nehemiah, (11) Chronicles. The Hebrew Bible lists them the same way to date (see chap. 1).

Several very important conclusions may be drawn from the foregoing data. First, the facts do not show that the present third classification of the Writings, containing eleven of the twenty-two books, is earlier than the fifth century CE.

Second, the earliest reference that enumerates the books in a third division is Josephus who lists them as four. This is strong evidence against the claim of the critics that Daniel, Chronicles, and Ezra–Nehemiah were late books, listed among the writings that were not canonized until the first century CE.

Third, the number of the twenty-two books that were placed in the Writings grew from four to eleven between the first and fifth centuries. None of these facts supports the standard liberal view that there was a group of books, inclusive of Daniel, Chronicles, and Ezra–Nehemiah, which were not brought into the Jewish canon until the first century CE. There was an early tendency to arrange the Old Testament into a threefold classification (for reasons not fully known), and the number of books in this section grew over the years. But the number and rearrangement of these books had no essential connection with the basic twofold division and development of the Old Testament canon.

The History of the Twofold Canonization Process

The earliest and most persistent references to the canon of the Old Testament indicate that it is one collection of prophetic books with two divisions, the Law of Moses and the prophets who followed him. Let us trace the evidence historically.

During the early post-Mosaic period. After Moses had written the books of the Law (Genesis–Deuteronomy), there was a continual line of references to the Law of Moses. His immediate successor, Joshua, was told to "observe to do according to all the law, which Moses my servant commanded" (Josh. 1:7 KJV) and instructions were given from it throughout Joshua's life (Josh. 4:10; 8:31; 9:24; 13:33; 17:4; 21:2). Likewise, during the time of the Judges they were reminded to "hearken unto the commandments of the LORD, which he commanded their fathers by the hand of Moses" (Judg. 3:4 KJV). First Samuel 12:6, 8 refers to what God had done for Israel through "Moses." During the time of the kings they were told of God's "commandments, and his rules, and his testimonies, as it is written in the law of Moses" (1 Kings 2:3). Likewise, 2 Kings 23:25 speaks of "all the Law of Moses." Parallel history in Chronicles also mentions what "Moses had commanded according to the word of the LORD" (1 Chron. 15:15) and what is "written in the law, in the Book of Moses" (2 Chron. 25:4).

In short, they possessed a written "law of Moses" which they used as a norm for their lives. There were other books written by prophets after Moses, such as Joshua, Samuel, and others (1 Sam. 19:20). These were called "prophets."

During the exile. By the time of the exile, Daniel had referred to "the books" as containing both "the Law of Moses" and "the prophets" (Dan. 9:2, 6, 11) including Jeremiah (v. 2) who was a contemporary of Daniel's. This is the first indication of a twofold Old Testament, the first written by the great lawgiver Moses and rest by prophets after Moses' time.[1]

The postexilic period. After the exile the prophet Zechariah mentions "the law and the words that the LORD of hosts had sent by his Spirit through the former prophets" (Zech. 7:12). Ezra "set the priests in their divisions, and the Levites in their divisions, for the service of God . . . as it is written in the book of Moses" (Ezra 6:18). And Nehemiah led a revival by reading "the Book of the Law of Moses" (Neh. 8:1, 13, 14). Nehemiah also spoke of how God had warned Israel by His "Spirit through your prophets" (Neh. 9:30), thus distinguishing between the Law and the Prophets.

During the Intertestamental Period. This same twofold distinction continues after the time of Malachi. Maccabees spoke of "the law and the prophets" (2 Macc. 15:9). Just before the time of Christ, the Qumran community consistently refers to the Old Testament as the law and the prophets (Manual of Discipline 1. 3; 8. 15; 9. 11).

During the New Testament Times. During the time of Jesus and the apostles, the consistent and repeated way to refer to the whole Old Testament was by phrases like "law and prophets," or what is the same, "Moses and the prophets."

These phrases occur about a dozen times (e.g., Matt. 5:17; Luke 16:16, 31; 24:27), often in a context where it emphasizes the whole canon of Old Testament Scripture (e.g., Luke 24:27; Matt. 11:13). So, several important

---

1. For a history of Hebrew text types and popular texts and translations, including scrolls brought to Babylon (in the deportations of 597 and 586 BCE) and returned from Babylon, see the chart in Norman L. Geisler and William E. Nix, *A General Introduction to the Bible* (Chicago: Moody, 1986), 375–78.

conclusions emerge from these facts.

First, the canonization of the Old Testament was in two stages: first, the Law, and then the Prophets. That was the whole Jewish canon. There was no third stage of canonization, certainly not after the time of Christ at Jamnia (ca. 90 CE) or later.

Second, the phrase "Law and Prophets" referred to the whole Jewish canon, the entire twenty-two books. For example, when Jesus said, "The law and the Prophets were until John" (Luke 16:16), He included every inspired writing prior to New Testament times in that phrase. Matthew 22:40 carries the same implication: "On these two [love] commandments depend all the Law and the Prophets." Jesus used the same phrase when stressing the comprehensive messianic truths of the Old Testament: "Beginning with Moses and all the Prophets, he interpreted to them in all the Scriptures the things concerning himself" (Luke 24:27). It will be remembered (see chap. 3) that some eighteen of the twenty-two books of the Hebrew Old Testament are cited authoritatively in the New Testament (all except Judges, Chronicles, Esther, and Song of Solomon). Although there are no clear citations of these four books there are allusions to them.

Third, as far as Jesus and the New Testament writers were concerned, the Jewish canon was closed before the time of Jesus. Luke informs us that "the Law and the Prophets" were read in the synagogue on the Sabbath (Acts 13:15). When attempting to convince the Jews of his complete orthodoxy, the apostle Paul said that he believed "everything laid down by the Law or written in the Prophets" (Acts 24:14; cf. 26:22). Elsewhere, he said he had declared to them "the whole counsel of God" (Acts 20:27). This could hardly be true unless the "law and prophets" contained it. The reference to the Old Testament as the law . . . the prophets in the Sermon on the Mount is crucial (Matt. 5:17; cf. Rom. 1:2). Jesus declared, "Do not think that I have come to abolish the Law or the Prophets; I have not come to abolish them but to fulfill them. For truly, I say to you, until heaven and earth pass away, not an iota, not a dot, will pass from the Law until all is accomplished" (Matt. 5:17–18). Such a forceful pronouncement could scarcely refer to less than the totality of the Jewish Scriptures.

Fourth, according to Judaism, the canon was completed by about 400 BCE. The Jewish historian Josephus said, "From Artaxerxes [fourth century BCE] until our time everything has been recorded, but has not been deemed worthy of like credit with what preceded, because the exact succession of the prophets ceased" (*Contra Apion* 1.8). The Talmud declares that "up to this point [fourth century BCE] the prophets prophesied through the Holy Spirit; from this time onward incline thine ear and listen to the sayings of the wise" (Seder Olam Rabba 30). It adds flatly, "With the death of Hagai, Zechariah and Malachai the latter prophets, the Holy Spirit ceased out of Israel" (Tos. Sotah 13:2). It adds elsewhere, "The books of the heretics do not make the hands unclean; the books of Ben Sira [ca. 180 BCE] and whatever books have been written since his time are not canonical" (Tosefta Yadaim 3:5).

In short, the Jewish canon contained two sections: Law and Prophets. And it was complete by the time of Malachi around 400 BCE. As evidence during the intertestamental period (the Apocrypha), the Qumran period, and in the New Testament, it is assumed that there was a closed canon. And that canon consisted of the twenty-two books of the Jewish Torah, referred to consistently as "Law and Prophets." Thus, the later tendency to divide the "prophets" into two sections of eight prophets and eleven writings is definitely not the basis for a progressive three-stage development of the canon and was not fixed in its present form until fourth century CE.

THE DEVELOPMENT OF THE OLD TESTAMENT CANON

There is not enough data to form a complete history of the Old Testament canon. Sufficient material is available, however, to provide an overall sketch and to illustrate some crucial links. The rest must be projected as a result of the exercise of reasonable judgment. The first significant factor in the development of the Old Testament canon was the immediate and progressive collection of prophetic books. These books were preserved as divinely authoritative writings.

Evidence of a Progressive Collection of Prophetic Books

From the very beginning, the inspired writings were collected by the people of God and revered as sacred and divinely authoritative. Moses' laws were stored by the ark in the tabernacle of God, beside the ark of the covenant (Deut. 31:24–26) and later in the temple (2 Kings 22:8). Joshua added his words "in the Book of the Law of God . . . and set it up . . . by the sanctuary of the LORD" (Josh. 24:26). Samuel informed the Israelites of the duties of their king "and he wrote them in a book and laid it up before the LORD" (1 Sam. 10:25).

Samuel headed up a school of the prophets whose disciples were called "sons of the prophets" (1 Kings 20:35). According to Ezekiel there was an official register of prophets and their writings in the temple (Ezek. 13:9). Daniel refers to "the books" which contained the "law of Moses" and "the prophets" (9:2, 6, 11). The writers of the books of Kings and Chronicles were aware of many books by prophets that covered the whole of preexilic history (see "Evidence of a Prophetic Continuity" below).

This general evidence of a growing collection of prophetic books is confirmed by specific usage of the earlier prophets by later ones. The books of Moses are cited throughout the Old Testament from Joshua (1:7) to Malachi (4:4), including most of the major books between (1 Kings 2:3; 2 Kings 14:6; 2 Chron. 14:4; Jer. 8:8; Dan. 9:11; Ezra 6:18; and Neh. 13:1). Both Joshua and events in his book are referred to in Judges (1:1; 2:6–8). The books of Kings cite the life of David as it was told in the books of Samuel (see 1 Kings 3:14; 5:7; 8:16; 9:5). Chronicles review Israel's history recorded from Genesis through Kings, including the genealogical link mentioned only in Ruth (1 Chron. 2:12–13). Nehemiah 9 reviews Israel's history as it is recorded from Genesis to Ezra. A psalm of David, Psalm 18, is recorded in 2 Samuel 22. Reference is made to Solomon's Proverbs and Songs in 1 Kings 4:32. Daniel cites Jeremiah 25 (Dan. 9:2). The prophet Jonah recites parts from many psalms (Jonah 2). Ezekiel mentions both Job and Daniel (Ezek. 14:14, 20). Not every prior book is cited by a later one, but enough are cited to demonstrate that there was a growing collection of divinely authoritative books available to and quoted by subsequent prophets.

Evidence of a Prophetic Continuity

In addition to the continuous collection of prophetic writings presented in the Old Testament, there appears to be a continuity among the writings themselves. Each of the leaders in the prophetic community seems to have linked his history to that of his predecessors to produce an unbroken chain of books.

Since the last chapter of Deuteronomy does not present itself as prophecy, it would seem that Moses did not write about his own funeral. It is more likely that Joshua, his God-appointed successor, recorded the death of Moses (Deuteronomy 34). The first verse of Joshua links itself to Deuteronomy, saying, "After the death of Moses the servant of the LORD, the LORD said to Joshua the son of Nun." Joshua added to the Mosaic law and put it by the tabernacle (Josh. 24:26). Judges picked up at the end of Joshua saying, "After the death of Joshua the sons of Israel inquired of the Lord," but the record was not completed until Samuel's time. This is repeatedly shown by the statement, "In those days there was no king in Israel" (Judg. 17:6; 18:1; 19:1; 21:25).

At this point the prophetic continuity was established in a school directed by Samuel (1 Sam. 19:20). From its ranks came a series of prophetic books that cover the entire history of the kings of Israel and Judah, as the following sample illustrates:

> The history of David was written by Samuel (cf. 1 Sam.), Nathan, and Gad (1 Chron. 29:29).
>
> The history of Solomon was recorded by the prophets Nathan, Ahijah, and Iddo (2 Chron. 9:29).
>
> The acts of Rehoboam were written by Shemaiah and Iddo (2 Chron. 12:15).
>
> The history of Abijah was added by the prophet Iddo (2 Chron. 13:22).
>
> The story of Jehoshaphat's reign was recorded by Jehu the prophet (2 Chron. 20:34).
>
> The reign of Hezekiah was written by Isaiah (2 Chron. 32:32).
>
> The life of Manasseh was recorded by unnamed prophets (2 Chron. 33:19).
>
> The other kings also have their histories recorded by prophets (2 Chron. 35:27).

Old Testament expert R. Laird Harris referred to the "colophon principle" as evidence of the prophetic continuity of books in the Old Testament canon. Professor Harris wrote: "Each book completes the preceding and links the prophetic history together. Ruth was originally appended to Judges. . . . Likewise, the last chapter of Kings parallels the material in Jeremiah 52, 39, 40, and 41. Similarly, the book of Chronicles ends with the same two verses that the Ezra–Nehemiah unit begins with."[2]

Anyone familiar with the biblical books that cover the period from David to the exile will see that the prophetic books listed above are not identical with the two-book sets of Samuel, Kings, and Chronicles. Each time a

---

2. R. Laird Harris, *Inspiration and Canonicity of the Bible* (Grand Rapids: Zondervan, 1957), 166.

cue is given in the repeated phrase "and the rest of the acts" of king so-and-so are written "in the book" of prophet such-and-such. The biblical books appear to be prophetic abridgements edited out of the more complete histories recorded by the prophetic succession beginning with Samuel.

Interestingly Jeremiah, who wrote just prior to and during the Jewish exile, is not mentioned as having written one of these histories. Yet Jeremiah was a writing prophet, as his books (Jeremiah and Lamentations) indicate, and as he explicitly claims on numerous occasions (eg., Jer. 30:2; 36:1, 2; 45:1–2; 51:60, 63). In fact the scribe Baruch tells us that Jeremiah had secretarial help. Speaking of Jeremiah, he confessed, "He dictated all these words to me, while I wrote them with ink on the scroll" (Jer. 36:18; see also 45:1). As noted, the last chapter of the Kings parallels earlier material in Jeremiah 52, 39, 40, and 41. This is still another indication that Jeremiah was responsible for both books. Later in the exile, Daniel claims to have had access to the books of Moses and the prophets. From them he not only names Jeremiah but quotes his prediction of the seventy-year captivity from chapter 25 (cf. Dan. 9:2, 6, 11). On the basis of these facts, it is reasonable to suppose that the abridgment of the prophetic writings, which took the form of the biblical books of the Kings, was the work of Jeremiah. Thus, the continuity of the preexilic prophets from Moses, Joshua, and Samuel would be completed with the works of Jeremiah.

During the exile, Daniel and Ezekiel continued the prophetic ministry. Ezekiel vouched to an official register of prophets in the temple records. He declared that false prophets "shall not be in the council of my people, nor be enrolled in the register of the house of Israel" (Ezek. 13:9). Ezekiel referred to Daniel by name as a noted servant of God (Ezek. 14:14, 20). Since Daniel possessed a copy of the books of Moses and the prophets, including Jeremiah's book, we may reasonably assume that the Jewish community in the Babylonian exile possessed Genesis through Daniel.

After the exile, Ezra the priest returned from Babylon with the books of Moses and the prophets (Ezra 6:18; Neh. 9:14, 26–30). In the Chronicles he undoubtedly carried his own priestly account of the history of Judah and the temple (see Neh. 12:23). Chronicles is connected with Ezra–Nehemiah by the repetition of the last verse of one as the second verse of the other.

With Nehemiah the chronology of prophetic continuity is complete. Each prophet from Moses through Nehemiah contributed to the growing collection that was preserved by the official prophetic community stemming from Samuel. As with the prophetic continuity, the canon of prophetic writings is complete with Nehemiah. All twenty-two (twenty-four)[3] books of the Hebrew Scriptures are written by the prophets, preserved by the prophetic community, and recognized by the people of God. So far there is no evidence to demonstrate that other books, called the Writings, were written and canonized after this time (ca. 400 BCE).

Evidence That the OT Canon Was Completed with the Prophets

To this point we have indicated that the complete Hebrew Testament was collected in two main sections: the five books of Moses and the nineteen prophets who followed him. We have also shown that there was continuity in those prophetic writings, with each prophet making authoritative use of the former prophets and adding his contribution to the growing collection of sacred writings. By the time of Nehemiah (ca. 400 BCE) this prophetic succession had produced and collected the twenty-two books of the Hebrew canon. Thus, no third section of the canon was written and recognized after this time. Briefly, the evidence is as follows:

It has been long held by critical scholars that the third section of the current Jewish Old Testament, called the Writings or Kethuvim, were not canonized until ca. 90 CE, when the so-called "Council of Jamnia" (Yavneh) met. However, this case seriously lacks supportive evidence.

First of all, it has been demonstrated that this gathering was nothing like a later church council which made official pronouncement for Judaism the way in which early Christian Creeds were supposed to do for the Christian Church. In a definitive article on the topic, Professor Jack P. Lewis affirmed that "Yavneh and the concerns of its scholars . . . contain nothing of the closing of the canon at a Council of Jamnia." In fact, "None of these terms or descriptions suggest that the Yavneh gatherings justify the use of the Christian terminology like 'synod' or 'council' for them. . . . These terms are not appropriate to Judaism."[4]

---

3. Listing the books as twenty-two makes it correspond with the twenty-two letters of the Hebrew alphabet, possibly indicating that the canon was complete. If Ruth is separated from Judges and Lamentations from Jeremiah, it makes twenty-four books, which is the way they have been listed from the fifth century to the present.

4. See Jack Lewis, "Jamnia after Forty Years," from The ALTA Serials collection (2004), 233, 252.

Second, as shown previously, the Old Testament was completed by 400 BCE, and no Jewish prophet arose from that time to the time of Christ. As the Talmud declared, "Up to this point [fourth century BCE] the prophets prophesied through the Holy Spirit; from this time onward incline thine ear and listen to the sayings of the wise" (Seder Olam Rabba 30), adding that with the death of Malachi, "the Holy Spirit ceased out of Israel" (Tos. Sotah 13:2).

Third, Jesus and the New Testament writers assume a fixed canon in "the law and the prophets" that was considered "all the Scriptures" (Luke 24:27), the whole of inspired Jewish history to that time (Matt. 23:35), and everything up to John the Baptist. Luke wrote: "The Law and the Prophets were until John; since then the good news of the kingdom of God is preached" (Luke 16:16).

Fourth, the critics' late dating of the book of Daniel (at 165 BCE) as part of this third section of the Jewish Bible called the Writings is also called into question. For Josephus (first century CE) clearly did not have Daniel in his third section of supposedly non-prophetic books. For of the twenty-two books, said Josephus, only "four books contain hymns to God and precepts for the conduct of human life" (*Against Apion*, 1.8). The four books were probably Job, Psalms, Proverbs, and Ecclesiastes. Daniel certainly did not fit into this category. Therefore, they must have been listed with the prophets. The reference by Jesus to "the prophet Daniel" (Matt. 24:15) supports this position.

Fifth, the New Testament cites almost every book of the Hebrew canon, including those called Writings (like Daniel and Chronicles). But it clearly lists them all under the twofold classification of law and prophets (cf. Matt. 5:17; and Luke 24:27). Thus, these book later out into a third section of the Old Testament (by the fourth century CE) for whatever reason, festal, liturgical, topical, etc., were clearly part of the Law and Prophets, the complete canon of the Old Testament.

Sixth, the book of Psalms, listed in the third section by Josephus, was clearly part of the Prophets. Jesus used the phrase "the law of Moses and the Prophets and the Psalms" as a parallel to the phrase "Moses and all the Prophets" (Luke 24:27, 44). Jesus spoke to the Jews and quoted a psalm as what is "written in your Law" (John 10:34–35), and then He identified it as the Scripture and the Word of God. All this clearly indicates that the Psalms were part of the canonical Jewish Scriptures known as "the Law and the Prophets." Indeed, the New Testament authoritatively quotes the Psalms as Scripture more than any other book in the Old Testament. This too verifies that they were held to be canonical before 100 CE.

Evidence from Later Redaction

There is some evidence of editorial changes by later Old Testament writers. Some evangelical writers have posited "inspired redactors" to account for these changes. However, no content changes could occur by "inspired" redactions since: (1) this is contrary to repeated warnings by God "not [to] add to the word which I [God] am commanding you" (Deut. 4:2; cf. Prov. 30:6, Rev. 22:18–19); (2) it confuses canonicity with textual criticism; (3) it is contrary to the biblical use of the word "inspired" which is limited to the writings, not the writers; (4) it transforms fixed autographs into a fluid process; (5) it undermines the test by which the original audience could verify the prophetic nature of the writing because they knew the author; (6) it shifts the locus of authority from the original writing of a prophet to a later community of believers; (7) it involves deception about a prophetic writing by the adding of another, later author's words to those of the original author as though he wrote all of them; (8) it confuses legitimate later scribal activity (involving grammatical form, updating names, and arrangement of prophetic material) with illegitimate later tampering with the content of the prophet's message; and (9) the redaction theory assumes, contrary to Jewish teaching (see above), that there were inspired prophets well beyond 400 BCE.

Some of the alleged later "redactions" actually were: (1) later prophetic writings like Moses' death written by Joshua (Deut. 34); (2) parenthetical sections written by Moses himself (e.g., Deut. 2:13); (3) simply adding new psalms or rearranging older ones; (4) adding proverbs by other prophets to those written by Solomon (e.g., Prov. 30 and 31); (5) having two inspired versions of a book (e.g., Jeremiah) in which the later one contained more of his prophecies than the former one; and (6) including other books mentioned as references (e.g., 1 Chron. 9:1; 29:29) which were merely reliable sources.

What the evidence does show is that there was a continuing prophetic community that preserved, arranged, and even updated names and places, sometimes adding new revelations, but never making content changes in former revelation. A divinely inspired and inerrant writing has no mistakes in it to correct.

SUMMARY AND CONCLUSION

Our investigation shows that as far as the evidence is concerned, the canon of the Old Testament was completed about 400 BCE. There were two main sections: the Law and the Prophets. Virtually all twenty-two books (twenty-four when Ruth is separated from Judges and Lamentations from Jeremiah) in both sections are cited as Scripture by the New Testament. There is no scriptural or historical support for the theory that a third division, known as the Writings, awaited canonization at a later date. Instead, the inspired books were brought into the canon as law and prophets. This canonization was a twofold process. Whatever the factors are that led to subsequent or parallel threefold categorization of these Old Testament books, this much seems clear—the complete canon of the Old Testament is consistently referred to as the law and the prophets (Matt. 5:17; Luke 16:16; 24:27).

8

THE EXTENT *of the* OLD TESTAMENT CANON

THE INITIAL ACCEPTANCE of the twenty-two books (same as our thirty-nine) of the Hebrew Scriptures (see chap. 7) did not settle the issue once and for all. Later scholars who were not always fully aware of the facts of the original acceptance raised questions about the canonicity of certain books.

The discussion gave rise to a technical terminology. The biblical books that were accepted by all were called "homologoumena" (lit., to speak as one). Those nonbiblical works rejected by all were entitled "pseudepigrapha" (false writings). A third category, comprised of biblical books that were occasionally questioned by some, were labeled "antilegomena" (to speak against). A fourth category, comprised of nonbiblical books that were (are) accepted by some but rejected by others, includes the disputed books of the "Apocrypha" (hidden, or doubtful). Our discussion will follow this fourfold classification.

THE BOOKS ACCEPTED BY ALL—HOMOLOGOUMENA

The canonicity of some books was never seriously challenged by any of the great rabbis within the Jewish community. Once these books were accepted by God's people as being from the hand of the prophet of God, they continued to be recognized as divinely authoritative by subsequent generations. Thirty-four of the thirty-nine books of the Old Testament may be classed as homologoumena. This includes every book except Song of Solomon, Ecclesiastes, Esther, Ezekiel, and Proverbs. Since none of these books has been seriously disputed, our attention may be turned to the other books.

THE BOOKS REJECTED BY ALL—PSEUDEPIGRAPHA

A large number of spurious religious writings which circulated in the ancient Jewish community are known as the pseudepigrapha. Not everything in these pseudepigraphal writings is false. In fact, most of them arose from within the context of a religious fantasy or tradition that has its source in some truth. Frequently the origin of these writings was spiritual speculation on something not explicitly covered in canonical Scripture. The speculative traditions about the patriarch Enoch no doubt lie at the root of the Book of Enoch. Likewise, curiosity about the death and glorification of Moses is undoubtedly behind the Assumption of Moses. Such speculation, however, does not mean that there are no truths in these books. On the contrary, the New Testament refers to truths embodied in both of these books (see Jude 14, 15), and even makes allusion to the *Penitence of Jannes and Jambres* (2 Tim. 3:8).

Nonetheless, these books are not cited authoritatively as Scripture by the New Testament. Like the quotations of Paul from the non-Christian poets Aratus (Acts 17:28), Menander (1 Cor. 15:33), and Epimenides (Titus 1:12), it is only a truth contained in the book that is verified by its citation and not by the authority of the book itself. Truth is truth no matter where it is found, whether it is uttered by a heathen poet, a pagan prophet (Num. 24:17), a dumb animal (Num. 22:28), or even a demon (Acts 16:17).

It is important to note that no formula such as "it is written" or "the Scriptures say" is used in referring to these pseudepigraphal works. Perhaps the most dangerous thing about these false writings is the fact that the elements of truth are presented in words of divine authority in a context of religious fancy which usually contains some theological heresy. It is important to remember that it is only the truth quoted, and not the book as such, that is given divine authority in the New Testament.

The Nature of the Pseudepigrapha

The Old Testament pseudepigrapha contain the extremes of Jewish religious fancy expressed between 200 BCE and 200 CE. Some books are theologically harmless (e.g., Psalm 151), while others contain historical errors and outright heresy. The genuineness of these books is particularly challenged, since it is claimed that they were written by biblical authors. The pseudepigrapha reflect the literary style of a period long after the close of the prophetic writings, and most of the books imitate the apocalyptic format of Ezekiel, Daniel, and Zechariah—speaking of dreams, visions, and revelations. Unlike these prophets, however, the religious fancy of pseudepigrapha often becomes magical.

Overall, the pseudepigrapha depict a bright messianic future of rewards for those who engage in lives of suffering and self-denial. Beneath the surface there is often an innocent albeit misguided religious motive. But the false claim to divine authority, the highly fanciful character of the events, and the questionable (even heretical) teachings have led the Jewish fathers to consider them spurious. As a result they have correctly received the label "pseudepigrapha."

The Number of the Pseudepigrapha

The standard collection of the pseudepigrapha contains seventeen books. Add to this Psalm 151 which is found in the Codex Vaticanus and the Septuagint version of the Old Testament, and the principal list is as follows:

Legendary	1. The Book of Jubilee 2. The Letter of Aristeas 3. The Book of Adam and Eve 4. The Martyrdom of Isaiah
Apocalyptic	1. 1 Enoch 2. The Testament of the Twelve Patriarchs 3. The Sibylline Oracle 4. The Assumption of Moses 5. 2 Enoch, or the Book of the Secrets of Enoch 6. 2 Baruch, or The Syriac Apocalypse of Baruch* 7. 3 Baruch, or The Greek Apocalypse of Baruch
Didactic	1. 3 Maccabees 2. 4 Maccabees 3. Pirke Aboth 4. The Story of Ahikar
Poetical	1. The Psalms of Solomon 2. Psalm 151
Historical	1. The Fragment of a Zadokite Work

---

* 1 Baruch is listed in the Apocrypha (see previous discussion).

This list is by no means complete. Other books are known, including some interesting ones brought to light with the Dead Sea Scrolls and Discoveries in the Judean Desert. Among those are the Genesis Apocryphon and the War of the Sons of Light Against the Sons of Darkness (see chap. 12).

THE BOOKS DISPUTED BY SOME—THE ANTILEGOMENA

The Nature of the Antilegomena

Of more interest to our study are the books that were originally and ultimately received as canonical but were subjected to rabbinical debate in the process. The previous chapter revealed how all thirty-nine books of the Old Testament were initially accepted by the people of God from His prophets. During the centuries that followed, a different school of thought developed within Judaism, which debated, among other things, the canonicity of certain books that had previously been received into the Old Testament. Ultimately these books were retained in the canon, as their original status prevailed. Nevertheless, because these books were at one time or another spoken against by some rabbis, they are called the antilegomena.

The Number of the Antilegomena

The canonicity of five Old Testament books was questioned at one time or another by some teachers within Judaism: Song of Solomon, Ecclesiastes, Esther, Ezekiel, and Proverbs. Each was questioned for a different reason, but in the end the divine authority of each was vindicated.

Song of Solomon. Some within the school of Shammai thought this canticle to be *sensual*. In an apparent attempt to cover over the controversy and defend the canonicity of the Song, Rabbi Akiba wrote, "God forbid!—no man in Israel ever disputed about the Song of Songs that it does not render the hands unclean [i.e., is not canonical], for all the ages are not worth the day on which the Song of Songs was given to Israel; for all the Writings are holy, but the Song of Songs is the Holy of Holies."[1]

As others have observed, the very fact of such a statement indicates that someone had doubted the purity of the book. The doubts, centered in the alleged sensual character of the Song of Solomon, were misdirected. It is

---

1. Herbert Danby, *The Mishnah* (Oxford: Oxford Univ. Press, 1933), 782.

more likely that the purity and nobility of marriage is part of the essential purpose of the book. Whatever the questions about the various interpretations, there should be no doubt about its inspiration, once it is viewed in a proper spiritual perspective.[2]

Ecclesiastes. The objection sometimes leveled against this book is that it seems *skeptical*. Some have even called it the "Song of Skepticism." Rabbi Akiba admitted that "if aught was in dispute the dispute was about Ecclesiastes alone." There is little question about the occasional skeptical *sound* of the book: "Vanity of vanities! All is vanity.... there is nothing new under the sun.... For in much wisdom is much vexation, and he who increases knowledge increases sorrow" (Eccl. 1:2, 9, 18).[3]

What is overlooked when the charge of skepticism is made is both the context of these statements and the general conclusion of the book. A man seeking ultimate satisfaction "under the sun" will certainly feel the same frustrations that Solomon felt, for eternal happiness is not found in this temporal world. Moreover, the conclusion and general teaching of the entire book is far from skeptical. When "all has been heard," the reader is admonished, "Fear God and keep his commandments, for this is the whole duty of man" (Eccl. 12:13). In Ecclesiastes, as in the Song, the basic problem is one of interpretation and not inspiration or canonization.

Esther. Because of the conspicuous absence of the name of God in this book, some have thought it to be unspiritual. They ask, How can a book be the Word of God when it does not even bear His name? In addition, the story of the book seems to be purely secular in nature. As a result, several attempts have been made to explain the phenomenon of God's apparent absence in the book of Esther. Some have suggested that the Persian Jews, not being in the theocratic line, did not have the name of the covenant God associated with them. Others have argued that the omission of the name of God is intentional to protect the book from the possibility of a pagan plagiarism by the substitution of the name of a false god. Still others see the name of Jehovah or Yahweh (YHWH, יהוה) in an acrostic at four crucial points in the story in such a way as to eliminate chance.[4]

---

2. Ibid.

3. Ibid.

4. See Norman L. Geisler, *A Popular Survey of the Old Testament* (Grand Rapids: Baker, 2000), chap. 29.

Whatever the explanation, this much is obvious: the absence of the name of God is overshadowed by the presence of God in the preservation of His people. Esther and her companions were deeply devout: a religious fast was held, and Esther exercised great faith (Esth. 4:16). The fact that God granted His people deliverance in the book serves as the basis for the Jewish Feast of Purim (Esth. 9:26–28). This alone is sufficient indication of the authority ascribed to the book within Judaism.

Ezekiel. There were those within the rabbinical school who thought the book of Ezekiel was anti-Mosaic in its teaching. The school of Shammai, for example, felt that the book was not in harmony with the Mosaic Law and that the first ten chapters exhibited a tendency toward Gnosticism. If there were actual contradictions then the book, of course, could not be canonical. However, no specific examples of contradictions with the Torah were provided. Here again it seems to be a question of interpretation rather than inspiration.

Proverbs. The dispute over Proverbs centered on the fact that some of the teachings within the book seemed contradictory with other proverbs. Speaking of this alleged internal inconsistency, the Talmud says, "The book of Proverbs also they sought to hide, because its words contradicted one to another" (Tractate "Shabbath," 30b). One supposed contradiction is found in chapter 26, where the reader is exhorted both to "answer a fool according to his folly" and not to do so (Prov. 26:4–5). But, as other rabbis have observed, the meaning here is that there are occasions when a fool should be answered according to his folly and other times when he should not. Since the statements are in successive verse, a legitimate form of Hebrew poetry, the composers obviously saw no contradiction. The qualifying phrase which indicates whether one should or should not answer a fool clearly reveals that the situations calling for different answers are not the same.

No contradiction exists in Proverbs 26, none has been demonstrated elsewhere in Proverbs, and hence nothing stands in the way of its canonicity.

THE BOOKS ACCEPTED BY SOME—APOCRYPHA

The most crucial area of disagreement on the Old Testament canon among Christians is the debate over the so-called Apocrypha. In brief, these books are accepted by Roman Catholics as canonical and rejected in Protestantism and Judaism. In point of fact, the meanings of the word *apocrypha* reflect the problem manifest in the two views on its canonicity. In classical Greek, the word *apocrypha* meant "hidden" or "hard to understand." Later it took on the connotation of *esoteric,* or something understood only by the initiated and not an outsider. By the times of Irenaeus and Jerome (third and fourth centuries) the term *apocrypha* came to be applied to the noncanonical books of the Old Testament, including what was previously classified as pseudepigrapha. Since the Reformation era, the word has been used to denote the noncanonical Jewish religious literature coming from the intertestamental period.

The issue before us is to determine whether the books were hidden in order to be preserved, because their message was deep and spiritual, or because they were spurious and of doubtful authenticity.

The Nature and Number of the Old Testament Apocrypha

There are fifteen books in the Apocrypha (fourteen if the Letter of Jeremiah is combined with Baruch, as it is in Roman Catholic Douay versions). With the exception of 2 Esdras (ca. 100 CE), these books bridge the gap between Malachi and Matthew and specifically cover the two or three centuries before Christ. Their dates and classification are as follows:

BOOKS OF THE APOCRYPHA

Book Type	Revised Standard Version	Douay
DIDACTIC	1. Wisdom of Solomon (ca. 30 BCE) 2. Ecclesiasticus (Sirach) (132 BCE)	Book of Wisdom Ecclesiasticus
RELIGIOUS	3. Tobit (ca. 200 BCE)	Tobias
ROMANCE	4. Judith (ca. 150 BCE)	Judith
HISTORIC	5. 1 Esdras (ca. 150–100 BCE) 6. 1 Maccabees (ca. 110 BCE) 7. 2 Maccabees (110–70 BCE)	3 Esdras+ 1 Maccabees 2 Maccabees
PROPHETIC	8. Baruch (ca. 150–50 BCE) 9. Letter of Jeremiah (ca. 300 BCE) 10. 2 Esdras (ca. 100 CE)	Baruch chaps 1–5 Baruch chap. 6 4 Esdras+
LEGENDARY	11. Additions to Esther (140–130 BCE) 12. Prayer of Azariah (2nd or 1st century BCE) 13. (Song of Three Young Men) 14. Susanna (2nd or 1st century BCE) 15. Bel and the Dragon (ca. 100 BCE) +Prayer of Manasseh (2nd or 1st cent. BCE)	Esther 10:4 16:24* Daniel 3:24–90* Daniel 13* Daniel 14* Prayer of Manasseh+

+Books not accepted as canonical at the Council of Trent (1546).

*Books not listed in Douay (and later Roman Catholic versions) table of contents because they are appended to other books.

Arguments for Accepting the Old Testament Apocrypha

The Old Testament Apocrypha have received varying degrees of acceptance by Christians. Most Protestants and Jews accept them as having religious and even historical value but not canonical authority. Roman Catholics since the Council of Trent have held these books to be canonical. The Apocrypha are still used to support extrabiblical doctrines and were proclaimed to be divinely inspired at Trent. Other groups, such as Anglicans and the various Orthodox churches, have views of varying respect for the Apocrypha. The following is a summary of the arguments advanced for accepting these books as having some kind of canonical status.

1. New Testament allusions. Proponents argue that the New Testament reflects the thoughts of and records some events from the Apocrypha. Hebrews, for instance, speaks of women receiving their dead by resurrection (Heb. 11:35), and makes reference to 2 Maccabees 7 and 12. The so-called wider Apocrypha or pseudepigrapha are also cited in the New Testament (Jude 14–15; 2 Tim. 3:8).

2. New Testament usages of the Septuagint. The Greek translation of the Hebrew Old Testament made at Alexandria is known as the Septuagint (LXX). It is the version most often cited by New Testament writers, for it was in many respects the Bible of the apostles and early Christians. The LXX contained the Apocrypha. The presence of these books in the LXX supports the broader Alexandrian canon of the Old Testament as opposed to the narrower Palestinian canon which omits them.

3. The earliest complete manuscripts of the Bible. The earliest Greek manuscripts of the Bible contain the Apocrypha interspersed among the Old Testament books. Manuscripts א (*Aleph*), A, and B (see chap. 12) all include these books, revealing that they were part of the early Christian Bible.

4. Early Christian art. Some of the earliest records of Christian art reflect usage of the Apocrypha. Catacomb scenes sometimes draw on the history of the faithful recorded in the intertestamental period.

5. The early church fathers. Some of the very early church fathers, particularly in the West, used the Apocrypha in their teaching and preaching. Even in the East, however, Clement of Alexandria recognized 2 Esdras as fully canonical. Origen added Maccabees as well as the Letter of Jeremiah to his canonical list. Irenaeus quoted from the Book of Wisdom, and other Fathers cited other Apocryphal books.

6. The influence of St. Augustine. St. Augustine (ca. 354–430) brought the wider Western tradition about the Apocrypha to its culmination by giving to them canonical status. He influenced the church councils at Hippo (393 CE) and Carthage (397 CE) which listed the Apocrypha as canonical. From this time forward, the Western church used the Apocrypha in public worship.

7. The Council of Trent. In 1546 the post-Reformation Roman Catholic Council of Trent proclaimed the Apocrypha as canonical, declaring,

> The Synod . . . receives and venerates . . . all of the books both of the Old and of the New Testament [including Apocrypha]—seeing that one God is the Author of both . . . as having been dictated, either by Christ's own word of mouth or by the Holy Ghost . . . if anyone receives not as sacred and canonical the said books entire with all their parts, as they have been used to be read in the Catholic Church . . . let him be anathema.[5]

Since the Council of Trent, the books of the Apocrypha have had binding and canonical authority in the Roman Catholic Church. They are usually called "deuterocanonical" (lit. "second canon").

8. Non-Catholic usage. Protestant Bibles ever since the Reformation have often contained the Apocrypha. Indeed, in Anglican churches the Apocrypha are read regularly along with the other books of the Old and New Testaments in public worship. The Apocrypha continues to be used by churches in the Eastern Orthodox tradition.

9. The Dead Sea community. Books of the Apocrypha were found among the scrolls of the Dead Sea community at Qumran. Discoveries in the Judean Desert (DJD) confirm this pattern (see chap. 12). Some of these books were written in Hebrew, indicating their use among Palestinian Jews even before the time of Christ.

In summary argument, this position argues that the widespread employment of the Apocrypha by Christians from the earliest centuries is evidence of their acceptance by the people of God. This long tradition was culminated by an official recognition of these books as inspired and canonical by the Council of Trent (1546).

---

5. Philip Schaff, ed., *The Creeds of Christendom*, 6th ed. (New York: Harper, 1919), 2:81. More recent and comprehensive is Jaroslav Pelikan, ed., *Credo*; and Jaroslav Pelikan and Valerie Hotchkiss, *Creeds and Confessions of Faith in the Christian Tradition*, 3 vols., with CD–ROM (New Haven: Yale Univ. Press, 2003).

To date, even non-Catholics give something of a quasi-canonical status to the Apocrypha, as indicated by the place they give them in their Bibles and in the churches. Oxford and Cambridge university presses have published the Apocrypha in recent editions of the KJV.[6]

Reasons for Rejecting the Canonicity of the Apocrypha

Opponents of the Apocrypha have offered many counterarguments for excluding it from the canon. These arguments will be presented in the same order as those presented by the advocates of the larger canon.

1. New Testament authority. The New Testament never cites an Apocryphal book as inspired. Alleged allusions to these books lend no more authority to them than do the New Testament references to the pagan poets. Further, the New Testament cites virtually every canonical book of the Old Testament and verifies the contents and limits of the Old Testament but never books from the Apocrypha; this supports the Jewish view that they were never part of the Jewish canon. Josephus, the Jewish historian, expressly rejects the Apocrypha by listing only twenty-two canonical books.

2. The Septuagint translation. Palestine was the home of the Jewish canon, not Alexandria, Egypt. The great Greek learning center in Egypt was no authority in determining which books belonged in the Jewish Old Testament. Alexandria was the place of translation, not of canonization. The fact that the Septuagint contains the Apocrypha only proves that the Alexandrian Jews translated the other Jewish religious literature from the intertestamental period along with the canonical books. But even Philo, an Alexandrian Jew, clearly rejected the canonicity of the Apocrypha at the time of Christ, as has official Judaism at all times. In fact, the extant copies of the LXX date from the fourth century CE and do not prove what books were in the LXX of earlier times (250 BCE and later).

3. The early Christian Bible. The early Greek manuscripts of the Bible date from the fourth century. They follow the LXX tradition which contains the Apocrypha. As was noted above, this is a Greek translation, not a Hebrew canon. Jesus and the New Testament writers quoted most often

---

6. See Robert Carroll and Stephen Prickett, eds., *Oxford World's Classics: The Bible: Authorized King James Version, with Apocrypha* (Oxford: Oxford Univ. Press, 1997, 1998, reissued 2008); and David Norton, ed., *The New Cambridge Paragraph Bible with the Apocrypha* (Cambridge Univ. Press, 2006). Both of these works exclude Psalm 151.

from the LXX, nonetheless never once from any book of the Apocrypha. At best, the presence of the Apocrypha in Christian Bibles of the fourth century shows only that these books were accepted by some at that time. It does not indicate that either the Jews or earlier Christians accepted these books as canonical, to say nothing of the universal church, which has not held all of them to be canonical.

4. Early Christian art. Artistic representations are not grounds for determining the canonicity of the Apocrypha. Catacomb scenes from the Apocrypha indicate only that believers of that period were aware of the events of the intertestamental period and considered them part of their religious heritage. Early Christian art does nothing to settle the question of the canonicity of the Apocrypha.

5. Early church fathers. Many of the great early church fathers, including Melito, Origen, Cyril of Jerusalem, and Athanasius, spoke against the Apocrypha. No important Father before Augustine accepted all the Apocryphal books canonized by the Council of Trent. Further, as one authority on the Old Testament canon observed,

> When one examines the passages in the early Fathers which are supposed to establish the canonicity of the Apocrypha, one finds that some of them are taken from the alternative Greek text of Ezra (1 Esdras) or from additions or appendices to Daniel, Jeremiah or some other canonical book, which . . . are not really relevant; that others of them are not quotations from the Apocrypha at all; and that, of those which are, many do not give any indication that the book is regarded as Scripture.[7]

6. The canon of St. Augustine. The testimony of Augustine is neither definitive nor unequivocal. First, Augustine admitted that the Apocrypha were not part of the Jewish canon. Further, his grounds of accepting them are unfounded, namely, that they contain "the extreme and wonderful suffering of certain martyrs" (*City of God* 18. 36). On these grounds, *Foxe's Book of Martyrs* should also be added to the canon! Further, the councils of Hippo and Carthage were small local councils influenced by Augustine and the tradition of the Greek Septuagint translation, a tradition that is

---

7. Roger Beckwith, *The Old Testament Canon of the New Testament Church* (Eugene, Oreg.: Wipf & Stock, 2008), 387.

Apocryphal.[8]

No qualified Hebrew scholars were present at either of these councils. The most qualified Hebrew scholar of the time, St. Jerome, argued strongly against Augustine in his rejecting the canonicity of the Apocrypha. Jerome refused even to translate the Apocrypha into Latin or to include it in his Latin Vulgate versions. It was not until after Jerome's day and literally over his dead body that the Apocrypha was brought into the Latin Vulgate (see chap. 18).

7. The Council of Trent. The actions of the Council of Trent were polemical, prejudicial, and unbiblical. In debates with Luther, the Roman Catholics quoted the Maccabees in support of prayer for the dead (see 2 Macc. 12:44–45). Luther, and other Protestants following him, challenged the canonicity of that book, citing the New Testament, the early church fathers, and Jewish teachers for support. The Council of Trent responded to Luther by canonizing the Apocrypha. Not only was the action of Trent obviously polemical, but it was also prejudicial, since not all of the fourteen (fifteen) books of the Apocrypha were accepted by Trent. The books of 1 and 2 Esdras and the Prayer of Manasseh were rejected.[9] The rejection of 2 Esdras is particularly suspect, for it contains a strong verse against praying for the dead (2 Esdras 7:45). In fact, some medieval scribe had cut this section out of the Latin manuscripts of 2 Esdras, and it was known by Arabic manuscripts until found again in Latin by Robert L. Bently in 1874 at a library in Amiens, France.

The decision at Trent did not reflect either a universal or indisputable consent within the Catholic church of the Reformation. Cardinal Thommas de Vio Cajetan, who opposed Luther at Augsburg in 1518, published a *Commentary on All the Authentic Historical Books of the Old Testament* (1532), which omitted the Apocrypha. Even before this, Cardinal Francisco de Cisneros Ximénes distinguished between the Apocrypha and the Old Testament canon in his *Complutensian Polyglot* (1514–1517). With this data in view, Protestants generally reject the decision of Trent as unfounded.

---

8. This legend claims that seventy Jewish scholars made seventy independent translations of the Old Testament from Hebrew to Greek (called the LXX or Septuagint), and when they compared them they were identical! Since the Apocryphal books were allegedly in this translation, it is assumed that this is a supernatural approval of them.

9. The Roman Catholic Douay version called them 3 and 4 Esdras because the names 1 and 2 Esdras are used for the canonical books of Ezra and Nehemiah in the Douay version.

In canonizing the Apocrypha, Trent does not live up to its own statement that such statements should be in accord with the unanimous consent of the Fathers. In fact, Trent shows how fallible a supposed infallible pronouncement of the Roman Catholic Church can be.[10]

8. Non-Catholic usage. The use of the Apocrypha among Orthodox, Anglican, and Protestant churches has been uneven. Some have used it in public worship. Many Bibles contain translations of the Apocrypha, although it is placed in a separate section, usually between the Old and New Testaments. Even though some non-Catholics have employed the Apocrypha, they have usually not given to it the same canonical authority of the rest of the Bible. Instead, its use has been more devotional than canonical.

9. The Dead Sea Scrolls. Many noncanonical books were discovered in the caves at Qumran, including commentaries and manuals (see discussion in chap. 12). These caves contained numerous books not believed by the community to be inspired. Since no commentaries on or authoritative quotes from the Apocrypha have been discovered at Qumran, there is no evidence to demonstrate that they held the Apocrypha to be inspired. We may assume that they did not regard the Apocrypha as canonical. Even if evidence to the contrary is found, the fact that the group was a sect which had broken off from official Judaism would mean that it was not expected to be orthodox in all its beliefs. As far as we can tell, however, they were orthodox in their view of the canonicity of the Old Testament; that is, they did not accept the canonicity of the Apocrypha.[11]

10. Failure to meet the tests for canonicity. As a collection, the Apocrypha fails to meet the tests for canonicity stated earlier (in chap. 6). It does not claim to be inspired by God, as is indicated by the facts that: (1) it was not written by prophets of God (1 Macc. 9:27); (2) it was not written by persons confirmed by acts of God (Heb. 2:3–4); and (3) it does not always tell the truth of God. (For example, it teaches praying for the dead [2 Macc. 12:44] and working for salvation [Tobit 12:9]). Further, the Apocrypha (4) does not have the life-transforming power of God that the canonical books have;

---

10. For more on the fallibility of Rome, see Norman L. Geisler and Joshua M. Betancourt, *Is Rome the True Church?* (Wheaton, Ill.: Crossway, 2008).

11. For a complete listing and discussion of the Apocryphal books found at Qumran, see James VanderKam and Peter Flint, *The Meaning of the Dead Sea Scrolls* (San Francisco: Harper Collins, 2002), chap. 8.

and (5) it was not accepted by the people of God (Judaism).

In addition to the above five standard tests for the canonicity of the Apocrypha, it also fails because: (6) it was not accepted by Jesus the Son of God, who never cited it (Matt. 5:17–18; Luke. 24:27); (7) it was not accepted by the apostles of God (who didn't quote it); (8) it was not accepted by the early church of God (who never canonized it); (9) it was rejected by the great Catholic translator of the Word of God (Jerome); and (10) it was not written during the period of the prophets of God (see chap. 7) which ended by 400 BCE, and all the Apocrypha books were written 200 BCE and following. Again, the Jewish historian Josephus affirmed that "from Artaxerxes [fourth century BCE] until our time everything has been recorded, but has not been deemed worthy of like credit with what preceded, because the exact succession of the prophets ceased" (Contra Apion 1.8).

SUMMARY AND CONCLUSION

The extent of the Old Testament canon up to the time of Nehemiah comprised twenty-two (sometimes listed as twenty-four) books in Hebrew and relisted as thirty-nine in Christian Bibles, and was determined by the fourth century BCE. The minor disputes since that time have not changed the contents of the canon. It was the books written after this time, known as the Apocrypha, which because of the influence of the Greek translation at Alexandria gained a wide circulation among Christians. Since some of the early Fathers, particularly in the West, made use of these books in their writings, the church (largely under the influence of Augustine) gave them a broader and ecclesiastical use. Their canonization by the Council of Trent stands unsupported by history. Even that verdict was polemical, prejudiced, and biblically unjustified.

That these books, whatever devotional or ecclesiastical value they may possess, are not canonical is substantiated by the following facts: (1) the Jewish community has never accepted them as canonical; (2) they were not accepted by Jesus nor the New Testament writers; (3) most great Fathers of the early church rejected their canonicity; (4) no church council, local or universal, held them to be canonical until the late fourth century; (5) Jerome, the great biblical scholar and translator of the Vulgate, strongly rejected the Apocrypha (see discussions in chaps. 8 and 18); (6) some Roman Catholic scholars, even through the Reformation period, rejected the canonicity of the Apocrypha; (7) neither Eastern Orthodox, Anglican, nor Protestant churches to this date have recognized the Apocrypha as inspired and canonical in the full sense of the word.

In view of this, it behooves Christians today not to use the Apocrypha as the Word of God, nor use it as an authoritative support for any point of doctrine. Indeed, when examined by the criteria for canonicity set forth in chapter 6, the Apocrypha is found wanting: (1) the Apocrypha does not claim to be prophetic; (2) it does not come with the authority of God; (3) it contains historical errors (see Tobit 1:3–5 and 14:11) and such theological heresies as praying for the dead (2 Macc. 12:42–45); (4) the value of its contents for edification is mostly repetitious of the material already found in the canonical books; (5) there is a conspicuous absence of prophecy such as is found in the canonical books; and (6) nothing new is added to our knowledge of messianic truth by the Apocrypha. Finally, (7) the reception by the people of God to whom it was originally presented was negative; and (8) the Jewish community has never changed its position. Some Christians have been less definitive, but whatever value is placed upon it, it is evident that the church as a whole has never accepted the Apocrypha as canonical Scripture.

9

THE DEVELOPMENT *of the* NEW TESTAMENT CANON

THE HISTORY OF THE NEW TESTAMENT CANON differs from that of the Old in several respects. In the first place, since Christianity was an international religion from the beginning, there was no tightly knit prophetic community that received all inspired books and collected them in one place. Local and somewhat complete collections were made from the very beginning, but there is no evidence of a central and official clearinghouse for inspired writings. Therefore, the process by which all of the apostolic writings became universally accepted took many centuries. Fortunately, because of the availability of source materials more data is available on the New Testament canon than the Old.

Another difference between the history of the Old and New Testament canons is that once discussions resulted in the recognition of the twenty-seven canonical books of the New Testament canon, there have been no moves within Christendom to add to it or take away from it. The extent of the New Testament canon has met with virtually universal agreement within the Christian church as a whole.

THE STIMULI FOR AN OFFICIAL COLLECTION OF BOOKS

Several forces at work in the early Christian world led to an official recognition of the twenty-seven canonical books of the New Testament. Three of these forces are of special significance: the ecclesiastical, the theological, and the political.

The Ecclesiastical Stimulus for a Canonical List

The early church had both internal and external needs for an official recognition of canonical books. From within there was the need to know which books should be read in the churches according to the practice indicated for the New Testament church by the apostles (1 Thess. 5:27). From outside the church was the need to know which books should be translated into the foreign languages of the converted peoples. Without a recognized list of books it would be difficult for the early church to perform either of these tasks. The combination of these forces put increasing pressure on the church fathers to make an official list of the canonical books.

The Theological Stimulus for a Canonical List

Another factor within early Christianity called for an ecclesiastical pronouncement on the canon. Since all Scripture is profitable for doctrine (2 Tim. 3:16–17), it became increasingly necessary to define the limits of the apostolic doctrinal bank. The need to know which books were to be used to teach doctrine with divine authority became even more pressing as a result of the multitude of apocryphal and heretical books claiming divine authority. When the heretic Marcion published a sharply abridged list of canonical books (ca. 140), including only the gospel of Luke and ten of Paul's epistles (omitting 1 and 2 Timothy and Titus), the need for a complete canonical list became acute. Caught in the tension between those who would add to the canon and others who would take from it, the burden fell on the early church fathers to define precisely the limits of the canon.

The Political Stimulus for a Canonical List

The forces for canonization culminated in the political pressures brought to bear on the early Christian church. The Diocletian persecutions (ca. 302–305) provided a strong motive for the church to settle on a definitive list of canonical books. According to the Christian historian Eusebius, an imperial edict of Diocletian in 303 ordered "the destruction by fire of the Scriptures." Ironically enough, within twenty-five years the Emperor Constantine had become a convert to Christianity and ordered Eusebius to prepare and distribute fifty copies of the Bible. The persecution had occasioned a serious look at just which canonical books should be preserved, and the call for Bibles by the Emperor Constantine also made an official list of canonical books necessary. As noted in chapter 6, the Council of Nicea in 325 dealt with the deity of Christ but not the inspiration of Scripture.

THE PROGRESSIVE COLLECTION
AND RECOGNITION OF CANONICAL BOOKS

There is evidence to indicate that the very first believers collected and preserved the inspired books of the New Testament. These books were circulated among the early churches and doubtlessly copied as well. But since no official listing was promulgated, universal recognition was delayed several centuries until the pressures had brought about the need for such a list.

New Testament Evidence for a Growing Canon

The New Testament was written during the last half of the first century. Most of the books were written to local churches (e.g., the bulk of Paul's epistles) and some were addressed to individuals (e.g., Philemon, 2 and 3 John). Others were aimed at a broader audience, in eastern Asia (1 Pet.), western Asia (Revelation), and even Europe (Romans). Some of the letters probably originated in Jerusalem (James) while others arose as far west as Rome (1 Pet.). With such a geographical diversity of origin and destination it is understandable that not all the churches would immediately possess copies of all the inspired New Testament books. Add to this the problems of communication and transportation and it is easy to see that gaining a general recognition of all twenty-seven books of the New Testament canon would take some time. These difficulties notwithstanding, the early churches immediately began to make collections of whatever apostolic literature they could verify.

Confirming authentic books. From the very beginning inauthentic and nonapostolic writings were in circulation. Paul warned the Thessalonians, "We beg you, brethren," he wrote, "not to be quickly shaken in mind or alarmed . . . by . . . a letter seeming to be from us, to the effect that the day of the Lord has come" (2 Thess. 2:2). In order to verify the authenticity of his epistle, he closed saying, "I, Paul, write this greeting with my own hand. This is the sign of genuineness in every letter of mine; it is the way I write" (3:17). In addition, the letter would be sent by personal envoy from the apostle.

The apostle John further informs us that "Jesus did many other signs . . . which are not written in this book" (John 20:30), for if every one were written, "I suppose the world itself could not contain the books that would be written" (John 21:25). From the multitude of His deeds that were not written by the apostles, there arose many beliefs about the life of Christ that demanded apostolic verification. While the original eyewitnesses of the life and resurrection of Christ were alive (Acts 1:21–22), everything could be subjected to the authority of the oral teaching or tradition of the apostles (1 Thess. 2:13; 1 Cor. 11:2, and their authorized agents (Titus 1:5). So, the apostolic church was called upon to be selective in determining the authenticity of the many stories and sayings about Christ. In his gospel, John put to rest a false belief circulating in the first-century church, which held that he would never die (John 21:23–24). The same apostle also issued a strong warning to believers when he wrote, "Beloved, do not believe every spirit, but test the spirits to see whether they are from God, for many false prophets have gone out into the world" (1 John 4:1).

In brief, there is every indication that within the first-century church, a selecting process was at work. Every alleged word about Christ, whether oral or written, was subjected to authoritative apostolic teaching. If word or work could not be verified by those who were eyewitnesses (Luke 1:2; Acts 1:21–22), it was rejected.

The apostles who could say, "That which we have seen and heard we proclaim also to you" (1 John 1:3), were the final court of appeal. As another apostle wrote, "We did not follow cleverly devised myths when we made known to you the power and coming of our Lord Jesus Christ, but we were eyewitnesses of his majesty" (2 Pet. 1:16). This primary source of apostolic authority was the canon by which the first church selected the writings through which they devoted themselves to the apostles' teaching and fellowship (Acts 2:42). Thus the living "canon" of eyewitnesses became the criterion by which the earliest canonical writings were recognized, and God Himself bore witness to the apostles (Heb. 2:3–4). This includes both apostles and prophets (Eph. 2:20) who were also given revelation from God and who were authorized agents of the apostles (Titus 1:5; 2 Tim. 1:6).

Public reading of apostolic books. Another indication that the process of New Testament canonization began immediately in the first-century church was the official public reading of apostolic books. Paul commanded the Thessalonians, "I put you under oath before the Lord to have this letter read to all the brothers" (1 Thess. 5:27). Likewise, Timothy was told to present Paul's message to the churches along with the Old Testament

Scriptures. "Until I come," Paul wrote, "devote yourself to the public reading of the Scripture, to exhortation, to teaching" (1 Tim. 4:13; see also v. 11).

Paul also wrote to the Colossians, "And when this letter has been read among you, have it read also in the church of the Laodiceans" (Col. 4:16). John promised a blessing for him who reads "aloud" this book (Rev. 1:3), which he sent to seven different churches. This clearly indicates that the apostolic letters were intended to have a broader application than merely one local congregation. They were binding on all the churches, and as the churches were receiving and reading those authoritative writings, they were thereby laying the foundation of a growing collection of received writings. In brief, they were involved in an incipient process of canonization. This original acceptance of a book as one authoritatively read in the churches would be crucial to later recognition of the book as canonical.

Public reading of authoritative words from God was a practice of long standing. Moses and Joshua did it (Ex. 24:7; Josh. 8:34). Josiah had the Bible read to the people of his day (2 Kings 23:2) as did Ezra and the Levites when "they read from the book, from the Law of God, clearly, and they gave the sense, so that the people understood the reading" (Neh. 8:8). The reading of apostolic letters to the churches is a continuation of this long prophetic tradition.

The circulation and collection of books. There was already in New Testament times something of a growing and circulating canon of inspired Scripture. At first no church possessed all the apostolic letters, but their collection grew as copies could be made and authenticated by apostolic signature or emissary. Undoubtedly the first copies of Scripture emerged from this procedure of circulating epistles. As the churches grew, the demand for copies became greater, so that more congregations could keep them for their regular readings and study along with the Old Testament Scriptures.

The Colossian passage previously cited (4:16) informs us that circulation was an apostolic practice. There are also other indications of this practice. John was commanded of God, "Write what you see in a book and send it to the seven churches [of Asia Minor]" (Rev. 1:11). Since it was one book and they were many churches, the book had to be circulated among them. The same is true of many of the general epistles. James is addressed to the twelve tribes in the Dispersion (James 1:1). Peter wrote a letter to "the elect exiles of the dispersion in Pontus, Galatia, Cappadocia, Asia and Bithynia" (1 Pet. 1:1). Some have held that Paul's Ephesian epistle was general since the term Ephesians is not in the earliest manuscripts. The letter is simply addressed "to the saints who are . . . faithful in Christ Jesus" (Eph. 1:1).

All these circulating letters reveal the beginning of a canonization process. First, the letters were obviously intended for the churches in general. Then, each church would be obliged to make copies of the letters so they would possess them for further reference and study. The commands to read and study the Scriptures in the New Testament (which include some apostolic letters) do not indicate a mere once-for-all reading. Christians were urged to continually read the Scriptures (1 Tim. 4:11, 13). The only way this could be accomplished among the ever-growing number of churches was to make copies so that each church or group of churches could have its own collection of authoritative writings.

Peter apparently possessed a collection of Paul's letters and placed them alongside the "other Scriptures" (2 Pet. 3:15–16). We may assume that Peter had a collection of copies of Paul's works, since there is no good reason that Peter would have possessed the original copies of Paul's epistles. After all, they were not written to Peter, but to the churches scattered throughout the world. This indicates other collections must have arisen to fulfill the needs of the growing churches. The fact that one writer quotes from another also indicates that letters with divine authority were collected. Jude quotes from Peter (Jude 17; cf. 2 Pet. 3:2), and Paul cites Luke's gospel as Scripture (1 Tim. 5:18; cf. Luke 10:7). Luke assumes that Theophilus had a first book or account (Acts 1:1). He also alludes to at least two gospels written before his (Luke 1:1).[1] In addition, most New Testament scholars acknowledge that later gospels refer to material recorded in earlier gospels, as evidenced by numerous similarities between accounts in the Synoptic Gospels.[2]

Thus, the process of canonization was at work from the very beginning. The first churches were exhorted to select only the authentic apostolic writings. When a book was verified as authentic either by signature or by apostolic envoy, it was officially read to the church and then circulated among other churches. Collections of these apostolic writings began to take form

1. Luke said "many" had written before him (Gk. *polloi* can mean as few as two). Since only two other books (Matthew and Mark) exist and almost all scholars agree they were written before Luke, these may be the two to which Luke alludes.

2. It matters not whether Matthew wrote first (as the early church believed) or Mark (as many in the contemporary church hold). In either case one is aware of the material in the other(s).

in apostolic times. By the end of the first century all twenty-seven New Testament books were written and received by the churches. The canon was complete and all the books were recognized by believers. Because of the multiplicity of false writings and the lack of immediate access to the conditions related to the initial acceptance of a book, the debate about the canon continued for several centuries, until the church universal finally recognized the canonicity of the twenty-seven books of the New Testament.

THE CONFIRMATION OF THE OFFICIAL COLLECTION OF BOOKS

Immediate Acceptance of New Testament Books. As the previous discussion shows, New Testament books inspired of God were accepted, collected, and passed on to other churches during the time of the apostles (Col. 4:16; 2 Pet. 3:15–16; Rev. 1:3–4). Since it is now a widely accepted fact, even by critical scholars, that the entire canon of twenty-seven New Testament books was composed by the end of the first century, they were obviously accepted by their original audience; otherwise we should not have copies of them today, nor would they have been available for citation by the sub-apostolic church.

Acceptance of New Testament Books by the Earliest Fathers. During the first century after the apostles the inspiration of all of the twenty–seven New Testament books became generally recognized, as shown in the chart at the end of the chapter. This period is sometimes called the "sub-apostolic" period. In fact, some of the authors overlapped with the time of the apostles. This period would include Pseudo-Barnabas (70–130), Clement of Rome (ca. 96), Ignatius (ca. 110), Polycarp (110–150), who was a disciple of the apostle John, the Didache (120–150), Papias of Hierapolis (130–140), 2 Clement (ca. 150), and the Shepherd of Hermas (140–160). These men alone cite the whole New Testament except 2 Corinthians, Colossians, Philemon, 2 Peter, 2 John, 3 John, Jude, and Revelation. Importantly the lack of citation does not mean rejection, but merely the lack of an occasion to cite it. Most of these book were tiny one-chapter books that afforded little occasion to cite. To illustrate this point, the reader might ask himself or herself when they last quoted 2 or 3 John.

By 200 CE, only a century after the close of the apostolic age, all twenty-seven books of the New Testament were cited (see chart below). This is proof positive that these books were considered part of the inspired canon of Scripture from the earliest times.

In fact, within about two hundred years after the first century, not only every book but nearly every verse of the New Testament was cited in one or more of the Fathers—over thirty-six thousand citations by the Fathers (see chap. 13). Since the patristic witness to New Testament Scripture has already been reviewed (see chap. 4), it will not be repeated here. The following chart shows exactly which Father cited what book as Scripture in the early centuries. Not every book of the New Testament is quoted by every Father, but every book is quoted as canonical by some Father. In the final analysis, this is sufficient to indicate that the book was recognized as apostolic from the very beginning.

EARLY CITATIONS OF THE NEW TESTAMENT BY THE CHURCH FATHERS

Writer	Gospels	Acts	Pauline Epistles	General Epistles	Revelation	Totals
Justin Martyr	268	10	43	6 (266) ALLUSIONS	3	330
Irenaeus	1,038	194	499	23	65	1,819
Clement of Alexandria	1,017	44	1,127	207	11	2,406
Origen	9,231	349	7,778	399	165	17,922
Tertullian	3,822	502	2,609	120	205	7,258
Hippolytus	734	42	387	27	188	1,378
Eusebius	3,268	211	1,592	88	27	5,176
Totals	19,368	1,352	14,035	870	664	36,289

THE WITNESS OF THE EARLY LISTS, AND TRANSLATIONS OF THE CANON

Other confirmations of the canon of the first century are found in the translations and canonical lists of the second and third centuries. Translations could not be made unless there was first a recognition of the books to be included in the translation.

The Old Syriac translation. A translation of the New Testament was circulated in Syria by the end of the fourth century which represented a text dating from the second century. It included all the twenty-seven New Testament books except 2 Peter, 2 and 3 John, Jude, and Revelation. Noted biblical scholar B. F. Westcott observed, "Its general agreement with our own [canon] is striking and important; and its omissions admit of easy explanation."[3] The omitted books were originally destined for the Western world, and the Syriac church was in the East. The distance and lack of verifying communications slowed down the final acceptance of these books in the Eastern Bible, which had come out before that evidence was available to them.[4]

The Old Latin translation. The New Testament was translated into Latin prior to 200 and served as the Bible for the early Western church, just as the Syriac version did for the East. The Old Latin version contained every book of the New Testament with the exception of Hebrews, James, and 1 and 2 Peter. These omissions are the reverse of those in the Syriac Bible. Hebrews, 1 Peter, and probably James were written to churches at the Eastern end of the Mediterranean world. Hence, it took time for their credentials to be finally recognized in the West. Second Peter presented a special problem that will be discussed in chapter 10. Significantly, though, between the two earliest Bibles in the Christian church all twenty-seven New Testament books received canonicity.

The Muratorian Canon (170 CE). Aside from the obviously abridged canon of the heretic Marcion (140 CE), the earliest canonical list is found in the Muratorian Fragment. The list of New Testament books corresponds exactly with that of the Old Latin translation, omitting only Hebrews, James, and 1 and 2 Peter. Westcott argues that there was probably a break in the manuscript, which may have at one time included these books.[5] For it is rather unusual that Hebrews and 1 Peter should be omitted while the less frequently cited Philemon and 3 John are included.

Codex Barococcio (206). Another supporting testimony to the early canon of the New Testament comes from a codex entitled "The Sixty Books." Upon careful examination, these sixty books actually include sixty-four of the familiar sixty-six canonical books of the Bible. Only Esther is omitted from the Old Testament, and Revelation from the New. The canonicity of

3. Brooke Foss Westcott, *A General Survey of the History of the Canon of the New Testament*, 7th ed. (New York: Macmillan, 1896), 249–50.

4. In the Syriac church, for example, the Peshitta used the *Diatessaron* in the place of the four gospels and had a truncated canon until the sixth century, when James, 1 Peter, 1 John, and Revelation were included in the Harclean Syriac version; see W. G. Kümmel, trans. by A. J. Mattill Jr., *Introduction to the New Testament*, 14th rev. ed. (Nashville: Abingdon, 1966), 2.

5. Westcott, *A General Survey*, 223. Everett Ferguson lists 3 John as questionable in "Muratorian Canon," ed. Everett Ferguson, *Encyclopedia of Early Christianity*, 2nd ed. (New York: Garland Publishing, 1999), 786–87.

Revelation is well attested elsewhere, being supported by Justin Martyr, Irenaeus, Clement of Alexandria, Tertullian, and the Muratorian list.

Eusebius of Caesarea (ca. 340). In his *Ecclesiastical History* (3. 25), the historian Eusebius summarized well the New Testament canon in the West at the beginning of the fourth century. He listed as fully accepted all twenty-seven New Testament books except James, Jude, 2 Peter, and 2 and 3 John. These he listed as disputed by some, while he rejected Revelation altogether. Thus all but Revelation had gained acceptance, although several of the general epistles were not without dispute.

Athanasius of Alexandria (ca. 373). Whatever doubts existed in the West about some of the general epistles and Revelation, they were dispelled in the fifty years following Eusebius's work. Athanasius, the father of Orthodoxy, clearly lists all twenty-seven books of the New Testament as canonical (Letters 3. 267.5). Within a generation both Jerome and Augustine had confirmed the same list of books, and these twenty-seven books remained the accepted canon of the New Testament (see Augustine, On Christian Doctrine 2. 8. 13).

The councils of Hippo (393) and Carthage (397). The supporting witness to the canon of the New Testament was not limited to individual voices. Two local councils ratified the twenty-seven canonical books of the New Testament. The variation on the Old Testament canon accepted by these councils has already been discussed in chapter 8. There is also a list from the Synod at Laodicea (343–381), which includes all except Revelation; but eleven scholars have questioned the genuineness of this list.

Since the fifth century the church has accepted these twenty-seven books as the New Testament canon. Although subsequently there have been disputes about the Old Testament, the Christian church in all of its main branches continues to this day to recognize only these twenty-seven books of the New Testament as apostolic.

Summary and Conclusion. The process of collecting authentic apostolic literature began within New Testament times. In the second century, there was verification of this literature by quotation of the divine authority of each of the twenty-seven books of the New Testament. In the third century, doubts and debates over certain books culminated in the fourth century with the decisions of influential Fathers and councils. Through the centuries since that time, the Christian church has maintained the canonicity of these twenty-seven books.

NEW TESTAMENT BOOKS CITED BY THE EARLY CHURCH FATHERS

	Matthew	Mark	Luke	John	Acts	Romans	1 Corinthians	2 Corinthians	Galatians	Ephesians	Philippians	Colossians	1 Thessalonians	2 Thessalonians	1 Timothy	2 Timothy	Titus	Philemon	Hebrews	James	1 Peter	2 Peter	1 John	2 John	3 John	Jude	Revelation
Pseudo-Barnabas (70–130)	✓	✓	✓																✓								
Clement of Rome (ca.96)	✓	✓	✓		✓	✓	✓									✓			✓	✓	✓						
Ignatius (ca.110)	✓						✓			✓			✓		✓								✓				
Polycarp (110–150)	✓	✓	✓		✓	✓	✓		✓	✓	✓		✓	✓	✓	✓					✓		✓				
Didache (120–150)	✓		✓																✓								
Papias of Hierapolis (130–140)	✓	✓		✓			✓																				
2 Clement (ca.150)	✓		✓				✓	✓							✓				✓								
Hermas (140–160)	✓		✓	✓														✓	✓	✓							
Justin Martyr (ca.138–165)	✓	✓	✓	✓					✓																		✓
Tatian's Diatessaron (ca.170)	✓	✓	✓	✓																							
Melito of Sardis (170–180)		✓	✓			✓							✓						✓								
Muratorian Canon (ca.170–200)	✓	✓	✓	✓	✓	✓	✓	✓	✓	✓	✓	✓	✓	✓	✓	✓	✓	✓					✓	✓	?	✓	✓
Theophilus of Antioch (168–188)	✓		✓	✓	✓	✓	✓			✓					✓				✓				✓				
Irenaeus of Lyons (182–188)	✓	✓	✓	✓	✓	✓	✓	✓	✓	✓	✓	✓	✓	✓	✓	✓	✓	✓		✓	✓		✓	✓		✓	✓
Old Latin (ca.200)	✓	✓	✓	✓	✓	✓	✓	✓	✓	✓	✓	✓	✓	✓	✓	✓	✓			✓	✓		✓	✓	✓	✓	✓
Tertullian (198–220)	✓	✓	✓	✓	✓	✓	✓	✓	✓	✓	✓	✓	✓	✓	✓	✓	✓		✓	✓	✓		✓			✓	✓
Hippolytus (222–236)	✓	✓	✓	✓	✓	✓	✓	✓	✓	✓	✓	✓	✓	✓	✓	✓			✓	✓	✓		✓			✓	✓
Origen (225–254)	✓	✓	✓	✓	✓	✓	✓	✓	✓	✓	✓	✓	✓	✓	✓	✓	✓	✓	✓	✓	✓	?	✓	?	?	✓	✓
Against Novatian (254–256)	✓		✓	✓			✓			✓	✓								✓	✓			✓			✓	✓
Cyprian of Carthage (ca.246–258)	✓	✓	✓	✓	✓	✓	✓	✓	✓	✓	✓	✓	✓	✓	✓	✓	✓			✓	✓		✓	✓			✓
Firmilian of Caesarea (256)	✓	✓	✓	✓		✓	✓		✓	✓	✓									✓	✓						
Dionysius of Alexandria (246–265)	✓	✓	✓	✓	✓	✓	✓									✓				✓			✓	✓	✓		✓
Archelaus (262–278)	✓	✓	✓	✓		✓	✓	✓	✓	✓	✓	✓			✓												
Apostolic Canon (ca.300)	✓	✓	✓	✓	✓	✓	✓	✓	✓	✓	✓	✓	✓	✓	✓	✓	✓	✓	✓	✓	✓	✓	✓	✓	✓	✓	✓
Peter of Alexandria (285–311)	✓			✓	✓	✓			✓	✓					✓								✓				
Methodius (260–312)	✓	✓	✓	✓	✓	✓	✓	✓	✓	✓	✓				✓						✓						✓
Athanasius before Nicea (318)	✓	✓	✓	✓	✓	✓	✓	✓		✓	✓									✓	✓						
Alexander of Alexandria (313–326)	✓		✓	✓		✓	✓	✓			✓				✓	✓			✓					✓			
Council of Nicea (325)	✓	✓	✓	✓	✓	✓	✓	✓	✓	✓	✓	✓	✓	✓	✓	✓	✓	✓	✓	?	✓	?	✓	?	?	?	✓
Vaticanus Ms. (325–350)	✓	✓	✓	✓	✓	✓	✓	✓	✓	✓	✓	✓	✓	✓	✓	✓	✓	✓	✓	✓	✓	✓	✓	✓	✓	✓	✓
Sinaiticus Ms. (340–350)	✓	✓	✓	✓	✓	✓	✓	✓	✓	✓	✓	✓	✓	✓	✓	✓	✓	✓	✓	✓	✓	✓	✓	✓	✓	✓	✓
Council of Hippo (393)	✓	✓	✓	✓	✓	✓	✓	✓	✓	✓	✓	✓	✓	✓	✓	✓	✓	✓	✓	✓	✓	✓	✓	✓	✓	✓	✓
Council of Carthage (397)	✓	✓	✓	✓	✓	✓	✓	✓	✓	✓	✓	✓	✓	✓	✓	✓	✓	✓	✓	✓	✓	✓	✓	✓	✓	✓	✓

Legend: ✓ = cited, ? = uncertain References for many of these can be found at www.biblequery.org/Bible/BibleCanon/EarlyChristianNTGridReferences.htm

Assembled with assistance from Steve Morrison.

10

The Extent *of the* New Testament Canon

Precisely which books of the New Testament canon were in dispute in the early church? On what basis did they gain their final acceptance? What were some of the New Testament Apocryphal books that hovered on the borders of the canon? How do we know the canon is closed? These questions will provide the basis for our discussion in the present chapter.

The Books Accepted by All—Homologoumena

Like the Old Testament, the vast majority of New Testament books were accepted by the church from the very beginning and never disputed. These are called *homologoumena* (lit. one word), because all the Fathers spoke in favor of their canonicity. The homologoumena appear in virtually all of the major translations and canons of the early church. Generally speaking, twenty of the twenty-seven books of the New Testament are homologoumena. This includes all but Hebrews, James, 2 Peter, 2 John, 3 John, Jude, and Revelation. Three more books, Philemon, 1 Peter, and 1 John, are sometimes lacking in recognition, but it is better to refer to these books as omitted rather than disputed. Since the books of the homologoumena were accepted by all, we will direct our attention to the other groups of books.

The Books Rejected by All—Pseudepigrapha

During the second and third centuries numerous spurious and heretical works appeared which have been called pseudepigrapha, or false writings. Eusebius called these books "totally absurd and impious."

The Nature of the Pseudepigrapha

So far as Christians are concerned, these books are mainly of historical interest. Their contents are heretical teachings of Gnostics, Docetics, and ascetics. The Gnostics were a philosophical sect claiming special knowledge into the divine mysteries. They held that matter is evil and denied the incarnation of Christ. Docetists held to the deity of Christ but denied His humanity, saying He only appeared to be human. The ascetic Monophysites taught that Christ had only one nature, which was a fusion of the divine and human.

At best, these books were revered by some cults but were rejected by all the orthodox Fathers. The mainstream of Christianity followed Eusebius and never considered them anything but spurious and impious. Like the Old Testament pseudepigrapha, these books manifested a wild religious fancy. They evidence an incurable curiosity to discover things not revealed in the canonical books (for example, about the childhood of Jesus) and display an unhealthy tendency to support doctrinal idiosyncrasies by means of pious frauds. There is perhaps a kernel of truth behind some of what is presented, but the pseudepigrapha must be carefully "demythologized" in order to discover that truth.

The Number of the Pseudepigrapha

The exact number of these books is difficult to determine. By the ninth century, Photius listed some 280 of them. Since then more have been brought to light. Some of the more important pseudepigrapha and the traditions traceable to them are listed below with brief citations from some to illustrate their apocryphal nature:

Gospels. Here are almost two dozen books among the gospels:
1. *The Gospel of Thomas* (first century) is a Gnostic view of the alleged miracles of the childhood of Jesus.
2. *The Gospel of the Ebionites* (second century) is a Gnostic Christian perpetuation of Old Testament practices.
3. *The Gospel of Peter* (second century) is a Docetic and Gnostic forgery.

4. *Protoevangelium of James* (second century) is a narration by Mary of King Herod's massacre of the babies.

5. *The Gospel of the Egyptians* (second century) is an ascetic teaching against marriage, meat, and wine.

6. *Arabic Gospel of Childhood* (?) records childhood miracles of Jesus in Egypt and the visit of Zoroastrian Magi.

7. *The Gospel of Nicodemus* (second or fifth century) contains the *Acts of Pilate* and the *Descent of Jesus*.

8. *The Gospel of Joseph the Carpenter* (fourth century) is the writing of a Monophysite cult which glorified Joseph.

9. *The History of Joseph the Carpenter* (fifth century) is a Monophysite version of Joseph's life.

10. *The Passing of Mary* (fourth century) relates the bodily assumption of Mary and shows advanced stages of Mary worship.

11. *The Gospel of the Nativity of Mary* (sixth century) promotes Mary worship and forms the basis of the *Golden Legend*, a popular thirteenth-century book of lives of the saints.

12. *The Gospel of Pseudo-Matthew* (fifth century) contains a narrative about the visit to Egypt by Jesus and some of His later boyhood miracles.

13. *The Gospel of Judas* (2nd century Coptic Gnostic) contains esoteric writing, makes Judas a hero, and denies a Creator God.[1]

14. *The Gospel of the Twelve, of Barnabas, of Bartholomew, of the Hebrews* (see Apocrypha), *of Marcion, of Andrew, of Mathias, of Peter, of Philip.*

Acts. Eight books describe the lives of many of the apostles:

1. *The Acts of Peter* (second century) contains the legend that Peter was crucified upside down.

2. *The Acts of John* (second century) shows influence from Gnostic and

---

1. A third-century Coptic manuscript was recently discovered and published. But this Gospel of Judas lacks authenticity because: (1) It claims to have been written by Judas; (2) It contains heretical Gnostic doctrines; (3) It portrays Judas as a hero and superior apostle; (4) It is contrary to epistles of Paul from 55–56 CE; (5) It has a false view of the body as evil (cf. Gen. 1:27; 1 Tim. 4:4; Rom. 14:14); (6) It claims salvation is by special mystical knowledge, not by grace through faith (Eph. 2:8–9); (7) It assumes a mystical, unverifiable way of knowing (see Col. 2); (8) It denies human depravity and deifies the inner man (vs. Rom. 3:10–11); (9) It claims there are errors in the Gospels (e.g., Judas's death); (10) It teaches that the Serpent is good, a clearly demonic teaching (1 Tim. 4:1–2; cf. 2 Cor. 11:14).

Docetic teachings.

3. *The Acts of Andrew* (?) is a Gnostic story of the imprisonment and death of Andrew.

4. *The Acts of Thomas* (?) presents the mission and martyrdom of Thomas in India.

5. *The Acts of Paul* describes Paul as small, large-nosed, baldheaded, and bowlegged.

6. *The Acts of Mattias, of Philip, of Thaddaeus.*

Epistles. A letter attributed to Jesus and eight others attributed to Paul are all forgeries. The nine epistles are:

1. *The Letter Attributed to Our Lord* is an alleged record of the response of Jesus to a request for healing by the king of Mesopotamia. It says He would send someone after His resurrection.

2. *The Lost Epistle to the Corinthians* (second, third century) is a forgery based on 1 Corinthians 5:9 found in a fifth-century Armenian Bible.

3. *The (six) Letters of Paul to Seneca* (fourth century) are forgeries recommending Christianity to Seneca's students.

4. *The Epistle of Paul to the Laodiceans* is a forgery based on Colossians 4:16. (We have also listed this letter under Apocrypha.)

Apocalypses.[2] Several books describing apocalypse appear in the pseudepigrapha, including:

1. *The Apocalypse of Peter* (also listed under Apocrypha)

2. *The Apocalypse of Paul*

3. *The Apocalypse of Thomas*

4. *The Apocalypse of Stephen*

5. *The Second Apocalypse of James*

6. *The Apocalypse of Messos*

7. *The Apocalypse of Dositheos*

These last three are third-century Coptic Gnostic works found in 1946 at Nag Hammadi, Egypt.

---

2. For an introduction to the apocalypses, see volume 1 of *New Testament Apocrypha*, Edgar Hennecke and Wilhelm Schmeemelcher, eds. (Philadelphia: Westminster, 1963).

Some other works. These three books are also from Nag Hammadi and were unknown before 1946: *Secret Book of John, Traditions of Matthias,* and *Dialogue of the Saviour.* They are part of the Discoveries of the Judean Desert (DJD) and will be discussed in chapter 12.

Reasons for Rejecting the Pseudepigrapha

Since the great teachers and councils of the church were virtually unanimous in rejecting these books because of their inauthenticity or heresies, they are properly called pseudepigrapha. There are many reasons for this.

First, they contain false claims to be written by apostles and associates who were long dead. These included Peter, James, John, and Mary Magdalene, among others.

Second, they have false miracle claims about Jesus' childhood, whereas John the apostle writes that Jesus' first miracle occurred when He was an adult (John. 2:11). For example, "the teacher [of Jesus] was annoyed [at His question] and struck him on the head. And the child was hurt and cursed him, and he immediately fainted and fell to the ground on his face" (The Account of Thomas the Israelite Philosopher Concerning the Childhood of the Lord 14.1–3). On another occasion, a playmate of Jesus

> took a branch of a willow and (with it) dispersed the water which Jesus had gathered together. When Jesus saw what he had done he was enraged and said to him: "You insolent, godless thunderhead, what harm did the pools and the water do to you? See now you also shall wither like a tree and shall bear neither leaves nor root nor fruit." And immediately that lad withered up completely. (The Account of Thomas the Israelite Philosopher 3.1–3)

Third, they have false claims about biblical events. Consider this embellished claim about Jesus' resurrection:

> In the night in which the Lord's day dawned . . . there rang out a loud voice in heaven, and they saw the heavens opened and two men come down from there in a great brightness and draw nigh to the sepulchre. That stone which had been laid against the entrance to the sepulchre started of itself to roll and give way to the side. And whilst they were relating what they had seen, they saw again three men come out from the sepulchre and two

of them sustaining the other, and a cross following them, and the heads of the two reaching to heaven, but that of him who was led of them by the hand overpassing the heavens. And they heard a voice out of the heavens crying, "Thou has preached to them that sleep," and from the cross there was heard the answer, "Yea." (Gospel of Peter 9.35–10.42)

Fourth, they have many false teachings on their pages. For example, the Gospel of Thomas (Plate 21), highly reputed by the liberal scholars of the "Jesus Seminar," taught numerous heresies, such as pantheism: [Jesus said,] "I am the All; the All has emerged from me, and the All has attained to me. Cleave a piece of wood—I am there; lift a stone up—and you will find me there" (Gospel of Thomas, Logion 77). That gospel also teaches preincarnation: Jesus said: "Blessed is he who was before he came into being" (ibid., Logion 19). Gnosticism is also embraced: "Wretched is the body which depends upon a body and wretched is the soul which depends upon these two" (Logion 87). It even contains a radical passage against women: "See, I shall lead her, so that I will make her male, that she too may become a living spirit, resembling you males. For every woman who makes herself male will enter the Kingdom of Heaven" (Logion, 114).

Further, the pseudepigrapha denies the deity of Christ (Arianism). The Gospel of Judas: "The first [angel] is Seth, who is called Christ. . . . The fifth is Adonaios. These are five who ruled over the underworld, and first of all over chaos" (The Gospel of Judas, sec. 52).

Other false writings from the second and third centuries teach these and many more heresies, such as modalism: "[Jesus said] he had revealed to his disciples that the Father, the Son, and the Holy Spirit are one and the same person" (The Gospel of the Egyptians in Hennecke, *New Testament Apocrypha*, 170); emanationism: "All the emanations of the Father, then, are pleromas, and all His emanations have their root in Him who caused them all to grow from himself and gave to their destiny" (The Gospel of Truth 41.4–20); Platonism: "By means of knowledge each will purify himself from diversity into unity, devouring matter within him like a fire, darkness by light, death by life. . . . It is fitting for us to take thought above all that the house may be holy and silent for the Unity" (The Gospel of Truth (25.23–25); and perfectionism: "Your god who is within you. . . . Let any one of you who is strong enough among human beings bring out the perfect human and stand before my face" (The Gospel of Judas).

In addition, some taught Gnosticism salvationism: "What did come from the Father was knowledge [gnosis], which was manifested in order that oblivion might be done away and that (men) might know the Father. As soon as men come to this knowledge, 'oblivion' (which is ignorance of God) will no longer exist, and this is the Gospel revealed to the perfect" (The Gospel of Truth 18.17–26). There was also mysticism (The Gospel of Truth (25.23–25) and allegorism (The Account of Thomas the Israelite Philosopher Concerning the Childhood of the Lord 14.1–3).

Fifth, they were rejected by the early Fathers of the church. Irenaeus (second century) declared: "It is not possible that the Gospels can be either more or fewer in number than they are. For . . . while the Church is scattered throughout all the world, and the 'pillar and ground' of the Church is the Gospel and the spirit of life; it is fitting that she have four pillars, breathing out immortality on every side, and vivifying men afresh."[3] He added,

> Indeed, they have arrived at such a pitch of audacity, as to entitle their comparatively recent writing, "the Gospel of Truth," though it agrees in nothing with the Gospels of the Apostles, so that they have really no Gospel, which is not full of blasphemy. . . . But that these Gospels [of the apostles] alone are true and reliable, and admit neither an increase nor diminution of the aforesaid number [four], I have proved by so many and such arguments.[4]

Summing up the early Fathers in the fourth century, Eusebius (*Ecclesiatical History*) called these books "totally impious and absurd."

Sixth, many modern experts reject these books as well. J. Donaldson (editor of *Ante-Nicene Fathers*) wrote: "The predominant impression which they leave on our minds is a profound sense of the immeasurable superiority, the unapproachable simplicity and majesty, of the Canonical Writings."[5] Noted scholar on Gnosticism, Edwin Yamauchi wrote: "The apocryphal gospels, even the earliest and soberest among them, can hardly compare with the canonical

---

3. Irenaeus, Against Heresies 3.11.8.

4. Ibid., 3.11.9.

5. Edwin Yamauchi, "The Word from Nag Hammadi," *Christianity Today*, 13 January 1978.

gospels. The former are all patently secondary and legendary or obviously slanted.... The extra-canonical literature, taken as a whole, manifests a surprising poverty. The bulk of it is legendary, and bears the clear mark of forgery."[6]

THE BOOKS DISPUTED BY SOME—ANTILEGOMENA

According to the historian Eusebius, by the early fourth century some church fathers disputed the genuineness of seven books. The books questioned were Hebrews, James, 2 Peter, 2 John, 3 John, Jude, and Revelation.

The Nature of the Antilegomena

The fact that these books had not gained universal recognition by the beginning of the fourth century does not mean that they did not have an initial recognition by the apostolic and subapostolic communities. On the contrary, these books are cited as inspired by a number of the earliest sources (see chaps. 3 and 9). Nor does the fact that they were once disputed by some in the church indicate that their present place in the canon is any less firm than other books. On the contrary, the basic problem of acceptance for most of these books was not the inspiration of the book but the lack of communication between East and West with regard to their divine authority. Once the facts were known by the Fathers, the final acceptance of all twenty-seven books of the New Testament was not long coming.

The Number of the Antilegomena

Each book was disputed for its own particular reasons. A brief survey of why each book was disputed and how it was finally recognized is in order at this juncture.

Hebrews. Since the author does not identify himself and disclaims being one of the apostles (Heb. 2:3), the book remained suspect among those in the West who were not aware of the authority and original acceptance of the book in the East. In addition, the fact that the heretical Montanists appealed to Hebrews to support some of their erroneous views slowed its acceptance in orthodox circles. By the fourth century, however, through the influence of Jerome and Augustine, the epistle to the Hebrews found a permanent place in the canon.

6.   Ibid.

The anonymity of Hebrews kept open the question of the apostolic authority of the epistle. In time, the Western church came to accept Hebrews as Pauline and, therefore, that issue was resolved for them. Once the West was convinced of the apostolicity of the book, there remained no obstacle to its full and final acceptance into the canon. However, even if Paul is not the author there should be no question of apostolic authority since the book meets the tests for canonicity (see chap. 6), the most basic of which is propheticity or apostolic authority. For the book was written by one who knew the apostles who "confirmed" the message to them (Heb. 2:3 KJV), and it was written during the time of the apostles since the author knew Timothy (Heb. 13:23) who was an associate of the apostle Paul (2 Cor. 1:1; 1 Tim. 6:20; 2 Tim. 1:2).

James. Critics challenged the veracity of the book of James and its authorship. As with the book of Hebrews, the author does not claim to be an apostle. The original readers and those after them could verify whether this was the James of the apostolic circle, the brother of Jesus (cf. Acts 15:13; Gal. 1:19). But the Western church did not have access to this original information. There was also the problem of the teaching on justification and works as presented in James. The supposed conflict with Paul's teaching of justification by faith plagued the book of James. Even Martin Luther called James a "right strawy epistle" and placed it at the end of his New Testament. But, as the result of the efforts of Origen, Eusebius (who personally favored James), Jerome, and Augustine, the veracity and apostolicity of the book came to be recognized in the Western church. From that time to the present, James has occupied a canonical position in Christendom. Its acceptance, of course, hinged on the understanding of its essential compatibility with the Pauline teachings on justification.

Second Peter. No other epistle in the New Testament had occasioned greater doubts as to its genuineness than 2 Peter. Jerome seemed to understand the problem and asserted the hesitancy to accept it as a genuine work of the apostle. The notable differences in style between these two epistles can be accounted for by his use of a scribe in 1 Peter (5:12) and the difference in time, topic, and recipients. And the similarities of content with Peter's speeches recorded in Acts 2, 3, 10, 15 strongly support his authorship.

Further, William F. Albright, noting the similarities to Qumran literature, dates the book before 80 CE. This would mean that it is not a second-century fraud but a work emanating from the apostolic period. The recently discovered Bodmer manuscript ($\mathfrak{P}^{72}$) contains a copy of 2 Peter from the third century in Egypt. This discovery also reveals that 2 Peter was in use and highly respected by the Coptic Christians at that early date. Both Clement of Rome and *Pseudo-Barnabas* cite 2 Peter in the first and second centuries, respectively. Then there are the testimonies of Origen, Eusebius, Jerome, and Augustine in the third through fifth centuries. In fact, there is more verification for 2 Peter than for such classics of the ancient world as the works of Herodotus and Thucydides.

Finally, there is positive internal evidence for the authentication of 2 Peter. There are marked Petrine characteristics and doctrinal interests. The differences in style can be explained easily because of the use of a scribe in 1 Peter and the lack of one in 2 Peter (see 1 Pet. 5:12). B. B. Warfield argued convincingly that there is more evidence for the authenticity of 2 Peter than for other books from antiquity.[7]

Second and Third John. The two shortest epistles of John were also questioned as to their genuineness. The writer identifies himself only as "the elder" (2 John 1:1), and because of their anonymity and limited circulation, these epistles did not enjoy a wide acceptance, albeit they were more widely accepted than 2 Peter. Both Polycarp and Irenaeus acknowledged 2 John as authentic. The Muratorian canon and the Old Latin version contained them as well. Their similarity in style and message to 1 John, which was widely accepted, made it obvious that they were from John the apostle (cf. 1 John 1:1–4). Who else was so familiar to the early Asian believers that he could write authoritatively under the affectionate title of "the elder"? The term *elder* was used as a designation by other apostles (see 1 Pet. 5:1), as it denoted their office (see Acts 1:20), and apostleship designated their gift (cf. Eph. 4:11).

Jude. Some questioned Jude's authenticity. The dispute centered mainly around the references to the pseudepigraphal Book of Enoch (Jude 14–15) and a possible reference to the Assumption of Moses (Jude 9). Origen hints at this problem in his day (*Commentary on Matthew 18:30*), and Jerome specifically declares this to be the problem (Jerome, *Lives of Illustrious Men,* chap. 4). Nevertheless, Jude was substantially recognized by the early Fathers. Irenaeus, Clement of Alexandria, and Tertullian all accepted the authenticity

---

7. B. B. Warfield, "The Canonicity of Second Peter," in *The Select Shorter Writings of B. B. Warfield*, John Meeter, ed. (Philadelphia: Presbyterian and Reformed, 1976).

of the book, as did the Muratorian canon. The explanation of the pseude-pigraphal quotes is that they are not essentially different from those citations made by Paul of the non-Christian poets (see Acts 17:28; 1 Cor. 15:33; Titus 1:12). In neither case are the books cited as authoritative, nor does the quote vouch for everything in the book—it merely cites a truth contained in the book. The recently discovered Bodmer papyrus ($\mathfrak{P}^{72}$) confirms the use of Jude, along with 2 Peter, in the Coptic church of the third century.

Revelation. Writers accepted and cited Revelation during the second century and after; nonetheless, it was labeled antilegomena in the early fourth century. This was due primary to their rejection of chiliasm (millennialism) based on Revelation 20. Strangely enough, Revelation was one of the first books to be recognized among the writings of the early Fathers. The writers of the *Didache* and the *Shepherd of Hermas* accepted it, as did Papias, Justin Martyr, and Irenaeus; it was also accepted by the Muratorian canon. But when the Montanists attached their deviant doctrines to the Revelation in the third century, the final acceptance of the book was considerably delayed. Dionysius, the Bishop of Alexandria, raised his influential voice against Revelation in the mid-third century. His influence waned when Athanasius, Jerome, and Augustine came to its defense. Once it became evident that the book of Revelation was being misused by cultic groups, although it originated with the apostle John (Rev. 1:4; cf. 22:8–9) rather than with them, its final place in the canon was confirmed.

In summary, the antilegomena books were spoken against by some Fathers. This was usually because of a lack of communication or because of misinterpretations which had attached themselves to those books. Once the truth was known by all, they were fully and finally accepted into the canon, just as they had been recognized by Christians at the very beginning.

THE BOOKS ACCEPTED BY SOME—APOCRYPHA

The distinction between the New Testament Apocrypha and pseude-pigrapha is not definitive. For the most part, the later books were not received by any of the orthodox fathers or churches as canonical, whereas the Apocryphal books were held in high esteem by at least one church father.

The Nature of the New Testament Apocrypha

The New Testament Apocrypha had only at best what Alexander Souter called a "temporal and local canonicity."[8] They were accepted by a limited group of Christians for a limited time but never gained very wide or permanent recognition. The fact that these books possessed more value than the pseudepigrapha undoubtedly accounts for the higher esteem given them by Christians. There are several reasons why they are an important part of the homiletical and devotional libraries from the early church: (1) they revealed the teachings of the second-century church; (2) they provide documentation for the acceptance of the twenty-seven canonical books of the New Testament; and (3) they provide other valuable historical information about the early Christian church concerning its doctrine and liturgy.

The Number of the New Testament Apocrypha

The enumeration of the New Testament Apocrypha is difficult because it depends upon the distinction made between Apocrypha and pseudepigrapha. If the criteria include acceptance by at least one of the orthodox fathers or lists of the first five centuries,[9] then discussion followed. If not, then the book was not considered part of the New Testament Apocrypha.

The Epistle of Pseudo–Barnabas (ca. 70–79). This widely circulated first-century letter is found in the Codex Sinaiticus manuscript (ℵ, *Aleph*) and is mentioned in the table of contents of Codex Bezae (D) as late as 550 CE. It was quoted as Scripture by both Clement of Alexandria and Origen. Its style is similar to Hebrews, but its contents are more allegorical, like the Shepherd of Hermas. Some have questioned whether it is really a first-century document. But as Westcott has said, "While the antiquity of the Epistle is firmly established, its Apostolicity is more than questionable."[10]

The Epistle to the Corinthians (ca. 96). According to Dionysius of Corinth, this letter by Clement of Rome was read publicly at Corinth and elsewhere. It is also found in Codex Alexandrinus (A) around 450, and Eusebius informs us that this letter had been read in many churches (*Ecclesiastical History* 3.16). The author was probably the Clement mentioned in Philippians 4:3, but the book does not claim divine inspiration. There is a rather fanciful use

8. Alexander Souter, *The Text and Canon of the New Testament* (London: Duckworth, 1913), 178–81.

9. "Orthodox" is defined here as being in accordance with the teachings of the creeds and councils of the first five centuries, such as the Apostles' Creed, Nicene Creed, etc.

10. Brooke Foss Westcott, *A General Survey of the History of the Canon of the New Testament*, 7th ed. (New York: Macmillan, 1896), 41.

made of Old Testament statements, and the Apocryphal Book of Wisdom is quoted as Scripture in chapter 27. The tone of the letter is evangelical but its spirit is decidedly subapostolica. There has never been a wide acceptance of this book, and the Christian church has never recognized it as canonical.

The "Real" First Corinthians. Some scholars have argued that a nonexistent epistle to which Paul referred in 1 Corinthians 5:9 should be in the New Testament canon. Paul said to the Corinthians in the canonical 1 Corinthians, "I wrote to you in my letter ..." (1 Cor. 5:9). This would imply that there was an epistle prior to the canonical 1 Corinthians. However, there are many reasons for rejecting this view. First, no such piece of literature exists. Second, no such book was ever quoted by any early Father. Third, "I wrote" is not past tense in Greek. It is in the aorist tense; that does not mean time of action but kind of action. It is probably an "epistolary aorist," which means one that refers very emphatically to the epistle in which it occurs. It would amount to saying, "I am now decisively writing this to you." Finally, Paul uses an epistolary aorist elsewhere in this very book (1 Cor. 9:15). So, it is not unknown to Paul's usage. In view of all these reasons, we conclude that no such book ever existed. Hence, it poses no real problem for New Testament canonicity.

Ancient Homily. The so-called *Second Epistle of Clement* (ca. 120–140) was once wrongly attributed to Clement of Rome. It was known and used in the second century. In Codex Alexandrinus (A) it is placed at the end of the New Testament along with 1 Clement and Psalms of Solomon. There is no evidence that this book was ever considered fully canonical. If it ever was, it certainly was not received on a large scale. The New Testament canon has excluded it to date.

Shepherd of Hermas (ca. 115–140). This was the most popular noncanonical book in the early church. It is found in Codex Sinaiticus (א, *Aleph*), in the table of contents of Bezae (D), and in some Latin Bibles, and was quoted as inspired by Irenaeus and Origen. Eusebius relates that it was read publicly in the churches and used for instruction classes in the faith. The Shepherd is a great Christian allegory and, like John Bunyan's *Pilgrims Progress* later, it ranked second only to the canonical books in circulation in the early church. Like the Wisdom of Sirach (Ecclesiasticus) of the Old Testament Apocrypha, the Shepherd has ethical and devotional value but was never recognized by the church as canonical. The note in the Muratorian Fragment summarizes the status of the Shepherd in the early church, "It ought to be read; but it cannot be publicly read in the church to the people, either among the Prophets, since their number is complete, or among the Apostles, to the end of time."[11]

The Didache [Teaching of the Twelve] (ca. 100–120). This early work was also held in high regard in the early church. Clement of Alexandria quoted it as Scripture, and Athanasius said it was used in catechetical instruction. Eusebius, however, listed it among the "rejected writings," as did the major Fathers after him and the church in general. Nonetheless, the book has great historical importance as a link between the apostles and the early Fathers, with its many references to the Gospels, Paul's epistles, and even the Revelation. However, it was not recognized as canonical in any of the official translations or lists of the early church.

The Apocalypse of Peter (ca. 150). This is one of the oldest of the noncanonical New Testament apocalypses and was widely circulated in the early church. It is mentioned in the Muratorian Fragment and in the table of contents of Bezae (D), and it is quoted by Clement of Alexandria. Its vivid imagery of the spiritual worlds had a wide influence on medieval thought from which Dante's *Inferno* was derived. The Muratorian Fragment had questions about its authenticity, claiming that some would not permit it to be read in the churches. The church universal has never recognized it as canonical.

The Acts of Paul and Thecla (170). This was quoted by Origen and is in the table of contents of Codex Bezae (D). Stripped of its mythical elements, it is the story of Thecla, an Iconian lady who supposedly was converted under Paul in Acts 14:1–7. Many scholars feel that the book embodies a genuine tradition, but most are inclined to agree with Adolf von Harnack that the book contains "a great deal of fiction and very little truth." The book has never really gained anything like canonical recognition.

Epistle to the Laodiceans (fourth century?). This forgery was known to Jerome, but it appears in many Bibles from the sixth to the fifteenth centuries. As J. B. Lightfoot noted, "The Epistle is a centro of Pauline phrases strung together without any definite connection or any clear object."[12] It has no doctrinal peculiarities and is as innocent as any forgery can be.

11. Henry Bettenson and Chris Maunder, eds., *Documents of the Christian Church,* 3rd ed. (Oxford: Oxford Univ. Press, 1999), 31–32. Also see B. F. Westcott, "Appendix C: The Muratorian Fragment on the Canon," *A General Survey of the History of the Canon of the New Testament,* 6th ed. (New York: Macmillan, 1889; repr. Grand Rapids: Baker, 1980), 521–38, esp. 537–38.

12. J. B. Lightfoot, *Saint Paul's Epistles to the Colossians and to Philemon* (Grand Rapids: Zondervan, 1965), 285.

Combined with the fact that a book by this name appears in Colossians 4:16, these factors no doubt account for its very late appearance in Christian circles. Although the Council of Nicea II (787 CE) warned against it, calling it a "forged epistle," it reappeared in the Reformation era in German and English Bibles. Nevertheless, it has never gained canonical recognition.

A book by this name is mentioned in the Muratorian Fragment, but some have thought this is the book mentioned by Paul in Colossians 4:16. However, this is mistaken since Paul never referred to the "epistle of the Laodiceans" but to the "epistle [coming] from Laodicea," which was probably Ephesians (or Philemon), written at the same time. This confusion has lent to the persistent reappearance of this noncanonical book, but the epistle is definitely not canonical.

The Gospel According to the Hebrews (ca. 65–100). This is probably the earliest extant noncanonical gospel and has survived only in fragments found in quotations from various Fathers. According to Jerome, some called it the true gospel, but this is questionable since it bears little resemblance to the canonical Matthew, for it is in many respects more pseudepigraphal than apocryphal in nature. Its usage by the Fathers was probably largely homiletical, and it never gained anything like canonical status.

Epistle of Polycarp to the Philippians (ca. 108). Polycarp, the disciple of John the apostle and the teacher of Irenaeus, is an important link with the first-century apostles. Polycarp laid no claim to inspiration, but said that he only taught the things he had learned from the apostles. There is very little originality in this epistle, as both the content and style is borrowed from the New Testament, and particularly from Paul's epistle to the Philippians. Even though Polycarp's work is not canonical, it is a most valuable source of information about many other New Testament books that he cites as canonical.

The Seven Epistles of Ignatius (ca.110). These letters reveal a definite familiarity with the teachings of the New Testament, especially the Pauline epistles. The style of the letters, however, is more Johannine. Irenaeus quotes from the epistle to the Ephesians, and Origen quotes from both the epistle to the Romans and the epistle to the Ephesians. Ignatius, whom tradition claims was a disciple of John, does not claim to speak with divine authority. To the Ephesians, for instance, he writes, "I do not issue orders to you, as if I were some great person. . . . I speak to you as fellow-disciples with me" (chap. 3). The letters are no doubt genuine but not apostolic and therefore not canonica. Such has been the consent of the Christian church through the years. The genuine writings from the subapostolic period are most helpful from a historical point of view, for they reveal the state of the church and the recognition of canonical books of the New Testament.

THE COMPLETION OF THE NEW TESTAMENT CANON

The foregoing discussion raises the question of the completion of the canon. How do we know the canon is closed? How do we know we have all the books God intended us to have? The answer to these questions is found in the following principles: (1) the authority of Christ, (2) the providence of God, (3) the testimony of history, and (4) the witness of the Spirit.

1. The authority of Christ. Jesus, who is the full and final revelation of God (see Hebrews), promised that the apostles would be led by the Holy Spirit "into all the truth" (John 16:13). He had taught them, and the Holy Spirit would help them to recall everything He had taught. Since He spoke with the authority of God (Matt. 28:18; John 8:26), then the apostolic teaching must contain what Jesus promised. But the only record we have of apostolic teaching is the New Testament. For every book of the New Testament was written either by an apostle or by a person under apostolic authority. Mark was an associate of Peter, and Luke was an associate of Paul. James and Jude were relatives of Jesus and part of the apostolic church. The early church was based on "the apostles and prophets" (Eph. 2:20)[13] and continued in the "apostles' teaching" (Acts 2:42). Even the apostle Paul, who was not one of the twelve apostles, had his message confirmed by the apostles lest he had "run in vain" (Gal. 2:2). So, every New Testament author was either an apostle or prophet whose revelation was under the watchful eye of an apostle and confirmed by an apostle.

2. The providence of God. It is a principle and practice of divine providence that God completes what He begins (cf. Rom. 8:29–30; Phil. 1:6). In view of God's providence, then, we must conclude that He would not inspire any books that He did not preserve. For it is contrary to God's nature and practice not to preserve truths He produced for the well-being (faith and

---

13. That Paul is referring to New Testament prophets is confirmed by (1) the order of words "apostle and prophets" (not prophets and apostles), (2) that they are the foundation of the New Testament church (Eph. 2:20), and (3) that they did not know the mystery of Christ in Old Testament times (Eph. 3:3–5; cf. Col. 1:26), but these New Testament apostles and prophets did.

practice) of His church. But the only record we have of the inspired writings of the apostles and prophets after Jesus is the New Testament. Therefore, we may conclude, based on the providence of God, that we have the completion of the revelation of God to His church in the New Testament.

3. The testimony of history. Since we have already covered this point earlier in this chapter, we need not repeat it here. But it is clear from the facts that God not only did preserve the apostolic books that are contained in the New Testament, but that the earliest Fathers recognized these books, and subsequently the Christian church has acknowledged them to be the only inspired books we have from the hands of the apostles and their authorized agents. So, it is not simply a matter of theological principle, but of historical fact, that we have the books that God inspired for the faith and practice of all future generations of believers.

This being the case, what Jesus "began to do and to teach" (Acts 1:1; cf. Luke 1:1) He continued to teach through the words and acts of the apostles. If there was any dispute, it was brought to the apostles for their disposal (Acts 15). Even the Holy Spirit, who inspired Scripture and illuminated minds to receive it, was given only "through the laying on of the apostles' hands" (Acts 8:18; cf. Acts 10 and 19).

Therefore, we can conclude that since Jesus promised "all truth" for faith and practice to the apostles, and since the New Testament is the only record of apostolic truth, then the New Testament canon must be complete. Otherwise, the divinely authoritative teaching of Jesus would be false—which is not possible.

4. The witness of the Spirit. Of course, from a strictly evidential perspective, we cannot be absolutely certain of what books are in the canon and whether the canon is closed. Historical evidence as such provides only probability, not certainty. Hence, many scholars have stressed the witness of the Holy Spirit as necessary for certitude on the matter of canonicity. Most Bible students are aware that the Holy Spirit "bears witness with our spirit that we are children of God" (Rom. 8:16). But it is also true that the Holy Spirit bears witness that the Bible is the Word of God. As John wrote, "If we receive the testimony of men, the testimony of God is greater, for this is the testimony of God that he has borne concerning his Son. Whoever believes in the Son of God has the testimony in himself. Whoever does not believe God has made him a liar, because he has not believed in the testimony that

God has borne concerning his Son" (1 John 5:9–10).

So, there is such a thing as subjective certitude about the canon. However, it is important to note that this subjective testimony of the Spirit *is in accord with* the objective evidence, not in isolation from it. It is the Holy Spirit working through Holy Scripture, not apart, who convinces us that the Bible truly is the Word of God. There are two real dangers here. First, this subjective certitude should not be sought apart from the objective historical evidence that these books were written by men of God, confirmed by acts of God and which tell the transforming truth of God as accepted by the people of God (see chap. 6). For Muslims, Mormons, and others have a subjective certitude about opposing Holy Books that are not the Word of God (see chap. 5). What they lack, and the Bible does not, is objective evidence that these books are the Word of God.

Second, contrary to some, it seems best to stress the communal nature of this witness of the Spirit that the Bible is the Word of God. That is, God's witness is to the church—God's people in general—and it is not simply up to each individual to determine whether the Bible is the Word of God. Of course, this witness is ministerial, not magisterial as Roman Catholics claim. That is, the community of believers, not each individual believer, has this witness of the Spirit to the canon. And when one section of Christendom assumes magisterial authority to contradict what the original people of God perceived (as in the case of Rome and the addition of the Apocrypha to the Old Testament—see chap. 8), then the ministerial authority of the original people of God takes precedence in determining the canon.

SUMMARY AND CONCLUSION

With respect to the extent of the New Testament canon, Christendom has been virtually unanimous, at least since the fourth century. Jesus promised, the apostles claimed, and history records the twenty-seven inspired books of the New Testament as the complete and final canon of Holy Scripture. This is confirmed by both the providence of God and the witness of the Holy Spirit; both by objective evidence and subjective testimony to the church as the people of God that the Bible is the Word of God. Each book bears its own claim and evidence, but the Book (the Bible) as a whole reveals both the hand of God and the Spirit of God to convince the people of God that the New Testament completes the Word of God.

PART THREE

Transmission

11

LANGUAGES *and* MATERIALS *of* THE BIBLE

TO THIS POINT our study has centered around the first two links in the chain from God to us. The first, inspiration, involved the giving and recording of God's revelation to man by the prophets. The second, canonization, involved the recognition and collection of the prophetic records by the people of God.

In order to share these records with new believers and with future generations, it was necessary to copy, translate, recopy, and retranslate them. This procedure is the third link in the chain of communication, and it is known as the transmission of the Bible.

Since the Bible has undergone nearly two thousand years of transmission, it is reasonable to ask if the twentieth-century English Bible is an accurate reproduction of the Hebrew, Aramaic, and Greek texts. In short, how much has the Bible suffered in the process of transmission? In order to address this issue, it will be necessary to look into the science of textual criticism (see chaps. 14 and 15), which includes the languages and materials of the Bible as well as the manuscript evidence itself (see chaps. 12 and 13).

THE IMPORTANCE OF WRITTEN LANGUAGES

Alternative Means of Communication

Several alternatives were open to God for communicating His truth to men (Heb. 1:1). He could have used any one or more of the media employed on various occasions in biblical times. For example, God used angels throughout the Bible (see Gen. 18–19; Rev. 22:8–16). The lot and the Urim and Thummim were also employed to determine God's will (Ex. 28:30; Prov. 16:33), as were the voices of conscience (Rom. 2:15) and creation (Ps. 19:1–6). In addition, God used audible voices (1 Sam. 3) and direct miracles (Judg. 6:36–40).

All these media suffered from some shortcoming. The sending of an angel to deliver each message of God to every man in every situation or the use of audible voices and direct miracles would be both cumbersome and repetitive. The use of the lot or the simple yes-or-no answer of the Urim and Thummim were too limited in scope when compared with the detailed descriptions available in other media of communication. On occasion, some means were too subjective and open to distortion or cultural corruption, as in the case of visions, dreams, and the voices of conscience or creation. This situation is especially true when compared to the more objective means of communication available in written language.[1]

Language in General

It would be incorrect to say that any or all of these media were not good, for they were in fact the various means by which God spoke to the prophets. Nevertheless, there was "a more excellent way" to communicate to the men of all ages through the prophets. God chose to make permanent and immortalize His message to men by means of a written record. This way was more precise, more permanent, more objective, and more easily disseminated than any other media He utilized.

Precision. One of the advantages of written language over other media is its precision. For a thought to be apprehended and expressed in writing, it must have been clearly understood by its author. In addition, the reader can understand more precisely the thought transmitted through written expression. Since mankind's most treasured knowledge to date is preserved in the form of written records and books, it is understandable that God should choose to convey His truth to man in the same manner.

Permanence. Another advantage of written language is the matter of its permanence. It provides a means whereby a thought or expression can

1. See F. F. Bruce, Walter C. Kaiser, Jr., Peter H. Davids, and Manfred T. Brauch, *The Hard Sayings of the Bible* (Downers Grove, Ill.: InterVarsity, 1996).

be preserved rather than lost through lapse of memory or vacillation of thought into other realms. In addition, a written record stimulates the reader's memory and stirs his imagination to include a host of personal implications latent in the words or symbols of the record. Words are not so wooden as to prevent personal enrichment for the reader.

Objectivity. The transmission of a communication in written form also tends to make it more objective. A written expression carries with it a note of finality not inherent in other modes of communication of the time. This finality transcends the subjectivity of each individual reader, thus complementing the precision and permanence of the message disseminated. In addition, it militates against misinterpretation and mistransmission of the message.

Dissemination. Still another advantage of written language over some other media of communication is its ability to be propagated, or disseminated. No matter how carefully an oral communication is related, there is always a greater chance for corruption and alteration than with recorded words. In short, oral tradition has tended to corrupt rather than to preserve a message. In the propagation of His revelation to mankind, especially for future generations, God chose a more accurate means of transmitting His Word.

Biblical Languages in Particular

The languages used in recording God's revelation in the Bible come from the Semitic and Indo-European families of languages. The Semitic family provided the basic languages of the Old Testament in Hebrew and Aramaic (Syriac). In addition to them, Latin and Greek represent the Indo-European family. Indirectly, the Phoenicians played a key role in the transmission of the Bible by providing the basic vehicle that made written language less cumbersome than it had been previously, namely the alphabet (see chap. 12).

Old Testament Languages. Aramaic was the language of the Syrians and was used throughout the Old Testament period. During the sixth century BCE it became the basic language of the entire Near East. Its widespread use is reflected in the place names and text portions of Ezra 4:7–6:18; 7:12–26; and Daniel 2:4–7:28.

Hebrew is the primary language of the Old Testament, and it is particularly suited for its task of relating the biography of God's people and His dealings with them. It is suited for this task because Hebrew is a *pictorial* language. It speaks with vivid, bold metaphors that challenge and dramatize the narrative of events. In addition, Hebrew is a *personal* language. It addresses itself to the heart and emotions rather than to the mind and reason alone. It is a language through which the message is felt rather than merely thought.

New Testament Languages. The Semitic languages were also used in the New Testament. In fact, Jesus and the disciples used Aramaic as their native tongue, since it had become the spoken language of Palestine by that time. During His agony on the cross, Jesus cried out in Aramaic, "'Eli, Eli, lema sabachthani?' that is, 'My God, my God, why have you forsaken me?'" (Matt. 27:46).[2] Hebrew made its influence felt through more idiomatic expressions. One such Hebrew idiom is, "and it came to pass." Another example of Hebrew influence may be seen in the use of a second noun to describe a quality rather than an adjective. Some examples would include the expressions, "work of faith and labor of love and steadfastness of hope" (1 Thess. 1:3).

In addition to the Semitic languages in the New Testament are the Indo-European: Latin and Greek. The former was influential mainly in its loan words, such as "centurion," "tribute," and "legion," as well as the inscription on the cross, which was written in Latin, Hebrew, and Greek.

The basic language of the New Testament, however, was Greek. Until the late nineteenth century, New Testament Greek was believed to be a special "Holy Ghost" language, but since that time it has come to be identified as one of the five stages in the development of Greek itself. This *koine* Greek was the most widely known language throughout the world of the first century. Its alphabet was derived from the Phoenicians; its cultural values and vocabulary encompassed a vast geographical expanse, and it became the official language of the empires into which Alexander the Great's conquests were divided. Its providential appearance, along with other cultural, political, social, and religious developments during the first centuries BCE, is implied in Paul's statement, "When the fulness of time had come, God sent forth his Son" (Gal. 4:4).

New Testament Greek was appropriately adapted to the objective of interpreting the revelation of Christ in theological language. It was especially suited for this task because Greek was an *intellectual* language. It was

---

2. The study note at Matthew 27:46, says, "Jesus quotes Ps 22:1. . . . The last two words are Aramaic (the everyday language spoken by Jesus), and the first two could be either Aramaic or Hebrew." See *ESV Study Bible: English Standard Version* (Wheaton, Ill.: Crossway, 2008), 1886.

more a language of the mind than of the heart, a fact to which the great Greek philosophers give ample evidence. Greek possessed a technical precision of expression not to be found in Hebrew. In addition, Greek was a nearly *universal* language. The Old Testament truth about God was initially revealed to one nation, Israel, in its own language, Hebrew. The fuller revelation given by Christ in the New Testament was not so restricted. Instead, the message of Christ was to "be proclaimed in his name to all nations" (Luke 24:47).

THE DEVELOPMENT OF WRITTEN LANGUAGES

Advances in Writing

Although the Old Testament does not say anything about the development of writing itself, three stages in that development may be discerned. These stages include *pictograms* (Plate 1), or crude representations that antedated the actual development of writing (pictures representing such objects as a man, an ox, a lion, or an eagle). As time passed, however, pictograms lost their dominant position as the means of written communication. They were replaced by *ideograms,* which were pictures representing ideas rather than objects. Such objects as a sun representing heat, an old man representing old age, an eagle representing power, an ox representing strength, and a lion depicting royalty gradually replaced pictograms. Still other extensions of pictograms were *phonograms,* representations of sound rather than ideas or objects. A sun might be used to depict a son, or a bear might be used to convey the notion of the verb *bear.* As a result, still another step was taken toward written languages.

After a long period, the Phoenicians developed their major innovation in the history of writing when they reduced their language to more specific elements—the alphabet. Still later, the Greek empire adapted the Phoenician alphabet to their own language by adding vowels to the consonantal alphabet of the Minoans (see chap. 12).

The Age of Writing

Although evidence of writing in antiquity is far from abundant, enough exists to indicate that it was the hallmark of cultural achievement. Writing seems to have been developed during the fourth millennium BCE. In the second millennium BCE several experiments led to the development of the alphabet and written documents by the Phoenicians. All this was completed before the time of Moses, who wrote not earlier than about 1450 BCE.

As early as ca. 3500 BCE cuneiform (Lat. *cuneus*, meaning "wedge") tablets were used by the Sumerians to record events in their history in Mesopotamia (Plates 2–3). The Sumerian flood narrative is an example of such writing, although it was recorded ca. 2100 BCE. In Egypt (ca. 3100 BCE) sacred objects and names were called hieroglyphs (*hiero*, sacred; *glyph*, symbol). Some 700 to 800 sacred symbols were utilized to write additional documents in hieroglyphic (pictographic) script. Among these early Egyptian writings were *The Teachings of Kagemni* and *The Teaching of Ptah-Hetep*, dating from ca. 2700 BCE. From ca. 2500 BCE pictographic signs were used at Byblos (Gebal) and Syria. At Knossos and Atchana, great commercial centers, additional written records appear that antedated the works of Moses. Other items for the mid- to late-second millennium BCE add still more evidence that writing had become well developed before the time of Moses. In short, Moses and the other biblical writers wrote during man's age of literacy.

WRITING MATERIALS AND INSTRUMENTS

Writing Materials

The writers of Scripture employed the same materials as were used throughout the ancient world. *Clay tablets,* for example, were not only used in ancient Sumer as early as ca. 3500 BCE, they were also utilized by Jeremiah (17:1) and Ezekiel (4:1). *Stone* was used to make inscriptions in Mesopotamia, Egypt, and Palestine for such records as the Code of Hammurabi, the Rosetta Stone, Tel el Amarna Tablet, and the Moabite Stone (Mesha stela; Plates 5–6, 8, 10). It was also employed at the Dog River in Lebanon and at Behistun in Persia (modern Iran) and by biblical writers (Ex. 24:12; 32:15–16; Deut. 27:2–3; Josh. 8:31–32).

Papyrus was utilized in ancient Gebal (Byblos) and Egypt about 2100 BCE. Formed into a scroll by pressing and gluing, these papyrus sheets were used by the apostle John in writing the Revelation (5:1) as well as his epistles (2 John 12). *Vellum, parchment,* and *leather* describe the various grades of writing material made from animal skins. Vellum was unknown before 200 BCE, so Jeremiah (36:23) must have had leather in mind. Parchments are indicated by Paul in 2 Timothy 4:13. Other materials for writing include *metal* (Ex. 28:36; Job 19:24; Matt. 22:19–20), *wax* (Isa. 8:1; 30:8; Hab. 2:2; Luke

1:63), *precious stones* (Ex. 39:6–14), and *potsherds* (ostraca), as indicated in Job 2:8. *Linen* was used in Egypt, Greece, and Italy, although there is no indication of its employment in the Bible record.

Writing Instruments

Several basic instruments were employed in the production of written records on the materials previously mentioned. Among these instruments were the *stylus,* a three-sided instrument with a beveled head for writing. It was especially used to make incursions into clay and wax tablets, although it was sometimes called a "pen of iron [*iron stylus* NASB]; with a point of diamond" by Jeremiah (see Jer. 17:1). A *chisel* was employed to make inscriptions in stone, as in Joshua 8:31–32. Job referred to a chisel as an "iron pen" (19:24) with which words could be engraved into rock. The *pen and ink* were utilized in writing on papyrus, leather, vellum, and parchment (3 John 13).

Scribes used other instruments to carry out their writing task. Jeremiah spoke of a *scribe's knife* used to destroy a scroll (Jer. 36:23 NASB). Its use indicates that the scroll was probably made of a material stronger than papyrus, which could be torn. The scribe's knife also helped the writer to sharpen his pen after it had begun to wear down. *Ink* was the necessary concomitant of the pen, and the *inkhorn* was employed to contain the ink for writing on papyrus, leather, parchment, and vellum. Thus, all the materials and instruments available to writers throughout the ancient world were available for use by the biblical writers.

THE PREPARATION AND PRESERVATION OF MANUSCRIPTS

The authentic writings produced under the direction and authorization of a prophet or apostle, called *autographa* (autographs), are no longer in existence. As a result, they must be reconstructed from early manuscripts and versions of the Bible text. The manuscripts provide tangible and important evidence about the transmission of the Bible from God to us.

The Preparation of Manuscript Copies

The Old Testament. Although Hebrew writing began before the time of Moses, it is impossible to determine just when it was introduced. No manuscripts exist that were written before the Babylonian captivity (586 BCE), but a great flood of Scripture copies date from the time of Ezra as the Jewish scribal tradition emerged. The earliest group of Jewish scribes were the Sopherim (fifth–third centuries BCE), active from Ezra to Antigonus of Soch. Under their leadership Jews preserved, at first by oral tradition and then in writing, an enormous amount of the Torah and other parts of the Old Testament that had been lost before and during the Babylonian Captivity (Plate 12). This mass of tradition was preserved in two major collections: the Midrash and the Talmud. The Zugoth (second–first centuries BCE), pairs of textual scholars, succeeded the Sopherim and were active during the period from Jose ben Joezer to Hillel.

After the Zugoth, a third group of scribes arose, the Tannaim (first century CE–after 200 CE). From the death of Hillel to the death of Judah Hannasi (after 200 CE), Tannaim teachings are preserved in the Mishnah, the Tosefta, the Baraihoh, and the Midrash. More than two hundred of the Tannaim "repeaters, or teachers" are named and entitled either Rabbi or Rabban (teacher) in these works.

The Amoraim (Speakers, Explainers) were sages who contributed to the Gemara. Finally, the Masoretes (500 CE–950 CE) were scholars who gave the final form to the text of the Old Testament.

During the Talmudic era (ca. 300 BCE–500 CE), two general classes of manuscript copies emerged: the *synagogue rolls* and the *private copies*. The synagogue rolls were regarded as "sacred copies" of the Old Testament text because of the strict rules employed in their transmission. As a result, these copies were used in public meeting places and at the annual feasts. Separate rolls contained the Torah (Law) on one roll, portions of the Nebhi'im (Prophets) on another, the Kethubhim (Writings) on two others, and the Megilloth ("Five Rolls") on five separate rolls. The Megilloth were undoubtedly produced on separate rolls in order to facilitate their being read at the annual feasts.

The private copies were regarded as common copies of the Old Testament text and were not used in public meetings. These rolls were prepared with great care, although they were not governed by the strict rules employed in making the synagogue roll copies. The desires of the purchaser determined the quality of the particular copy. Seldom did an individual have a collection of scrolls that contained the entire Old Testament.

The Masoretes were so named because they preserved in writing the oral tradition (*masorah*) concerning the correct vowels and accents and the number of occurrences of rare words of unusual spellings. The main Masorete centers were in Babylon, Palestine (Tiberia), and Egypt. They received the unpointed consonantal text of the Sopherim and inserted vowel points that gave to each word its exact pronunciation and grammatical form.

The Masoretes also engaged in moderate textual criticism. When they observed an erroneous reading in the consonantal text, they introduced a unique procedure: they inserted vowel points in the text (above or below the consonantal words) and added smaller consonants in the margin to indicate the correct reading. They invented the system of kethib (K), "it is written" and qerê (Q), "read" to preserve the actual text and to introduce the variant. Most famous (and frequent) is the qerê reading for the covenant name of God, YaHWeH (Jehovah). His name is written with four consonants: YHWH, going back to the original pronunciation YaHWeH. As early as the time of Ezra, Jews accepted the practice of substituting the title Lord ('aDōNāY) for the name Yahweh whenever reading it aloud. By substituting the vowels for ('aDōNāY) over the consonants YaHWeH they produced the appearance JeHōWāH (Jehovah). The American Standard Version, ASV (1901), the Jehovah's Witnesses New World Translation, the Jerusalem Bible, and the New Jerusalem Bible used Jehovah or Yahweh in their translations. The Jewish Publication Society (JPS, NJPS) Hebrew-English translations of TANAKH have appended the יהוה (YHWH) in their English translations, while the New Catholic Bible, NCB (2007), and *The Bible in Its Traditions* (2008 and ongoing) followed the request of Pope Benedict XVI (2007) not to use Jehovah (Yahweh) in future English translations largely for the sake of doctrinal integrity and out of deference to Jewish readers (see discussions in chap. 20).

The New Testament. The autographs of the New Testament have long since disappeared, but there is much evidence to warrant the assumption that these documents were written on rolls and books made of papyri. Paul indicated that the Old Testament had been copied into books and parchments (2 Tim. 4:13), but the New Testament was probably written on papyrus rolls between 50 and 100 CE. By the early second century, papyrus codices were introduced, but they too were perishable. With the introduction of persecutions within the Roman Empire, the Scriptures became jeopardized and were not systematically copied until the time of Constantine. With the Letter of Constantine to Eusebius of Caesarea, systematic copying of the New Testament began in the West. From that time, vellum and parchment were also employed in making manuscript copies of the New Testament. Not until the Reformation era were printed copies of the Bible available.

The Preservation (and Age) of Manuscript Copies

Prior to the Reformation and the development of printing processes, the West produced books as handwritten manuscript copies. Manuscript copies made during this time are dated by the age and preservation of earlier manuscript copies in lieu of a publication date on the opening pages. Scholars determine a manuscript's age by inspecting the *materials* used, *letter size and form*, *punctuation*, *text divisions*, and some *miscellaneous factors*.

Materials are an important clue. For present purposes, only those materials usable in making rolls or books are considered. The earliest of these were animal skins, although they made heavy, bulky rolls of the Old Testament. Papyrus rolls were used in the New Testament period because they were inexpensive when compared with vellum and parchment. Papyrus codices were introduced by the beginning of the second century CE to gather individual rolls together. Vellum and parchment were employed for the Old Testament during New Testament times (2 Tim. 4:13), and for the New Testament following the end of the persecutions in the fourth century. Redressed parchment was employed in copying manuscripts after the original writings had become faded.

Sometimes parchments were erased and rewritten, as in the case of the Codex Ephraemi Rescriptus (C). These manuscripts are also called *palimpsest* (Gk., rubbed out again) or *rescriptus* (Lat., rewritten). Paper was invented in China in the second century CE, introduced into Eastern Turkestan as early as the fourth century, manufactured in Arabia in the eighth, introduced into Europe in the tenth, manufactured there in the twelfth, and commonly used by the thirteenth century. Other developments in the manufacture of paper also help to determine manuscript age from its materials.

Letter size and form also provides evidence for determining the date of a given manuscript. The earliest form of letters in Hebrew resembled the prong shape of Phoenician script. This style prevailed until the time of Nehemiah (ca. 444 BCE). After that time the Aramaic script was employed, since it became the vernacular language of Israel during the fifth century BCE. After 200 BCE the Old Testament was copied in the square letters of Aramaic script. The discovery of the Dead Sea Scrolls at Qumran in 1947 and the Discoveries in the Judean Desert during the 1950s cast further light on the study of Hebrew paleography. These manuscripts revealed three different types of text as well as differences in matters of spelling, grammatical forms, and, to some extent, wording from the Masoretic (traditional, from *masorah*) Text. The Hebrew word *masorah* (tradition) from *masar* (transmit, or hand over) means to "fetter" the exposition of the text of Scripture. In the course of time, the Masorah connected with the verb ("to hand down") and acquired the general meaning of "tradition." By the time of the Masoretes—Jewish scribes who standardized the Hebrew text of the Old Testament (ca. 500–1000 CE)—the principles of the late Talmudic period became rather stereotyped.

Greek manuscripts during the New Testament period were generally written in two styles: literary and nonliterary. The New Testament was undoubtedly written in the nonliterary style. During the first three centuries, the New Testament was probably circulated outside the regular channels of ordinary book trade because of the political status of Christianity. During the first three formative centuries of the church and its canon of New Testament Scriptures, various oral and written traditions followed the whims of individual interpreters and prevailing fashions among scribes. Not until the fourth century were serious attempts made at recension, a critical, systematic revision of the manuscripts.

The style of letters used in these revisions and early manuscripts is called *uncial* (capital). The letters were written separately, and there were no breaks between words or sentences. Until the tenth century this slow process of copying a manuscript was employed. By that time the demand for manuscripts was so great that a faster writing style was developed. This *cursive* style employed smaller, connected letters with breaks between words and sentences. The name *minuscule* was applied to these manuscripts, which became the dominant form during the golden age of manuscript copying, the eleventh through fifteenth centuries.

Punctuation adds further light to the age of a manuscript. At the outset words were run together and very little punctuation was used. During the sixth century scribes began to make more liberal use of punctuation. By the eighth they had come to utilize not only the spaces, but periods, commas, colons, breath, and accent marks, and they added interrogatives later. This slow process was completed by the tenth century, in time to be employed with cursive writing in the golden age of manuscript copying.

Text divisions were begun in the Old Testament autographs in some instances, such as the book of Lamentations and Psalm 119. Additional sections were added to the Pentateuch prior to the Babylonian captivity, called *sedarim* (plural). During the captivity the Torah was divided into fifty-four sections called *parashiyyoth* (pl.; *parashah*, sing.). The parashiyyoth were public recitations of the Torah used during a three-year cycle. They were later subdivided even further. The Maccabean sections were made during the second century BCE. These were divisions in the prophets, called *haphtaroth* (plural), corresponding to the *sedarim* of the law. During the Reformation era the Hebrew Old Testament began to follow the Protestant chapter divisions for the most part. Some chapter divisions, however, had been placed in the margins as early as 1330. The Masoretes added vowel points to the Hebrew text during the sixth through tenth centuries, but it was not until 900 CE that the versification of the Old Testament began to become standardized. In 1571, Arius Montanus published the first Hebrew Old Testament to have verse markings in the margin as well as chapter divisions.

Prior to the Council of Nicea (325 CE) the New Testament was divided into sections. These sections, called *kephalaia* (Gk., "headings"), differed from modern chapter divisions. Another system was utilized in the Codex Vaticanus (B) during the fourth century, and still another was employed by Eusebius of Caesarea. These divisions were longer than modern verses, but shorter than modern chapters.

Not until the thirteenth century were these divisions modified, and then only gradually. Stephen Langton (ca. 1150–1228), a professor at the University of Paris who became Archbishop of Canterbury (1207–1228), completed the modification, although others may give the credit to Cardinal Hugo of St. Cher (d. 1263). The Wycliffe Bible (1382) followed this pattern. Since it provided the basis for subsequent versions and translations, the system became standardized. Modern verses had not yet appeared, although they were employed in the Greek New Testament published by Robert Stephanus in 1551 and introduced into the English Bible in 1557. In 1555 they were placed into a Latin Vulgate edition published by Stephanus. The first English Bible to employ both the modern chapter and verse divisions was the Geneva Bible (1560).

Miscellaneous factors involved in the dating of a manuscript include the size and shape of letters, the ornamentation of a manuscript, spelling, ink color, and the texture and coloration of parchment. The ornamentation of manuscripts became more and more elaborate in the uncial manuscripts during the fourth to late ninth centuries. From that time onward the ornamentation declined as uncials were less carefully copied. These factors were paralleled in the minuscules from that time until the introduction of printed editions and translations of the Bible in the sixteenth century. At the outset, only black ink was used in writing a manuscript. Later green, red, and other colors were employed. Just as the spoken language changes through the centuries, so do these physical components. Then, the changing quality and texture of materials can be coupled with the aging process in determining the age of a manuscript.

Results

A cursory survey of the evidence available concerning the age and preservation of manuscripts presents us with some important information about the relative value of a given manuscript in the transmission of the Bible.

Old Testament manuscripts generally come from two broad periods of production. The Talmudic period (300 BCE–500 CE) produced manuscripts which were used in the synagogues and for private study. By comparison with the later Masoretic period (500–1000), these earlier manuscript copies were few in number but they were carefully transmitted "official" copies. During the Masoretic period the Old Testament manuscript copying underwent a complete review of established rules, and a systematic renovation of transmission techniques resulted.

New Testament manuscripts may be classified into four general periods of transmission:

1. During the first three centuries the integrity of the New Testament Scriptures comes from a combined testimony of sources because of the illegal status of Christianity. Not many complete manuscripts from this period can be found, but the ones extant are significant.
2. From the fourth and fifth centuries, following the legalization of Christianity, a multiplication of New Testament manuscripts appeared. These manuscripts were on vellum and parchment instead of the papyrus used earlier.
3. From the sixth century onward manuscripts were copied by monks, who collected and cared for them in monasteries. This was a period of rather uncritical reproduction, increased production, and a generally decreased quality of text.
4. After the introduction of minuscule manuscripts in the tenth

century, manuscript copies were multiplied rapidly and the decline in quality of textual transmission continued.

As the following chart, "The Reliability of the New Testament Documents," indicates, the preservation of literary works survived from the ancient world. The care and accuracy of New Testament copyists is apparent when their work is compared to other literary works. This is still another reason to regard the Old and New Testament texts as reliable.

THE RELIABILITY OF THE NEW TESTAMENT DOCUMENTS

Author/ Book	Date Written	Earliest Copies	Time Gap	No. of Copies	Percent Accuracy
Hindu *Mahābhārata*	13th cent. B.C.				90
Homer, *Iliad*	800 B.C.			643	95
Herodotus, *History*	480–425 B.C.	ca. A.D. 900	ca. 1,350 yrs.	8	?
Thucydides, *History*	460–400 B.C.	ca. A.D. 900	ca. 1,300 yrs.	8	?
Plato	400 B.C.	ca. A.D. 900	ca. 1,300 yrs.	7	?
Demosthenes	300 B.C.	ca. A.D. 1100	ca. 1,400 yrs.	200	?
Caesar, *Gaelic Wars*	100–44 B.C.	ca. A.D. 900	ca. 1,000 yrs.	10	?
Livy, *History of Rome*	59 B.C.– A.D. 17	4th cent. (partial) mostly 10th cent.	ca. 1,350 yrs.	1 partial 19 copies	?
Tacitus, *Annals*	A.D. 100	ca. A.D. 1100	ca. 1,000 yrs.	20	?
Pliny Secundus, *Natural History*	A.D. 61–113	ca. 850	ca. 750 yrs.	7	?
New Testament	A.D. 50–100	ca. 114 (fragment) ca. 200 (books) ca. 250 (most of N.T.) ca. 325 (complete N.T.)	±50 yrs. 100 yrs. 150 yrs. 225 yrs.	5800	99+

SOURCE: Norman L. Geisler and William E. Nix, *A General Introduction to the Bible*, rev. ed. (Chicago: Moody, 1986), 408.

PLATES

Plate 1 **Pictograms**—Earliest form of writing from Southern Iraq (Sumer), dating to the 4th millennium BCE, is known as the proto-literate age of logographic (pictures standing for words). *Zev Radovan / BibleLandPictures.com*

Plate 2 **Pictograms**—Earliest known writing, it eventually led to the development of cuneiform. By the beginning of the 2nd millennium BCE it became the standard script in most Mesopotamian regions. *Zev Radovan / BibleLandPictures.com*

Plate 3 **Ebla Tablet** (ca. 2500–2250 BCE)—One of 1,800 complete clay tablets in Sumerian cuneiform script (logograms) discovered near Tel Mardikh (Ebla), Syria in 1974–75.

Plate 4 **Gilgamesh Deluge Tablet**—Tablet 11 of the twelve Gilgamesh tablets (ca. 18th–17th cent. BCE) was discovered near ancient Nineveh.

Plate 5 **Prologue Hammurabi Code Louvre** (18th cent. BCE)—shows the first of 305 inscripted squares on the Hammurabi Code Stele.

Plate 6 **Tel el Amarna Tablet** (1395–1335 BCE)—The tablet is a letter from Abimelech.

Plate 7 **Menerptah Stele**–This hieroglyphic slab, 7.5 feet tall, was found in Pharaoh Merneptah's funerary temple in western Thebes. It contains Merneptah's exploits and the earliest mention (1230 BCE) of "Israel" in any *official* document outside the Bible (see inset below). *Zev Radovan / BibleLandPictures.com*

Plate 8 **Mesha Stela (Moabite Stone)**—Ninth century BCE record of conflicts between King Mesha of Moab and Kings Omri and Ahab of Israel (2 Kings 1-3). Epigrapher Andre Lamaire has noted that the dynastic phrase "House of D[avid]" may also be present. *Zev Radovan / BibleLandPictures.com*

Above (inset): **Menerptah Stele, Line 27**–"Israel is laid waste; its seed is not"

D W D T Y B

Across (inset): **The Tel Dan Stele:** "The house of David**"**

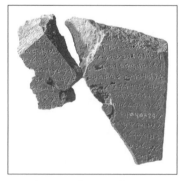

Plate 9 **Tel Dan Stele**–An 8th century victory stele, it mentions the "House of David." It is the first extrabiblical reference to the Davidic line. *Joseph Holden / Veritas Evangelical Seminary*

Plate 10 **Rosetta Stone**—This 1,700 pound trilingual black basalt slab provided the key to decipher hieroglyphic (top), Demotic (middle), and Greek (bottom) scripts. *Joseph Holden / Veritas Evangelical Seminary*

Plate 11 **Ancient Egyptian Scribe at Luxor** *Courtesy Antiquité éqyptienne, Musée de Luxour, Memphis, Egypt*

Plate 12 **Orthodox Jewish Scribe**—Talmudic and Masoretic scribes preserved the Scriptures by skillfully copying the text according to strict guidelines and standards.

Plate 13 **Samaritan High Priest and Old Pentateuch**—Samaritans claim to be lineal descendants of ancient Israel; they most certainly represent Samaritans from the time of Christ.

Plate 14 **Ketef Hinnom Silver Scroll** (ca. 600 BCE)—This Hebrew inscribed amulet is the oldest biblical text known to date. Of special importance is the scroll's contents, which mention the name "YHWH" several times within the priestly benediction of Numbers 6:24–26. *Zev Radovan / BibleLandPictures.com*

Plate 15 **Copper Scroll (3Q15)**—Discovered in Qumran Cave 3, two Hebrew copper scrolls list more than 60 sites of buried treasure (i.e., ingots, gold) in the Judean desert. *Zev Radovan / BibleLandPictures.com*

Plate 16 **Qumran Cave 4**—The cave contained some 100 biblical books and more than 50,000 fragments. It included partial copies/fragments of Genesis, Daniel 7:28 to 8:1 (Aramaic changes to Hebrew), and commentaries on Psalms, Isaiah, and Nahum. *Joseph Holden / Veritas Evangelical Seminary*

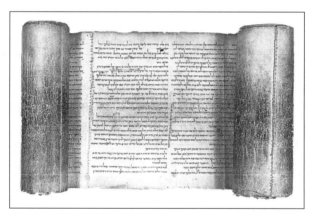

Plate 17 **Isaiah A Scroll (1QIsa A)** —Qumran cave 1 yielded a complete copy of the book of Isaiah, written in Hebrew on parchment (animal skin) dating to 125 BCE. The scroll is approximately 26 feet long and is open to Isaiah 38:9–40:28. *©John C. Trever, Ph.D., digital image by James E. Trever*

Plate 18 **Psalm (11QPs)**—This Hebrew psalm was discovered in cave 11. Scholars now possess nearly 40 psalms, ranging from Psalm 90 to 150 (and the noncanonical Psalm 151). *Zev Radovan / BibleLandPictures.com*

Plate 19 **Habakkuk (1QpHab)**—Findings in cave 1 include a Hebrew text commentary (*pesher*) of Habakkuk dating to the 1st century BCE. *Zev Radovan / BibleLandPictures.com*

Plate 20 **Messianic Testimony (4Q175)**—This 1st century BCE Hebrew manuscript, discovered in cave 4 at Qumran, contains assorted Messianic passages from Deuteronomy, Numbers, and Joshua. *Zev Radovan / BibleLandPictures.com*

Plate 21 **Gospel of Thomas**—Discovered in 1945 near Nag Hammadi, Egypt, the Coptic text of Gnostic Gospel of Thomas contains 114 sayings attributed to Jesus. *Zev Radovan / BibleLandPictures.com*

Plate 22 **St. Catherine's Monastery,** Sinai, Egypt—Here Constantin von Tischendorf (1815–1874) discovered the earliest known complete Bible, Codex Sinaiticus (ca. 350 CE). *Joseph Holden / Veritas Evangelical Seminary*

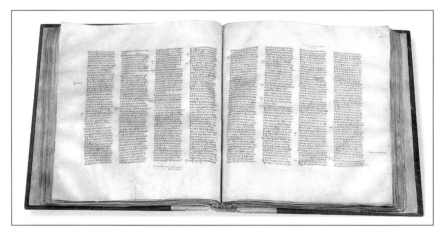

Plate 23 **Codex Sinaiticus (ℵ, *Aleph* 01)** —The oldest complete Greek Bible is written in four columns and dates to ca. 350 CE. *Zev Radovan / BibleLandPictures.com*

Plate 24 **Codex Vaticanus (B 02)** —This early 4th century CE manuscript contains the complete Old Testament and most of the New Testament written with Greek (Alexandrian text type). Isaiah 52:10–54:2 is shown above. *William E. Nix*

Plate 25 **Codex Vaticanus (B 02)** —New Testament, in three columns, of 2 Thessalonians 3:4–18—Hebrews 1:1–2:2 is shown. *Zev Radovan / BibleLandPictures.com*

Plate 26 **Codex Alexandrinus (A 03)**—This Greek manuscript from 5th century CE contains the entire Old Testament and most of the New Testament. Text of Luke 24:32–53 is shown here.

Plate 27 **Codex Alexandrinus (A 03)**—This recto page of the two-column Greek New Testament manuscript shows John 1:1–18.

Plate 28 **Codex Bezae (D^ea 05)**—The codex is a bilingual Greek (verso) and Latin (recto) diglot; here it shows the end of Luke and the beginning of John.

Plate 29 **Pontius Pilate Inscription**—Latin inscription (1st cent. CE) identifies Pontius Pilate as prefect in Judea during the reign of Caesar Tiberius at the time of Christ's crucifixion. *Zev Radovan / BibleLandPictures.com*

Plate 30 **Bodmer Papyrus $\mathfrak{P}^{66}$**—The Bodmer Collection consists of nearly two dozen biblical and nonbiblical papyri originally discovered in 1952. The earliest biblical text in the Library ($\mathfrak{P}^{66}$) dates to ca. 200 CE. John 1:1–14 is shown.

Plate 31 **Chester Beatty Papyrus $\mathfrak{P}^{46}$**—This papyrus collection consists of nearly one dozen biblical papyri written in Greek (3rd cent. CE). Folio text of 2 Corinthians 11:33–12:9 (ca. 200) is shown.

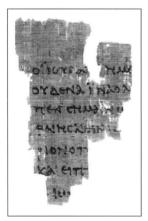

Plate 32 **John Rylands Papyrus $\mathfrak{P}^{52}$**—This double-sided Greek fragment (front shown above) of John 18:31–33, 37–38 is currently the oldest Peshitta New Testament text (ca. 125). *Zev Radovan / BibleLandPictures.com*

Plate 33 **Peshitta (Peshito) Old Testament**—Syriac text (464 CE) is the oldest dated biblical manuscript in existence. Exodus 13:14–16 is shown. (British Museum Add. MS. 14; 425)

Plate 34 **Peshitta (Peshito) New Testament**—The oldest complete eastern (Aramaic Peshitta) New Testament text is written in unvocalized Estangelo script. This text omits 2 Peter, 2 John, 3 John, Jude, and Revelation (restored in later editions).

Plate 35 **Lectionary 152—** Codex Harleianus 5787, Lectionary 152 (Gregory-Aland); Folio 95 of this 9th century codex is shown.

Plate 36 **Carolingian Gospel Minuscule—**Anonymous text (British Library, MS 11848) written in Carolingian minuscule script. Luke 23:14–26 is shown.

Plate 37 **Aleppo Codex—**Hebrew Old Testament (900 CE) includes vowel points used by Masoretes. It serves as the basis for most modern English Old Testament translations. *Zev Radovan / Bible-LandPictures.com*

Plate 38 **Targum Codex** (first quarter 11th cent.)—This page shows Aramaic first word (Exodus 12:24) and then Hebrew square book script of Exodus 12:25–31.

Plate 39 **Leningrad Codex—** Cover of the oldest complete Hebrew Bible (ca. 1008–10). The codex is used today for reconstructing missing texts from the earlier Aleppo Codex.

Plate 40 **Leningrad Codex** (ca. 1008–10 CE)—Probably written at Cairo, Egypt, the Leningrad Codex is considered one of the best examples of the Masoretic text by Ben-Asher family**.**

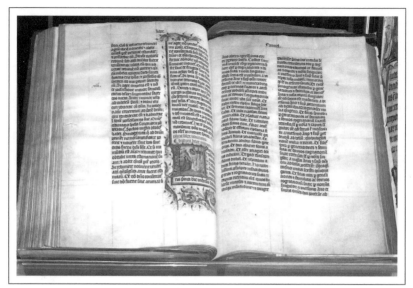

Plate 41 **Malmesbury Latin Bible** (1407)—Handwritten Latin Bible contains the end of Leviticus and beginning of Numbers; on display in Malmesbury Abbey, Wilshire, England.

To ye corint. i.

as ye ertheli man is: suche ben ye ertheli men/and suche as ye heuenli man is: suche ben al so ye heuenli men/þfor as we han bore ye ymage of ye erþ li man: bere we also ye ymage of ye heuenli man/Bri þ en y seie þis þing. þt fleisch and blood moun not welde ye kingdom of god/neþ corrup cioun schal welde uncorrupci oun// lo y seie to ʒou þ pucte of hooli þingis/and alle we schul len rise aʒen: but not alle we

of ye lord euermore witinge þt ʒoure trauel is not idel in ye lord// xvi

But of ye gaderingis of monei þat ben maad in to seyntis. as y ordei nede in ye chirchis of galathi: so also do ʒe o dai of ye woke/ ech of ʒou kepe at hym silf. kepinge þat þat plesiþ to him: þat whanne y come ye gade ringis ben not maad/& whanne y schal be þsent. whiche men þuen: y schal sende hem bi

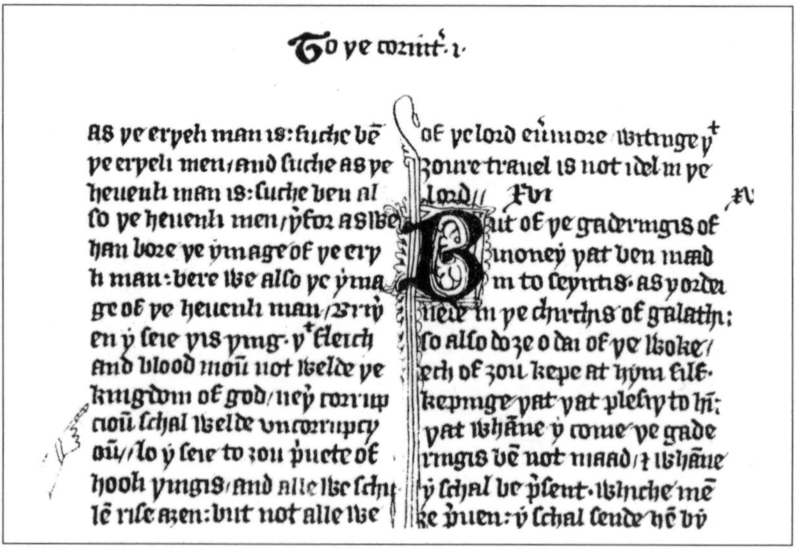

Plate 42 **Wycliffite New Testament**—A handwritten translation from the Latin Vulgate. Shown are the early and later versions of 1 Corinthians 15–16 updated by John Purvey (ca. 1400–1425). *Donald L. Brake Sr.*

Plate 43 **Gutenberg Bible** (also known as the 42-line Bible, the Mazarin Bible or the B42)—This vellum Bible is the first major book printed in the Western world with a movable-type printing press invented by Johannes Gutenberg in Mainz, Germany (1454–55). Only eleven complete vellum Bibles are known to exist. *Mark Pellegrini photo Rovl654 / U.S. Library of Congress.*

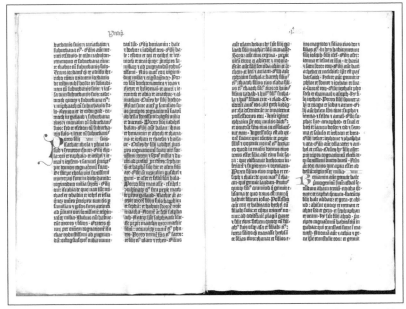

Plate 44 **Gutenberg II (Bamberg) 36-line Bible**—First printed Bible using Gutenberg's movable type but limiting the lines per page to thirty-six, this image shows Latin text of 1 Chronicles 6:76b–8:6.

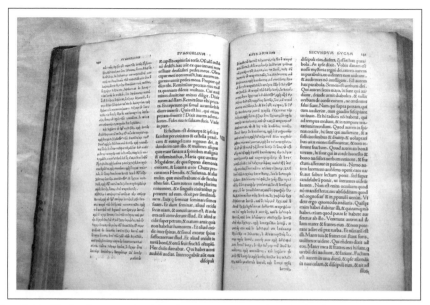

Plate 45 **Desiderius Erasmus Greek/Latin New Testament** (1516)—The first published Greek New Testament in the West, this diglot text shows Luke 7:46–8:22. *Jim M. Bolton; courtesy of the Rawlings Foundation*

Plate 46 **Complutensian Polyglot** (1514–1517)—Printed but not published until sanctioned by Pope Leo X in 1520 from Alcalá (Complutum). This shows the beginning of Matthew. *Jim M. Bolton; courtesy of the Rawlings Foundation*

Plate 47 **Tyndale Bible** (1526)—
The plate shows the first chapter of the Gospel of John.

Plate 48 **Coverdale Bible**—Title
Page (1635)

Plate 49 **Coverdale Bible** (1635)—
First Kings 22:18–50 is shown.

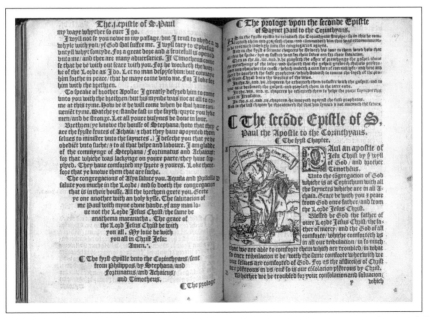

Plate 50 **William Tyndale Open Bible (1536)**—This open Bible shows the end of 1 Corinthians and the
beginning of 2 Corinthians. *Donald L. Brake Sr.*

Plate 51 **Matthew's Bible** (1538)—This is the first English Bible issued with a royal license, to Thomas Matthew, a pseudonym for John Rogers (1500–1555), the first martyr in the persecution during the reign of Mary Tudor. *Jim M. Bolton; courtesy of the Rawlings Foundation*

Plate 52 **Matthew's Bible** (1537)—Title page with date and royal license. *Jim M. Bolton; courtesy of the Rawlings Foundation*

Plate 53 **The Great Bible** (1539)—This title page depicts Henry VIII receiving the Word of God and bestowing it upon his archbishops and bishops, who deliver it to the priests, and then to the laity. *Jim M. Bolton; courtesy of the Rawlings Foundation*

Plate 54 **The Geneva Bible** (NT 1582; OT 1609)—Published by English exiles in Geneva, it includes annotations, study notes, cross references, and maps. This is the Bible of Shakespeare, Milton, Bunyan, Knox, Puritans, and Pilgrims on the *Mayflower* (1620). *Jim M. Bolton; courtesy of the Rawlings Foundation*

Plate 55 **Bishops' Bible** (1569)—Upon the ascension of Elizabeth I, a new translation was needed to counteract the influence of the Geneva Bible. *Jim M. Bolton; courtesy of the Rawlings Foundation*

Plate 56 **Bishops' Bible** (1538)—Old Testament translation of the Apocrypha; the translation is of uneven quality and is best known for its lavish production. *Jim M. Bolton; courtesy of the Rawlings Foundation*

Plate 57 **Rheims New Testament** (1582)—Roman Catholic exiles during the reign of Elizabeth I (1558–1603) translated from the Latin Vulgate, comparing it with Greek texts. *Donald L. Brake Sr.*

Plate 58 **Douai Old Testament** (1609)—Roman Catholic exiles at Douai during reign of James I (1603–1625) translated the Latin Vulgate comparing it with Hebrew and Greek manuscripts. *Courtesy of Northwest Christian University.*

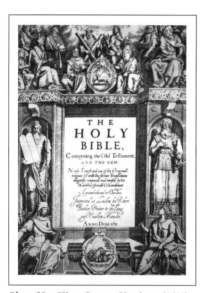

Plate 59 **King James Version** (1611)—Originated at Hampton Court Conference in January 1604 when King James I appointed a committee of fifty-four scholars to do the translation. *Jim M. Bolton; courtesy of the Rawlings Foundation*

Plate 60 **Challoner–Douai Bible** (1749)—Major revision of Douai–Rheims Bible became the standard Roman Catholic English Bible until the 20th century.

12

The Major Manuscripts *of* the Bible

THE CLASSICAL WRITINGS OF GREECE AND ROME illustrate the character of biblical manuscript preservation quite strikingly. As of the present, a total of over 5,800 New Testament manuscripts have been catalogued. By contrast, other religious and historical books of the ancient world pale in significance. Only 643 copies of Homer's *Iliad* have survived in manuscript form. Titus Livy's *History of Rome* has only twenty manuscripts, and Caesar's *Gallic Wars* is known from a mere nine or ten manuscripts. *History of the Peloponnesian War* of Thucydides remains in only eight manuscripts and the *Works* of Tacitus are to be found in only two manuscripts. A survey of the manuscript evidence of the Old Testament, although not as vast as the available New Testament manuscripts, indicates the nature and amount of documentary evidence for the original text of the Hebrew Bible.

Manuscripts of the Old Testament

Before the discovery in 1947 of the Dead Sea Scrolls (DSS) there were relatively few early manuscripts of the Old Testament text. During the 1950s Scripture scrolls were discovered in the Judean desert ruins at Masada (used by followers of Bar Kochba), and at Wadi Murabba'at and Nahal Hever. We now consider those discoveries as we review the Masoretic Text (MT), Dead Sea Scrolls (DSS), and Discoveries of the Judean Desert (DJD).

The Masoretic Text

Until the discovery of the Cairo Genezah manuscripts in 1890, only 731 Hebrew manuscripts had been published. In fact, Hebrew Bibles edited by Rudolph Kittel (*Biblia Hebraica I, BHK1, 1906; Biblia Hebraica* II, BHK2, 1913), Paul Kahle, *Biblia Hebraica* III (BH3, 1937), *Biblia Hebraica Stuttgartensia* (BHS, 1967–77), I (BHQ), and the Biblia Hebraic Quinta (BHQ, since 1996) are all based on the Masoretic Text and the Leningrad Codex (B 19 A or L) and are commonly known as "diplomatic" editions. Following the Qumran and Judean Desert discoveries, two new editions of the Hebrew text have been initiated that incorporate those materials into "critical" editions of the Old Testament text. The Hebrew University Bible (HUB, 1995–2004+) and the Oxford Hebrew Bible (OHB, 1995–2008+) are currently being produced as a series of individual critical editions of the Old Testament published by Oxford University Press.

A digitized electronic transcription of the print edition of *Biblia Hebraica Stuttgartensia* (1983) has been made available in the MCWT (Michigan-Claremont-Westminster Text) catalogued at Oxford University. It was based on only four major Hebrew manuscripts, and primarily on just one of those, the Leningrad Codex (B 19 A or L). This text began as the work of Richard Whitaker (Princeton Seminary) and H. van Parunak (University of Michigan), continued by Robert Kraft (University of Pennsylvania) and Emmanuel Tov (Hebrew University), and completed by Professor Alan Groves (Westminster Seminary). The transcription was completed and archived at the Oxford Text Archive in 1987 as the Michigan-Claremont-Westminster Electronic Hebrew Bible (MCWT). Variously known as "eBHS" or "CCAT" text, it has been modified in many hundreds of places to conform to the photofacsimile of the Leningrad Codex, Firkovich B19A, residing at the Russian National Library, St. Petersburg; hence the name change.[1]

Beginning in 1987, a team of Westminster scholars under the direction of Professor Alan Groves began to perfect a computerized version of the morphological analysis of the Hebrew text based on Richard Whitaker's (Claremont, Princeton Seminary) database and referred to as the Groves-Wheeler Westminster Hebrew Morphology (version 4.8 as of July 2007), in recognition of the contribution of Professor Dale Wheeler (Multnomah) and others. Logos Bible Software and many other Bible software producers

---

1. This discussion follows the "Projects" page at Westminster Theological Seminary: http://www.wts.edu.

have incorporated the Westminster Hebrew Morphology (WM).[2]

On a different track, the print edition of *Biblia Hebraica Stuttgartensia* (BHS) was used by the Jewish Publication Society (JPS) as the text for the *TANAKH: A New Translation of THE HOLY SCRIPTURES According to the Traditional Hebrew Text* (NJV, NJPS, 1985, 1999).[3] More recently, the *Biblia Hebraica Leningradensia* (BHL, 2001) presented a thoroughly revised, reset, and redesigned edition of the Hebrew Bible meticulously prepared by renowned Masoretic scholar Aron Dotan. BHL (Leningrad Codex or L) is the oldest dated manuscript of the complete Hebrew Bible (1008 CE). It is not a photographic reproduction, but a reprinting of the text with modern Hebrew fonts, and is the most accurate edition of the Leningrad Codex in print. The MCWT (see above) was collated manually using Aron Dotan's Hebrew Bible. The Westminster 4.2 Morphology (WM) database adds a complete morphological analysis for each word/morpheme of the Hebrew text.[4]

The major texts in this tradition were copied during the Masoretic period. The *Cairo Codex,* or *Codex Cairensis* (C) (895 CE) is perhaps the oldest known Masoretic manuscript of the prophets, and it contains both the former and the latter prophets. The *Leningrad Codex of the Prophets, or Babylonian Codex of the Latter Prophets* (MX B 3), also known as the [St.] Petersburg Codex (916 CE), contains only the latter prophets (Isaiah, Jeremiah, Ezekiel, and the Twelve), and was written with a Babylonian punctuation. The Aleppo Codex (930 CE) of the entire Old Testament is no longer complete (Plate 37). It was to be the primary authority of the Hebrew Bible to be published in Jerusalem, and it was corrected and punctuated by Aaron ben Asher in 930 CE. The British Museum Codex (Oriental 4445) dates from 950 CE and is an incomplete manuscript of the Pentateuch. It presently contains only Genesis 39:20 through Deuteronomy 1:33.

The largest and only complete manuscript of the entire Old Testament is the Leningrad Codex (B 19 A or L) (1008 CE). Written on vellum, it has

---

2. Ibid. Among Windows (Win) users of the Westminster Hebrew Morphology are BART by SIL/ Wycliffe; BibleWorks by Hermeneutika; Logos by Logos Research Systems, and WORDSearch by iExalt Electronic Publishing. Accordance by Oak Tree Software has a Macintosh (Mac) version.

3. TANAKH is an acronym for "Law," (*Torah*, חורה), "Prophets," (*Nebhi'im*, נביאמ), and "Writings," (*Kethuvim*, כחובים).

4. See http://logos.com, *Biblia Hebraica Stuttgartensia* (BHS Hebrew): With Westminster 4.2 Morphology.

three columns of twenty-one lines each per sheet(Plates 39–40). The vowel points and accents follow the Babylonian custom, being placed above the line. The Reuchlin Codex (MS *Ad.* 21161) of the prophets (1105 CE) contains a recension text that attests to the fidelity of Leningrad. The Cairo Genezah fragments (500–800 CE), discovered in 1890 at Cairo, are scattered throughout various libraries. Ernst Wurthwein says there are some 10,000 biblical manuscripts and fragments from this storehouse, although recent catalogues of American and European libraries require a considerable adjustment to this observation.[5]

The scarcity of early Old Testament manuscripts, with the exception of the Cairo Genezah, may be attributed to several factors. First and most obviously, the very antiquity of these manuscripts combined with their destructibility virtually assured that most would not survive. A second factor working against their survival is the fact that the Israelites were subject to the ravages of deportation during the Babylonian captivity and to foreign domination following their return to Palestine. In its history, from 1800 BCE to 1948 CE, Jerusalem was conquered forty-seven times. This also explains why those Masoretic texts discovered have been found outside Palestine proper. A third factor involved in the scarcity of Old Testament manuscripts centers around the sacred scribal laws demanding the burial of worn or flawed manuscripts. According to Talmudic tradition, any manuscript that contained a mistake or error, and all those that were aged beyond use, were systematically and religiously destroyed. Such practice undoubtedly decreased the number of discoverable manuscripts appreciably.

Finally, during the fifth and sixth centuries CE, when the Masoretes (Jewish scribes) standardized the Hebrew text, it is believed that they systematically and completely destroyed all the manuscripts that did not agree with their vocalization (adding of vowel letters) and standardization of the Scripture text. Archaeological evidence, the absence of surviving early manuscripts, tends to support this judgment. As a result, the printed Masoretic Text (MT) of the Old Testament as it appears today is based on relatively few

---

5. Additional fragments were found in the Basatin cemetery east of Old Cairo, and the collection includes a number of old documents bought in Cairo in the later nineteenth century. Presently dispersed among a number of libraries, including fragments in the Taylor-Schechter collection at Cambridge (193,000), the John Rylands Library at Manchester (11,000), and a further 31,000 fragments at the Jewish Theological Seminary of America.

manuscripts, none of which antedates the tenth century CE.

Although there are relatively few early Masoretic manuscripts, the quality of the extant manuscripts is very good. This too is to be attributed to several factors. First, very few variants appear among the available texts because they are all descendants of one text type that was established about 100 CE. Unlike the New Testament, which bases its textual fidelity on the multiplicity of manuscript copies, the Old Testament text owes its accuracy to the ability and reliability of the scribes who transmitted it. With respect to the Jewish Scriptures, however, scribal accuracy alone does not guarantee the product. Rather, their almost superstitious reverence for the Bible is paramount. According to the Talmud only certain kinds of skins could be used, the size of columns was regulated, and the ritual a scribe followed in copying a manuscript followed religious rules. If a manuscript was found to contain even one mistake, it was discarded and destroyed. This scribal formalism was responsible, at least in part, for the extreme care exercised in copying the Scriptures.

One line of evidence that supports the integrity of the Masoretic Text is the Samaritan Pentateuch (SamP). According to the *Encyclopedia Judaica*, 2nd ed., the first copy of the Samaritan Pentateuch to reach Western Bible scholars was obtained by Pietro della Valle in 1616. The first edition printed was in the Paris Polyglot Bible (1629–45) and the London Polyglot (1657). These and other early editions were inadequate for textual study until W. Gesenius published his detailed examination (1815). He compared approximately 6,000 textual differences with the Masoretic Text (MT). His dictum was that the SamP always presents the lectio facilio against the more archaic and difficult forms of the Masoretic Text. The sacred and zealously guarded tradition of the Samaritan sect shows clear affinity to the language of the Qumran Scrolls (Q). The best known difference of substance is the additional text regarded by the Samaritans as the tenth command of the Decalogue (after Ex. 20:14 [17] and Deut. 5:18), where a lengthy addition is inserted (based largely on Deut. 27:2, 3, 4–7; and 11:30).

This interpolation supports the Samaritan claim that Gerizim is the "chosen place." Most authorities agree that the Samaritan Pentateuch existed in the third century BCE, based on approximately 2,000 agreements between the Samaritan Pentateuch and the Septuagint (LXX) against the Masoretic Text. All this suggests that the Masoretic Text, Samaritan Pentateuch, and Septuagint were all recensions of earlier editions of the Pentateuch. The chief textual value of the Samaritan Pentateuch is its indirect witness that the Masoretic Text is a superb, disciplined text. In addition, its earliest preserved manuscript (about 100 CE) indicates that the Masoretes preserved a text tradition that is much older and purer than that of the Samaritan Pentateuch.

Another line of evidence for the integrity of the Masoretic Text is found in the comparison of duplicate passages of the Old Testament Masoretic Text itself. Psalm 14, for example, occurs again in Psalm 53, much of Isaiah 36–39 is also found in 2 Kings 18–20, Isaiah 2:2–4 parallels Micah 4:1–3, and large portions of the Chronicles are to be found in Samuel and Kings. An examination of these and other passages shows not only substantial textual agreement but, in some cases, almost a word-for-word identity. As a result, we can conclude that the Old Testament texts have not undergone radical revisions, even if the parallel passages stem from identical sources.

Still another substantial proof for the accuracy of the Masoretic Text comes from archaeology. Robert Dick Wilson and William F. Albright, for example, have made numerous discoveries that confirm the historical accuracy of the biblical documents, even to obsolete names of foreign kings. Wilson's *A Scientific Investigation of the Old Testament* and Albright's *From the Stone Age to Christianity* support this view. Scrolls discovered in the Judean desert, and possessed by the Pharisees and Zealots at Masada, reveal that the books of the Bible used by them can be identified with the current Masoretic Text. Scripture texts used by the followers of Bar Kochba show clear ties with the present-day MT. Remnants of Scripture scrolls used by Bar Kochba's soldiers found at Wadi Murabba'at and items from Nahal Hever show that they also used the same text (with only the slightest differences) which we call the Masoretic Text.[6]

Perhaps the best line of evidence to support the integrity of the Masoretic Text comes from the Greek translation of the Old Testament known as the Septuagint (LXX). This work was performed during the third and second centuries BCE in Alexandria, Egypt. For the most part it was almost

---

6. Menachem Cohen, "The Idea of the Sanctity of the Biblical Text and the Science of Textual Criticism," translated from *HaMikrah V'anachnu*, Uiel Simon, HaMachon L'Yahadut U'Machshava Bat-Z'mananu and Dvir, eds. (Tel Aviv, 1979), with very minor changes. The English version was edited by Isaac B. Gottlieb.

a book-by-book, chapter-by-chapter reproduction of the MT, containing common stylistic and idiomatic differences. Furthermore, the LXX was the Bible of Jesus and the apostles, and most New Testament quotations are taken from it directly. The Septuagint, accepted first by Alexandrian Jews and afterward by all the Greek-speaking countries, helped introduce into Greek the theological terminology of Scripture. Even Palestinian Jews recognized the Septuagint as a legitimate text. The Septuagint remains the official text in the Greek Church and it was the basic text used for early Latin translations of the Bible adopted in the Western church. On the whole, the Septuagint closely parallels the MT and tends to confirm the fidelity of the tenth-century CE Hebrew text.

LINEAGE OF OLD TESTAMENT MANUSCRIPTS

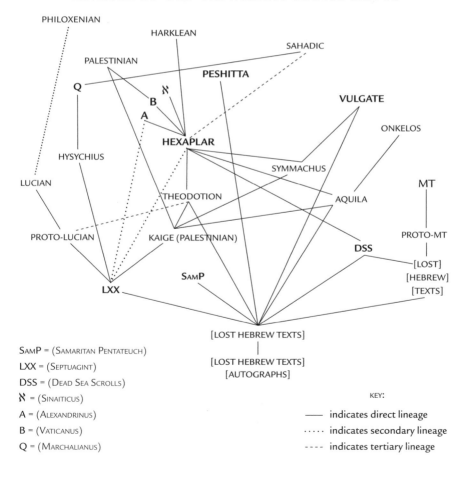

SᴀᴍP = (Sᴀᴍᴀʀɪᴛᴀɴ Pᴇɴᴛᴀᴛᴇᴜᴄʜ)
LXX = (Sᴇᴘᴛᴜᴀɢɪɴᴛ)
DSS = (Dᴇᴀᴅ Sᴇᴀ Sᴄʀᴏʟʟs)
א = (Sɪɴᴀɪᴛɪᴄᴜs)
A = (Aʟᴇxᴀɴᴅʀɪɴᴜs)
B = (Vᴀᴛɪᴄᴀɴᴜs)
Q = (Mᴀʀᴄʜᴀʟɪᴀɴᴜs)

KEY:
—— indicates direct lineage
····· indicates secondary lineage
---- indicates tertiary lineage

Critical corrections were made by Origen, Lucian, and Hesychius before being published in the celebrated Codex Vaticanus (B) and Sinaiticus (א *Aleph*) in the fourth century, and Codex Alexandrinus (A) in the fifth century. Written in Egypt on fine vellum, Codex Marchalianus (Q) is a most valuable sixth-century copy of the Prophets. Its text is a result of the Hesychian recension and its marginal readings contain additions by Origen as well as a great number of variant readings from the Hexaplar text written by an almost contemporary hand. Codex Q is used in discussion about the Tetragrammaton (YHWH, יהוה) in Isaiah 45:18. All the printed editions of the Septuagint are derived from these recensions, with Codex Vaticanus representing the purest textual tradition. The edition princeps from Origen's Hexaplar text was produced in the Complutensian Polyglot (1514–1518). The purer Aldine edition, closer to Vaticanus, was published in Venice (1518). American Charles Thomson published the first English translation of the Septuagint without the Apocrypha (1808), revised and enlarged by C. A. Muses (1954). The second was by Sir Lancelot Charles Lee Brenton, *The Septuagint Version of the Old Testament According to the Vatican Text* (1844); Brenton's *The Septuagint with Apocrypha: Greek and English* (1851) became the long-time standard edition. His Septuagint was revised as *The Apostles' Bible* (2008). A third English translation of the Septuagint was published as *The Apostolic Bible Polyglot* (1996) as "a numerically coded Greek-English Interlinear Bible," utilizing the "Strong numbering system" of James Strong, *The Exhaustive Concordance of the Bible.*[7] A *New English Translation of the Septuagint* (NETS), edited by Albert Pietersma and Benjamin G. Wright, with the subtitle: *and the Other Greek Translations Traditionally Included under That Title* (2007), is a fourth English translation of the Septuagint. The Greek text of NETS frequently departs from Alfred Rahlfs's *Septuaginta* (1935) and is based on the 24 volume Göttengin Septuagint (1931–2006). The NETS aims to translate the text in present-day literary language to communicate to the well-educated constituency familiar with and accustomed to the New Revised Standard Version (NRSV, 1989) upon which it is based.

---

7. Charles Van der Pool, *The Apostolic Bible Polyglot: Η ΠΑΛΑΙΑ ΚΑΙ Η ΚΑΙΝΗ ΔΙΑΘΗΚΗ* (Newport, Oreg.: The Apostolic Press, 1996).

THE DEAD SEA SCROLLS;
DOCUMENTS IN THE JUDEAN DESERT

The major manuscript discovery known as the Dead Sea Scrolls came about in March 1947, when a young Arab boy (Muhammad adh-Dhib) was pursuing a lost goat in the caves seven and one-half miles south of Jericho and a mile west of the Dead Sea. In one of the caves he discovered some jars containing several leather scrolls. Between that time and February 1956, eleven caves containing scrolls and fragments were excavated near Qumran.

In these caves the Essenes, a Jewish religious sect dating from about 300 BCE to 50 CE (including the time of Christ), housed their library. Together with the 1950s scrolls discovered in the Judean desert ruins at Masada, Wadi Murabba'at and Nahal Hever, jointly known as Discoveries in the Judean Desert, they are being published by Oxford University Press in a series entitled Discoveries in the Judean Desert (DJD). Altogether the thousands of manuscript fragments constituted the remains of some six hundred manuscripts, about 60 percent proto-Masoretic, 5 percent pre-Samaritan, 5 percent the Hebrew text underlying the Septuagint, and about 30 percent mixed texts. During the period 100 BCE–100 CE, the Proto-Masoretic Text began to predominate over the others, and became the so-called official text during the period (70–150 CE). Although it was not a pristine text, it did have a very old post-captivity textual tradition.

Of particular interest to us are those manuscripts that bear on the text of the Old Testament. Cave 1 was discovered by the Arab boy, and it contained seven more or less complete scrolls and some fragments, including the earliest known complete book of the Bible (Isaiah A), a manual of discipline, a commentary on Habakkuk, a Genesis Apocryphon, an incomplete text of Isaiah (Isaiah B), the War Scroll, and about thirty thanksgiving hymns (Plates 16–19).

Additional manuscripts were found in Cave 2, although it had been discovered by Bedouins who pilfered it. Fragments of about a hundred manuscripts were found here, but nothing was discovered so spectacular as what was found in other caves. In Cave 3 two halves of a copper scroll were discovered which provided directions to sixty or more sites containing hidden treasures mostly in and around the Jerusalem area.

Cave 4 (Partridge Cave) had also been ransacked by Bedouins before it was excavated in September 1952. Nevertheless, it proved to be the most productive of all caves, for literally thousands of fragments were recovered either by purchase from the Bedouins or as a result of archaeological sifting of the dust on the floor of the cave. The fragment of Samuel found here is thought to be the oldest known piece of biblical Hebrew, dating from the fourth century BCE. Cave 5 revealed some biblical and Apocryphal books in an advanced stage of deterioration. Cave 6 produced mostly papyrus fragments rather than leather. Caves 7–10 provided data of interest to the professional archaeologist, but nothing of relevance to the present study. Cave 11 was the last to be excavated, in early 1956. It produced a well-preserved copy of some of the psalms, including the Apocryphal Psalm 151 which was hitherto known only in Greek texts. In addition, it contained a very fine scroll of a portion of Leviticus and an Aramaic targum (paraphrase) of Job.

Prompted by these original finds, the Bedouins pursued their search and discovered caves to the southwest of Bethlehem. Here at Murabba'at they discovered some self-dated manuscripts and documents from the Second Jewish Revolt (132–135 CE). These manuscripts helped to establish the antiquity of the Dead Sea Scrolls, and they produced another scroll of the Minor Prophets (Joel through Haggai) which closely supports the Masoretic Text. In addition, the oldest known Semitic papyrus, a palimpsest, inscribed the second time in the ancient Hebrew script of the seventh and eighth centuries BCE, was discovered here.

Several lines of evidence were used to date the DSS. First, Carbon 14, 1950 process gave a 168 BCE to 233 CE DATE. Second, more recent (1991–98) scientific dating from accelerator mass spectrometry (AMS) placed the Isaiah scroll at 202 to 93 BCE. Third, paleography (writing form) and orthography (spelling) gave a 168 BCE to 233 CE range. Fourth, by use of pottery and coins, archaeologists provided a 150 BCE to 100 CE range. Finally, the self-dated later Murabba'at discoveries (of 1952) of 132–135 CE reveal an early date for the DSS, as the other evidence indicates.

The nature and number of these Dead Sea discoveries produced the following general conclusions about the integrity of the Masoretic Text. The scrolls give overwhelming confirmation to the fidelity of the Masoretic Text. Millar Burrows, in his work *The Dead Sea Scrolls,* indicates that there is very little alteration in the text in something like a thousand years. R. Laird Harris, in *Inspiration and Canonicity of the Bible,* argues that there is less variation in these two traditions in a thousand years than there is in two of the families of New Testament manuscripts. Gleason Archer advocates the integrity of "our standard Hebrew Bible" (i.e., the Masoretic Text) by stating that it agrees virtually word for word with the Isaiah manuscript from Cave 1 in 95 percent of its contents, with the remaining 5 percent being comprised of obvious slips of the pen and variations in spelling[8] that developed in the interim. The vast majority of these do not affect the meaning of the text. And none of them affect any basic Christian doctrine.

MANUSCRIPTS OF THE NEW TESTAMENT

The integrity of the Old Testament text was established primarily by the fidelity of the transmission process, which was later confirmed by the Dead Sea Scrolls. The fidelity of the New Testament text, however, rests in the multiplicity of the extant manuscripts. Whereas the Old Testament had only a few complete manuscripts, all of which were of good quality, the New Testament has many more copies which are of generally poorer quality. A manuscript is a handwritten literary composition in contrast to a printed copy. As indicated in the previous chapter, the New Testament was written in a formal printed style known as uncials (or majuscules). After the sixth century this style went into decline as it was gradually displaced by minuscule manuscripts. These minuscules gained dominance in the period from the ninth to the fifteenth centuries.

Testimony to the fidelity of the New Testament text comes from three basic sources: Greek manuscripts, ancient translations, and patristic citations. The first of these sources is the most important and can itself be divided into three classes. These classes of manuscripts are commonly termed the papyruses, the uncials, and the minuscules because of their most distinguishing characteristics.

The Papyrus Manuscripts

The manuscripts classified as papyruses date from the second and third centuries, when Christianity was illegal and its Scriptures were transcribed on the cheapest possible materials. There are some seventy-six of these papyrus manuscripts of the New Testament. Their witness to the text is invaluable since they range chronologically from the very threshold of the second

---

8.   Gleason Archer, *A Survey of Old Testament Introduction,* rev.ed. (Chicago: Moody, 1994), 25.

century, a mere generation removed from the autographs, and contain most of the New Testament.

The more important representatives of the papyrus manuscripts are treated here. $\mathfrak{P}^{52}$, the John Rylands Fragment (117–138), is the earliest known and attested fragment of the New Testament. It was written on both sides and contains portions of five verses from the gospel of John (18:31–33, 37–38). $\mathfrak{P}^{45}$,$\mathfrak{P}^{46}$, $\mathfrak{P}^{47}$, the Chester Beatty Papyri (250), consists of three codices containing most of the New Testament. $\mathfrak{P}^{45}$ is comprised of thirty leaves of a papyrus codex containing the Gospels and Acts. $\mathfrak{P}^{46}$ contains most of Paul's epistles, as well as Hebrews, although portions of Romans and 1 Thessalonians, and all of 2 Thessalonians, are missing. $\mathfrak{P}^{47}$ contains portions of Revelation. $\mathfrak{P}^{66}$, $\mathfrak{P}^{72}$, $\mathfrak{P}^{75}$, the Bodmer Papyri ($\mathfrak{P}^{75-225}$), comprise the most important New Testament papyrus discoveries since the Chester Beatty Papyri (Plates 30–32). $\mathfrak{P}^{66}$ dates from 200 and contains portions of the gospel of John. $\mathfrak{P}^{72}$ is the earliest known copy of Jude, 1 Peter, and 2 Peter. Dating from the early third century, it contains several Apocryphal and canonical books. $\mathfrak{P}^{75}$ contains Luke and John in clear and carefully printed uncials dated between $\mathfrak{P}^{75}$ and $\mathfrak{P}225$. Consequently, it is the earliest known copy of Luke.

The Uncial Manuscripts

As a whole, the most important manuscripts of the New Testament are generally considered to be the great uncials written on vellum and parchment during the fourth to ninth centuries. There are about 310 of these uncial manuscripts, the most important are Codex Siniaticus ($\aleph$, *Aleph*, 01, S), Alexandrinus (A, 02), Vaticanus (B, 03), Ephraemi Rescriptus (C, 04), and Bezae (D, 05). Only Bezae (D) was available to the translators of the King James Bible, and it was used only slightly by them.[9] This fact alone was sufficient to call for a new translation of the Bible after these great uncials were discovered.

Codex Vaticanus (B, 03) is perhaps the oldest uncial on either parchment or vellum (325–350 CE) and one of the most important witnesses to the text of the New Testament (Plates 24–25). It was unknown to biblical scholars until after 1475, when it was catalogued in the Vatican Library. It was published

---

9. See "Major Uncials" discussion by Carol F. Ellertson, "New Testament Manuscripts," in Kent P. Jackson and Frank F. Judd Jr., eds., *How the New Testament Came to Be* (Provo, Utah: Religious Studies Center, Brigham Young Univ., 2006), 97–99. Also see Metzger, *The New Testament*, 4th ed., 310–12, and Greenlee, *Introduction to New Testament Criticism*, 85–86.

in a complete photographic facsimile for the first time in 1889–1890. In 1904–1907 another facsimile edition of the New Testament was published making the Codex widely available. The Patriarchal Text (PT) was published in 1904. Based primarily on Codex Vaticanus, it is the official Greek text of the Greek Eastern/Orthodox Church.[10] It contains most of the Old Testament (LXX), the New Testament in Greek, and the Apocrypha with some omissions. Also missing from this codex is Genesis 1:1–46:28; 2 Kings 2:5–7, 10–13; Psalms 106:27–138:18; as well as Hebrews 9:14 to the end of the New Testament. Mark 16:9–20 and John 7:58–8:11 were purposely omitted from the text which was written in small and delicate uncials on fine vellum. Previously published editions of Codex Vaticanus (B, 03) (1209) were eclipsed by the very fine reproduction of Bibliorum Sacrorum Graecorum Codex Vaticanus B (1999) which stimulated renewed interest among biblical scholars.[11]

Codex Sinaiticus (ℵ, Aleph, 01, S) is the fourth-century Greek manuscript generally considered to be the most important witness to the text because of its antiquity, accuracy, and lack of omissions. The story of its discovery is one of the most fascinating and romantic in the history of the biblical text. German Count Tischendorf found the manuscript in the monastery of St. Catherine at Mount Sinai (Plates 22–23). In 1844 he discovered forty-three leaves of vellum, containing portions of the Septuagint (1 Chronicles, Jeremiah, Nehemiah, and Esther) in a basket of scraps which were used by the monks to light their fires. He secured the manuscript and took it to Leipzig, Germany, where it remains as the Codex Frederico-Augustanus. On a second visit in 1853, Tischendorf found nothing new, but in 1859 he made a third visit, under the direction of Czar Alexander II.

Just before he was to depart for home, the monastery steward showed

---

10. It was published as *H KAINH DIQHKAH EGKRISKEI THS MEGALHS TOU CRISTOU EKKLHSIAS* (*EN KONSTANTINOUPOLKI: EK TOU PATRIARCIKOU TUPOGRAFKIOU*, 1904). This edition includes versification in the margins and critical notes at the bottom of each page. The text is being republished with the Old Testament and the New Testament (with or without versification) and as of June 30, 2011, without critical notes, although the New Testament does incorporate judicious input from the Nestle-Aland Critical Text of UBS4/NA27.

11. *Biblioteca Apostolica Vaticana, Bibliorum sacrorum Graecorum Codex Vaticanis B, or Bibliothecae apostolicae Vaticanae Codex Vaticanus Graecus 1209* (Roma: Istituto Poligrafico e Zecca della Stato [the Italian State Printing House and Mint], 1999). For the first time ever, the Biblioteca Apostolica Vaticana published a limited edition of a very fine reprint in full color, an exact scale facsimile (with distinctive individual shape of each page including holes in the vellum) of Codex Vaticanus Graece 1209 along with an additional 74-page *Prolegomena* volume with gold and silver impressions.

to him an almost complete copy of the Scriptures and some other books. These were subsequently acquired for the Czar as a "conditional gift." Now known as *Codex Sinaiticus* (ℵ, *Aleph*), this manuscript contains more than half the Old Testament (LXX) and all the New, with the exception of Mark 16:9–20, John 7:58–8:11 and a few others, all the Old Testament Apocrypha, the Epistle of Barnabas, and the Shepherd of Hermas. The material is good vellum, made from antelope skins. The manuscript underwent several scribal "corrections," known by the seglum ℵ (*Aleph*). At Caesarea in the sixth or seventh century a group of scribes introduced a large number of alterations known as N^{ca} or N^{cb}.

In 1933 the British government purchased the Codex Sinaiticus for £100,000. H. J. M. Milne and T. C. Skeat published *Scribes and Correctors of Codex Sinaiticus* (1938) which gave new insights into the questions of the original contents of the MS, the scribes, the supplementary apparatus, the correctors, orthography, date, provenance, and bindings of the MS with numerous full-page plates of figures showing types of writing, corrections, numberings, titles, and subscriptions. *Scribes* illustrated fully the points discussed so the reader might follow the descriptions and arguments without turning to the often inaccessible facsimile edition by Kirsopp Lake of the *Codex Sinaiticus Petropolitanus: The New Testament* (1911). Lake also published the *Codex Sinaiticvs Petropolitanvs et Friderico–Avgvstanvs Lipsiensis*. The Old Testament preserved in the public library of Petrograd, in the library of the Society of ancient literature in Petrograd, and in the library of the University of Leipzig, was now reproduced in facsimile from photographs of the Old Testament (1922). A facsimile edition of Codex Sinaiticus, including a 31-page "Reference Guide" with a concordance (2010), was published based on the digital photographs taken as part of the Codex Sinaiticus Project at the British Library in London.[12]

Codex Alexandrinus (A, 02) is a well-preserved fifth-century manuscript that ranks immediately following B and ℵ (*Aleph*) as representative of the New Testament text (Plates 26–27). Although some have dated this codex in the late fourth century, it was probably the result of scribal work at Alexandria, Egypt, about 450. In 1078 this codex was presented to the Patriarch of Alexandria, for which it received its designation. In 1621 it was taken to

---

12. The facsimile was made possible through an agreement among the British Library Board, the National Library of Russia, the Library of the Monastery of Saint Catherine at Mount Sinai, and the University Library at Leipzig.

Constantinople before being presented to Sir Thomas Roe, English ambassador to Turkey, in 1624, for presentation to King James I. He died before the manuscript reached England, and it was presented to Charles I in 1627. This made it unavailable for use by the translators of the King James Bible in 1611, although the manuscript was known to be in existence at that time. In 1757, George II presented the codex to the National Library of the British Museum. It contains the entire Old Testament, except for several mutilated portions (Gen. 14:14–17; 15:1–5, 16–19; 16:6–9; 1 Kingdoms [1 Samuel] 12:18–14:9; Pss. 49:19–79:100; and most of the New Testament, missing only Matthew 1:1–25:6; John 6:50–8:52; and 2 Corinthians 4:13–12:6. The codex does contain 1 and 2 Clement and the Psalms of Solomon, with some missing parts. The large square uncial letters are written on very thin vellum and are divided into sections marked by large letters.

Ephraemi Rescriptus Codex (C, 04) probably originated in Alexandria, Egypt, around 345. It was brought to Italy in about 1500 by John Lascaris and later sold to Pietro Strozzi. Catherine de Medici, an Italian who was the wife and mother of French kings, acquired it in 1533. Following her death, the manuscript was placed in the National Library at Paris, where it remains today. Most of the Old Testament is missing from this codex, except portions of Job, Proverbs, Ecclesiastes, Song of Solomon, and two Apocryphal books—the Wisdom of Solomon and Ecclesiasticus. The New Testament lacks 2 Thessalonians, 2 John, and parts of other books. The manuscript is a *palimpsest* (rubbed out, erased) *rescriptus* (rewritten) that originally contained the Old and New Testaments. These texts were erased to make space for sermons written by Ephraem, a fourth-century Syrian father. By chemical reactivation, Count Tischendorf was able to decipher the almost invisible writing on the parchment leaves of the codex. Located in the National Library at Paris, this manuscript shows evidence of two sets of corrections: the first, C^2 or C^b, was done in sixth-century Palestine and the second, C^3 or C^c, was added in ninth-century Constantinople.

Codex Bezae (D, 05), also known as Codex Cantabrigiensis, was transcribed in 450 or 550. It is the oldest known bilingual manuscript of the New Testament, written in Greek and Latin in the general region of southern Gaul (France) or northern Italy. This was discovered in 1562 by Théodore de Bèze (Lat., Beza), the French theologian, at St. Irenaeus Monastery in Lyons, France. In 1581 Bèze gave it to Cambridge University. This codex

(Plate 28) contains the four gospels, Acts, and 3 John 11–15, with variations from other manuscripts indicated. It has many omissions in its text, and only the Latin text of 3 John 11–15 remains.

This manuscript has a remarkable number of variations and was so far removed from the accepted standard Byzantine text that it has been corrected by scribes many times over the centuries. For example, it is the only known Greek text to substitute Luke's version of Jesus' genealogy with a form of Matthew's genealogy in reverse order (beginning with "Joseph, husband of Mary," instead of Abraham).[13]

Codex Claromontanus (D² or D^{p2}, 06) is a sixth-century complement of Codex D dated 550. It contains much of the New Testament which is missing in D. D² seems to have originated in Italy or Sardinia and receives its name from a monastery at Clermont, France, where it was found by Beza. Following Beza's death, the codex was owned by several private individuals before it was purchased by King Louis XIV for the National Library in 1656. It was fully edited by Count Tischendorf in 1852. The codex contains all of Paul's epistles and Hebrews, although Romans 1:1–7, 27–30, and 1 Corinthians 14:13–22 are missing in Greek, and 1 Corinthians 14:8–18 and Hebrews 13:21–23 are missing in Latin. This bilingual manuscript was artistically written on thin, high quality vellum. The Greek is good, but the Latin grammar is inferior in places.

Codex Washingtonianus I (W, 032) dates from the fourth or early fifth century. It was purchased by Charles F. Freer of Detroit in 1906 from a dealer in Cairo, Egypt. Between 1910 and 1918 it was edited by Professor H. A. Sanders of the University of Michigan, and it is currently located in the Smithsonian Institution, Washington, D.C. The manuscript contains the four gospels, portions of Paul's epistles (except Romans), Hebrews, Deuteronomy, Joshua, and Psalms. Its arrangement of the Gospels is Matthew, John, Luke, and Mark. Mark contains the long ending (Mark 16:9–20); however, an additional insertion is added following verse 14. This thick vellum codex is comprised of a curiously mixed text type.

The remaining uncial manuscripts add supportive evidence to the various textual traditions of those already presented. For all practical purposes, the major vellum and parchment manuscripts have been indicated and our attention may now turn to the minuscules.

---

13. Ellertson, *New Testament Manuscripts,* 98. Also see Metzger, *The New Testament,* 70–73.

The Minuscule Manuscripts

The dates of the minuscule manuscripts (ninth through fifteenth centuries) indicate that they are generally of inferior quality when compared to either the papyrus or uncial manuscripts (eg., Plate 28). Their main importance rests on the accent they place on their textual families rather than their quantity. Currently, the New Testament Textual Research (INTF) in Münster, Westphalia, Germany, has catalogued 5,339 manuscripts: 2,907 minuscule codices and 2,432 lectionaries (early church-service books containing the text of selections of the Scriptures appointed to be read on the several days of the ecclesiastical and the civil calendar (see Plates 35–36). Some of the more important minuscule manuscripts are identified below.

Minuscules in the Alexandrian family are represented by manuscript 33, the "queen of the cursives," which dates from the ninth or possibly the tenth century. It contains the entire New Testament except Revelation and is in the possession of the Bibliothèque Nationale in Paris.

The Caesarean text type has survived in family 1 of the minuscules. This family contains manuscripts 1, 118, 131, and 209; and they all date from the twelfth to the fourteenth centuries. The Italian subfamily of the Caesarean text type is represented by about a dozen manuscripts known as family 13. These manuscripts were copied between the eleventh and fifteenth centuries and include manuscripts 13, 69, 124, 230, 346, 543, 788, 826, 828, 983, 1689, and 1709. Some of these manuscripts were formerly thought to be of the Syrian text type.

Many of the remaining minuscule manuscripts may be placed into one or another of the various text type families, but they stand on their own merits rather than belonging to one of the families of manuscripts mentioned above. In all, however, they were copied from earlier uncial or minuscule manuscripts and add little new evidence to the text of the New Testament. They do provide a continual line of transmission of the biblical text, whereas the manuscripts of other classical works have breaks of nine hundred to a thousand years between the autographs and their manuscript copies, as may be seen in the examples of Caesar's *Gallic Wars* and the *Works* of Tacitus. In view of the ongoing and enormous investment in bringing Bible manuscripts into the digital age, prospects for additional interest and development for textual studies has a bright future.

13

ADDITIONAL WITNESSES
to the BIBLE TEXT

THE TRANSMISSION OF THE BIBLICAL TEXT can be traced rather clearly from the late second and early third centuries to modern times by means of the great manuscripts. The linking of these manuscripts to the first century, however, rests on a few papyrus fragments and some quotations from the apostolic fathers. In addition to these lines of evidence, there are materials from archaeological discoveries such as the nonbiblical papyruses, biblical and related papyruses, ostraca, and inscriptions.

THE NONBIBLICAL PAPYRUSES

The epochal discovery of papyruses, ostraca, and inscriptions transformed some basic notions about the very nature of the New Testament itself. Prior to that, the New Testament had been regarded as a mysteriously written book communicated to man in a supposedly Holy Ghost language. Three works in the early twentieth century would change the thinking: Moulton and Milligan's *Vocabulary of the Greek New Testament, Illustrated from the Papyri and Other Non-Literary Sources* (1914); A. T. Robertson's *A Grammar of the Greek New Testament in Light of Historical Research* (1914); and Adolf Deissman's *Light from the Ancient East* (trans. 1923). Their works combined with the efforts of others proved indisputably that the New Testament was a lucid example of first-century colloquial speech—koine Greek. They discovered that the New Testament was not written in a "perfect language," as some of

212 FROM GOD TO US

the Latin Fathers had assumed, but that in phonology, vocabulary, syntax, and style, the New Testament is really a record of late colloquial Greek.

In addition, they discovered among the nonbiblical papyruses that background which formed the cultural and religious backdrop of the first century. By looking into the cultural similarities between these papyruses and the New Testament, they saw that there were competing cults which were also missionary religions. The ancient world became an open book that reflected the same patterns of life and interests as reflected in the Bible. The phraseology of the New Testament was like that of the broader setting; in fact, the language of popular religion, law, and emperor worship were similar to the New Testament.

That a common language was used in the New Testament and its setting does not imply that the two had the same meanings in their expressions. In other words, the same words used by the different religions could, at best, be expected to have parallel but not identical meanings with Christianity.

There are some unavoidable conclusions, however, that the nonbiblical papyruses indicate. Among these are the facts that the New Testament was not written in a so-called Holy Ghost language. Instead, it was written in the common (*koine*) trade language of the Roman world, the language of the masses and the marketplace. In addition, the "Pauline" and other styles of Greek syntax and vocabulary were all commonly used throughout the first century. These facts imply that if the Greek of the New Testament was the common language of the first century, then the New Testament must have been written in the first century.

PAPYRUSES, OSTRACA, INSCRIPTIONS, LECTIONARIES

Biblical Papyruses

In addition to the materials discussed in chapter 12, a few supplementary papyruses add further light on the New Testament text. A group of noncanonical Logia of Jesus (Sayings of Jesus) were discovered among the papyruses. A comparison of their contents with the canonical papyrus texts indicates their apocryphal tone. There can be little doubt that these so-called sayings have local and possibly heretical appeal, but they did give rise to collections of "sayings" which can be used to reflect the popular religious experience of the first and second centuries.

Ostraca

Ostraca are broken pieces of pottery that were frequently used as a writing material by the lower classes in antiquity. According to Metzger and Ehrman (2005), "Short portions of six New Testament books have been preserved on ostraca, or broken pieces of pottery used by the poorest people as writing material. Twenty-five of these have been catalogued." One example of the use of this means of transmitting the Bible text is to be found in a seventh-century copy of the Gospels recorded on twenty pieces of ostraca. This represents what may be called a "poor man's Bible." Long overlooked by scholars, these pieces of potsherds have cast additional light on the biblical text. Allen P. Wikgren has listed some 1,624 specimens of these humble records of history in his work entitled *Greek Ostraca*.

Inscriptions

The wide distribution and variety of ancient inscriptions testify to the importance of the biblical text as well as to its very existence. There is an abundance of engravings on walls, pillars, coins, monuments, and other items that have preserved a witness to the New Testament text. This witness, however, is merely supportive and is not of importance in establishing the text of the New Testament.

Lectionaries

Still another witness to the text of the New Testament that has been generally undervalued is the numerous lectionaries (church-service books) containing selected readings from the Bible itself (Plate 35). These lectionaries served as manuals and were used in religious services throughout the calendar year. Most of the lectionaries probably originated between the seventh and the twelfth centuries, although a dozen leaves and fragments have survived dated between the fourth and sixth. Only five or six lectionaries have survived which were copied onto papyrus, and they utilized uncial script even after it had been superseded by the minuscule type script.

Although Caspar René Gregory listed about 1,545 Greek lectionaries in his *Canon and Text of the New Testament* (1912), approximately 2,200 have been utilized in the critical apparatus of the United Bible Societies' edition of *The Greek New Testament* (UBS2, 1966). Based on the Greek Lectionary Project at the University of Chicago, fifty-two additional lectionaries were

added to NA27 and UBS3 (1975). Barbara Aland and Johannes Karavidopoulos replaced Matthew Black and Allen Wikgren on the editorial committee of NA27 and UBS4 (1993). A thorough review and new selection of
manuscripts from a completely new collation of manuscripts was made
under the direction of Johannes Karavidopoulos in the Lectionary Research
Center of the University of Thessaloniki.

The great majority of lectionaries consist of readings taken from the
Gospels. The remainder contain portions of Acts, either with or without
the epistles. Although they were often elaborately adorned, and sometimes
even included musical notations, it must be admitted that the lectionaries
are only of secondary value at best in establishing the New Testament text.
They do, however, play an important role in the understanding of specific
passages of Scripture, such as John 7:53–8:11 and Mark 16:9–20.

PATRISTIC REFERENCES TO THE BIBLE TEXT

In addition to the manuscripts and the miscellaneous items witness-
ing to the New Testament text, the student of textual criticism has available
the patristic citations of the Scriptures to aid in his quest for the true text.
The Fathers who made these references and citations lived during the early
centuries of the church. Their closeness to the apostles and their use of the
text provide information about the precise area, date, and type of text used
throughout the early church.

When the Fathers Lived

Since the Old Testament canon was closed and recognized prior to the time
of Christ, the attitude of the early church fathers (first to the fourth centuries) may be summarized in the words of B. F. Westcott:

> They continued to look upon the Old Testament as a full and lasting
> record of the revelation of God. In one remarkable particular they carried
> this belief yet further than it had been carried before. With them the indi-
> viduality of the several writers falls into the background. They practically
> regarded the whole Book as one Divine utterance.[1]

---

1.   Brooke Foss Westcott, *The Bible in the Church*, 2nd ed. (New York: MacMillan, 1887), 83–84.

When considering their use of the New Testament, the picture is more diverse and the role of the Fathers is much more significant, since the New Testament canon was not finally and completely recognized until the fourth century. As a result of this situation, it will be helpful to trace again briefly the history of the recognition of the canon in order to bring the position of the Fathers into sharper focus.

The last half of the first century saw the process of selecting, sorting (Luke 1:1–4; 1 Thess. 2:13), reading (1 Thess. 5:27), circulating (Col. 4:16), collecting (2 Pet. 3:15–16), and quoting (1 Tim. 5:18) apostolic literature. All twenty-seven books of the New Testament were written and copied and began to be distributed among the churches before the close of the first century. In the first half of the second century the apostolic writings became more generally known and more widely circulated. By this time almost every book of the New Testament was explicitly cited as Scripture. The writings of the Fathers were also widely read and circulated in the churches, and they quoted the New Testament as authoritative in their struggles against heretical groups, dialogues with unbelievers, and exhortations against vice. They tell much about the history, doctrine, and practices of the early church.

In the last half of the second century, the New Testament books were widely recognized as Scripture, as were those of the Old Testament. This was a period of missionary activity, and the Scriptures were translated into other languages as the church spread beyond the confines of the Roman Empire. It was also during these years that commentaries began to appear, such as Papias's *Exposition of the Lord's Oracles,* Heracleon's *Commentary on the Gospels,* and Melito's *Commentary on the Apocalypse.* The *Diatessaron* of Tatian also came into being. The writings of the Fathers were profuse with citations from the New Testament as authoritative Scriptures, and all but five were listed as such in the Muratorian Fragment (ca. 170).

During the third century the New Testament books were collected into a single catalog of "recognized books" and separated from other types of Christian literature. It was during this century that a great surge of intellectual activity within the church occurred, as Origen's *Hexapla* (six-column Bible) and other works attest. No longer were there merely two classes of Christian literature (Scripture and writing of the Fathers), as a body of apocryphal and pseudepigraphal literature emerged. The rise of these diverse kinds of literature gave impetus to the sorting and sifting tests for all religious literature in the church. These tests and others led ultimately to the recognition of the canonical New Testament and the erasure of doubts about the disputed books belonging to it.

By the time the fourth century dawned, the New Testament canon was fully settled and acknowledged. The writings of the Fathers indicate the general agreement of all Christians about the New Testament canon as indicated in the discussion in chapters 9 and 10.

What the Fathers Did

While the testimony of the Fathers is quite early, actually older than the best codices, it is not always reliable. A Father may have quoted a variant reading from an existing manuscript which would perpetuate the error. In addition, the writing of a particular Father might itself have been subject to alteration or corruption during its transmission, just as the Greek text of the New Testament was. A third factor involved is the method itself of the particular Father's quotation. It may have been verbatim, a loose citation, a paraphrase, or perhaps even a mere allusion. Even if the quote were verbatim, it would be important to discern whether it was cited from memory or read from a written text. Even if the text were being read, it would be significant to determine whether he was a member of some heretical group. If a Father cited a given passage more than once, it would be necessary to compare those examples to determine whether they are identical or divergent. Finally, if an amanuensis was employed, it could be that he would take notes and search for the particular passage at a later time.

All of these difficulties notwithstanding, the evidence from the patristic writers is of such great importance that the labor of refining the ore from the dross is well worth the effort. Their importance may be summarized in a fourfold manner: they show the history of the text of the New Testament, render the best evidence as to the canon of the New Testament, provide a means of dating the manuscripts of the New Testament, and assist in determining just when translations, versions, and revisions of the New Testament text occur.

Who the Principal Fathers Were

During the period before the Council of Nicea (325) there were three broad classes of patristic writers: the apostolic fathers (70–150), the Ante-Nicene fathers (150–300), and the Nicene and Post-Nicene fathers (300–430). Their writings give overwhelming support to the existence of the New Testament canon in two ways. First, they cited as authoritative every book of the New Testament. Second, they quoted with authority virtually every verse of the twenty-seven books of the New Testament. The print edition of the Ante-Nicene, Nicene, and Post-Nicene fathers is complemented by the Patristic texts published in the "Monachos.net" library of the Orthodox Church to make the patristic corpus more readily available in a variety of means online. They also maintain an extensive listing of patristic texts available elsewhere to provide patristic writings on the Internet. According to Metzger and Ehrman (2005), "The importance of patristic quotations lies in the circumstance that they serve to localize and date readings and types of text in Greek manuscripts and versions."

Citation of New Testament Books by Church Fathers

The chart "New Testament Books Cited by the Early Church Fathers" (see chap. 9) should be reviewed at this point. By the end of the first century, some fourteen books of the New Testament were cited. By 110 CE there were nineteen books recognized by citation. And within another forty years (150 CE) some twenty-four New Testament books were acknowledged. Before the century ended, which is about one hundred years after the New Testament was written, twenty-six books had been cited. Only 3 John, perhaps because of its lack in size and significance, remained without corroboration. But within about a generation Origen confirmed the existence of 3 John, as did the Old Latin version and possibly the Muratorian canon (see chap. 9). Most of the twenty-seven books are acknowledged many times by several Fathers within the first century after the books were written.

Quotations of New Testament Verses by Church Fathers

Not only did the early Fathers cite all twenty-seven books of the New Testament, they also quoted virtually all of the verses in all of these twenty-seven books. Five Fathers alone from Irenaeus to Eusebius possess almost 36,000 quotations from the New Testament (see first chart in chap. 9).[2] We know

---

2. Norman L. Geisler and William E. Nix, *A General Introduction to the Bible*, rev. ed. (Chicago: Moody, 1986), 431.

of no other book from the ancient world that exists largely in toto by way of thousands of individual and selected quotations of it. It is an amazing fact that the New Testament could be reconstructed simply from quotations made within two hundred years of its composition. The evidence from the church fathers has been treated differently since the NA26 and UBS3 (1975), which took their citations "almost wholly from printed editions of the Greek New Testament" without having "yet been checked." In UBS4 (1993), "the whole field of NT citations in the church fathers has been thoroughly reviewed," resulting in the establishment of two criteria for inclusion: the citation must be capable of verification (i.e., the manuscript must be identifiable) and the citation must relate clearly to a specific passage in the NT. "Patristic paraphrases, variations, and allusions have no place in this edition."[3]

WITNESS FROM EARLY APOCRYPHAL LITERATURE

Despite its heretical nature and religious fancy, the apocryphal literature from the second and third centuries CE provides a corroborative witness to the existence of the books of the New Testament canon. This it does in several ways. First, the names of the books with their alleged apostolic authors are a clear imitation of the real books of the apostles in the New Testament (see chap. 10). Second, there is often both literary and doctrinal dependence on the canonical books reflected in these false writings. Third, their style and literary type is imitative of the first century books. Fourth, some books (for example, the Epistle of the Laodiceans, supposedly fourth century) are similar in content to biblical books (specifically, Ephesians and Colossians). Fifth, some of the third-century Gnostic books from Nag Hammadi, Egypt, (discovered 1946) cite several New Testament books.[4] The Gospel of Truth cites most of the New Testament, including Hebrews and Revelation. The Epistle of Reginus cites 1 and 2 Corinthians, Romans, Ephesians, Philippians,

---

3. See "Introduction," par. 6, "The Evidence from Church Fathers," UBS4 (1993), 29–37.

4. These texts and their interaction with early Christianity may be studied in a collection of essays Charles W. Hedrick and Robert Hodgson, Jr., eds., *Nag Hammadi, Gnosticism, and Early Christianity* (1985). The books themselves are available in James M. Robinson, gen. ed., *The Nag Hammadi Library*, third completely revised edition (1988), and Marvin Meyer, *The Nag Hammadi Scriptures: The International Edition* (2007). Photographic reproductions of papyrus pages and leather covers were published by James M. Robinson ed., *The Facsimile Edition of the Nag Hammadi Codices* (Leiden, Netherlands: Brill, 1972–1984).

Colossians, and the Transfiguration narrative from the Gospels, and uses Johannine language in places.

SUMMARY AND CONCLUSION

In addition to the three thousand Greek manuscripts, some two thousand lectionary manuscripts support the text of the New Testament. Besides the nonbiblical literary support for the New Testament from the papyruses, there are numerous ostraca and inscriptions with biblical quotations. And from the early church fathers' quotations alone, much of the entire New Testament is preserved. In addition to all these witnesses, there are from the second and third centuries numbers of allusions and citations in apocryphal books that give direct testimony to the existence of most of the twenty-seven books of the New Testament. In totality, this is a highly significant corroborative witness to the biblical text.

14

The Development *of* Textual Criticism

Once all the manuscripts and other evidence bearing witness to the text of the Scriptures have been gathered, the student of textual criticism becomes the heir to a great tradition. He has at his disposal much of the material used to determine the true reading of the biblical text. This chapter is concerned with the historical development of the science of textual criticism.

Higher and Lower Criticism Distinguished

Much confusion and controversy has arisen over the matter of "higher" (historical) and "lower" (textual) criticism of the Bible. Some of this controversy has resulted from a misunderstanding of the term *criticism* as it is applied to the Scriptures. In its grammatical sense the term refers merely to the exercise of judgment. When applied to the Bible it is used in the sense of exercising judgment about the Bible itself. But there are two basic types of criticism, and two basic attitudes toward each type. The titles ascribed to these two types of criticism have nothing at all to do with their importance, as the following discussion will illustrate.

Higher (Historical) Criticism

When scholarly judgment is applied to the *genuineness* of the biblical text, it is classified as higher or historical criticism. The subject matter of this type of scholarly judgment concerns such matters as the date of the text, its literary style and structure, its historicity, and its authorship. As a result, higher criticism is not actually an integral part of a general introduction to the Bible. Instead, higher criticism is the very essence of special introduction. The result of higher critical study by the heirs to the destructive theology of the late eighteenth century has been a kind of destructive criticism.

The Old Testament. The late date ascribed to Old Testament documents led some scholars to attribute its supernatural elements to legend or myth. This resulted in the denial of the historicity and genuineness of much of the Old Testament by skeptical scholars. In an attempt at mediation between traditionalism and skepticism, Julius Wellhausen and his followers developed the documentary theory, which proposed to date the Old Testament books in a less supernaturalistic manner. As a result they developed the JEDP Theory of the Old Testament.

This theory was based largely on the argument that Israel had no writing prior to the monarchy, and that an Elohist (E) Code and a Yahwist or Jehovahist (J) Code were based on two oral traditions about God ("E" using the name *Elohim* and "J" using *Jehovah* [Yahweh]). To these were added the Deuteronomic (D) Code (documents ascribed to the time of Josiah) and the so-called Priestly (P) documents associated with postexilic Judaism. These views were not palatable to orthodox scholars and a wave of opposition arose. This opposition emerged only after a considerable period of time, and the scholarly world largely followed the theory of Wellhausen, W. Robertson Smith, and Samuel R. Driver. When opposition finally raised its voice against this "destructive criticism," it was generally written off as an insignificant minority and ignored. Among the opposition were such proponents of "constructive criticism" as William Henry Green, A. H. Sayce, Franz Delitzsch, James Orr, Wilhelm Moller, Eduard Naville, and Robert Dick Wilson and others (see discussion in chap. 7).

The New Testament. Application of similar principles to the New Testament writings appeared in the Tubingen school of theology following the lead of Heinrich Paulus, Wilhelm De Wette, and others. They developed principles to challenge the authorship, structure, style, and date of the New Testament books. The destructive criticism of modernism led to the form criticism in the Gospels and to a denial of Paul's authorship of most of the Pauline epistles. It came to recognize as *genuinely* Pauline only the "Big Four" (Romans, Galatians, 1 and 2 Corinthians).

Toward the end of the nineteenth century, capable orthodox scholars began to challenge the destructive criticism of the higher critical school. Among these orthodox scholars were George Salmon, Theodor von Zahn, and R. H. Lightfoot. Their work in higher criticism must surely be regarded as constructive criticism. Much of the recent work done in the field of higher criticism has revealed itself as rationalistic in theology, although it makes claim to be upholding orthodox Christian doctrine. This recent rationalism manifests itself most openly when it considers such matters as miracles, the virgin birth of Jesus, and His bodily resurrection.

Lower (Textual) Criticism

When scholarly judgment is applied to the *authenticity* of the biblical text, it is classified as lower or textual criticism. Lower criticism is applied to the form or text of the Bible in an attempt to restore the original text. It should not be confused with higher criticism, since the textual (lower) critic studies the form of the words of a document rather than its value as a document. Many examples of lower criticism may be seen in the history of the transmission of the Bible text. Some of these examples were done by staunch supporters of orthodox Christianity, while others were done by its sharpest opponents. Those who are interested in obtaining the original reading of the text by application of certain criteria or standards of quality are textual critics. In general, their work is constructive and their basic attitude positive. Some of these individuals follow the example of B. F. Westcott, Sir Frederic G. Kenyon, Bruce M. Metzger, and others. Those who use these criteria to undermine the text are fault-finders and their work is basically negative and destructive.

Since many adherents of higher criticism have also spent considerable time and energy in the study of textual criticism, there has been a tendency to classify all textual critics as "modernists," destructive critics, or higher critics. In so doing, some Christians have virtually "thrown the baby out with the bathwater." To avoid textual criticism merely because certain higher critics have used its method in their work is hardly a justifiable position to maintain. The issue of importance is not whether criticism is higher, but whether it is sound. That is a matter of evidence and argument, not one of a priori assumptions.

HISTORICAL DEVELOPMENT OF TEXTUAL CRITICISM

The history of the text of the Bible in the church may be divided into several basic periods, especially with reference to the New Testament: (1) the period of reduplication (to 325), (2) the period of standardization of the text (325–1500), (3) the period of crystallization (1500–1648), and (4) the period of criticism and revision (1648–present). During the period of criticism and revision, a struggle has been waged between the proponents of the "received text" and those advocating the "critical text." In this struggle the critical text has come into the position of dominance. Although not many modern scholars seriously defend the superiority of the received text, it should be noted that there is no substantial difference between it and the critical text. What differences there are between these two textual traditions are merely technical rather than doctrinal, for the variants are doctrinally inconsequential.[1] Nevertheless, the "critical" readings are often helpful in interpreting the Bible, and for all practical purposes both text traditions convey the *content* of the autographs even though they are separately garnished with their own minor scribal and technical differences.

The Period of Reduplication (to 325)

From as early as the third century BCE scholars in Alexandria attempted to restore the texts of the Greek poets and writers of prose. It was at this center that the LXX version of the Old Testament was produced about 280–150 BCE. Alexandria was also a center of Christianity during the early centuries of the church, a position it retained until the rise of Islam in the seventh century. It is understandable that this city would be a center of activity in attempts at restoring the Bible text prior to 325. Basically, however, there was no real textual criticism of New Testament books during these centuries. Instead,

---

1. While making some good points on particular passages, Wilbur Pickering's challenge to this conclusion fails (in "What Difference Does It Make?" in a revision of 'Appendix G' ['H' in the Online version]) in his book *The Identity of the New Testament Text II* 3rd ed. (Eugene, Oreg.: Wipf and Stock Publishers, 2003). There are several reasons for this: (1) Even he admits that "it is usually assumed that no cardinal Christian doctrine is at risk" (p. 1); (2) He cannot point to any major doctrine that is overthrown as a result of rejecting the Majority Text (MT); (3) His attempt to show a logical connection between rejecting the MT and undermining the doctrine of inerrancy fails logically by overdrawing his premise. At best, he only shows that sometimes one must accept the MT reading to preserve consistence, and (4), most inerrantist scholars do not accept the MT and yet they work out the alleged inconsistencies without accepting the MT in toto.

it was a period of reduplication of manuscripts rather than one of textual evaluation. In contrast to Alexandria, however, diligent textual work was performed on the Old Testament by rabbinical scholars in Palestine 70–100 CE.

Copies of the autographs (to 150). During the second half of the first century the New Testament books were written under the direction of the Holy Spirit and were inerrant. Undoubtedly written on papyrus, these autograph copies have all subsequently been lost. Before they perished, however, they were providentially copied and circulated. The Hebrew autographs or other paleo-Hebrew copies of the Torah that were made following God's directive (Deut. 17:18–20) and discovered in the temple by Hilkiah the priest under King Josiah (2 Kings 22:8–13; 2 Chron. 34:14–21) were lost, as were the copies recorded during the exilic period and the Hebrew prophecies of the postexilic period (The Twelve). Palestinian Jews recognized these paleo-Hebrew and proto-Masoretic copies as early as 95 CE. These writings were supplemented during the Maccabean period by the so-called deuterocanonical or Apocryphal books. They were also written on papyrus rolls, and later recopied in papyrus codices; parchment and vellum were employed later. Very few, if any, of these early copies are extant today.

While there were many early copies of the autographs, not all of them were of the same quality, for as soon as copies began to appear errors and misprints crept into the text. The quality of a copy depended upon the capabilities of the particular scribe. Highly accurate copies were quite expensive, for they were the work of professional scribes. Less capable scribes made poorer copies, although their very cost made them more widely distributed. Still other copies were of quite poor quality since they were done by nonprofessionals for use by individuals or groups.

Copies of the copies (150–325). As the apostolic period drew to a close, persecution became more widespread against the Christian church. The sporadic persecutions culminated in two imperial persecutions under Decius and Diocletian. In addition to their confrontation with intense persecution, suffering, and even death, Christians frequently saw their sacred writings confiscated and destroyed. As a result of this destruction, the Scriptures were in danger of being lost to the church. Therefore, Christians often made copies of whatever manuscripts they had, however hastily it was deemed necessary. Since scribes were in danger of persecution if apprehended, the Scriptures were often copied "unprofessionally," or in an amateur manner by members of a given church. The possibility of errors creeping into the text became even more pronounced in this situation.

Meanwhile, during these very years, the church at Alexandria began to do pioneer work at the local level and compared and published texts in the period around 200–250. Their leadership was followed in other parts of the empire as well, and some basic work in textual criticism was done by the time of the persecution under Decius (249–251). Origen in Alexandria worked on his *Hexapla*, although it was never published in its entirety. In addition to this work in the Old Testament, he wrote commentaries on the New Testament and became something of a textual critic in that area as well. Other examples of early textual criticism include such works as the *Lucian Recension*, Julius Africanus's work on *Susanna*, and Theodore of Mopsuestia's *Song of Songs* in the area about Caesarea. These early textual critics did some elementary selection and editorial revision of the text materials, but their work did not stem the tide of casual, unsystematic, and largely unintentional creation of variant readings in the New Testament text.

The Period of Standardization (325–1500)

After the church was released from the threat of persecution following the Edict of Milan (313 CE), the influence was soon felt on the copying of biblical manuscripts. This period was marked by the introduction of parchment and vellum codices, and paper books toward its close. During this period Greek uncials gave way to minuscules; i.e., printed works were replaced by those written in a modified cursive script. Throughout the period critical revisions of the texts were relatively rare, except for the efforts of such scholars as Jerome (ca. 340–420) and Alcuin of York (735–804). Nevertheless, the particular period between 500 and 1000 witnessed the Masoretic work on the text of the Old Testament, which resulted in the Masoretic Text.

When the Emperor Constantine wrote to Eusebius of Caesarea instructing him to make fifty copies of the Christian Scriptures, a new direction in the history of the New Testament began. This was the period of standardization of the text, as the New Testament began to be carefully and faithfully copied from existing manuscripts. The text of a particular region was copied by copyists of that region. When Constantine moved the seat of the empire to the city named after him (Constantinople) it was only reasonable that that city would come to dominate the Greek-speaking world and that its

Scripture text would become the dominant text of the church. This was especially true in light of the emperor's patronage in producing careful copies of the New Testament text.

As a result of the precedent set by Constantine, great numbers of carefully copied manuscripts were produced throughout the Middle Ages, but official and carefully planned revision of the text was rare. Since a standardized text was developed, there was little need for classification and critical evaluation of the earlier manuscripts of the New Testament. As a result, the text remained relatively unchanged throughout the entire period. Toward the end of the period a completely standardized text with unlimited more-or-less identical copies became possible with the introduction of cheap paper and the printing press. Paper copies of the Bible became more abundant after the twelfth century. About 1454 Johann Gutenberg developed movable type for the printing press (Plates 43–44), and the door was open for efforts at more careful textual criticism during the Reformation era.

The Period of Crystallization (1500–1648)

In the Reformation era the biblical text entered into a period of crystallization in printed rather than manuscript form. Attempts were made to publish printed texts of the Bible as accurately as possible. Frequently these were published in polyglot (multilingual) form, including such titles as the Complutensian Polyglot (1514–17; Plate 46), the Antwerp Polyglot (1569-72), the Paris Polyglot (1629–45), and the London Polyglot (1657–69). It was also during this period that a standard edition of the Masoretic Text was published (ca. 1525) under the editorship of Jacob Ben Chayyim, a Hebrew Christian, based on manuscripts dating from the fourteenth century. The text is essentially a recension of the Masorete Ben Asher (fl. ca. 920), and it became the basis for all subsequent copies of the Hebrew Bible, whether in manuscript or printed form. Work on the New Testament text was more varied and sweeping in its outreach as a result of Gutenberg's invention.

Cardinal Francisco Ximénes de Cisneros (1437–1517) of Spain planned the first printed Greek New Testament to come off the press in 1502. It was to be a part of the Complutensian Polyglot, consisting of the Hebrew, Aramaic, Greek, and Latin texts, and published in the university town of Alcalá (*Complutum* in Latin), after which the polyglot received its name when printed there in 1514 and 1517. Although this was the first printed New Testament, it was not the first to be placed on the market. Pope Leo X did not give his sanction until March 1520. The Greek manuscripts underlying Ximénes' work have never been adequately determined; and there was some question about Ximénes' statements in the dedication about them.

Desiderius Erasmus (ca.1466–1536) of Rotterdam, the Dutch scholar and humanist, had the honor of editing the first Greek New Testament to be published. As early as 1514 Erasmus discussed such a work with the printer Johann Froben of Basel. Erasmus traveled to Basel in July 1515 in an attempt to find Greek manuscripts to set alongside his own Latin translation. Although the manuscripts he found needed editing, he proceeded with his task. Hasty in his work, his first edition, published in March 1516 (Plate 45), as Erasmus himself declared later, was "precipitated rather than edited" (*praecipitatum verius quam editum*).[2] Owing to the haste of production the 1,000-page volume contained numerous errors, including hundreds of typographical and mechanical mistakes. Bruce M. Metzger indicates that Erasmus' text, which was later to become the basis for the so-called Textus Receptus (thanks to printer Robert Estienne, below), was not based on early manuscripts, not reliably edited, and consequently not trustworthy. Even the reception of Erasmus' edition of the Greek New Testament was quite mixed. Nevertheless, by 1519 a new edition was needed. This second edition became the basis for Luther's German translation, although only one additional manuscript was used in its preparation. Further editions appeared in 1522, 1527, and 1535. All these editions were based on the Byzantine type text, contained readings from very late manuscripts, and included such spurious readings as 1 John 5:7–8 as well as Erasmus' translation into Greek of the Latin text of some verses in Revelation.

Robert Estienne (Etienne; Lat., Stephanus), royal printer in Paris, published the Greek New Testament in 1546, 1549, 1550, and 1551. The third edition (1550) was the earliest edition to contain a critical apparatus, although it was a mere fifteen manuscripts. This edition was based on Erasmus' fourth edition and became the basis for the Textus Receptus. After its publication this third edition became the dominant text in England. In his fourth edition, Estienne indicated his conversion to Protestantism and demonstrated

---

2. As quoted in Bruce M. Metzger, *The Text of the New Testament*, 4th ed. (New York: Oxford Univ. Press, 2005), 143–45.

the modern verse divisions which he produced for the first time.

Théodore de Bèze (Beza) (1519–1605) was the successor to John Calvin at Geneva. He published nine editions of the New Testament after the death of his famous predecessor in 1564, as well as a posthumous tenth edition in 1611. The most outstanding edition published by Beza came in 1582, when he included a few readings from Codex Bezae (D) and Codex Claromontanus (D²). His spare use of these manuscripts may be attributed to the fact that they differed too radically from the Erasmusan and Complutensian texts. As a result, Beza's Greek New Testament editions were in general agreement with the 1550 edition of Estienne. Their influence lies in the fact that they tended to popularize and stereotype the Textus Receptus (TR). The King James translators made use of Beza's 1588/89 edition.

Bonaventure and Abraham Elzevir (1583–1652 and 1592–1652) produced the Received Text (Textus Receptus). While the text of Stephanus held sway over England, this text became the most popular on the Continent. The uncle and nephew were quite enterprising as publishers, and their Leiden company released seven editions of the New Testament between 1624 and 1787. The 1624 edition drew basically from Beza's 1565 edition, and their second edition (1633) is the source of the title given to their text, as the preface reads, *"Textum ergo habes, nunc ab omnibus receptum: in quo nihil immutatum aut corruptum damus."* Thus, a publisher's blurb became the catchword (*textus receptus* means "received text") to designate the Greek text which they had derived from the editions of Ximénes, Beza, and Stephanus. This text is almost identical to that of Stephanus, which was the basis for the King James translation. Nevertheless, the textual basis was actually very late, from only a handful of manuscripts, and several passages were inserted that have no textual support. Only new manuscript discoveries, classification, and comparison could remedy such a state of affairs.

The Period of Criticism and Revision (1648–Present)

At the close of the Reformation era the Bible entered into a period of criticism and revision, which actually consisted of three shorter periods. Each of these subperiods was characterized by an important phase of criticism and revision, namely, they were periods of preparation, progression, and purification. It is important to remember that each of these phases of criticism was constructive rather than destructive in nature.

The period of preparation (1648–1831) was characterized by the gathering of textual materials and their systematic collection. When Brian Walton (1600–1661) edited the London Polyglot, he included the variant readings of Estienne's 1550 edition. This Polyglot contained the New Testament in Greek, Latin, Syrian, Ethiopic, Arabic, and Persian (in the Gospels). In the annotations the variant readings of the recently discovered Codex Alexandrinus (A) and a critical apparatus by Archbishop Ussher appeared. In 1675 John Fell (1625–1686) published an anonymous edition of the Greek New Testament at Oxford that contained evidence for the first time of the Gothic and Bohairic versions. Then, in 1707, John Mill (1645–1707) reprinted the 1550 Estienne text and added some thirty thousand variants from nearly one hundred manuscripts. This work was a monumental contribution to subsequent scholars as it provided them with a broad basis of established textual evidence.

Richard Bentley (1662–1742) was an outstanding classical scholar who issued a prospectus for a New Testament text which he never completed. Nevertheless, he challenged others to gather available textual materials and translations for intensive study. Among those scholars was Johann Albrecht Bengel (1687–1752), who established one of the basic canons of textual criticism: the difficult reading is to be preferred to the easy. One of Bentley's collators who had showed an early disposition for textual criticism was Johann Jakob Wettstein (1693–1754), who published the first apparatus identifying the uncial manuscripts by capital Roman letters and the minuscules by Arabic numerals. He also advocated the sound principle that manuscripts must be evaluated by their weight rather than by their numbers. The fruit of his forty-year efforts was published in 1751–1752 at Amsterdam.

A reprint of Wettstein's *Prolegomena* was made in 1764 by Johann Salomo Semler (1725–1791) who is known as the "father of German rationalism." He followed Bengel's pattern of classifying manuscripts by groups, but carried the process farther. Semler was the first scholar to apply the term *recension* to groups of New Testament witnesses. He identified three of these recensions: Alexandrian, Eastern, and Western. All later materials were regarded by Semler as mixtures of these.

The individual who actually carried Bengel's and Semler's principles to fruition was Johann Jakob Griesbach (1745–1812). He classified the New Testament manuscripts into three groups (Alexandrian, Western, and Byzantine), and laid the foundation for all subsequent work on the Greek New Testament. In his work Griesbach established fifteen canons of criticism. Shortly after he published the first edition of his New Testament (1775–1777), several other scholars published collations which greatly increased the availability of textual evidence from the church fathers, early versions, and the Greek text.

Christian Friedrich Matthaei (1744–1811) published a valuable critical apparatus in his Greek and Latin New Testament, for he added new evidence from the Slavonic translations. Frary Karl Alter (1749–1804), a Jesuit scholar from Vienna, added evidence from the Slavic manuscripts from twenty additional Greek manuscripts and other manuscripts as well. In 1788–1801 a group of Danish scholars published four volumes of textual work under the direction of Andrew Birch (1758–1829). In these volumes the readings from Codex Vaticanus (B) appeared in print for the first time.

Meanwhile, two Roman Catholic scholars were intense in their textual work. Johann Leonhard Hug (1765–1846) and his pupil Johannes Martin Augustinus Scholz (1794–1852) developed the theory that a "common edition" *(koine ekdosis)* followed the degeneration of the New Testament text in the third century. Scholz added 616 new manuscripts to the growing body of available textual materials and stressed, for the first time, the importance of ascribing geographical provenance represented by several manuscripts. This last point was elaborated by B. H. Streeter in 1924 as part of his theory of "local texts." After some time, Scholz adopted Bengel's classification of manuscripts and published a New Testament in 1830–1836 which indicated a regression toward the Textus Receptus, as he followed the Byzantine rather than the Alexandrian text. Only in 1845 did Scholz retract this view in favor of the Alexandrian readings.

The period of progression (1831–1881) brought the constructive critics to the fore in their grouping of textual materials. The first complete break with the Received Text was made by such men as Karl Lachmann (1793–1851), who published the first Greek New Testament resting wholly on a critical text and evaluation of variant readings; Lobegott Friedrich Constantin von Tischendorf (1815–1874), who sought out, discovered, and published manuscripts and critical texts; Samuel Prideaux Tregelles (1813–1875), who was instrumental in directing England away from the Received Text; and Henry Alford (1810–1871), who wrote numerous commentaries and otherwise demolished the unworthy and pedantic reverence for the Received Text.

Several other great scholars played key roles in the development of textual criticism. Caspar Rene Gregory completed the last edition of Tischendorf's Greek Testament with a prolegomenon (1894). This work provided the chief source of textual materials upon which scholars still depend as well as the basis for the universally accepted catalogue of manuscripts. Later revived by Kurt Aland and universally recognized as the Gregory-Aland list, it is catalogued at the Institute for New Testament Textual Research (INTF) in Münster, Westphalia, Germany (http://intf.uni-muenster.de/vmr/NTVMR/IndexNTVMR.php).

Two Cambridge scholars, Brooke Foss Westcott (1825–1901) and Fenton John Anthony Hort (1828–1892), rank with Tischendorf as making outstanding contributions to the study of the New Testament text. They published *The New Testament in the Original Greek* (1881–1882) in two volumes. The text of this work had been made available to the revision committee, which produced the English Revised New Testament in 1881. Their views were not original but were based on the work of Lachmann, Tregelles, Griesbach, Tischendorf, and others. The use of their text for the English Revised Version and the thoroughness of the explanation of their views in their introduction added to the acceptance of their critical text.

Nevertheless, some scholarly advocates for the Received Text spared no efforts in arguing against the text of Westcott and Hort. Three of these were John W. Burgon (1813–1888), who vehemently denounced the critical text; F. H. A. Scrivener (1813–1891), who was somewhat milder in his criticism; and George Salmon (1819–1904), who decried the lack of weight ascribed to "Western" readings by Westcott and Hort.

The "genealogical theory" of Westcott and Hort divided the textual materials into four types: Syrian, Western, Neutral, and Alexandrian. The Syrian text type included the Syrian, Antiochian, and Byzantine texts, such as A, E, F, G, H, S, V, Z, and most of the minuscules. The Western text type for Westcott and Hort had its roots in the Syrian church but was carried farther west, as observed in *Delta* (Δ), Old Latin, Syriac^c, and the *Theta* (Θ) family so far as it was known. The Neutral text type was supposedly of Egyptian origin and included the codices B and *Aleph* ($\aleph$). Their fourth text type was Alexandrian and comprised of a small number of witnesses in Egypt which were not of the Neutral type. This family contained C, L, family 33, the Sahidic, and the Bohairic texts. According to Westcott and Hort, there was a common ancestor (X) to both the Neutral and Alexandrian text types that was quite early and pure. The accompanying chart illustrates the relationships of each of these text-type families of the New Testament:

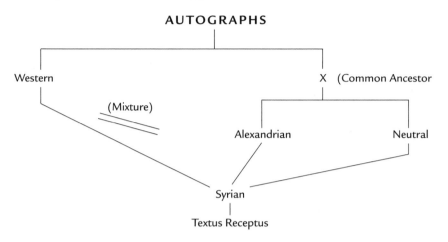

SOURCE: Norman L. Geisler and William E. Nix, *A General Introduction to the Bible*, rev. ed. (Chicago: Moody, 1986), 456.

The period of purification (1881–present) witnessed the reaction against the theory of Westcott and Hort, which had all but dethroned the Received Text as well as the further growth of materials utilized in textual criticism. The chief opponents of the critical text were Burgon and Scrivener, while its major proponents included Bernhard Weiss (1827–1918), Alexander Souter (1873–1949), and others. The arguments against the critical text may be summarized as follows: (1) the traditional text used by the church for fifteen hundred years must be correct because of its duration; (2) the traditional text had hundreds of manuscripts in its favor, whereas the critical text had only a few early ones; and (3) the traditional text is better because it is older. Following the deaths of Burgon and Scrivener, opposition to the critical text became less seriously considered by scholars.

Another critic of the Westcott-Hort position was Hermann Freiherr von Soden (1852–1914). He began his work on a different basis than Westcott and Hort, but confirmed many of their findings in his New Testament work. Although he had vast financial assistance for his work, von Soden's enterprise has been regarded as a magnificent failure. Nevertheless, he did agree with other opponents in indicating that Westcott and Hort had a non-acceptable notion about the Syrian recension as well as the Syrian text.

This situation resulted in a reinvestigation of the textual materials utilized by Westcott and Hort. The results of this scholarly and constructive
criticism may be seen in the current status of the Westcott-Hort theory (see
discussion in chap. 12). The text types have been reclassified as a result of
von Soden and other critics. The Syrian family has been renamed as Byzantine or Antiochian because of the possibility of being confused with the Old
Syriac version. At present there is a general recognition of more intermix-
ture between the Alexandrian and Neutral text types, and that both these
text types are actually only slightly different variations of the same family.
Hence, the Alexandrian designation now includes the Neutral text.

In a reevaluation of the Western type text, scholars have determined
that there are actually three subgroups (Codex D, Old Latin and Old Syriac)
and they agree that the text is not generally reliable when its readings stand
alone. Since the deaths of Westcott, Hort, and von Soden, a new text type
has been discovered (Caesarean). This family lies midway between the Alexandrian and Western texts, or possibly closer to the Western. J. Harold
Greenlee set out the distribution of New Testament manuscripts by family,
but other manuscript discoveries and developments in the definitive introduction to New Testament textual studies by Kurt and Barbara Aland and
utilized in the publication of the Nestle-Aland *Novum Testamentum Graece*
(NA26/NA27) and the United Bible Societies publication of *The Greek New
Testament* (UBS3/UBS4) have revealed the shortcomings of Greenlee's classification.[3] The following charts and discussion illustrate the changed situation by the beginning of the twenty-first century.[4]

> Category I: Manuscripts of very special quality which should always be
> considered in establishing the original text (e.g., the Alexandrian text
> belongs here). The papyri and uncials up to the third/fourth century
> also belong here almost automatically because they represent the text
> of the early period (those whose witness is slight are shown in paren-
> thesis).

> Category II: Manuscripts of special quality, but distinguished from manu-
> scripts of category I by the presence of alien influences (particularly of

---

3. J. Harold Greenlee, *Introduction to New Testament Textual Criticism*, rev. ed. (Peabody, Mass.:
   Hendrickson, 1995), 117–18.

4. Data for the following discussion follows Kurt Aland and Barbara Aland, *Text of the New Testament*
   (Grand Rapids: Eerdmans, 1989), 96–103, as well as the NA 27/UBS4 "Introduction," 6*–19*.

DISTRIBUTION OF GREEK MANUSCRIPTS BY CENTURY

	NEW TESTAMENT MANUSCRIPTS			LECTIONARIES	
Century	Papyri	Uncials	Minuscules	Uncials	Minuscules
2nd	2	–	–	–	–
ca. 200	4	–	–	–	–
2nd/3rd	1	1	–	–	–
3rd	28	2	–	–	–
3rd/4th	8	2	–	–	–
4th	14	14	–	1	–
4th/5th	8	8	–	–	–
5th	2	36	–	1	–
5th/6th	4	10	–	–	–
6th	7	51	–	3	–
6th/7th	5	5	–	1	–
7th	8	28	–	4	–
7th/8th	3	4	–	–	–
8th	2	29	–	22	–
8th/9th	–	4	–	5	–
9th	–	53	13	113	5
9th/10th	–	1	4	–	1
10th	–	17	124	108	38
10th/11th	–	3	8	3	4
11th	–	1	429	15	227
11th/12th	–	–	33	–	13
12th	–	–	555	6	486
12th/13th	–	–	26	–	17
13th	–	–	547	4	394
13th/14th	–	–	28	–	17
14th	–	–	511	–	308
14th/15th	–	–	8	–	2
15th	–	–	241	–	171
15th/16th	–	–	4	–	2
16th	–	–	136	–	194

SOURCE: Kurt Aland and Barbara Aland, *The Text of the New Testament*, trans. Erroll F. Rhodes, 2nd ed. (Grand Rapids: Eerdmans 1989), 81. Reprinted by permission of the publisher; all rights reserved.

the Byzantine text) and yet of importance for establishing the original text (e.g., the Egyptian text belongs here).

Category III: Manuscripts of a distinctive character with an independent text, usually important for establishing the original text, but particularly important for the history of the text (e.g., f1, f13).

Category IV: Manuscripts of the D text.

Category V: Manuscripts with a purely or predominantly Byzantine text.[5]

The new approach to Greek manuscript collation was introduced by Kurt and Barbara Aland, *The Text of the New Testament* (1981, English translation 1987) revised and amplified (1989) into five (and one unclassified) categories, as follows:

Category I	Category II	Category III	Category IV	Category V	Unclassified*
𝔓[4] 𝔓[5]	𝔓[1] 𝔓[6]	𝔓[2] 𝔓[3]	𝔓[38] 𝔓[48]	𝔓[73]	𝔓[25] 𝔓[89]
𝔓[9] 𝔓[10]	𝔓[8] 𝔓[11]	𝔓[21] 𝔓[36]	𝔓[69]		𝔓[90] 𝔓[91]
𝔓[12] 𝔓[13]	𝔓[14] 𝔓[17]	𝔓[41] 𝔓[50]			𝔓[92] 𝔓[93]
𝔓[16] 𝔓[18]	𝔓[19] 𝔓[33]	𝔓[54] 𝔓[59]			𝔓[94] 𝔓[95]
𝔓[20] 𝔓[22]	𝔓[34] 𝔓[42]	𝔓[60] 𝔓[68]			𝔓[96] [lost].
𝔓[23] 𝔓[24]	𝔓[43] 𝔓[44]	𝔓[76] 𝔓[83]			
𝔓[26] 𝔓[27]	𝔓[51] 𝔓[55]	𝔓[84] 𝔓[88]			
𝔓[28] 𝔓[29]	𝔓[56] 𝔓[57]				
𝔓[30] 𝔓[31]	𝔓[58] 𝔓[61]				
𝔓[32] 𝔓[35]	𝔓[62] 𝔓[63]				
𝔓[37] 𝔓[39]	𝔓[71] 𝔓[79]				*Not classified
𝔓[40] 𝔓[45]	𝔓[81] 𝔓[82]				in the Aland
𝔓[46] 𝔓[47]	𝔓[85] 𝔓[86]				categories.
𝔓[49] 𝔓[52]					
𝔓[53] 𝔓[64]					
𝔓[65] 𝔓[66]					
𝔓[67] 𝔓[70]					
𝔓[72] 𝔓[74]					
𝔓[75] 𝔓[77]					
𝔓[78] 𝔓[79]					
𝔓[80] 𝔓[87]					

Only four of these papyri are from scrolls (𝔓[12] 𝔓[13] 𝔓[18] 𝔓[22]) either as opisthographs (written on both sides) or written on reused material. In Category I 𝔓[67] duplicates 𝔓[64]; in Category II, 𝔓[58] duplicates 𝔓[33] and 𝔓[63] is influenced by

5. Kurt Aland and Barbara Aland, *The Text of the New Testament*, translated from *Der Texte dies Neuen Testaments* (1981) by Erroll F. Rhodes, 2d ed. rev. (Grand Rapids: Eerdmans 1989), 106, 159–62, 332–37.

Category V; in Category III 𝔓⁸⁴ is influenced by Category V; in Category V 𝔓⁹⁶ is lost. During the twentieth century the dominance of the great uncial codices, ℵ (*Aleph*) 01, Codex Siniaticus; A 02, Codex Alexandrinus; B 03, Codex Vaticanus; C 04, Codex Ephraemi Rescriptus; Dea 05, Codex Bezae Cantabrigiensis; D 06, Codex Claromontanus, et al. has been diminished by the papyri, and is being further diminished by the influence of a group of minuscules currently being studied in addition to the 264 catalogued uncial manuscripts.[6]

In addition to the uncial papyri and codices, the NA27 and UBS4, under the direction of J. Karvidopoulos in the Lectionaries Research Center of the University of Thessaloniki, have added seventy Greek lectionaries (30 for the Gospels and 40 for the Apostolos) to those already utilized in earlier editions of *The Greek New Testament*. The symbol *Lect* is used to indicate the agreement of the majority text of the selected lectionaries with the standard edition of the lectionary used by the Greek Church.[7] Individual lectionaries that differ from the standard edition are cited individually by the *l* symbol. Early versions of the text are utilized only when their underlying Greek text may be determined with certainty or a high degree of probability. The major versions of Latin, Syriac, Coptic, Amenian, Georgian, Ethiopic, and Old Church Slavonic were examined by editors of NA2/UBS4. The Old Latin is cited with all its important manuscripts. The Vulgate, having over 8,000 manuscript copies has a textual tradition of its own. These Aland collations of textual materials appear in the *Greek New Testament* of the Deutsche Bibelgesellschaft and the United Bible Societies, edited by K. Aland and others (e.g., NA26, NA27/UBS3, UBS4). They generally rank the manuscript evidence in the following descending order of importance: Alexandrian, Caesarean, Western, and Byzantine. Since the Received Text basically follows the Byzantine text, it is almost redundant to indicate that its authority is not highly regarded by most critical text scholars. The underlying reason seems to be that it does not move beyond the Westcott-Hort "Byzantine/non-Byzantine" dichotomy of Eberhard Nestle's *Novum Testamentum Graece* (editions 1–25).

6. Data for these charts and discussion follow Kurt Aland and Barbara Aland, *Text of the New Testament*, rev. ed., 1989), pp. 96-103, as well as the NA 27/UBS4 "Introduction," 6*-19*.

7. B. Antoniadis, *H KAINH DIAQHKH KATA THN EKAOSIN TOU OIKOUMENIKOU PATRIARCEIOU*. (Athens: Apostoliki Diakonia, 1988.)

Recent collations of the materials are available based on other criteria for the normative Greek New Testament presented in the various editions of Nestle-Aland *Novum Testamentum Graece* and *The Greek New Testament* by the United Bible Societies. Kurt and Barbara Aland provide an excellent overview of "creating the *de facto* standard text" of the New Testament. *A Reader's Greek New Testament* differs from the UBS text in 285 places.[8]

8.   Richard J. Goodrich and Albert L. Lukaszewski, *A Reader's Greek New Testament*, rev. ed. (Grand Rapids: Zondervan, 2003, 2007), 9, n. 4. They refer to Kurt Aland and Barbara Aland, *Text of the New Testament*, rev. ed., 1989), 30–36.

15

Restoration *of the* Bible Text

ALTHOUGH THERE ARE NO KNOWN AUTOGRAPHS of the Old and New Testaments, numerous manuscript copies and quotations are available to assist biblical scholars in their efforts to restore the original Bible text. In addition to the evidence we have discussed in the past few chapters, there is supportive evidence for the Bible text from its various translations, but these items will be the basic subject matter of part 4. For the present, our concern will be the matter of textual criticism in restoring the text itself rather than its translation into various languages.

As previous discussions illustrate, the landscape of textual criticism and of making a critical edition has changed dramatically in the past quarter century. Four basic changes are observable: (1) the introduction of the computer on collecting and analyzing manuscript evidence, (2) significant changes in the study of manuscripts involving the development of Christian thought as well as recovery of variant readings, (3) ongoing publication of new manuscript discoveries, and (4) the number of research tools that have been published.[1] "In recent decades it has become common to make the separate discipline of codicology out of the study of the

---

1. See chapters 11–17 passim, as well as D. C. Parker, *An Introduction to the New Testament Manuscripts and Their Texts* (Cambridge: Cambridge Univ. Press, 2008), 1–2.

material and makeup of the pages, and restricting palaeography to the study of the script. Whether this is a necessary or an advisable distinction is uncertain."[2] Peter M. Head argues that the double dots now known as distigmai (marking textual variation in Codex Vaticanus) belong to one unified system that was added sometime in the sixteenth century.[3] Contrast Philip Payne, who discovered these distigmai in the first place, and thinks that some of them (approximately fifty) are original to the scribe working in the fourth century.[4]

THE PROBLEM OF TEXTUAL CRITICISM

The problem of textual criticism centers on three basic issues: genuineness and authenticity, manuscript evidence, and variant readings in the text. Although each of these issues has been mentioned repeatedly in earlier discussions, a more detailed treatment of them is in order.

Genuineness and Authenticity

Genuineness is used in the matter of textual criticism as it relates to the truth of the origin of a document, that is, its authorship. As indicated in chapter 14, genuineness is primarily the subject of studies in special introduction to the Bible, since it relates to such things as the authorship, date, and destiny of biblical books. A class on general introduction to the Bible is concerned with such topics as inspiration, authority, canonicity, and authenticity of the books of the Bible. The question answered by genuineness is simply this: Is this document really from its alleged source or author? Is it genuinely the work of the stated writer?

Authenticity refers to the truth about the facts and content of the

---

2. Parker, *Introduction to the New Testament*, 32–33. Also see the discussions of the relevance of the newly advanced tool of codicology, 58–60, 317.

3. Philip B. Payne and Paul Canart, "Distigmai Matching the Original Ink of Codex Vaticanus: Do They Mark the Location of Textual Variants?" in Patrick Andrist, ed., *Le manuscript B de la Bible* (Vaticanus graecus 1209), Lausanne, 2009. Also see SBL *New Orleans 2009: Peter Head Putting the Distigmai in the Right Place*; "The Marginalia of Codex Vaticanus: Putting the Distigmai (Formerly known as 'Umlauts') in Their Place."

4. See http://evangelicaltextualcriticism.blogspot.com for an extended dialog arising from Peter M. Head's Society for Biblical Literature (Nov. 2009) response to Philip B. Payne and Paul Canart, "The Originality of Textual-Critical Symbols in Codex Vaticanus," *Novum Testamentum*, XLII, 2 (2000): 105–13.

documents of the Bible. It deals primarily with the integrity (trustworthiness) and the credibility (truthfulness) of the record. In short, a book may be genuine without being authentic, if the professed writer is the real one, even if the content is untrue. Then again, a book may be authentic without being genuine, if the content is true but the professed writer is not the actual one. In general introduction, then, the concern is with the integrity of the text based on its credibility and authority. It is assumed that a biblical book, which has divine authority and hence credibility, and has been transmitted with integrity, will automatically have genuineness. If there were a lie in the book regarding its origin or authorship, how could its contents be believed?

Manuscript Evidence

A summary review of the manuscript evidence pertaining to the biblical text will prove beneficial at this point. It will reveal the basic difference in approach to the textual criticism of each Testament.

The Old Testament has survived in few complete manuscripts, most of which date from the ninth century CE or later. There are, however, abundant reasons for believing that these copies are good. (See discussion in chapter 12.) Several lines of evidence support this contention: (1) the few variants existing in these Masoretic manuscripts; (2) the almost literal agreement of most of the Septuagint (LXX) with the Hebrew of the Masoretic Text (MT); (3) the scrupulous rules of the scribes who copied the manuscripts; (4) the similarity of parallel Old Testament passages; (5) archaeological confirmation of historical details of the text; (6) the agreement, by and large, of the Samaritan Pentateuch (SamP); (7) the thousands of Cairo Genezah manuscripts (see chap. 12); and (8) the phenomenal confirmation of the Hebrew text by the Dead Sea Scroll (DSS) and Documents in the Judean Desert (DJD) discoveries.

The New Testament manuscripts are numerous but so are the variant readings. Consequently, the science of textual criticism is necessary to the restoration of the New Testament text. Over five thousand Greek manuscripts, dating from the second century onward, bear witness to the text. In contrast to the Old Testament which has few but good early manuscripts, the New Testament has many manuscripts that are of poorer quality, that is, they possess more variant readings.

Variant Readings in the Text

The multiplicity of manuscripts produces a corresponding number of variant readings, for the more manuscripts that were copied, the greater the possible number of errors made by copyists. Instead of being a hindrance to reconstructing the biblical text, this situation actually becomes extremely beneficial.

Old Testament variants are relatively rare for several reasons: (1) because there is only one major manuscript tradition, the total number of possible errors is less; (2) copies were made by official scribes who labored under strict rules; and (3) the Masoretes systematically destroyed all copies with "mistakes" or variant readings. The discovery of the DSS and DJD have provided overwhelming confirmation of the fidelity of the Masoretic Text, as may be observed in the conclusions of such Old Testament scholars as Millar Burrows, *The Dead Sea Scrolls;* R. Laird Harris, *Inspiration and Canonicity of the Bible;* Gleason L. Archer Jr., *A Survey of Old Testament Introduction;* and F. F. Bruce, *Second Thoughts on the Dead Sea Scrolls.* The sum of their testimony is that there are so few variant readings between the MT and DSS that the latter confirm the integrity of the former. Where there are differences, the DSS tend to support the readings found in the Septuagint (LXX). Since the MT stemmed from a single source which was standardized as the Proto-Masoretic text by Hebrew scholars about 100 CE, the discovery of manuscripts antedating this period casts new light on the history of the Old Testament text prior to that time.

In addition to the three basic textual traditions of the Old Testament that had been recognized already (Proto-Masoretic, Samaritan, and Greek), the Dead Sea Scrolls revealed a Proto-Masoretic text type, a Proto-Septuagint text type, and a Proto-Samaritan text type. Attempts at drawing the lines of relationship between these textual families are in the embryonic stage, and the situation calls for dedicated scholarship. For the present, the Masoretic Text is considered basic, since both the Samaritan Pentateuch (SamP) (see chap. 16) and Septuagint (see chap. 17) texts are based on translations of the Proto-Hebrew documents. Nevertheless, the DSS have indicated that there are places where the LXX contains the preferred reading. The basic problem is to determine how great the difference is between the Hebrew, Samaritan, Aramaic, and Greek traditions.

With emerging discoveries and cooperative efforts of scholars internationally, Old Testament textual studies have entered into a new era of development (see discussion in chap. 12). Two examples are observable. First is the cooperative effort of the Codex Sinaiticus Project at the British Library in London (2010), by agreement with the British Library Board, the National Library of Russia, the Library at the Monastery of Saint Catherine at Mount Sinai, and the Library at University of Leipzig. Second is the republication of Codex Vaticanus (B) by the Vatican Library (1996, 1999).

New Testament variants are much more abundant than their Old Testament counterparts because of the numerous manuscripts and because many private and unofficial copies were produced. Every time a new manuscript is discovered, the gross number of variants increases. Thus John Mill estimated approximately 30,000 variants existed in 1707; in 1874 F. H. A. Scrivener counted 150,000 variants; and today more than 200,000 known variants exist.

Yet there is an ambiguity in saying 200,000 variants exist, since these represent only about 10,000 places in the New Testament. If a single word were misspelled in 3,000 different manuscripts, they are counted as 3,000 variants. Once the counting procedure is understood, and the mechanical (orthographic) variants have been eliminated, the remaining significant variants are surprisingly few in number. In his recent popular book, *Misquoting Jesus*, agnostic New Testament critic Bart Ehrman contends there are so many "errors" (variants) that we don't know how many there are, perhaps 4,000. He asserts, "These copies differ from each other in so many places that we don't even know how many differences there are."[5]

Ironically, the way Ehrman counts "errors" (variants), there were 1.6 million errors in the first printing of his book. For there were 16 errors, and the book printed an alleged 100,000 copies.[6] Yet Ehrman would be shocked if someone denied the credibility of his book based on this count. Similarly, no one should deny the credibility of the Bible on Ehrman's count. Ehrman himself admits the biblical variants do not affect the central message of the Bible. He wrote, "In fact, most of the changes found in early Christian manuscripts have nothing to do with theology or ideology. Far and away the most changes are the result of mistakes pure and simple—slips of the pen, accidental omissions, inadvertent additions, misspelled words, blunders of one sort or another."[7]

5. Bart Ehrman, *Misquoting Jesus* (New York: HarperCollins, 2007), 10.

6. See Bart Ehrman, "Millions and Millions of Variants, part 1 of 2," posted 16 September 2010 (www.truefreethinker.com).

7. Ehrman, *Misquoting Jesus*, 55.

Ways That Variants Appear

To fully understand the significance of variant readings, and to determine which are correct (or original) readings, it is first necessary to examine just how these variants came into the text. Although these principles also apply to the Old Testament, they are here used with reference to the New Testament only.

In general, careful students of textual criticism have suggested two classes of errors: *unintentional* and *intentional.*

(1) Unintentional changes of various kinds all arise from the imperfection of some human faculty. These have resulted in the vast number of transcriptional errors in the text. Errors of the eye, for example, have resulted in several kinds of variant readings. Among these are wrong divisions of words that resulted in the introduction of new words. Since early manuscripts did not separate words by spaces, such divisions would have a bearing on the resultant reading of the text. To use an English example, HEISNOWHERE could mean either HE IS NOW HERE or HE IS NOWHERE. Even more amusing is this: DIDYOUEVERSEEABUNDANCEONTHETABLE (with its clever secondary reading, Did you ever see a bun dance on the table). Omissions of letters, words, and even whole lines of text occurred when an astigmatic eye jumped from one group of letters or words to a similar group. This particular error is caused by *homeoteleuton* (similar ending). When only one letter is missing, the error is called *haplography* (single writing). *Repetitions* are the opposite of errors of omission. When the eye picked up the same letter or word twice, it is called *dittography.* It is from such an error in some minuscules that the following reading emerged: "Whom do you want me to release for you: Jesus Barabbas or Jesus?" (Matt. 27:17, marg.).

Transposition is the reversal of position of two letters or words, technically known as *metathesis.* In 2 Chronicles 3:4, the transposition of letters altered the measurements of the porch of Solomon's temple to 120 cubits instead of 20 cubits, as it correctly appears in the LXX. Other confusions of spelling, abbreviation, and scribal insertions account for the remainder of scribal errors. This is especially true of Hebrew letters that were used as numerals too. The confusion of such numbers in the Old Testament may be seen in the conflicts of parallel passages: see, for example, 40,000 in 1 Kings 4:26 as opposed to 4,000 in 2 Chronicles 9:25; the 42 years in 2 Chronicles 22:2 (RSV) in contrast to the correct reading of 22 years in 2 Kings 8:26 (RSV) also fits into this category.

Errors of the ear occurred only when manuscripts were copied by a scribe listening to a reader. This may explain why some manuscripts (after the fifth century CE) read *kamelos* (rope) instead of *kamēlos* (a camel) in Matthew 19:24, *kauthasomai* (he burns) instead of *kauchasomai* (he boasts) in 1 Corinthians 13:4, and other such alterations in the text of the New Testament.

Errors of memory are not so numerous, but occasionally a scribe forgot the precise word in a passage and substituted a synonym. He may have been influenced by a parallel passage or truth, as in the case of Ephesians 5:9, possibly confused with Galatians 5:22, as well as the addition to Hebrews 9:22 (ASV) of "there is no remission [of sins]."

Errors of judgment are generally ascribed to dim lighting and poor eyesight at the occasion of copying the manuscript. Sometimes marginal notations were incorporated into the text in such instances, or perhaps they were the product of a sleepy scribe at work. No doubt one of these causes is to be blamed for the variant readings in John 5:4, 2 Corinthians 8:7, etc. It is difficult at times to tell whether a variant is the result of faulty judgment or intentional doctrinal changes. No doubt 1 John 5:8, John 7:53–8:11, and Acts 8:37 fit into one of these categories.

Errors of writing are attributed to scribes who, due to imperfect style or accident, wrote indistinctly or imprecisely and set the stage for future sight or judgment errors. On some occasions, for example, a scribe might neglect to insert a number or word into the text he transcribed, as in the case of the omitted number in 1 Samuel 13:1.

(2) Intentional changes account for a good number of textual variants, although the vast majority are attributed to unintentional errors. These intentional errors may have been motivated by good intentions, and no doubt they were, but nonetheless they were deliberate alterations of the text. Among the factors involved in making intentional alterations in a biblical manuscript were the grammatical and linguistic variations.

Orthographic variations in spelling, euphony, and grammatical form are abundant in the papyruses, and each scribal tradition had its own idiosyncrasies. Within these traditions a scribe might tend to modify his manuscript in order to make it conform to them. Such changes include spelling of proper names, verb forms, smoothing of grammar, gender changes, and syntactical alterations.

Liturgical changes are widely observable in the lectionaries. Minor changes might be made at the beginning of a passage, and sometimes a passage might be summarized for liturgical use. On occasion some of these changes would creep into the biblical text itself, as in the case of the "doxology" of the Lord's Prayer (Matt. 6:13).

Harmonizational changes frequently appear in the Gospels when one account is brought into agreement with its parallel passages (see Luke 11:2–4 and Matt. 6:9–13), or in Acts 9:4–6, which was brought into more literal agreement with Acts 26:14–15. In the same manner some Old Testament quotations were enlarged in some manuscripts to conform more precisely to the Septuagint (cf. Matt. 15:8 with Isa. 29:13, where the phrase *this people* is added).

Historical and factual changes were sometimes introduced by well-meaning scribes. John 19:14 was changed in some manuscripts to read "third" instead of "sixth" hour, and Mark 8:31, where "after three days" was changed to read "on the third day" in some manuscripts.

Conflational changes result from combining two or more variants into a single reading, as in the likely case of Mark 9:49 and Romans 3:22 (KJV).

Doctrinal changes constitute the last category of intentional scribal changes. Most of the deliberate doctrinal changes have been in the direction of orthodoxy, as is the reference to the Trinity in 1 John 5:7–8. Other alterations, while springing from good intentions, have had the effect of adding to the text what was not part of the original teaching at that point. Such is probably the case with the addition of "fasting" to "prayer" in Mark 9:29 and the so-called long ending to that gospel itself (Mark 16:9–20). But even here the text is not heretical. It is well to remember at this point that no Christian doctrine hangs on a debatable text, and that a student of the New Testament must beware of changing the text simply on the basis of doctrinal considerations.

When a comparison of the variant readings of the New Testament is made with those of other books that have survived from antiquity, the results are little short of astounding. For instance, although there are 200,000 (and some assert there are 400,000) "errors" among the New Testament manuscripts, these appear in only about 10,000 places, and only about one-sixtieth rise above the level of trivialities. Westcott and Hort, Ezra

Abbot, Philip Schaff, and A. T. Robertson have carefully evaluated the evidence and concluded that the New Testament text is 99+ percent pure. A. T. Robertson said, "The real concern is with a thousandth part of the entire text" (which equals 99.9 percent accuracy). Philip Schaff added that only fifty variants were of real significance, and there is no "article of faith or a precept of duty which is not abundantly sustained by other and undoubted passages, or by the whole tenor of Scripture teaching."[8] In light of the fact that there are over 5,800 Greek manuscripts, some 19,000 versions and translations, the evidence for the integrity of the New Testament is beyond question. And none of the variants affects any of the basic doctrines of the Christian faith.

This is especially true when some of the greatest writings of antiquity have survived in only a handful of manuscripts (see chap. 12). A comparison of the nature or quality of those writings sets the biblical text in bold relief for its integrity. Bruce M. Metzger made an excellent study of Homer's *Iliad* and the Hindu *Mahabhārata* in *Chapters in the History of New Testament Textual Criticism*. In that study he demonstrated that the textual corruption of those sacred books is much greater than the New Testament.

The *Iliad* is particularly appropriate for this study because it has so much in common with the New Testament. Next to the New Testament the *Iliad* has more extant manuscripts than any other book (453 papyri, 2 uncials, and 188 minuscules for a total of 643). Like the Bible, it was considered sacred, and experienced textual changes and criticism of its Greek manuscripts. While the New Testament has about 20,000 lines, the *Iliad* has about 15,000. Only 40 lines (400 words) of the New Testament are in doubt, whereas 764 lines of the *Iliad* are in question. Thus the 5 percent corruption of the *Iliad* stands against the less than 1 percent of the New Testament text. The national epic of India, the *Mahabhārata,* has suffered even more corruption. It is about eight times as long as the *Iliad* and the *Odyssey* combined, roughly 250,000 lines. Of these, some 26,000 lines are textually corrupt, or just over 10 percent.

British textual scholar Frederick Kenyon may have stated it best: "The

---

8. A. T. Robertson, *An Introduction to Textual Criticism of the New Testament* (Nashville: Broadman, 1925), 22; and Philip Schaff, *Companion to the Greek Testament and the English Version* 3rd ed. rev. (New York: Harper & Brothers, 1883), 177.

interval between the dates of original composition and the earliest extant evidence becomes so small as to be in fact negligible, and the last foundation for any doubt that the Scriptures have come down substantially as they were written has now been removed. Both the authenticity and the general integrity of the books of the New Testament may be regarded as finally established."[9]

Thus, the New Testament has not only survived in more manuscripts than any other book from antiquity, but it has survived in a much purer form than any other great book, whether or not they are sacred works, a form that is over 99 percent pure. Even the Qu'ran, which is not an ancient book since it originated in the seventh century CE, has suffered from a large collection of variants that necessitated the Orthmanic revision. In fact, there are still seven ways to read the text (vocalization and punctuation), all based on Orthman's recension, which was made about twenty years after the death of Muhammad himself.

THE PRINCIPLES OF TEXTUAL CRITICISM

The full appreciation of the arduous task of reconstructing the New Testament text from thousands of manuscripts containing tens of thousands of variants can be derived, in part, from a study of just how textual critics proceed about their task. They use two kinds of textual evidence: external and internal.

External Evidence

External evidence falls into three basic varieties: chronological, geographical, and genealogical. *Chronological* evidence pertains to the date of the text type rather than to the particular manuscript itself. The earlier text types have readings that are preferred over later ones by textual critics. *Geographical* distribution of independent witnesses that agree in support of a variant are preferred to those having closer proximity or relationship. *Genealogical* relationships between manuscripts follow the discussion presented in chapter 14. Of the four major textual families, the Alexandrian is considered to be the most reliable, although it sometimes shows a "learned" correction. Readings supported by good representatives of two or more text types are to

---

9. Sir Frederick Kenyon, *The Bible and Archaeology* (New York: Harper, 1940), 288.

be preferred to a single text type. The Byzantine text is generally considered to be the poorest. When the manuscripts within a given text type are divided in their support of a variant, the true reading is probably the reading of the manuscripts most generally faithful to their own text type, the reading that differs from that of the other text types, the reading that is different from the Byzantine textual family, or the reading that is most characteristic of the text type to which the manuscripts in question belong.

Internal Evidence

Internal evidence is classified in two basic varieties: transcriptional (depending on the habits of scribes) and intrinsic (depending on the habits of authors).

Transcriptional evidence renders four general assertions: the more difficult reading (for the scribe) is preferred, especially if it is sensible; the shorter reading is preferred unless it arose from an accidental omission of lines because of similar ends *(parablepsis)* or intentional deletion; the more verbally dissonant readings of parallel passages is preferred, even if they are quotations of the Old Testament; and the less refined grammatical construction, expression, word, etc., is preferred.

Intrinsic evidence depends upon the probability of what the author is likely to have written. It is determined by the author's style throughout the book (and elsewhere), the immediate context of the passage, the harmony of a reading with the author's teaching elsewhere (as well as with other canonical writings), and the influence of the author's background.

In considering all the internal and external factors in textual criticism, it is essential to realize that their use is not merely one of science, it is also a delicate art. A few observations may assist the beginner in getting acquainted with the process of textual criticism. In general, external evidence is more important than internal, since it is more objective. Decisions must select internal as well as external evidence in textual evaluation, since no manuscript or text type contains all the correct readings in itself. On some occasions different scholars will come to conflicting positions, because of the subjective element in internal evidence.

Gleason Archer cautiously suggests the priority which should be utilized in the event that a textual variant is encountered: (1) the older reading is preferred; (2) the more difficult reading is preferred; (3) the shorter reading is preferred; (4) the reading which best explains the variants is preferred;

(5) the widest geographical support for a reading makes it preferred; (6) the reading which conforms best with the author's style and diction is preferred; and (7) the reading which reflects no doctrinal bias is preferred.[10]

THE PRACTICE OF TEXTUAL CRITICISM

The most practical way to observe the results of the principles of textual criticism is to compare the differences between the Authorized Version (KJV) of 1611, which is based on the Received Text, and the American Standard Version (ASV) of 1901 or the Revised Standard Version (RSV) of 1946 and 1952, which are based on the Critical Text. A survey of several passages will serve to illustrate the procedure used in reconstructing the true text.

Old Testament Examples

Deuteronomy 32:8 provides another interesting exercise on Old Testament textual criticism. The Masoretic Text, followed by the KJV and the ASV, reads, "The Most High gave to the nations their inheritance. . . . He set the bounds of the peoples according to the number of the children of Israel." The RSV followed the Septuagint (LXX) rendition: "According to the number of the sons [or angels] of God." A fragment from Qumran now supports the Septuagint (LXX) reading. According to the principles of textual criticism indicated earlier, the RSV is correct because it (1) has the more difficult reading, (2) is supported by the earliest known manuscript, (3) is in harmony with the patriarchal description of angels as "sons of God" (cf. Job 1:6; 2:1; 38:7; and possibly Gen. 6:4), and (4) explains the origin of the other variant.

Zechariah 12:10 illustrates this same point. The KJV and ASV follow the Masoretic Text (MT): "They shall look upon me [Jehovah speaking] whom they have pierced." The RSV follows the Theodotian version (ca. 180 CE; see chap. 17) in rendering it, "When they look on him whom they have pierced." The Masoretic Text preserves the preferred reading because it (1) is based on the earlier and better manuscripts, (2) is the more difficult reading, and (3) can explain the other readings on the grounds of theological prejudice against the deity of Christ or the influence of the New Testament change from the first to the third person in its quotation of this passage (cf. John 19:37).

---

10. Gleason L. Archer Jr., *A Survey of Old Testament Introduction*, rev. ed. (Chicago: Moody, 1974), 58–60.

Some other important variants between the Masoretic Text and Septuagint (LXX) texts were clarified with the Dead Sea Scrolls (DSS) and Documents in the Judean Desert (DJD) discoveries, and in these instances they tend to support the LXX. Among those passages are Hebrews 1:6 (KJV) which follows the LXX quotation of Deuteronomy 32:43, the famous Isaiah 7:14 rendition of "His name shall be called," instead of the MT reading, "[she] shall call his name." The Greek LXX version of Jeremiah is sixty verses shorter than the MT, and the Qumran fragment of Jeremiah tends to support the Greek text. These illustrations should not be construed as a uniform picture of the Dead Sea Scrolls supporting the LXX text, since there are not many variants from the MT among the manuscripts found at the Dead Sea site. In general the scrolls have tended to confirm the integrity of the MT. The passages indicated here are merely indications of the problems and principles of textual criticism as they are practiced by Old Testament textual critics.

New Testament Examples

Mark 16:9–20 (KJV) produces one of the most perplexing of all textual problems. These verses are lacking in many of the oldest and best Greek manuscripts, such as ℵ, B, Old Latin manuscript k, the Sinaitic Syriac, many Old Armenian manuscripts, and a number of Ethiopic manuscripts. Many of the ancient fathers show no knowledge of it, and Jerome admitted that this portion was omitted from almost all Greek copies. Among the witnesses that have these verses, some also have an asterisk (※ or ⁑) or obelus (−) to indicate that they are a spurious addition to the text. There is also another ending which occurs in several uncials, a few minuscules, and several manuscript copies of ancient versions. The familiar long ending of the KJV and the Received Text is found in a vast number of uncial manuscripts (C, D, L, W, and Θ), most minuscules, most Old Latin manuscripts, the Latin Vulgate, and in some Syriac and Coptic manuscripts. In Codex W the long ending is expanded after verse 14.

A decision as to which of these endings is preferred is still a moot point, since none of them commends itself as original because of the limited textual evidence, the apocryphal flavor, and the non-Marcan style of the endings. On the other hand, if none of these endings is genuine, it is difficult to believe that

VARIOUS SCHOOLS OF NEW TESTAMENT TEXTUAL CRITICISM

Wescott-Hort Text	Critical Text	Eclectic Text	Majority Text	Received Text
⇨	⇨		⇦	⇦
Tends toward Alexandrian Family		Takes each variant individually		Tends toward Byzantine Family

(The purpose of textual criticism is to ascertain the original reading)

SOURCE: Norman L. Geisler and William E. Nix, *A General Introduction to the Bible*, rev. and expanded ed. (Chicago: Moody, 1986), 482.

Mark 16:8 is not the original ending. A defense of the Received Text (Mark 16:9–20) was made by John W. Burgon, and more recently by M. van der Valk, although it is admittedly difficult to arrive at a solution about which text best represents the original. On the basis of known textual evidence, it seems more likely that the original end of the gospel of Mark was verse 8. Practically speaking, it makes no difference in any basic Christian teaching with or without the longer endings since no essential doctrine is gained or lost by it.

John 7:53–8:11 (KJV) relates the story of the woman taken in adultery. It is placed in brackets in the ASV with a note that most ancient authorities omit it. The RSV places the passage in brackets at the end of the gospel of John, with a note that other ancient authorities place it there, at the end of John's gospel, or after Luke 21:38. The evidence that this passage is part of John's gospel is decidedly lacking because (1) it is not in the oldest and best Greek manuscripts; (2) neither Tatian nor the Old Syriac betrays any knowledge of it, and it is also omitted in the best Peshitta manuscripts, the Coptic, several Gothic, and Old Latin manuscripts; (3) no Greek writer refers to it until the twelfth century; (4) its style and interruption do not fit into the context of the fourth gospel; (5) its earliest appearance is in Codex Bezae (ca. 550); (6) several scribes placed it in other locations (for example, following John 7:36; John 21:24; John 7:44; or Luke 21:38); and (7) many manuscripts which included it indicated doubts about its integrity by marking it with an obelus. As a result, the passage may well preserve a true story, but from the standpoint of textual criticism it should be placed as an appendix to John with a note that it has no fixed place in the ancient witnesses.

First John 5:7 (KJV) is completely omitted in the ASV and RSV renditions without any explanation. There is an explanation for this omission, however, and it provides an interesting scene in the history of textual criticism. There is virtually no textual support for the KJV reading in any Greek manuscript, although there is ample support in the Vulgate. Thus, when Erasmus was challenged as to why he did not include the reading in his Greek New Testament of 1516 and 1519, he hastily responded that he would include it in his next edition if anyone were to find even one manuscript in its support. One sixteenth-century Greek minuscule was produced to support it, the 1520 manuscript of the Franciscan friar Froy, or Roy. Erasmus complied with his promise and included the reading in his 1522 edition. The KJV followed Erasmus's Greek text; and, on the basis of a single, late, and insignificant witness, all the weight and authority of all other Greek manuscripts were disregarded. In fact, the inclusion of this verse as genuine breaks almost every major canon of textual criticism.

Luke 23:34a. The statement of Jesus from the cross "Father, forgive them, for they know not what they do" (KJV and other English translations) is challenged in the critical text of NA26/UBS3 and NA27/UBS4, which reject it as not being a part of the original text. Proponents of this "shorter" reading tend to emphasize external evidence, while defenders of the longer reading focus on internal probability.[11] Nathan Eubank presents arguments by eight proponents of the "shorter" reading and eight advocates of the "longer" reading. He concludes that shorter reading proponents overstate their case and that longer reading advocates offer strong intrinsic evidence but it needs a more credible explanation, which he finds in the writings of the church fathers. He surmises that the original reading was regarded as Jesus' prayer for the Jews, and the omission of the text was a later development, during a time of fierce Christian-Jewish polemics. He rightly concludes: "The growing awareness of the influence of the social realities of early Christianity on the text of the NT has enriched our understanding of scribal proclivities, but this approach can only be enhanced by more careful attention to ancient exegesis."[12]

---

11. This discussion follows the excellent and balanced treatment by Nathan Eubank, "A Disconcerting Prayer: On the Originality of Luke 23:34a," *Journal of Biblical Literature* 129, no. 3 (2010): 521–36.

12. Eubank, "A Disconcerting Prayer," 536. He goes on to illustrate how the prayer of Jesus was difficult for early Christian exegesis in its historical development, pp. 528–36.

On the basis of the above-mentioned case studies, it should be clear that textual criticism is both a science and an art. Not only is the Bible the most well-preserved book to survive from the ancient world, its variant readings of significance amount to less than one-half of one percent, none of which affect any basic Christian doctrine. In addition, the textual critic has at his disposal a series of canons that for all practical purposes enables him to completely restore the exact text of the Hebrew and Greek autographs of the Scriptures—not only line for line, but in most cases even word for word. Evaluation of disputed readings should incorporate exegetical and historical evidence as well as external and internal criteria.

PART FOUR

Translation

16

Aramaic, Syriac, *and* Related Translations *and* Bibles

The transmission of the revelation from God to us centers on three significant historical developments: the invention of writing before 3000 BCE, the beginnings of translation before 200 BCE, and the developments in printing before ca. 1600 CE (all discussed in chap. 11). Earlier we looked into the matter of writing and copying the original manuscripts of the Bible as well as the role, method, and practice of textual criticism in preserving the text of those original writings. Here we shall direct our attention to the translation of God's Word.

The goal of translation is to transfer the meaning of a text from one language (the "source") to another (the "target" or "receptor").[1] There are two main philosophies of translation, known to specialists as formal equivalence and functional equivalence. Formal equivalence is also called "literal" or "word-for-word" translation. Functional equivalence is also known as "dynamic equivalence, "idiomatic equivalence," or "thought-for-thought" translation.

The present chapter will be devoted to a study of the earliest of the translation efforts, and to those related to them by language. Before turning to these translations, however, certain technical terms involved in the history of Bible translation need to be clearly understood.

---

1. Mark L. Strauss, "Understanding New Testament Translation," in John R. Kohlenberger III, gen. ed., *The Evangelical Parallel New Testament* (New York: Oxford Univ. Press, 2003), xv.

DEFINITIONS AND DISTINCTIONS

There are more precise definitions of some of the basic words involved in Bible translation than are generally used in popular discussion. The careful student of the Bible should avoid confusing these terms.

Definitions

Translation, literal translation, and transliteration.[2] Those three terms are closely related. A translation is merely the rendering of a given literary composition from one language into another. For example, if the Bible were rendered from the original Hebrew and Greek into Latin, or from Latin into English, it would be a translation. If these later translations were rendered back into the original languages, those too would be translations. *The New English Bible,* or NEB (1961, 1970), is a translation. A literal translation is an attempt to express, as far as possible, the exact meaning of the original words of the text being translated. It is a word-for-word rendering of the text. As a result, it is somewhat rigid. Such is the case with *Young's Literal Translation of the Holy Bible* (1898). A transliteration is the rendering of the letters of one language into the corresponding letters of another. Of course, a complete transliteration of the Bible would be meaningless for one who did not understand Hebrew and Greek. However, transliteration of words such as "angel," "baptize," and "evangel" have been introduced into English.

Version, revision, revised version, and recension. Again, these are closely related terms. Technically speaking, a *version* is a translation from (or with direct reference to) the original language into any other language, although common usage neglects this distinction. The key to this is that it involves the original language of a given manuscript. For all practical purposes, the *New English Bible* (NEB, 1961, 1970), and its revision, the *Revised English Bible* (REB, 1989), are versions in this sense of the term. However, *The Rheims-Douay,* or *Douay-Rheims Bible* (1582, 1609), and the *King James Version* (AV, *Authorized Version; or KJB, King James Bible,* 1611), and their successors, all fail the test of being translated from the original languages. The Douay-Rheims was translated from the Latin Vulgate, itself a translation, while the KJV (KJB) was the fifth revision of Tyndale's version. However, *The Revised Version* (RV or ERV, 1881, 1885, 1897), *The American Standard Version* (ASV, 1901),

---

2. See discussions in chapters 19 and 20.

and *the Revised Standard Version* (RSV, 1946, 1952) are all versions in the more common use of the word. Again, the crucial factor is that a version must be translated from the original language.

A revision, or *revised version*, is a term used to describe those translations, usually from the original languages, that have been carefully and systematically reviewed and critically examined with a view to correcting errors or making other necessary emendations. The KJV is an example of such a revision, as are the Douay-Rheims-Challoner editions and the RSV. A recension is the critical and systematic revision of a text, although such works are generally and popularly called "revisions." The most outstanding example of a recent recension is the *New American Standard Bible,* NASB (1963, 1971, 1995).

Paraphrase and commentary. A *paraphrase* is a "free" or "loose" translation. It attempts to translate idea for idea rather than word for word. Hence, it is more of an interpretation than a literal translation. In the history of Bible translation this format has been very popular. As early as the seventh century, for instance, Caedmon made paraphrases of the Creation. Recent paraphrases include J. B. Phillips' *New Testament in Modern English* (1958), the American Bible Society's *Good News for Modern Man: The New Testament in Today's English,* TEV (1966), Kenneth Taylor's The Living Bible (1971), and the Holy Bible: New Living Translation (1996, 2004).

A *commentary* is simply an explanation of Scripture. The earliest example of such a work is the Midrash or Jewish commentary on the Old Testament. In recent years some Bible translations known as amplified or expanded translations have contained implicit, and sometimes explicit, commentary within the text of the translation itself. Two examples will suffice to illustrate this popular approach: Kenneth S. Wuest, *Expanded Translation of the New Testament* (1956-1959), carried the same principles to various parts of speech; and the Lockman Foundation made the fullest attempt at translating The Amplified Bible (1965), and The Amplified Bible, Expanded Edition (1987), as commentaries by the use of dashes, brackets, parentheses, and italicized words.

Distinctions

In order to appreciate fully the role of Bible translations, it is important to understand that the very process of translation itself indicates the vitality the Bible has among the people of God. At first, translations were an integral part of the religious life of the ancient Hebrews. They set the tone for all later translations. In the early church, missionary activity was accompanied by diverse translations of the Bible into various languages. As time progressed, still another phase of Bible translation arose with the developments in printing. As a result, we should carefully distinguish between three general categories of Bible translations: the ancient, medieval, and modern translations.

Ancient Translations of the Bible. The ancient translations of the Bible contained portions of the Old Testament, and sometimes the New. They appeared before the period of the church councils (ca. 350 CE) and include such works as the Samaritan Pentateuch, the Aramaic targums, the Talmud, the Midrash, and the Septuagint (LXX). Following the apostolic period, these ancient translations were continued in Aquila's version, Theodotion's revision, Symmachus's revision, Origen's *Hexapla,* and the Syriac versions of the Old Testament. Translations of the New Testament into Aramaic and Latin also appeared prior to the Council of Nicea (325).

Medieval Translations of the Bible. Medieval translations of the Bible generally contained both the Old and the New Testaments. They were completed during the period 350–1400. During this period the Latin Vulgate of Jerome (ca. 340–420) dominated the Bible translations. The Vulgate provided the basis for commentaries as well as thought throughout the Middle Ages. From it arose the paraphrases of Caedmon, the *Ecclesiastical History* by the Venerable Bede, and even the translation of the Bible into English by Wycliffe. The Bible continued to be translated into other languages throughout this period.

Modern Translations. Modern translations came into being about the time of Wycliffe and his successors. Following the example of Wycliffe, since his was the first complete English Bible, William Tyndale (1492–1536) made his translation directly from the original languages instead of the Latin Vulgate (Plate 47). Since that time multitudes of renderings have been produced containing all or parts of the Old and New Testaments. Following the development of movable typeset by Johann Gutenberg (ca. 1454), the history of Bible transmission, translation, and distribution enters into a new era.

The translation of the Bible helped to keep Judaism pure during the last centuries before Christ, as our discussion of the Samaritan Pentateuch and the targums will indicate. The Septuagint (see chap. 17) was translated into

Greek at Alexandria, Egypt, (beginning 280–250 BCE), and it set the tone for such translations into Latin and other languages (see chap. 18). These translations were vital to the evangelization, expansion, and establishment of the church. Since the Reformation era, the dissemination of the Bible has resulted in translations into numerous other languages. The role of the English Bible has been paramount among modern translations (see chaps. 19 and 20). Our discussion will follow these general topical lines, beginning with the Aramaic, Syriac, and related translations.

PRIMARY TRANSLATIONS

Early Bible translations had a twofold purpose that cannot be minimized: They were used to disseminate the message of the autographs to the people of God and assisted them in keeping their religion pure. Their proximity to the autographs also indicates their importance, since they take the Bible scholar back to the very threshold of the autographs.

The Samaritan Pentateuch

The Samaritan Pentateuch (SamP) may date from the period of Nehemiah's rebuilding of Jerusalem; and, while it is not really a translation or version, it does indicate the need for careful study in tracing the true text of Scripture. This work was actually a manuscript portion of the text of the Pentateuch itself. It contains the five books of Moses and is written in a paleo-Hebrew script quite similar to that found on the Moabite Stone (Mesha Stele) Siloam Inscription, Lachish Letters, and some of the older biblical manuscripts of Qumran (see chap. 11 discussion). The textual tradition of the Samaritan Pentateuch is independent of the Masoretic Text. It was not discovered by Christian scholars until 1616, although it had been known to such fathers of the church as Eusebius of Caesarea and Jerome, and it was first published in the Paris Polyglot (1645) and then in the London Polyglot (1657).

The roots of the Samaritans can be traced back to the time of David. During the reign of Omri (880–874 BCE) the capital was established at Samaria (1 Kings 16:24), and the entire northern kingdom came to be known as Samaria. In 732 BCE the Assyrians, under Tiglath-pileser III (745–727 BCE), conquered the northeast portion of Israel and established a policy of deportation of inhabitants and importation of other captive peoples into the area. Under Sargon II (in 721 BCE) the same procedure was followed when he captured the rest of Israel. Intermarriage was imposed by Assyria on those Israelites who were not deported in order to guarantee that no revolt would occur by automatically denationalizing and commingling the cultures of their captive peoples (2 Kings 17:24–18:1). At first, the colonists worshiped their own gods. By the time, or shortly after, the Jews returned from their own Babylonian captivity, these colonists seemed to want to follow the God of Israel. The Jews rebuffed the Samaritans who in turn opposed Israel's restoration (see Ezra 4:2–6; Neh. 5:11–6:19). About 432 BCE, however, the daughter of Sanballat was married to the grandson of the high priest Eliashib. This couple was expelled from Judah and the event provided the historical incident for the break between the Jews and the Samaritans (see Neh. 13:23–31).

The Samaritan religion as a separate system of worship actually dates from the expulsion of the high priest's grandson, about 432 BCE. At this time, a copy of the Torah may have been taken to Samaria and placed in the temple built on Mount Gerizim at Shechem (Nablus), where a rival priest-hood was established. This fifth-century date may account for both the paleo-Hebrew script and the twofold categorization of the Samaritan Pentateuch into the Law and the noncanonical books. Samaritan adherence to the Torah and their isolation from the Jews resulted in a separate textual tradition for the Law.

The earliest manuscript of the Samaritan Pentateuch dates from the mid-eleventh century as a fragmentary portion of a fourteenth-century parchment, the Abisha scroll. The oldest SamP codex bears a note about its sale in 1149–50 CE, although it is much older, and the New York Public Library owns another copy dating from about 1232. Immediately after it was discovered in 1616, the SamP was acclaimed as superior to the Masoretic Text. After careful study, however, it was relegated to an inferior status.

Only recently has it regained some of its former importance, although it is still regarded as less important than the Masoretic Text of the law. The merits of the SamP text tradition may be seen in the fact that its approximately 6,000 variants from the Masoretic Text are relatively few, mainly ortho-graphic and rather insignificant. It does claim that Mount Gerizim rather than Jerusalem is the center of worship, and adds to the accounts follow-ing Exodus 20:2–17 and Deuteronomy 5:6–21. Whenever the SamP and the LXX agree on a reading that differs from the Masoretic Text, they probably represent the original reading of the text. Otherwise, the SamP reflects cultural trends in the Hebrew setting, such as sectarian insertions, repetition of God's commands, trends toward popularizing the Old Testament text, tendencies to modernize antique word forms, and attempts to simplify difficult portions of Hebrew sentence construction.

The Aramaic Targums

The origin of the targums. There is evidence that the scribes were making oral paraphrases of the Hebrew Scriptures into Aramaic as early as the time of Ezra (Neh. 8:1–8). These were not actually translations so much as aids in understanding the archaic language of the Torah. The Levitical "teacher" gave way to the lay "interpreter, translator" (Chaldean, *methurgeman,* or *meturgeman*) who made paraphrases that played an important role in communicating the quaint-sounding Hebrew into the everyday language of the people. Before the birth of Christ, almost every book in the Old Testament had its own oral paraphrase or interpretation (targum). During the next few centuries these targums were committed to writing and an official text emerged.

The earliest Aramaic targums were probably written in Palestine during the second century CE, although there is evidence of some Aramaic targums from the pre-Christian period. These early official targums contained the Law and the Prophets, although unofficial targums of later times also included the Writings. Several unofficial Aramaic targums were found in the Qumran caves, but they were superseded by the official texts of the second century CE. During the third century, the official Palestinian targums of the law and the prophets were practically swallowed up by another family of paraphrases of the law and the prophets, the Babylonian Aramaic targums. Targums on the Writings continued to be made on an unofficial basis.

The outstanding targums. During the third century CE, an Aramaic targum on the Torah appeared in Babylonia. It was possibly a recension of an earlier Palestinian tradition, but may have originated in Babylonia, and has been traditionally ascribed to Onkelos (Ongelos), although the name is probably confused with Aquila (see chap. 17). The Babylonian Talmud mentions the Targum Didan ("our Targum"), thus acknowledging its official status for public reading in the synagogues of Talmudic times.

The Targum of Jonathan ben Uzziel is another Babylonian Aramaic targum that accompanies the prophets (former and latter). It dates from the fourth century and is a freer rendering of the text than Onkelos. Both these targums were read in synagogues: Onkelos along with the Torah, which was read in its entirety, and Jonathan along with selections from the prophets (haphtaroth, pl.). In modern times, Yemenite Jews continue to use the targum as a liturgical text. Since the kethuvim (writings) were not read publicly in the synagogues, no official targum was made, although unofficial copies were used by individuals. Most of the kethuvim have targumim, originating mostly in Palestine (western) rather than Babylonia (eastern). Daniel and Ezra–Nehemiah have no targums, since they contain Aramaic portions, and Daniel foretells the date of Messiah's coming. Poorly preserved and less well known, the Palestinian Targum Kethuvim tradition made its way to Italy and from there to medieval Ashkenaz and Sepharad.

During the middle of the seventh century the Pseudo-Jonathan Targum on the Pentateuch appeared. It is a mixture of the Onkelos Targum and some Midrash materials. Still another targum appeared about 700, the Jerusalem Targum, but it survives in fragments only. None of these targums is important on textual grounds, but they do provide significant information for the study of hermeneutics since they indicate the manner in which Scripture was interpreted by rabbinical scholars. Even after Jewish communities had largely ceased speaking Aramaic, the targum never ceased to be a major source for Jewish biblical exegesis. The targum continues to be printed alongside the text in Jewish editions of the Bible with commentaries.

The Talmud and Midrash

A second period of the Old Testament scribal tradition appeared between 100–500 CE known as the Talmudic period. The Talmud (lit., instruction) grew up as a body of Hebrew civil and canonical law based on the Torah. The Talmud basically represents the opinions and decisions of Jewish teachers from about 300 BCE to 500 CE, and it consists of two main divisions: the Mishnah and the Gemara. The Mishnah (repetition, explanation) was completed about 200 CE as a Hebrew digest of all the oral laws since the time of Moses. It was highly regarded as the second law, the Torah being the first. The Gemara (completion) was an Aramaic expanded commentary on the Mishnah. It was transmitted in two traditions: the Palestinian Gemara (ca. 200) and the larger, more authoritative Babylonian Gemara (ca. 500).

The Midrash (lit. textual study) is actually a formal doctrinal and homiletical exposition of the Hebrew Scriptures written in Hebrew and Aramaic. About 100 BCE–300 CE these were gathered into a body consisting of the *Halakah* (procedure), a further expansion of the Torah only, and the *Haggadah* (declaration, explanation), being commentaries on the entire Old Testament. The Midrash actually differs from the targums in that they are commentaries instead of paraphrases. The Midrash contains some of the earliest extant synagogue homilies on the Old Testament, as well as some proverbs and parables.

Syriac Translations

The Syriac (Aramaic) language of the Old Testament, and indeed of the Gospels, was comparable to the koine in Greek and the Vulgate in Latin. It was the common language of the market. Since Palestinian Jews of our Lord's time undoubtedly spoke Aramaic, the language of this entire region, it is reasonable to assume that the Jews in nearby Syria also spoke it. In fact, Josephus relates that first-century Jews proselytized in the areas east of ancient Nineveh, near Arbela. After the martyrdom of Stephen, disciples "traveled as far as Phoenicia and Cyprus and Antioch, speaking the word to no one except Jews. But there were some of them, men of Cyprus and Cyrene, who on coming to Antioch spoke to the Hellenists also, preaching the Lord Jesus. . . . And in Antioch the disciples were first called Christians" (Acts 11:19–20, 26). Following the Jewish example, early Christians went into the same area and then on into Central Asia, India, and even China. The basic language of this entire branch of Christianity was Syriac, or what F. F. Bruce has called "Christian Aramaic." Once the church began to move out from Syria in its missionary efforts, the need for a version of the Bible for that area became urgent.

The Syriac Peshitta. The Bible translated into Syriac was comparable to the Vulgate in Latin. It is known as the Peshitta (lit., simple). The Old Testament text of the Peshitta stems from a mid-second- and early-third-century text, although the name Peshitta dates from the ninth century. The Old Testament was probably translated from Hebrew, but it was revised to conform to the Septuagint (LXX). Where the Peshitta follows the Masoretic Text (MT), it gives valuable support to the text, but it is not too reliable as an independent witness to the Old Testament text. Its main contribution is in

the area of the Old Testament canon. It omits the Apocryphal or deuterocanonical books of the Alexandrian Canon (see chap. 9).

The standard edition of the Syriac New Testament is believed to stem
from a fifth-century revision by Rabbula, Bishop of Edessa (411–435).
His revision was actually a recension of earlier Syriac versions which were
brought closer to the Greek manuscripts then in use in Constantinople
(Byzantium). This edition of the Syriac New Testament, plus the Christian recension of the Syriac Old Testament, has come to be known as the
Peshitta. Following Rabbula's order that a copy of his recension be placed in
every church in his diocese, the Peshitta had widespread circulation during
the middle and late fifth century. The Peshitta became the authorized version of the two main branches of Syriac Christianity, the Nestorians and the
Jacobites. From the fifth century onward the Peshitta had a wide circulation
in the East, and was accepted and honored by all the numerous sects of the
greatly divided Syriac Christianity. It had a great missionary influence on
the Armenian, Georgian, Arabic, and Persian versions. The famous Nestorian tablet of Sing-an-fu witnesses to the presence of the Syriac Scriptures in
the heart of China in the seventh century.

Brought west to Vienna by Moses of Minde (1555), Immanuel Tremel-
lius, the converted Jew whose scholarship was so valuable to the English
reformers and divines, made use of the Peshitta, and in 1569 issued a Syriac
New Testament in Hebrew letters. In 1645 the editio princeps of the Old
Testament was prepared by Gabriel Sionita for the Paris Polyglot, and in
1657 the whole Peshitta found a place in Walton's London Polyglot. The
choice of books included in the Old Testament Peshitta changes from
one manuscript to another. Usually most of the deuterocanonical books
(1 Esdras, 3 Maccabees, 4 Maccabees, Psalm 151) can be found in some manuscripts. The manuscript of Biblioteca Ambrosiana (discovered in 1866)
includes also 2 Baruch (Syriac Apocalypse of Baruch). The Peshitta version
of the New Testament continues the *Diatessaron* and Old Syriac traditions,
with some "Western" renderings in Acts, combined with some of the more
complex "Byzantine" readings of the fifth century. The Peshitta New Testament omits 2 Peter, 2 John, 3 John, Jude, and Revelation, although modern
Syriac Bibles add sixth- or seventh-century translations of these five books
to a revised Peshitta text. Almost all Syriac scholars agree that the Peshitta
gospels are translations of the Greek originals.

A minority viewpoint argues an Aramaic primacy that the Peshitta represents the original New Testament and that the Greek is a translation of it. Advocates of the Aramaic primacy include the Holy Bible from the Ancient Eastern Text, George M. Lamsa's translation from the Aramaic of the Peshitta (1968), as the authorized Bible.[3] The Patriarchate of the Church of the East states (Modesto, California, April 5, 1957), that "the Church of the East received the scriptures from the hands of the blessed Apostles themselves in the Aramaic original, the language spoken by our Lord Jesus Christ himself, and that the Peshitta is the text of the Church of the East which has come down from the Biblical times without any change or revision."[4] The Peshitta represents a Byzantine text type.

The Syro-Hexaplaric Version. The Syro-Hexaplar text of the Old Testament was a Syriac translation of the fifth column of Origen's *Hexapla* (see chap. 17). Although it was translated about 616 by Paul, Bishop of Tella, it never actually took root in the Syrian churches. This was partly because it was an excessively literal rendering of the Greek text in violation of Syriac idiom. The literal character of its translation makes the Syro-Hexaplar text a valuable aid in determining the correct text of the *Hexapla*. Manuscript portions of it have survived in the Codex Mediolanensis (M), Milanese Codex (Latin), consisting of 2 Kings, Isaiah, the Twelve, Lamentations, and the Poetical books (except Psalms). The Pentateuch and historical books survived until about 1574, but they have subsequently disappeared. Like the Peshitta, the text of this version is basically Byzantine.

The Diatessaron of Tatian (ca. 170). Tatian was an Assyrian Christian and follower of Justin Martyr in Rome. After the death of his mentor, Tatian returned to his native country and made a "scissors-and-paste" harmony of the Gospels known as the *Diatessaron* (lit., through the four). According to D. C. Parker,

> Tatian was a Syrian who came to Rome and was converted to Christianity at some time between 150 and 165, returning to the east after 172. At an unknown point he made his *Diatessaron*, a Gospel harmony in which the

---

3. George M. Lamsa, *Holy Bible from the Ancient Eastern Text* (San Francisco: Harper Collins, 1968).

4. See George Lamsa, "Preface," attested by Mar Eshai Shimun, by Grace, Catholicos Patriarch of the East, ii.

four narratives are woven into a single fabric (he may in fact have drawn also on a fifth source, but this is by no means clear). This was a very popular text in ancient times, especially in Syrian circles. In spite of this, no copy is known to survive. It is not known whether the *Diatessaron* was composed in Greek or in Syriac. . . .[5]

In the absence of any copies of the *Diatessaron*, we are wholly dependent upon a range of indirect witnesses. These are divided into two branches, one Eastern and one Western. The most valuable Eastern evidence is provided by the *Commentary on the Diatessaron* by Ephraem (ca. 306–373; the commentary was probably written after 363). An Armenian version published in 1836 was an important impetus to the growth of Diatessaronic study, which until then had not existed. The discovery and publication (1963) of a Syriac manuscript containing more than half of the work was a major step forward.[6]

Tatian's work is known mainly through indirect references, but it was a popular and widely used work until it was abolished by Rabbula and Theodoret, bishop of Cyrrhus, in 423, because Tatian had belonged to the heretical sect known as the Encratites. Tatian's work was so popular that Ephraem, a Syrian father, wrote a commentary on it before Theodoret had all copies of it (about two hundred) destroyed. In its place, Theodoret presented another translation of the Gospels of the Four Evangelists.

Since the *Diatessaron* has not survived, it is impossible to determine whether it was originally written in Syriac or, more likely, in Greek and later translated into Syriac. Ephraem's commentary on the *Diatessaron* was written in Syriac, but it too has been lost. An Armenian translation of the commentary has survived, however, as have two Arabic translations of the *Diatessaron*. Although the original *Diatessaron* would bear heavily on New Testament textual criticism, its secondary witness from the translation and the commentary in translation add little additional weight to the text. One fact is observable, however: the *Diatessaron* was influenced by both the Eastern and Western texts of the New Testament.

The Old Syriac Manuscripts. The *Diatessaron* was not the only form of

---

5. D. C. Parker, *An Introduction to the New Testament Manuscripts and Their Texts* (Cambridge: Cambridge Univ. Press, 2008), 135. Also see D.C. Parker, "A Copy of the Codex Mediolanensis," *Journal of Theological Studies* 41 (1990), 537–41.

6. Ibid., 331–35.

the Gospels used among the Syrian churches. Among scholars there was a tendency to read them in one or another of several separate forms. Even before the time of Tatian, such writers as Hegesippus quoted from another Syriac version of the Bible. This Old Syriac text of the Gospels was typical of the Western text type, and it has survived in two manuscripts. The first of these is a parchment known as the Curetonian Syriac, and the second is a palimpsest known as the Sinaitic Syriac. These gospels were called "the Separated Ones," because they were not interwoven in the manner of Tatian's *Diatessaron.* Although there are differences between the readings of these two texts, they both reflect the same version of a text dating from the late second or early third century. No Old Syriac texts of the remainder of the New Testament have survived, although they have been reconstructed on the basis of citations in the writings of the Fathers of the Eastern church.

Other Syriac Versions. Three additional Syriac versions require a comment, even though they reflect texts later than those already discussed. In 508 a new Syriac New Testament was completed that included the books omitted by the Peshitta (2 Peter, 2 John, 3 John, Jude, and Revelation). This work was actually a Syriac revision of the entire Bible by Bishop Polycarp under the direction of Zenaia (Philoxenus), a Jacobite bishop at Mabbug in eastern Syria. This Philoxenian Syriac translation reveals that the Syrian church had not accepted the entire New Testament canon until the sixth century. In 616 another bishop of Mabbug, Thomas of Harkel (Heraclea), reissued the Philoxenian text, to which he either added some marginal notes or thoroughly revised in a much more literal style. His revision is known as the Harklean version, although the Old Testament portion was done by Paul of Tella, as indicated earlier. The critical apparatus of the Harklean book of Acts is the second most important witness to the Western text, being surpassed in this respect only by Codex Bezae.

The third Syriac version is known as the Palestinian Syriac. No complete New Testament book from this translation exists. Its text probably dates from the fifth century and it survives in fragmentary form only, mostly from lectionaries of the Gospels dating from the eleventh and twelfth centuries.

Secondary Translations

Although the Samaritan Pentateuch, the Talmud, and the earliest Midrash manuscripts were written in paleo-Hebrew and Hebrew characters and thus

270 FROM GOD TO US

do not even qualify as translations, they did provide a basis for later works of translation by making the Scriptures available for use by the people of God. The Aramaic targums and various Syriac translations of the Bible further underscored this trend by placing them into the basic languages of Jewish and early Christian believers. While Greek and Latin texts, whatever their date and whatever the script in which they were produced and transmitted in manuscript form, are printed and written today in a single script, Syriac printed New Testament books may be found in one of three scripts. Estrangelo, the oldest of the three, is the script of the Old Syriac Gospel manuscripts.

The other two scripts owe their separate existence to the division between those Syrian Christians who accepted the decisions of the Council of Chalcedon and those who did not, preferring the views of Nestorius. There are exceptions, but by and large the former used the Serta script (sometimes called Jacobite) and the Maronite script among the Syrians of India. The third script is Madnhaya ("eastern"), also called Nestorian and Assyrian. Serta is found mostly within the Roman empire, Madnhaya further east.[7] From these basic versions arose several secondary translations. These secondary translations have little textual merit, but they do indicate the basic vitality of Christian missions and the desire of new believers for the Word of God in their own language.

Nestorian translations. When the Nestorians were condemned at the Council at Ephesus (431) their founder, Nestorius (d. ca. 451), was placed in a monastery as part of a compromise that brought many of his followers into the camp of his opponents. The Persian Nestorians, however, broke away and became a separate schismatic church. They spread into Central and even into East Asia and translated the Bible into several languages as they moved along their way. Among their translations are the so-called Sogdian versions. These translations were based on the Syriac Scriptures rather than the Hebrew and Greek Testaments. Scant remains of their work have survived, and all this is from the ninth, tenth, and later centuries. Textually speaking, none of these translations is significant, since each is a translation of a translation. The devastating work of Tamerlane, "the Scourge of Asia," almost exterminated the Nestorians and their heritage toward the close of the fourteenth century.

---

7. This discussion follows Parker, *Introduction to the New Testament Manuscripts*, 65.

Arabic translations. Subsequent to the rise of Islam (following the *hejirah,* the flight of Muhammad in 622 CE), the Bible was translated into Arabic from Greek, Syriac, Coptic, Latin, and various combinations of them. The earliest of the various Arabic translations appears to have stemmed from the Syriac, possibly the Old Syriac, about the time Islam emerged as a major force in history (ca. 720). Muhammad (570–632), the founder of Islam, knew the gospel story through oral tradition only, and this was based on Syriac sources. The only standardized Old Testament translation into Arabic was done by the Jewish scholar Saadia Gaon (ca. 930). Similar to the Nestorian translations, the Arabic translations range from the ninth to the thirteenth centuries. Except for the Old Testament, Arabic translations are based on translations rather than the original texts, and thus offer little if any textual assistance.

One of the noted characteristics of this is that the word for *God* in Arabic used in these transalations is the word "Allah." This does not mean, of course, that the Christian concept of God is the same as that of Islam. It is not. It simply means that "Allah" is the common word for God in Arabic, just as "Theos" is in Greek, and "Deus" is in Latin. So, it is natural to use "Allah" when translating the Bible into Arabic.

Old Persian translations. Two Old Persian translations of the Gospels are known, but they are themselves translations of the fourteenth-century Syriac text and a later Greek text. The latter has some resemblance to the Caesarean text, but it is of little use in textual criticism.

17

GREEK *and* RELATED TRANSLATIONS

DURING THE CAMPAIGNS of Alexander the Great (336–323 BCE), Jews were shown considerable favor. As Alexander moved on in his conquests, he established centers of population to administer his newly acquired territories. Many of these cities were named Alexandria, and they became centers of culture where Jews were given preferential treatment. Just as they had abandoned their native Hebrew tongue for Aramaic in the Near East, so they abandoned Aramaic in favor of Greek in such centers as Alexandria, Egypt.

Following the sudden death of Alexander in 323 BCE, his empire was divided into several dynasties by his generals. The Ptolemies gained control over Egypt, the Seleucids dominated Asia Minor, the Antigonids took Macedonia, and several minor kingdoms emerged. As far as the Bible is concerned, the Egyptian dynasty of the Ptolemies is of primary importance. It received its name from Ptolemy I Soter, the son of Lagus, who was governor from 323 to 305 and king from that time until his death in 285. He was succeeded by his son Ptolemy II Philadelphus (285–246), who married his sister Arsinoë after the example of the Pharaohs.

During the reign of Ptolemy II Philadelphus, the Jews received full political and religious privileges. It was also during this time that Egypt itself experienced a tremendous cultural and educational program under the patronage of Arsinoë. Included in this program were the founding of the museum at Alexandria and the translation of great works into Greek. Among the works which began to be translated into Greek at this time was the Hebrew Old Testament. It was, indeed, the very first time that it had been extensively translated into any language, as chapter 16 indicates. Our present discussion will center on this translation and those closely related to it.

The Septuagint

The leaders of Alexandrian Jewry produced a standard Greek version of the Old Testament known as the Septuagint (LXX), the Greek word for seventy. Although the term applies strictly to the Pentateuch, the only portion of the Hebrew Bible completely translated during the time of Ptolemy II Philadelphus, it has come to denote the entire Greek translation of the Old Testament. The Jewish community itself later lost interest in preserving their Greek version when Christians began to use it extensively for their own Old Testament Scriptures. Apart from the Pentateuch, the remainder of the Old Testament was probably translated during the third and second centuries BCE. Certainly it was completed before 150 BCE, since it is discussed in a letter of Aristeas to Philocrates (ca. 130–100 BCE).

This letter of Aristeas relates how the librarian at Alexandria persuaded Ptolemy to translate the Torah into Greek for use by the Jews in Alexandria. He goes on to report how six translators from each of the twelve tribes were chosen and that their work was completed in only seventy-two days. Although the details of this event are fictitious, they do indicate that the translation of the LXX for use by Alexandrian Jews is authentic.

For the most part it was a book-by-book, chapter-by-chapter reproduction of the traditional (Heb., *masoreh*) Hebrew text in use following the loss of the original by the time of the Babylonian captivity. The koine Greek of the Septuagint contains common stylistic and idiomatic differences from the traditional Hebrew. It was accepted first by Alexandrian Jews and afterwards by all the Greek-speaking peoples. It helped introduce into Greek the theological terminology of Scripture. Even Palestinian Jews recognized the LXX as a legitimate text. The Septuagint was the Bible of Jesus and the apostles, and the majority of New Testament quotations are taken from the Septuagint directly. It was the basic text of the Greek codices and was used for early Latin translations of the Bible adopted in the Western church. It remains the official authoritative text in the Eastern (Orthodox) church. On the whole, the LXX closely parallels the Masoretic Text and tends to confirm the fidelity of Hebrew texts produced by the Masoretes during the tenth century CE.

The quality of the translation of the Septuagint is not consistent throughout, and this leads us to several basic observations. First, the LXX ranges from a slavishly literal rendition of the Torah (Pentateuch) to free translations of the writings. Second, there must have been a different purpose in view for the LXX from that of the Hebrew Bible, such as public readings in the synagogues as opposed to scholarly work by the scribes. Third, the LXX was a pioneer effort in translation of the Old Testament text and an excellent example of such an enterprise. Finally, the LXX is generally faithful to the reading of the Old Testament Hebrew text, as indicated in chapter 12.

One question that is raised by the LXX, however, comes from the fact that there are places where it differs from the Masoretic Text (MT), and where the Dead Sea Scrolls (DSS) and Discoveries in the Judean Desert (DJD) agree with it as opposed to the Hebrew text. Several passages may be indicated that underscore this point, such as Deuteronomy 32:8; Exodus 1:5; Isaiah 7:14; and Hebrews 1:6 (KJV), which quotes Deuteronomy 32:43. In addition, the DSS also contain some of the Apocryphal books of the Old Testament, such as Psalm 151, which are known only through the Septuagint. From the available evidence about these variant readings between the texts, we are able to observe three basic textual traditions of the Old Testament: the MT, the Samaritan Pentateuch (SamP) (see chap. 16), and the LXX. On the whole, the MT is the best, but in several passages the LXX is better. The SamP reflects sectarian and cultural differences from the Hebrew text, and the LXX is itself a translation rather than the original text. Nevertheless, when the SamP and LXX agree against the MT, they probably witness to the original reading. Still, the Septuagint is generally faithful to the Masoretic Text readings, as are the Dead Sea Scrolls.

A comparison of the variants in a given chapter of the Bible may be used to illustrate this point. In Isaiah 53, for example, there are 166 words. The only significant change is the addition of the single word, "light," which is added to verse 11 and does not significantly affect the meaning. Furthermore, this word is supported by both the LXX and the Dead Sea Scrolls 1Q(Isaᵃ). This example is typical of the entire Isaiah A manuscript. It compels the reader to note the dependability of the Old Testament text in such a way that he recognizes that all the variant readings do nothing to change our understanding of the religious teaching of the Bible.

As a result of this quality, the importance of the LXX is easily observable. It bridged the religious gap between the Hebrew- and Greek-speaking peoples, as it met the needs of the Alexandrian Jews. It also bridged the historical gap between the Hebrew Old Testament of the Jews and the Greek-speaking Christians who would take the LXX as their Old Testament and use it alongside their own New Testament Scriptures. In addition, it provided an important precedent for missionaries and Christian scholars to make translations of the whole Bible into various languages and dialects. On textual grounds, it bridges the gap between the Hebrew Old Testament and the great codices of the church (*Aleph*, A, B, C, et al.). Although the LXX does not have the excellence of the Hebrew text, it does indicate its integrity.

Critical corrections were made to the Septuagint by Origen, Lucian, and Hesychius before it was published in the celebrated Codex Vaticanus (B, 02) and Sinaiticus (‎א‎, *Aleph*, 01, S) in the fourth century, and Codex Alexandrinus (A, 03) in the fifth century. Written in Egypt on fine vellum, Codex Marchalianus (Q) is a most valuable sixth-century copy of the Prophets. Its text is a result of the Hesychian recension and its marginal readings contain additions by Origen as well as a great number of variant readings from the *Hexaplar* text written by an almost contemporary hand. Codex Q is used in discussion about the Tetragrammaton (‎יהוה‎, YHWH) in Isaiah 45:18. All printed editions of the Septuagint are derived from these recensions, with Codex Vaticanus representing the purest textual tradition of the Septuagint. The edition princeps from Origen's *Hexaplar* text was produced in the Complutensian Polyglot (1514–1518), and a purer Aldine edition, closer to Vaticanus, was published in Venice (1518). American Charles Thomson published the first English translation of the Septuagint without the Apocrypha (1808), revised and enlarged by C. A. Muses (1954). The second was by Sir Lancelot Charles Lee Brenton (1844).[1] His *The Septuagint with Apocrypha: Greek and English* (1851) became the long-time standard edition. Paul W. Espisito revised Brenton's Septuagint as *The Apostles' Bible* (2008). *The Apostolic Bible: Polyglot* (1996)[2] was followed by a fourth translation: *A New*

---

1. Sir Lancelot Charles Lee Brenton, *The Septuagint Version of the Old Testament According to the Vatican Text*, translated into English (1844).

2. Charles Van der Pool published the *Apostolic Bible: Polyglot* (Newport, Oreg.: The Apostolic Press, 1996). A digitized version released at apostolic.com, 2006.

English Translation of the Septuagint (NETS, 2007).[3] The Greek text of NETS frequently departs from Alfred Rahlf's Septuaginta (1935) and is based on the 24 volume Göttengin Septuagint (1931–2006). The NETS aims to translate the text in present-day literary language to communicate to the well-educated constituency familiar with and accustomed to the New Revised Standard Version (NRSV, 1989) upon which it is based.

OTHER GREEK VERSIONS

As a result of Jewish criticism during the early centuries of Christianity, a reaction set in among the Jews against the Septuagint. Their rejection produced a new wave of translations of the Old Testament, such as the Greek translations known as Aquila's version and Symmachus's version, and even led to the first great work of textual criticism in the mid-third century, the *Hexapla* of Origen. All of these works play an important role in the study of textual criticism, since they are actually closer to the autographs than many of the Hebrew manuscript copies still extant.

F. F. Bruce has suggested that there are two basic reasons why the Jews rejected the Septuagint in the first centuries of the church. First, the LXX had been adopted by Christians as their own Old Testament text and freely used it in the propagation and defense of their faith. Second, a revised edition of the standard Hebrew text was established about 100 CE. At first it included the Pentateuch and later on the rest of the Old Testament. The end result of this revision process was the establishment of the Masoretic Text. Since there was no basic text acceptable to both Christians and Jews, Jewish scholars decided to correct the situation by making new Greek translations of their Scriptures.

Aquila's Version (ca. 130–150 CE). A new translation of the Old Testament was made for Greek-speaking Jews during the first half of the second century. It was done by Aquila, a man reported to have been a relative of the Emperor Hadrian who had moved to Jerusalem from Sinope as a civil servant. While at Jerusalem, Aquila was converted to Christianity, but found himself unable to forsake his pre-Christian ideas and habits. He was publicly

---

3. Albert Pietersma and Benjamin G. Wright, eds., *A New English Translation of the Septuagint* (NETS), and the other Greek translations traditionally included under that title (New York: Oxford Univ. Press, 2007).

rebuked by the elders of the church, took offense, and left Christianity for Judaism. As a Jewish proselyte, he studied under the famed Rabbi Aqiba and translated the Old Testament into Greek.

Much of this story is undoubtedly fabricated, but Aquila was probably a Jewish proselyte from the area of the Black Sea who flourished during the first half of the second century. He did make a new translation of the Old Testament from Hebrew into Greek, and is the Aquila wrongly associated with the Onkelos Targum as mentioned in chapter 16. Aquila's version of the Old Testament was a rigidly slavish translation of the Hebrew text. Although he used Greek words, the thought patterns and sentence structures followed Hebrew rules of composition. Nevertheless, Aquila's text became the official Greek version of the Old Testament used among non-Christian Jews. It has survived only in fragments and quotations.

Theodotion's Revision (ca. 150–185). The next important Greek translation of the Old Testament is attributed to Theodotion. The exact place and date of this work is disputed, although it appears to have been a revision of an earlier Greek version: either of the LXX, possibly Aquila's, or perhaps of some other Greek version. It seems most probable that it was done by Theodotion, a native of Ephesus, who was either a Jewish proselyte or an Ebionite Christian. His revision was much freer than Aquila's version, and in some instances he even replaced some of the older Septuagint renderings of the Hebrew text. Theodotion's translation of Daniel soon replaced the LXX version among Christians (e.g., Irenaeus of Lyons), and appeared in some of the early catalogs of the Scriptures. His rendition of Ezra–Nehemiah may have superseded the LXX version as well. Theodotion included deuterocanonical fragments of Daniel, postscripts of Job, and the Book of Baruch, but omitted the book of Esther. Origen used it in the *Hexapla* and from it supplied missing parts of the Septuagint.

Symmachus's Revision (ca. 185–200). Symmachus seems to have followed Theodotion in time as well as theological commitment, although some date this work prior to Theodotion's. Jerome believed that Symmachus was an Ebionite Christian, but Epiphanius asserts that he was a Samaritan convert to Judaism. Their disagreement makes little difference, however, since the purpose of Symmachus's work was to make an idiomatic Greek rendition of the text. As a translator, Symmachus stands at the opposite pole from Aquila. He was concerned with the sense of his translation rather than the exactness of its meaning. From this perspective, Symmachus exhibited high standards of accuracy that have had a profound influence on later Bible translators. His turning of Hebrew phrases into good and idiomatic Greek brings Symmachus nearer than any of his rivals to the modern conception of a translator's duty. Curiously, Symmachus had more influence on the Latin Bible than on later Greek translations, for Jerome made considerable use of him in his preparation of the Vulgate.

Origen's Hexapla (ca. 240–250). The translations of the Hebrew Bible into Greek resulted in the four different textual traditions by the beginning of the third century CE: the LXX, Aquila's version, and the revisions of Theodotion and Symmachus. This conflicted state of affairs opened the door for the first really outstanding attempt at textual criticism. This work was undertaken by Origen of Alexandria (185–254). Because of the many divergences existing among the various manuscripts of the LXX, the discrepancies between the Hebrew text and that of the LXX, and the various attempts at revising the Greek translations, Origen seems to have decided to provide a satisfactory Greek text of the Old Testament for the Christian world. His work was essentially a recension rather than a version or a revision, since he corrected textual corruptions and attempted to unify the Greek and Hebrew texts. He seems to have had a threefold objective: to correct the text of the Septuagint that was current in the church of his day, to provide an apologetic tool for Christians in their disputes with the Jews, and to bring understanding from the multiple ways of reading Scripture as an exegetical endeavor.[4] He used various revisions of the Old Testament LXX text to provide a comparative view of the existing Hebrew text along with divergent LXX texts.

The arrangement of the *Hexapla* (sixfold) was in six parallel columns. Each column contained a particular version of the Old Testament, making it an extremely bulky work. In the first column Origen placed the Hebrew text. In column two was a Greek transliteration of the Hebrew text. The literal

---

4. T. M. Law, "Origen's Parallel Bible: Textual Criticism, Apologetics, Exegesis," *Journal of Theological Studies*, vol. 89, pt. 1 (April 2008): 1–21. In his article, Law argues that the best approach to understanding why Origen compiled the *Hexapla* is something of an "exegetical maximalism," following A. Kamesar's definition that " 'exegetical maximalism' is the process of allowing both the Hebrew and the Greek texts to speak from multiple senses of interpretation. The perspective of this method is that it looks forward in a sense rather than backwards toward some 'original text' " (p. 17).

translation of Aquila was placed in column three, with the idiomatic revision of Symmachus in column four. Origen placed his own revision of the LXX text in column five, and added Theodotion's revision in column six.

In his *Hexapla* of the Psalms, Origen added three further columns, but only two of them were different translations. He also made a separate work called the *Tetrapla,* which was the *Hexapla* with columns one and two omitted. Origen's tremendous work has not survived the ravages of time, although Eusebius and Pamphilus did publish the fifth column (Origen's own translation of the LXX) with additions. It has survived in the fourth or fifth century Codex Sarravianus (G), which contains portions of Genesis through Judges. It is the only Greek edition of any significance that has been preserved, although there is a Syriac translation of the *Hexapla* dating from the seventh century, and some individual manuscripts have also survived, such as Codex Marchalianus (Q), which contains the text of the Twelve Prophets, Isaiah, Jeremiah, Baruch, Lamentations, Ezekiel, and Daniel (Theodotion version), with Susanna and Bel.

One accomplishment of Origen is observable in what has been discovered and disclosed about his techniques of textual criticism. He had discovered many corruptions, omissions, additions, and transpositions in the copies of the LXX of his day. Many of these discoveries were made by comparing the various revisions of the Greek Old Testament, but Origen was primarily concerned about bringing the LXX texts into greater conformity with the Hebrew text of column one of his *Hexapla.* He developed an elaborate system of critical markings to disclose the problems he uncovered in arriving at his own translation in column five. This enabled the reader to see which corruptions had been corrected, which omissions and additions had been made, and where words had been transposed among the various Greek texts.

Origen used an obelus (−), a horizontal stroke, to indicate when a reading appeared in the LXX that was not in the Hebrew text. When a reading appeared in the Hebrew text but was omitted in the LXX, Origen supplied the reading from Theodotion's revision and marked its beginning with an asterisk (※ or ⁎). He indicated the end of these corrections with a metobelus (✕). Where short passages were transposed, Origen would leave them where they appeared in the LXX and indicate them with a combination asterisk-obelus sign (※− or ⁎−) at the beginning and a metobelus at the close. In long transposed passages the Hebrew order would be restored.

In addition to its textual-critical importance, Origen's *Hexapla* was an important apologetic tool used by Christians as they encountered Jewish opponents. Instead of trying to establish a corrected text, Origen's purpose was "to provide a convenient tool for Christians to compare their Scriptures with those of the Jews when the need arose to defend the Bible of the Church." T. M. Law says, "If this text were to be used solely for debates against the Jews, it would seem to be counterproductive to use three Jewish translations. Origen's apologetic would have been hampered by an appeal to the Jewish revisions; his conviction was that the Septuagint was a new dispensation for the Church apart from, even if closely following, the Jewish Scriptures."[5] Origen gave no indication that his text was intended for use outside the church, and Law goes on to follow J. Wright that Origen's apologetic agenda was merely fit for the momentary need to defend the Septuagint against its critics.

T. M. Law, who finds these two most common explanations for Origen's motivation to be inadequate in themselves, adds that the primary purpose for his project cannot be reduced to one single explanation. Instead, he argues that Origen's whole lifetime experience, from both Alexandria and Caesarea, provided varying and powerful influences from prevailing methods of interpretation. His academic background developed his theological skill, and his pastoral experience enabled him to preach with clarity and persuasiveness. Origen is antipathic toward dogmatism when he interprets the text. When he "presents several interpretations of the same passage, all of [them] remain hypothetical. He insists on only what is decisively taught by the Church. Origen refuses to declare a single interpretation on everything else."[6]

After completing the *Hexapla*, Origen continued to comment on the Septuagint. Occasionally addressing the dissimilarities between the Greek and Hebrew texts, he allows both to speak. This methodology of allowing both versions to speak is called "exegetical maximalism," a method that is driven by multiple senses of interpretation, resulting in an expansion of the size of the Bible in order to increase the exegetical possibilities. Thus, Origen's exegetical work uses the recensions in addition to the Septuagint text so that he might work "forward" to a sense, rather than "backward" toward

---

5. Ibid., 13–14.
6. Ibid., 16–17.

some "original text." According to Law, "In the end, the best approach to answering the question of why Origen compiled the Hexapla might actually [be] a sort of 'exegetical maximalism' described above. A bit of all three positions is better than any one."[7] The standard two-volume edition of the remains of Origen's *Hexapla* (1875) by Field is now outdated by the Göttingen Septuagint (1931–2006) and is a vital part of the Hexaplaric tradition.

While Origen's task was of monumental significance, it is important for us to observe that his basic objective was different from that of the modern textual critic. His purpose was to produce a Greek version corresponding as closely as possible to the Hebrew text. The modern textual critic endeavors to recover the original text of the LXX itself as evidence for what the Hebrew text was before the development of the Masoretic Text. The transmission of Origen's LXX text without the accompanying diacritical markings he supplied has led to the dissemination of a corrupted Greek Old Testament text rather than the production and preservation of a Septuagint version which conformed to the Hebrew text of that day. Had Origen's *Hexapla* survived, it would be a treasure beyond price, for it would provide us with a copy of the standard Hebrew text of the third century CE, help solve the dispute over Hebrew pronunciation, and provide information about the Greek versions and translations of Origen's day. Only a translation of the fifth column has survived, largely through the work of Bishop Paul of Tella, in the Syro-Hexaplar text, in an eighth-century copy which is currently housed in the museum at Milan.

Other Recensions of the Septuagint. Early in the fourth century, Eusebius of Caesarea and his friend Pamphilus published their own editions of Origen's fifth column. As a result, they advanced the version of the LXX, which became the standard edition in many places. Two other scholars attempted to revise the Greek text of the Old Testament too. Hesychius, an Egyptian bishop martyred in 311, made a recension which is preserved only in the quotations from the text made by church writers in Egypt. The recovery of his work is dependent upon quotations of such writers as Cyril of Alexandria (d. 444). The works of Chrysostom (d. 407) and Theodoret (d. 444) may be used to recover still another recension of the Old Testament Greek text known as the Lucian Recension. Lucian was a resident of Samosata and

---

7. Ibid., 21.

Antioch who was also martyred in 311.

These two recensions, coupled with the works of Aquila, Theodotion, Symmachus, and Origen, provided Christians with the Old Testament text in Greek in North Syria, Asia Minor, Greece, Egypt, and the regions of Jerusalem and Caesarea. All of this was accomplished before the time of Jerome. As far as the modern textual scholar is concerned, the various translations of the Old Testament provide valuable witnesses to the Hebrew text.

THE SEPTUAGINT AND EARLY CHRISTIAN LITERATURE

A table of versions of the Septuagint depicts the vital connection to early Bible (LXX) translations, as shown in *The Septuagint in Context*, by Natalia Fernandez Marcos. Each translation includes (in parentheses) an approximate date for each version. The oldest translation for a language is indicated, not the date of later revisions or translations.

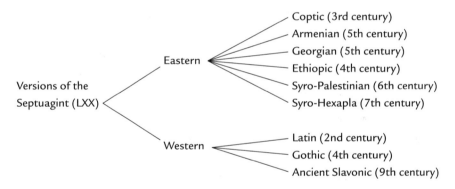

SOURCE: Natalia Fernandez Marcos, *The Septuagint in Context: Introduction to the Greek Version of the Bible*, Wilfred G. E. Watson, ed. (Leiden, Netherlands: Brill, 2000), 361.

TRANSLATIONS OF THE GREEK TEXT

Among the multitudes present in Jerusalem on the day of Pentecost were "Parthians and Medes and Elamites and residents of Mesopotamia, Judea and Cappadocia, Pontus and Asia, Phrygia and Pamphilia, Egypt and the parts of Libya belonging to Cyrene, and visitors from Rome, both Jews and proselytes, Cretans and Arabians" (Acts 2:9–11). These individuals would undoubtedly need the Scriptures in their own tongues if they were to be able to study them and use them to propagate their faith. We discussed the translation of the Old and New Testament texts into Syriac (Aramaic) in chapter 16 because of the close relationship those translations had with the translation of the Old Testament by Aramaic-speaking Jews. As a result, our attention here will be directed to other translations of the Greek text.

Coptic

Coptic is the latest form of ancient Egyptian writing. It followed earlier developments such as the hieroglyphic, hieratic, and demotic scripts (see chap. 11). Egyptian merchants used Greek elements and pagan priests used demotic characters to make religious amulets in their commerce with Phoenician traders from Crete, Carthage, and elsewhere. These elements of the Greek language, with seven demotic characters added to it, became the written mode of Coptic by the beginning of the Christian era. This system of writing had several dialects into which the Bible was translated. Of these dialects, Sahidic and Bohairic are most important for early versions of the Bible.

Sahidic (Thebaic). The Coptic dialect of southern Egypt (Upper Egypt) was Sahidic (Thebaic). Its center was in the region of ancient Thebes, where it was used to translate virtually all of the New Testament by the beginning of the fourth century. Manuscripts in this dialect represent the earliest Coptic versions of the New Testament, which Pachomius (ca. 292–346), the great organizer of Egyptian monasticism, required his followers to study diligently. The early date of the Sahidic version makes it an important witness to the text of the New Testament. It is basically related to the Alexandrian text type, although the Gospels and Acts follow the Western text type.

Bohairic (Memphic). In Lower (northern) Egypt near Memphis in the Delta region, another Coptic was used alongside the Greek language. This was near Alexandria, and its central location and importance in early church history is reflected in that Bohairic Coptic became the basic dialect of the Christian church in Egypt. The nearness of this region to Alexandria and the continued use of Greek in that center probably explain why the Bohairic versions of the New Testament appeared later than their Sahidic counterparts. The only early Bohairic manuscript to have survived is the Bodmer papyrus manuscript of the gospel of John (Papyrus Bodmer III). It has a badly mutilated beginning, but its condition is much better following John 4. This manuscript casts important light on two textual problems: John 5:3b–4 and John 7:53–8:11 (see chap. 15). The Bohairic version appears to be closely related to the Alexandrian text type.

Middle Egyptian dialects. A third area of Coptic dialects resides between the centers of Thebes and Alexandria. The Middle Egyptian dialects, also known as Oxyrhynchite, are classified as Fayumic, Achmimic, and sub-Achmimic by J. Harold Greenlee. No entire New Testament book is extant in these dialects, although John is nearly complete. One fourth-century papyrus codex in the Fayumic dialect contains John 6:11–15:11. It is closer to Sahidic than to Bohairic, which places it in the Alexandrian text type. Metzger and Ehrman relate that one fourth-century papyrus codex, now at Princeton University, contains one of the earliest copies of the gospel of Matthew, along with Vaticanus (B), Sinaiticus (ℵ, *Aleph*), and Washingtonianus (W). The Acts manuscript in Middle Egyptian was purchased by the late William S. Glazier and is at present in the keeping of the Pierpont Morgan Library of New York City. Preliminary analyses of the text indicate that it is a notable representative of the so-called Western type of text. Middle Egyptian dialect portions of ten Pauline epistles dating from the early fifth century are in fragmentary form at Istituto di Papirologia of the University of Milan.[8] All of the Old Testament manuscripts in the Coptic dialects follow the Septuagint.

Ethiopic

As Christianity spread through Egypt into Ethiopia, a need arose for another translation of the Bible. Although no authoritative statement can be made about it, the Ethiopic translation of the Greek Old Testament seems to have been revised in light of the Hebrew text beginning in the fourth century. By the seventh century this translation was completed and the New Testament was then translated. The complete translation into Ethiopic was probably accomplished by Syrian monks who moved into Ethiopia during the Monophysite Controversy (fifth and sixth centuries) and the rise of Islam (seventh and eighth centuries). Their influence was profound, as indicated by the fact that the Ethiopic church continues to be Monophysite.

Two recensions of the Ethiopic New Testament have been made in the fifth and the twelfth centuries. Coptic and Arabic translations later

---

8. See Metzger and Ehrman, *Text of the New Testament*, 4th ed. (2005), 113–14. *Das Matthaus-Evangelium im Mittelagyptischen Dialekt des Koptischen (Codex Scheide)*, ed. by Hans-Martin Schenke (Texte und Untersuchungen, cxxvii; Berlin, 1981), with facsimile reproduction of selected folios of the codex. Vaticanus and Sinaiticus are fourth century and Washingtonius is fifth century.

influenced the Ethiopic, and it may actually have been based on Syriac rather than Greek manuscripts. These manuscripts probably date from the fourth or fifth centuries, which further reduces the importance of the Ethiopic Bible in terms of textual criticism. The manuscripts that do survive reflect textual admixture, but they are basically Byzantine in origin. The Old Testament includes the noncanonical 1 Enoch (which is quoted in Jude 14–15) and the Book of Jubilees. This indicates that the Ethiopic church accepted a broader canon than the church at large. Over one hundred manuscript copies of the Ethiopic Bible have survived, but none are earlier than the thirteenth century. While these manuscripts may deserve further study, they will probably be neglected because of their late date.

Gothic

It is not clear exactly when Christianity moved into the area of the Germanic tribes between the Rhine and Danube rivers. The area was evangelized before the Council of Nicea (325), since Theophilus, bishop of the Goths, was in attendance. The Goths were among the chief Germanic tribes, and they played a significant role in the events of European history during the fifth century. The first of their tribes to be evangelized was the Ostrogoths, in the region of the lower Danube. Their second bishop, Ulfilas (311–381), the "Apostle of the Goths," led his converts into the area now known as Bulgaria. There he translated the Greek Bible into Gothic.

This enterprise was of great importance, especially if Ulfilas accomplished the task attributed to him. He reportedly created a Gothic alphabet and reduced the spoken language to writing. Whether or not he actually accomplished this feat, he did make a remarkably faithful translation of the Lucian recension of the Old Testament into Gothic during the fourth century (ca. 350). Very little remains of his Old Testament, and Ulfilas did not translate all of it in the first place. He felt that the books of Samuel and Kings were too warlike to be transmitted to the Gothic tribes who were themselves quite warlike.

Much more remains of the Gothic New Testament translated by Ulfilas. It is the earliest known literary monument in the Germanic dialect, but it is not found in a single complete manuscript copy. The translation adheres almost literally to the Greek text of the Byzantine type. As such it tells little to the textual critic. The chief value of the Gothic version lies in the fact that it is the earliest literary work in the Germanic language group to which English belongs. Six fragmentary manuscripts have survived, including the Codex Argenteus, "the silver codex," written on purple vellum in silver and some gold letters. All other Gothic manuscripts are palimpsests except a vellum leaf of a bilingual Gothic-Latin codex. Gothic, like Coptic, is a language which took script form expressly for the writing of the Scriptures into the language of the people. All its manuscripts are from the fifth and sixth centuries.

Armenian

Armenia claims the honor of being the first kingdom to accept Christianity as its official religion. As the Syrian churches carried out their evangelistic tasks, they contributed to several secondary translations of the Bible. These secondary translations are so called because they are derived from translations rather than manuscripts in the original languages. One of the foremost of these secondary translations is the Armenian, although not everyone agrees that it is a translation of a translation.

Two basic traditions about the origin of the Armenian translation are generally set forth. The first says that St. Mesrob (d. 439), a soldier turned missionary, created a new alphabet to assist Sahak (Isaac the Great, 390–439) in translating the Bible from the Greek text. The second tradition asserts that this translation was made from the Syriac text. Although both views have merit, the second best fits the actual situation, which stems from the nephew and disciple of Mesrob himself. The earliest Armenian translations were revised prior to the eighth century in accordance with "trustworthy Greek codices" which were brought from Constantinople after the Council at Ephesus (431). This revision rose to dominance by the eighth century and continues to be the most common Armenian text in use today.

The oldest surviving manuscript of this revised text dates from the ninth century. Its late date and its closeness to the Caesarean or Byzantine text type make it rather insignificant in matters of textual criticism. Although the matter is not settled, the text of the Gospels tends toward the Caesarean type. The first Armenian translation of the Old Testament, made in the fifth century, reveals a marked influence from the Syriac Peshitta. Its rendition of the Hexaplaric recension was revised in accordance with the Peshitta (see discussion in chap. 16).

Georgian

Georgia, the mountainous region between the Black and Caspian seas to the north of Armenia, received the Christian message during the fourth century. By the middle of the fifth century, it had its own translation of the Bible. Since Christianity spread into Georgia from Armenia, it is no surprise to learn that this was the same route taken by its Bible translation. Accordingly, if the Armenian Old Testament were translated from the LXX or the Syriac Peshitta and the New Testament were translated from the Old Syriac, they would be secondary translations. The Georgian translation was another step removed, since it was translated from Armenian. Even if the Armenian translations were from the original text, the Georgian would be a secondary translation.

The Georgian alphabet, like the Armenian and Gothic, was developed expressly for transmission of the Bible. In keeping with this cultural dependence, all the surviving manuscripts of the Georgian Bible indicate that it follows the Armenian textual tradition. The continuation of Bible translations by the people of God, as they followed the precedent set by the Jews who had made Aramaic and Syriac translations of the Old Testament, brought about the first actual attempts to place the entire Old Testament into another language, Greek. The LXX was produced in the third and second centuries BCE.

Although its quality as a translation varies, the Georgian Bible has provided the textual critic with invaluable information about the Hebrew text of the Old Testament. In addition, it was an example for other translators to follow as they sought means of transmitting God's Word. With the rise of Christianity, Jews turned away from the LXX, and other translations, revisions, and recensions appeared. This culminated in the great work of Origen, the *Hexapla*. As Christianity continued to spread, additional translations were made. In order to accomplish this task, missionaries developed many new written languages. This fact alone made the translation of the Bible a major force in history. It also offers a reason why Bible translators did not make their secondary translations directly from the original languages of the Old and New Testaments.

18

LATIN *and* RELATED TRANSLATIONS

WESTERN CHRISTIANITY produced only one great translation of the Bible which was transmitted through the Middle Ages, the Latin Vulgate of Jerome. Once his translation emerged to its dominant position, it remained unchallenged for a thousand years. Others had translated the Scriptures into Latin before Jerome performed his task; and, in order for us to better understand his accomplishment, we will look at those earlier translations.

THE LINGUISTIC SETTING OF THE ANCIENT WORLD

Before an accurate picture of the Latin translations of the Bible can be presented, we need to have a grasp of the linguistic setting of the ancient world in general and the Roman Empire in particular. We will look at the linguistic and cultural aspects of life in the ancient world through its geographical structure before turning to the Old Latin (Vetus Latina) translation itself.

The Near East

The fortunes of the Near East had become quite varied in terms of language, politics, and society by the time the New Testament was written. At any given moment in ancient times, several languages were spoken in the area around Palestine. Following the political fortunes of time, the official language of this region underwent radical shifts. The important languages of the Scriptures were discussed in chapter 11, but their periods of dominance need to be reviewed so we can have a sense of perspective on the overall process of the transmission of the Bible.

Aramaic. Following the Babylonian captivity, the official language of Palestine became Aramaic. It was used by the Hebrew scribes as early as the time of Ezra (Neh. 8:1-8). In fact, writers employed Aramaic to construct the targums during the Sopherim period (400 BCE-200 CE) and the Talmud and Midrash in the period between 100 BCE and 500 CE (see chap. 16). During New Testament times Aramaic was the language of Christ and His disciples.

Greek and Latin. After the campaigns of Alexander the Great (335-323 BCE), Greek became the official language within the confines of his conquests. Much of this territory was later incorporated into the Roman Empire, including the Near East, and Hellenistic Greek prevailed as the dominant official language of both Egypt and Syria under the Ptolemaic and Seleucid empires, and even Palestine during the Hasmonean independence (142-63 BCE). At the death of Attalus III (133 BCE), the kingdom of Pergamum was bequeathed to Rome, and by 63 BCE the Mediterranean (called Mare Nostrum) basin was incorporated into the Roman Republic. Accompanying this growth, Roman military and diplomatic language (Latin) spread across the ancient Near East.

Greece

Hellenic dialects. Hellenic Greek is applied to Greek culture of the Classical Age. Derived from the Greek word for Greece, *Hellas,* the various dialects of Hellenic Greek appeared during three waves of immigration into the southern part of the Balkan Peninsula during the second millennium BCE: the Ionian, Achaean, and Dorian. In turn, the Ionians were pushed across the Aegean Sea into Ionia, and other Greeks immigrated or founded colonies in the Near East, in North Africa, and even in southern Italy and the islands of the Mediterranean.

Although the Greeks were divided into a series of small states, they were united by their common language in its various dialects. The most famous of these dialects was Attic, which came into its own following the one great example of Greek unification when the Greek states joined together to oppose the Persians (490-480 BCE), who were led by Darius I and his son Xerxes (Ahasuerus, Esth. 1:1). During the next fifty years the Athenian

Empire raised Greek culture to its most glorious heights.

The Peloponnesian War (431–404 BCE) brought about the defeat of Athens, and the Greek city-states struggled as they moved their separate ways. Philip II, king of Macedonia (359–336 BCE), was succeeded by his son Alexander (356–323 BCE), who realized his father's dream of reuniting the Greeks by crushing their revolts in 335 BCE. With his ascendancy the Hellenic Age became the Hellenistic Age.

Hellenistic Greek. Unlike Hellenic culture, which belongs to those peoples who spoke Greek as their native language, Hellenistic culture was superimposed upon those peoples whose language was not Greek, following the conquests of Alexander the Great. This intentional advancement of Greek culture and civilization used as its basic language a new and common speech *(koine dialektos)* derived from a blending of the various Greek dialects, although it was primarily derived from Attic. During the centuries following the death of Alexander, this koine dialect became the official language of the Near East and Egypt as well as Greece and Macedonia. In fact, it was the dialect of the Septuagint translation written at Alexandria (see chap. 17).

As the Romans moved into Greece and the Near East, and especially after the Battle of Actium (31 BCE), Latin was the language used by military personnel as Octavian and his successors transformed the Roman Republic into the Roman Empire by (27 BCE–14 CE). Latin was the language also used by commercial interests. Although the Greeks and Jews continued to expend their energies in independent activity, they were no longer in the place of leadership in the ancient world.

Italy

During the first century BCE and the centuries following, all roads truly led to Rome. Here was the greatest empire the West had ever seen. Its progress was continual from the tenth century BCE, before the city of Rome itself was founded (ca. 753 BCE). About 509 BCE the Tarquin kings were expelled from the city and the Roman Republic was born. From this time the chief city of Latium and its allies began to spread until a nearly three-hundred-square-mile territory along the Tiber River controlled most of the Italian Peninsula (ca. 265 BCE) and Latin became the common speech. From 264 to 146 BCE Rome came into conflict with Carthage, an African colony of Phoenicia, resulting in the Punic Wars. Before these wars were half over, Rome became involved in the eastern Mediterranean area of Illyria and Macedonia (ca. 229–148 BCE). By 148 BCE Macedonia had become a Roman province, and in 133 BCE Attalus III bequeathed his kingdom (Pergamum) to Rome. Rome had become enmeshed in the Near East, and its intrusion introduced Latin as the military and commercial (but not official) language of the East.

In Italy, and especially Rome, the people were bilingual. The literary language of the upper classes was generally Greek, and even Latin literature followed the Greek models. Although both slaves and freedmen were bilingual, the military and commercial language was Latin. During the early years of the church, Christians in Rome were largely Greek speaking, as Paul's epistles and the epistles of Clement of Rome show. Only later on did Roman Christians begin to use Latin as the language of their writings. During the fourth and fifth centuries, the Germanic tribes used Latin instead of the more literary Greek as their written language. This is easily understood when it is recalled that the Germanic tribes came into more immediate contact with the Roman legions and merchants long before they did their literature.

Africa

The basic languages of North Africa were Greek, Latin, Berber, and Coptic in Egypt. Greek was used among the educated classes in Egypt under the Ptolemies, while Coptic emerged among the non-educated classes (see chap. 17). Alexandria was the center where Jews translated the Hebrew Old Testament and other literary works into Greek. Farther west, Latin became the basic language among Romans in North Africa, even before the Punic Wars. Under the influence of Roman military, commercial, and administrative contacts, Latin became the predominant language of North African native peoples.[1] It was the native tongue of such early Christian writers as Tertullian (who wrote in both Greek and Latin), Cyprian, and others. The early church within the Roman Empire used Greek as its literary language, and only later did Latin and other languages become necessary and widespread.

---

1.   See Salem Chaker, "Berber, a 'Long-Forgotten' Language of France," Laurie and Amar Chaker, trans. (Paris: INALCO, 2003), 215–27. Also see Katherine E. Hoffman, "Berber Language Ideologies, Maintenance, and Contraction," *Language & Communications* 26 (2006): 144–67.

THE OLD LATIN (VETUS LATINA) TRANSLATIONS

Although Latin was the official as well as the common language in the West, Greek retained its position as the literary language of Rome and the West until the third century. By that time native Berbers made the first translations of the Greek New Testament into Old Latin (Vetus Latina) for circulation throughout North Africa and Europe, indicating that Christians had already begun to express their desire for a Latin translation of the Bible in the second century.

The Old Testament. One of the earliest known translations of the Hebrew Scriptures in the West was the Old Latin, composed prior to 200 CE. The Old Latin translation of North Africa was made from the Septuagint (LXX) with some Jewish influence exerted on the translation itself. The Old Latin translation was widely used and quoted in North Africa, and may have been the Old Testament translation used by Tertullian and Cyprian during the second century. Apparently an unrevised Old Latin was added posthumously to Jerome's Vulgate Old Testament. Apart from citations and fragmentary remains of the Old Latin text of the Old Testament, nothing remains of this translation, so its value to the textual scholar is minimal at best.

The New Testament. The Old Latin version of the New Testament is an entirely different matter. Some twenty-seven manuscripts of the Gospels have survived, along with seven from Acts, six from the Pauline epistles, and some fragments of the general epistles and Revelation. These manuscripts date from the fourth through the thirteenth centuries, but no codex copy is extant. This evidence indicates that the Old Latin version continued to be copied long after it had been displaced by the Vulgate.

The Old Latin New Testament of early date is among the most valuable witnesses to the condition of the New Testament in the West. It is represented by two, and possibly three, different texts. The African text was used by Tertullian and Cyprian, a European text appears in the writings of Irenaeus and Novatian and an Italian (*Itala*) text is mentioned in the works of Augustine. Instead of regarding Augustine's text as a precursor to the Vulgate, recent trends have been to indicate it as simply a reference to the Vulgate itself. If this be the case, then there are only two different Old Latin texts of the New Testament. The African is reflected in Codex Bobiensis (k), and is a free and rough translation of the Greek text dating from the second century. The European text is represented in two codices: Codex Vercellensis (a), written by Eusebius of Vercelli before his death in 370 or 371, and Codex Veronensis (b), the basis of Jerome's translation of the Vulgate.

THE LATIN VULGATE

The numerous texts of the Old Latin Bible that appeared by the last half of the fourth century led to an untenable situation. Because of the variety of texts, Damasus, bishop of Rome (366–384), commissioned a revision of the Old Latin (Vetus Latina) text, which resulted in the Vulgate.

The Purpose of the Translation

Damasus of Borne demonstrated a keen interest in the Scriptures as well as in scholars whom he befriended and patronized. He was quite concerned about the diversity of Bible versions, translations, revisions, and recensions in the fourth century and felt that a new and authoritative edition of the Scriptures was needed. This was especially true in light of the fact that the church in the West had always demonstrated an attitude toward outward conformity that was uncommon and almost unknown in the East. There are several reasons why Damasus saw the need for a new and authoritative edition of the Bible.

Confusion of Latin texts. As indicated earlier, the diverse Latin texts of the Bible had created confusion. This diversity resulted from the fact that the Old Testament in Latin was actually a translation of the LXX, and the New Testament was translated on informal and unofficial occasions, such as the Old Latin translation used by Tertullian. He was bilingual, being able to read and write in Greek and Latin, and used the African text of the Old Latin when he did not make his own translation as he went along. These on-the-spot citations and translations caused no end of problems for scholars, especially when they tried to verify Tertullian's underlying textual authority.

Many existing translations. Many translations of the Scriptures existed, but Latin was rapidly becoming the official language of the church. In addition to those translations mentioned in chapters 16 and 17, there were the two basic Old Latin texts in the West. There is little wonder that Damasus desired a new, authoritative translation upon which the official doctrines of the church could be based.

Heresies and disputes. Within the Roman Empire there were many disputes between Christians and Jews. Even within the church, numerous disputations followed the emergence of such heretical groups as the Marcionites, the Manichaeans, and the Montanists, who based their doctrines on their own Bible canons and translations. The Arian controversy led to the councils at Nicea (325), Constantinople I (381), and Ephesus (431). The controversy surrounding Jerome's translation of the Old Testament from Hebrew reflects not only the conflicts between Christians and Jews, but the even more problematic notion that was held by many church leaders, including Augustine, that the LXX was actually the inspired and authoritative (infallible and inerrant) Word of God rather than a noninspired translation of the Hebrew originals.

The need for a standard text. Other factors calling for a new and authoritative translation included demands by scholars for an authentic and authoritative standard text to carry out the teaching activities of the church, its missionary programs, and its defense of doctrines established at the great councils. The transmission of copies of the Scriptures to the churches in the Empire required a trustworthy (authentic) text, and the existing situation underscored the need.

The Author of the Translation

Sophronius Eusebius Hieronymus, better known as St. Jerome (ca. 340–420),[2] was born to Christian parents at Stridon, Dalmatia. He was trained in the local school until he went to Rome at the age of twelve. For the next eight years he studied Latin, Greek, and pagan authors before becoming a Christian at the age of nineteen. Following his conversion and baptism, Jerome devoted himself to a life of rigid abstinence and service to the Lord. He spent many years pursuing a semi-ascetic and later a hermitic life. During the years 374–379 he employed a Jewish rabbi to teach him Hebrew while he was living in the East, near Antioch. He was ordained a presbyter at Antioch before going to Constantinople, where he studied under Gregory Nazianzen. In 382 he was summoned to Rome to be secretary to Damasus, bishop of Rome, and commissioned to revise the Latin Bible. Jerome was selected for his outstanding qualifications as a scholar. He probably undertook the project because of his devotion to Damasus, as he knew that the less educated would strongly oppose his translation.

---

2. J. N. D. Kelly, *Jerome: His Life, Writings, and Controversies* (New York: Harper and Row, 1975), xi–353, provides a rich and detailed account.

The Date and Place of the Translation

Jerome received his commission in 382 and began his work almost immediately. At the request of Damasus he made a slight revision of the Gospels, which he completed in 383. The Latin text he used for this revision is not known, but it was probably of the European type which he corrected in accordance with an Alexandrian-type Greek text. Shortly after his revision of the Gospels was completed, his patron died (384), and a new bishop of Rome was elected. Jerome, who aspired to that position, had already completed a hasty revision of the so-called Roman Psalter when he returned to the East and settled at Bethlehem. Before his departure, however, he made an even more cursory revision of the remainder of the New Testament. Since the exact date of this revision is unknown, some scholars believe that he did not even do the work.

Back in Bethlehem Jerome turned his attention to a more careful revision of the Roman Psalter and completed it in 387. This revision is known as the Gallican Psalter, which appears in the Vulgate Old Testament. This Psalter was actually based on Origen's *Hexapla,* the fifth column, and is only a translation instead of a version of the Psalms. As soon as he had completed his revision of the Psalter, Jerome began a revision of the LXX, although this had not been his original objective. While at Bethlehem he had begun to work on perfecting his knowledge of Hebrew so he could make a fresh translation of the Old Testament directly from the original language.

While his friends applauded his efforts, those more remote from him began to suspect that he might be Judaizing and even became outraged when he cast doubts on the "inspiration of the Septuagint." From this time he became more involved with his translation and the supervision of the monks at Bethlehem. He translated the Hebrew Psalter based on the Hebrew text then in use in Palestine. This translation never actually surpassed the Gallican Psalter or the Roman Psalter in liturgical use even though it was based on the original language instead of a translation. Jerome kept on translating the Hebrew Scriptures in spite of opposition and poor health. Finally, in 405, he completed his Latin translation of the Hebrew Old Testament, but it was not readily received. During the last fifteen years of his life Jerome continued writing, translating, and revising his Old Testament translation.

Jerome's Rejection of the Apocrypha

Jerome rejected the inspiration of the Apocrypha (see chap. 8).[3] He cared little for the Apocrypha and only reluctantly made a hasty translation of portions of it—Judith, Tobit, the rest of Esther, and the additions to Daniel—before his death. As a result, the Old Latin (Vetus Latina) version of the Apocrypha was brought into the Latin Vulgate Bible during the Middle Ages over Jerome's dead body.

Reaction to the Translation

When Jerome published his revisions of the Gospels, there was a sharp reaction. Because his work was sponsored by the bishop of Rome, however, the opposition was silenced. His reluctance to proceed with the revision of the remainder of the New Testament indicates that Jerome may have been aware of the approaching death of Damasus, his sponsor. The fact that Jerome left Rome just a year following his benefactor's death supports this notion, and the milder revisions he made when he did finally revise the remainder of the New Testament show that he was concerned to win the approval of his critics. The adoption of the Roman Psalter by the church at Rome reveals that it was first used there and that Jerome's scholarship was already apparent. Since the Gallican Psalter was accepted by churches outside Rome, it seems that Damasus was not so influential over those critics of Jerome's earlier work.

When Jerome began to study Hebrew at Bethlehem, and when he had translated the Hebrew Psalter, sharp cries of accusation arose against him. He was accused of presumption, making unlawful innovations, and sacrilege. Not being one to take criticism lightly, he used the prefaces of his translations and revisions as tools for counterattack. These items merely added fuel to the flames, and Jerome's translation was opposed by many of the outstanding leaders of the church. Among those critics was Augustine, who was outspoken against Jerome's Old Testament translation but wholeheartedly favored his New Testament revisions after 398.

Augustine's attitude provides us with a capsule view of what actually happened to the Vulgate Old Testament historically. During the early years of that translation, Augustine, and a large majority of influential church

---

3. See Jerome, preface to Jerome's *Commentary on Daniel*, Gleason Archer, trans. (Grand Rapids: Baker, 1977), 17.

leaders, opposed the translation because it was not based on the LXX. In fact, Augustine and others used Jerome's New Testament revision while they urged him to make his translation of the Old Testament from the LXX, which many held to be inspired.

Shortly after the great scholar's death in 420, his Old Testament translation gained a complete victory over other translations. Whether this fact is attributed to the sheer weight of the translation cannot be known with certainty, for the biting criticism and denouncing of his translation by its critics would scarcely be set aside merely on the basis of its merits. During the four centuries following Jerome's death, the Vulgate was triumphant and emerged as the unofficially recognized standard text of the Bible throughout the Middle Ages. By the thirteenth century this revision had come to be called the versio vulgata ("commonly used translation") of the Bible. This was due primarily to three factors: (1) the importance of Italy and southern Gaul for the production and dissemination of good texts of the Latin Bible, (2) the pull of liturgical tradition, and (3) the tendency toward local homogeneity and waves of missionary activity.[4]

There were no written native languages of the peoples who were evangelized by Christians. If they existed in any form, they consisted of symbols, runes, or other primitive objects. It was this missionary enterprise that brought written languages to the non-Christian world of the Middle Ages. For example, "Anglo-Saxons knew of three sacred languages, Hebrew, Greek, and Latin, but in practice Latin alone was accepted as the language of high knowledge. Alcuin explained to Charlemagne that the whole temple of Christian wisdom was borne upon the seven pillars of the Latin liberal arts, as these had been taught in the schools of Rome. Culture and learning for the Anglo-Saxons meant Roman culture."[5]

It was not until the Council of Trent (1546–1563), however, that the Roman Catholic Church officially elevated the Vulgate to that position. In the meantime it was published in parallel columns with other translations. When Latin became the dominant language of European scholars, other

4. See discussion in Robert C. Loewe, "The Medieval History of the Latin Vulgate," in G. W. H. Lampe, ed., *The Cambridge History of the Bible*, vol. 2: *The West from the Fathers to the Reformation* (Cambridge: Cambridge Univ. Press, 1969), 102–54.

5. Geoffrey Shepherd, "English Versions of the Scriptures before Wyclif," G. W. H. Lampe, ed., *The Cambridge History of the Bible*, vol. 2 (Cambridge: Cambridge Univ. Press, 1969), 363.

translations and versions faded and fell into the background behind the majestic Vulgate of Jerome.

The Results of the Translation

Of primary concern to the modern Bible student is the relative weight of the Latin Vulgate. It must be considered in the light of history. As has been indicated, the Vulgate New Testament was merely a revision of the Old Latin text, and not a critical revision at that. The Vulgate text of the Apocrypha was of even less value, since it is simply the Old Latin text attached to Jerome's Old Testament translation, with minor exceptions. The Vulgate Old Testament was an entirely different matter, however, since it was actually a version made from the Hebrew text rather than simply another translation or revision. Today the Vulgate is usually credited as being the first translation of the Old Testament into Latin directly from the Hebrew Tanakh, rather than the Greek Septuagint. It is difficult to determine just how direct the conversion of Hebrew to Latin was, however, because of Jerome's extensive use of exegetical material written in Greek, his use of the Aquiline and Theodotionic columns of the *Hexapla*, as well as the somewhat paraphrastic style of his translations.[6] Nonetheless, his reliance on the Hebrew text makes the Old Testament translation much more important to Bible scholars than the New.

It was inevitable that the Vulgate text would be corrupted in its transmission during the Middle Ages. Sometimes this corruption was the result of careless transcription and the intermingling of elements from the Old Latin text, with which it was often published. Throughout the Middle Ages the monastic scribes made several attempts at revision and recension of the Vulgate text. This led to the accumulation of over eight thousand extant Vulgate manuscripts. Among these manuscripts the greatest amount of

---

6. According to the website www./en.wikipedia.org/wiki/Vulgate, some, following P. Nautin (1986) and perhaps E. Burstein (1971), suggest that Jerome may have been almost wholly dependent on Greek material for his interpretation of the Hebrew. A. Kamesar (1993), on the other hand, sees evidence that in some cases Jerome's knowledge of Hebrew exceeds that of his exegetes, implying a direct understanding of the Hebrew text. Pierre Nautin, "Hieronymus," *Theologische Realenzyklopädie*, vol. 15; Walter de Gruyter, Berlin/New York 1986), 304–15, here 309–10; Adam Kamesar, *Jerome, Greek Scholarship, and the Hebrew Bible: A Study of the Quaestiones Hebraicae in Genesim* (Oxford: Clarendon Press, 1993), 97, which cites E. Burstein, "La compétence en hébreu de saint Jérôme" (Diss.), Poitiers (1971); Kelly, *Jerome*, passim.

"cross-contamination" of text types is evident. Still, the Council of Trent issued a "Decree Concerning the Edition, and the Use, of the Sacred Books," which held "of all the Latin editions, . . . the said old and Vulgate edition . . . [is] held as authentic."

It may be asked just which of the over eight thousand manuscript copies—and which particular edition of the Vulgate—should be regarded as the ultimate authority. As a result, the Council of Trent ordered that an authentic edition of the Vulgate be prepared. A papal commission undertook the task, but it was unable to overcome the many difficulties before it. Finally, in 1590, Pope Sixtus V published an edition of his own, just a few months before he died. This Sixtene edition was quite unpopular among scholars, especially the Jesuits, and was circulated for only a short time. Gregory XIV (1590–1591) succeeded to the papal chair and was immediately prepared to revise the Sixtene text drastically. His sudden death would have brought an end to the revision of the Sixtene text had it not been for the renewed interest of his successor, Clement VIII (1592–1605). In 1604 a new "authentic" Vulgate edition of the Bible appeared, which is known as the Sixto-Clementine edition. It differed from the Sixtene edition in some 4,900 variants, and became the dominant Vulgate text, surpassing even the Gutenberg edition printed at Mainz between 1450 and 1455.

Three centuries later, under a charge of Pope Pius X, the Benedictine order began in 1907 a critical revision of the Vulgate Old Testament. Meanwhile the Vulgate New Testament underwent critical revision by a group of Anglican scholars at Oxford. It was begun by Bishop John Wordsworth and Professor H. J. White between 1877 and 1926, and was completed by H. F. D. Sparks in 1954.

The *Nova Vulgata* (*Bibliorum Sacrorum nova vulgata editio*), also called the Neo-Vulgate, is currently the typical Latin edition published by the See of Rome for use in the Roman rite. It does not contain some books found in the earlier editions but omitted by the canon of Trent, namely the Prayer of Manasses, the 3rd and 4th books of Esdras, and the Epistle to the Laodiceans. The Second Vatican Council in Sacrosanctum Concilium mandated a revision of the Latin Psalter in accord with modern textual and linguistic studies, while preserving or refining its Christian Latin style. In 1965 Pope Paul VI appointed a commission to revise the rest of the Vulgate following the same principles. The Commission published its work in eight annotated sections, inviting criticism from Catholic scholars as the sections were published. The Latin Psalter was published in 1969; the New Testament was completed by 1971.

After decades of preparation, the entire *Nova Vulgata* was published in 1979 (second ed. in 1986). The foundational text of most of the *Nova Vulgata* Old Testament is the critical edition done by the monks of the Benedictine Abbey of St. Jerome under Pius X. The foundational text of the books of Tobit and Judith are from manuscripts of the Vetus Latina rather than the Vulgate.

The New Testament is based on the 1969 edition of the Stuttgart Vulgate. All of these base texts were revised to accord with the modern critical editions in Greek, Hebrew, and Aramaic. There are also a number of changes where the modern scholars felt that Jerome had failed to grasp the meaning of the original languages, or had rendered it obscurely. The *Nova Vulgata* has not been widely embraced by conservative Catholics, many of whom see it as being in some verses of the Old Testament a new translation rather than a revision of Jerome's work. Also, some of its readings sound unfamiliar to those who are accustomed to the Clementine.

In 1906, Kurt Aland published a critical edition of the *Novum Testamentum Latine* (Stuttgart). The Latin New Testament of Wordsworth and White provided variant readings from the diverse manuscripts and printed editions of the Vulgate and compared different wordings in their footnotes. The Stuttgart Vulgate attempts, through critical comparison of important, historical manuscripts of the Vulgate, to re-create an early text, cleansed of the scribal errors of a millennium. In 1984 and 1992 Kurt and Barbara Aland updated and entirely revised Nestle's edition of 1906 and republished it under the same name, Novum Testamentum Latine. The new text is a reprint of the New Testament of the *Nova Vulgata*, to which has been added a critical apparatus giving the variant readings of earlier editions.[7]

In 2001, the Vatican released the instruction Liturgiam Authenticam, establishing the *Nova Vulgata* as a point of reference for all translations of the liturgy of the Roman rite into the vernacular from the original languages,

---

7.   The editions described in the apparatus are the Stuttgart edition, the Gutenberg Bible (1452), the Latin text of the Complutensian Polyglot (1514), the edition from Wittenberg, which was favored by Luther (1529), and the editions of Desiderius Erasmus (1527), Robertus Stephanus (1540), Hentenius of Louvain (1547), Christophorus Plantinus (1583), Pope Sixtus V (1590), Pope Clement VIII (1592), and Wordsworth and White (1954).

"in order to maintain the tradition of interpretation that is proper to the Latin Liturgy."[8] The Stuttgart edition of *Biblia Sacra Vulgata*, or *Biblia Sacra iuxta vulgatam versionem*, first published in 1969 (5th edition, 2007) by the German Bible Society, is a "manual edition" (editio minor) in that it reduces much of the information in the big multi-volume critical editions that preceded it into a single compact volume. It is based on earlier critical editions of the Vulgate, including the Benedictine edition and the Latin New Testament produced by Wordsworth and White.

The consistency of the Vulgate text is quite mixed after the sixth century, and its overall character is rather faulty. Nevertheless, the influence of the Vulgate on the language and thought of Western Christianity has been immense, but its value to the textual critic is not nearly so high. When the text of Jerome is discovered from its own textual criticism, it reveals that Jerome's New Testament was a late fourth-century revision of the Old Latin, and his Old Testament was a late fourth- or early fifth-century version of the Hebrew text then in use in the East.

Only a few individuals acknowledged their error in accepting the LXX Old Testament as authoritative and inspired, and supported the accuracy of the Hebrew text underlying Jerome's Vulgate version. Among these was Augustine, bishop of Hippo, who would become the dominant voice in the next several centuries of church history. During those centuries the Vulgate became the dominant edition of the Bible in the Middle Ages. It also served as the basis for most modern Bible translations prior to the nineteenth century.

SECONDARY TRANSLATIONS

In the middle of the ninth century, a Moravian empire formed in east-central Europe. This kingdom came under the sway of Christianity, and its church leaders used Latin in their liturgy. The laity were not familiar with Latin, and Rostislav, the founder of the kingdom, requested that Slavonic priests be sent to conduct church services in the language of the people. At this time only Slavonic was spoken in this region of Europe.

In response to Rostislav's request, the Byzantine Emperor Michael III sent two monks to Moravia from Byzantium (Constantinople). The monks were the brothers Methodius and Constantinus, natives of Thessalonica.

---

8. According to website www./en.wikipedia.org/wiki/Vulgate.

Constantinus changed his name to Cyril when he entered the monastery. In order to accomplish their task, the brothers devised a new alphabet, known as the Cyrillic alphabet. It is comprised of thirty-six letters and is still the basis of Russian, Ukrainian, Serbo-Croatian, and Bulgarian. The Cyrillic alphabet superseded the local alphabet, the Glagolithic, in the tenth century.

Shortly after their entry into the region, Cyril and Methodius began translating the Gospels into Old Slavonic. Then these "Apostles to the Slaves" began translating the Old Testament. At one time it was believed that their translation was from the LXX, but recent evidence indicates that it was actually made from the Latin. The New Testament follows the Byzantine text, although it has many Western and Caesarean readings. Most of the known Slavonic manuscripts are lectionaries, and the first translation itself may have been in the form of a lectionary.

Of the other translations based on the Latin text, only the Anglo-Saxon and the Frankish translations demand a word of information. The Anglo-Saxon text will be discussed in chapter 19, and the Frankish translation appears in a bilingual edition. It is known from one fragmentary eighth-century manuscript containing portions of Matthew, facing a Latin text.

19

EARLY ENGLISH TRANSLATIONS

THE CHAIN FROM GOD TO US takes a new direction at this point. The Bible text in the original languages and early translations gives way to the particular transmission of the text in the English language. For although the Old Testament was recorded primarily in Hebrew, and the New was written basically in Greek, more modern translations of the Bible are in English than any other language. The English language of today reflects many centuries of development in England and North America, and an international scale that makes it the most universal language for modern Bible translations.[1]

PARTIAL TRANSLATIONS IN OLD AND MIDDLE ENGLISH

English is a sort of tag-end dialect of Low German, which itself belongs to the West Teutonic branch of the Teutonic group of languages in the Indo-European family. In order to place it in its proper setting, it is necessary for us to sketch the background of the English language and the place of the Bible in it.

The Late Development of the English Language

Just how the English language developed is not known for certain, but most scholars follow the lead of the Venerable Bede (ca. 673–735), who dates its

---

1. Albert C. Baugh and Thomas Cable, *A History of the English Language*, 5th ed. (Upper Saddle River, N.J.: Pearson Education, 2002), 2.

beginning to about 450 CE. The period 450–1100 is called Anglo-Saxon, or
Old English, because it was dominated by the influence from the Angles,
Saxons, and Jutes in their various dialects (using runes but not written language). Following the Norman invasion of England in 1066, the language
again came under the influence of the Scandinavian dialects, and the period
of Middle English appeared from 1100–1500. This was the period of both
Geoffrey Chaucer (1340–1400) and John Wycliffe (ca. 1320–1384). Following the invention of a movable typeset by Johann Gutenberg (ca. 1454), English entered into its third period of development: Modern English (1500
to the present). This period of development was precipitated by the great
vowel shift (the effect of which was to bring the pronunciation within mea-
surable distance of that which prevails today)[2] during the century following
the death of Chaucer and preceding the birth of William Shakespeare. With
this background in mind, our survey of the various translations of the Bible
into English should be more meaningful.[3]

Old English (Anglo-Saxon) Partial Translations (ca. 450–ca. 1100)

At the beginning of this period some five hundred different Bible translations existed. With the disintegration of the Roman Empire in the West,
however, they were diminished to Latin, the only officially recognized translation of the church. The Bible was presented to the laity in oral form and
later in written form. At first only pictures, wood carvings, paintings, preaching, poems, and paraphrases were employed to communicate the message
of the Bible to the Britons. Later on, stained glass windows depicted biblical
stories. "The classics of medieval Englishmen were to be found in the Bible.
It existed in a learned language, accessible only to an elite, but the moder-
ately educated person, usually a monk, a clergy by definition, seldom saw
the Bible as a whole."[4] The early translation of portions of the Scriptures

2. See Baugh and Cable, *A History*, 236–51, for a discussion of the importance of pronunciation in the
development of English during the period between Chaucer and Shakespeare (1564–1616).

3. Bruce M. Metzger, *The Bible in Translation* (Grand Rapids: Baker, 2001). Also see an expanded treatment in Bruce M. Metzger, "Translating the Bible: An Ongoing Task," delivered at the W. H. Griffith
Thomas Lectures, Dallas Theological Seminary, 4–7 February 1992, and published in *Bibliotheca Sacra*,
1993, vol. 150 (597): 34–49; (598): 139–50; (599): 272–84; and (600): 396–415.

4. Geoffrey Shepherd, "English Versions of the Scriptures before Wyclif," G. W. H. Lampe, ed.,
The Cambridge History of the Bible, vol. 2: *The West from the Fathers to the Reformation* (Cambridge:
Cambridge Univ. Press, 1969), 363.

were based on the Old Latin and Vulgate translations rather than the original Hebrew and Greek languages, and none of them contained the text of the entire Bible. Nevertheless, they do illustrate the manner by which the Bible entered into the English tongue.

Caedmon (d. ca. 680). The story of Caedmon is recorded in Bede's *Ecclesiastical History of the English People.* It involves an ungifted laborer at the monastery at Whitby in Yorkshire, Northumbria, who left a party one night for fear that he might be called upon to sing. Later that night he dreamed that an angel had commanded him to sing about how things were first created.[5] Other paraphrases and poems sung by Caedmon included the full story of Genesis, Israel's exodus from Egypt, the incarnation, passion, resurrection, and ascension of the Lord, the coming of the Holy Spirit, the teachings of the apostles, etc. His work became the basis for other poets, writers, and translators, for it became the popularized people's Bible of the day. As a result, Caedmon's songs were memorized and disseminated throughout the land.

Aldhelm (640–709). Aldhelm was the first bishop of Sherborne in Dorset. Shortly after 700 he translated the Psalter (Latin Vulgate) into Anglo-Saxon (Old English). It was the first straightforward translation of any portion of the Bible into the English language.

The Venerable Bede (674–735). The greatest scholar in England, and one of the greatest in all Europe in his day, Bede was situated at Jarrow-on-the-Tyne in Northumbria. From there he wrote his famous *Ecclesiastical History* and other works. Among these works was a translation of the gospel of John, which was probably meant to be a supplement to the three translated by Egbert. According to traditional accounts, Bede finished his translation in the very hour of his death.

Egbert (fl. ca. 700). Egbert of Northumbria became archbishop of York shortly before the death of Bede. He was also the teacher of Alcuin of York, who was later called by Charlemagne to establish a school at the court of Aix-la-Chapelle (Aachen). About 705, Egbert translated the Gospels into Old English for the first time.

Alcuin (ca. 735–804) was educated under Egbert at York before Charlemagne brought him to Aachen in 781, where he compiled a standardized

---

5. F. F. Bruce, *The English Bible: A History of Translations from the earliest English Versions*, 3rd ed. (New York: Oxford Univ. Press, 1978), 2–3.

text and standardized interpretation of Jerome's Latin Vulgate. Alcuin developed an educational program for Charlemagne's ministers (missi dominici). In doing this he developed a new style of handwriting—the Carolingian minuscule. This script included both small and capital letters, which made documents easier to read. The Carolingian minuscule became the standard script until the Reformation.

Alfred the Great (849–901). Alfred was a scholar of the first rank as well as being king of England (870-901). During his reign the Danelaw was established under the Treaty of Wedmore (878). The treaty contained only two stipulations for the new subjects: Christian baptism and loyalty to the king. Along with his translation of Bede's *Ecclesiastical History* from Latin into Anglo-Saxon (Old English), he also translated the Ten Command-ments, extracts from Exodus 21-23, Acts 15:23-29, and a negative form of the Golden Rule. It was during his reign that Britain experienced a revival of Christianity.

Aldred (fl. ca. 950). Another element was introduced into the history of the English Bible when Aldred wrote a Northumbrian gloss between the lines of a late seventh-century Latin copy of the Gospels. It is from the Latin copy of Eadfrid, bishop of Lindisfarne (698-721), that Aldred's work receives its name, the *Lindisfarne Gospels.* A generation later the Irish scribe MacRegol made another Anglo-Saxon gloss known as the Rushworth Gospels.

Aelfric (fl. ca. 1000). Aelfric was bishop of Eynsham in Oxfordshire, Wes-sex, when he translated portions of the first seven books of the Old Testa-ment. This translation, and other Old Testament portions which he trans-lated and cited in his homilies, were based on the Latin text. Even before Aelfric's time the *Wessex Gospels* (ca. 700) were translated into the same dia-lect. These items constitute the first extant independent translation of the Gospels into Old English.

Middle English Partial Translations (ca.1150–1500)

The Middle English period (ca.1150–1500) was "marked by momentous changes in the English language, changes more extensive and fundamental than those that have taken place at any time before or since."[6] The Norman Conquest (1066) came as a result of the dispute over the throne of Edward

6. Baugh and Cable, *A History*, 158.

the Confessor. With it the period of Saxon domination in Britain came to an end, and a period of Norman-French influence exerted itself on the language of the conquered peoples and Middle English (ca. 1150–ca. 1500) emerged by the middle of the twelfth century.

The pre-Conquest English vernacular survived as the common speech and commingled with French culture, the social language, and Latin, the principal language of religion and learning. Almost immediately, Norman invaders intermarried with their conquered subjects. Following the impetuous actions of King John Lackland (1199–1216), England lost its Continental territories and turned to domestic interests. Long before the outbreak of hostilities with France known as the Hundred Years War (1337–1453), English was making a comeback at both the spoken and written levels.[7] During this period additional attempts were made at translating the Bible into English.

Orm, or Ormin (fl. ca. 1200). Orm was an Augustinian monk who wrote a poetic paraphrase of the Gospels and Acts with an accompanying commentary. This work, *The Ormulum*, is preserved in only one manuscript of 20,000 words. Although the vocabulary is purely Teutonic, the cadence and syntax show Norman influence.

William of Shoreham (fl. ca. 1320). In 1313 William became Vicar of Chart Sutton, in Kent. He is often credited with producing the first prose version of the Psalter and other poems (1320). The poems and Psalter, both on the same manuscript and in the same handwriting, are preserved in the British Library (Additional MSS, No. 17376). Because this translation was into a Southern (Mercian) dialect of English instead of Kentish, there is some question about whether William was actually the translator of this 1320 work.[8]

Richard Rolle (fl. ca. 1320–1340). Rolle is known as the "Hermit of Hampole." He was responsible for the second literal translation of the Scriptures into English. Living near Doncaster, Yorkshire, he translated the Scriptures from the Latin Vulgate into the North English dialect. His translation of the Psalter was widely circulated, and it reflects the development of English Bible translation to the time of John Wycliffe.

7. Robert McCrum, William Cran, and Robert MacNeil, *The Story of English* (New York: Viking Penguin Inc., 1986), 73–80.

8. Michael Ott, "William of Shoreham," Catholic Encyclopedia.

COMPLETE TRANSLATIONS IN MIDDLE AND
EARLY MODERN ENGLISH

Although no complete Bibles existed in English prior to the fourteenth century, several indicators suggest one would soon appear. Rolle's literal Psalter circulated widely at the very time the papal court was experiencing struggles associated with the so-called Babylonian Captivity (1309–1377) and the Great Schism (1378–1417). This event and its aftermath provided a backdrop for the work of other Bible translators. The decision to translate the Bible into English must be seen in the context of the rise of lay literacy, the emergence of a vernacular culture, and the opposition to biblical translation.[9]

Fourteenth and Fifteenth Century Bible Translations

Following tradition, comments of the Fathers had been brought together into a standard commentary, or Glossa ordinaria, covering the whole Bible. Nominally completed in the twelfth century, it continued to evolve in the thirteenth century as "postills" (perhaps from "post illa" [verba textus], "after these words in the text") by Hugh of St. Cher (ca. 1200–1263).[10] Two distinct vehicles of interpretation were used to illuminate the text of Scripture: sermons and academic lectures.[11]

John Wycliffe (ca. 1320–1384). Wycliffe, "the Morning Star of the Reformation," lived during the "Babylonian captivity," along with Geoffrey Chaucer (ca. 1340–1400) and John of Gaunt (1340–1399). He would build on the precedents established by Bernard of Clairvaux (1091–1153), Robert Grosseteste (ca. 1175–1253), Nicholas of Lyra (ca. 1270–1340), and Richard Fitz-Ralph (ca. 1295–1360)—men who challenged the moral laxity and wealth of recently established monastic orders. They also opposed the extreme theory of dominion (dominium) advanced by Giles of Rome (ca. 1243/47–1316) who claimed that papal authority overrides temporal authority.

In his recoil from the spiritual apathy and moral degeneracy of the clergy in England, Wycliffe was thrust into the limelight as an opponent

---

9. Mary Dove, *The First English Bible: The Text and Context of the Wycliffite Versions* (Cambridge: Cambridge Univ. Press, 2007), 1.

10. Beryl Smalley, *The Study of the Bible in the Middle Ages*, 3rd ed. (Notre Dame, Ind.: Univ. of Notre Dame Press, 1978), 270.

11. G. R. Evans, *John Wycliffe: Myth and Reality* (Downers Grove, Ill.: InterVarsity, 2005), 114.

of the papacy and the established church. He opposed their requirement of an intermediary (priest or pope) between God and mankind. Late in life (ca. 1379–1381) Wycliffe took up his controversial position by rejecting the Eucharistic doctrine of transubstantiation. Wycliffe's notes indicate he probably lectured on the whole Bible (ca. 1371–1376). During his university years, Wycliffe enjoyed the support of John of Gaunt (Duke of Lancaster, fourth son of Edward III) until the end of the Avignonese Papacy (1377) and the Peasants' Revolt (1383), when John withdrew his support and realigned himself with Wycliffe's opponents.[12]

Like so many of his forebears and colleagues, Wycliffe cast aside scholastic Latin as a vehicle of communication and directed his appeal to the English people in their common language. His appeal was directed through the Lollards, an order of itinerant preachers, also known as the "poor priests." The Lollards identified themselves with Wycliffe[13] as they went throughout the countryside preaching, reading, and teaching the English Bible. In order to help them with their task, a new translation of the Bible was needed. After judicious study, Mary Dove reinforces the view that Wycliffe instigated the project begun in the early 1370s in the Queen's College, Oxford, and that Wycliffe, Nicholas of Hereford, and John Trevisa all played a part in the translation. This concurs with early evidence which became obscured in pre-Reformation copies. "Only twenty complete Wycliffite Bibles survive, with evidence of perhaps seventeen more."[14] The New Testament translation was completed in 1380. The Old Testament appeared in 1382. A second edition of the New Testament was published in 1388.

Apparently the first edition (Earlier Version) was never intended to be a translation in its own right, and translators of the second edition (Later Version) lost control of the first edition during the early 1380s.[15] (See the table "Major English Bible Translations through the 17th Century" on the next page to note the role of Wycliffe's Bible as the first English Bible.) In 1850 Josiah Forshall and Frederic Madden completed *The Holy Bible, Containing the Old and New Testaments, with the Apocryphal Books, in the Earliest English*

---

12. Ibid., 182–92.

13. Ibid., 250–56.

14. Dove, *The First English Bible*, 2, and Appendix 4, 235–66.

15. Ibid., 3.

MAJOR ENGLISH BIBLE TRANSLATIONS
THROUGH THE 17TH CENTURY

Original Bible Manuscripts
Old Testament in Hebrew and Aramaic
15th-5th cent. B.C.

Greek translation
of Old Testament
Septuagint (ca. 250 B.C.)

Original Bible mss
New Testament in Greek
ca. A.D. 30-100
Scholars of Jamnia (A.D. 90)
Old Testament Canon fixed

Syriac, Old Latin,
and Coptic translations
(2nd-4th centuries)

New Testament Canon fixed
(4th century)

Latin Vulgate
Jerome (ca. A.D. 400)

Anglo-Saxon Paraphrases
(ca. 700-1000)
Gospel of John
Bede (735)

9th-century Bible mss
Oldest known until 1947

English Bible
Wycliffe (ca. 1380-1384)

Printed Latin Bible
Gutenberg (ca. 1456-1457)

Printed Hebrew OT (1482)

Printed English NT
Tyndale (1525, 1535)
English Pentateuch

Printed Greek NT
Erasmus (1516)

German NT
Luther (1522)

Printed Latin Bible
Pagninus (1528)

Printed English Bible
Coverdale (1535)
Matthew's Bible (1537)
Great Bible (1539)
Taverner Bible (1539)

German OT
Luther (1534)

Greek New Testament
Stephanus (1550)
Greek New Testament
Beza (1557)

Geneva Bible (1560)
Bishops' Bible (1568)

Rheims NT (1582)
Douay OT (1610)

Textus Receptus
(1624)

King James Bible [KJV] (1611)

SOURCE: Norman L. Geisler and William E. Nix, *A General Introduction to the Bible*, rev. ed. (Chicago: Moody, 1986), 285.

Versions Made from the Latin Vulgate by John Wycliffe and His Followers.[16] They presented two versions of the translation side by side. The Earlier Version is a closely literal rendering of the Latin Bible[17] and the much more numerous copies of the Later Version provide a more idiomatic revision. "As a result of the Wycliffite enterprise, the biblical canon in its entirety was made accessible for the first time to the reader literate in English but not in Latin."[18]

The translations were made from contemporary manuscripts of the Latin Vulgate. The manuscripts upon which these translations were based reflect a generally poor quality and textual tradition, but they provided the basis for the first complete translation of the Bible into English. With the Wycliffe Bible translation, a new epoch in the history of the Bible was opened. One of Wycliffe's basic principles was that laid down by Hampole, namely, that the translators would seek no strange English, and use the easiest and commonest English, which would be most like the Latin, so that those who knew no Latin might by the English come to know many Latin words.

John Purvey (ca. 1354–1428). John Purvey served as Wycliffe's secretary and is credited with making a revision of the Earlier Wycliffite Bible (Plate 42). This revision is commonly known as the Later Wycliffite Version (LV), and the first as the Earlier Wycliffite Version (EV), although the term *version* does not strictly apply to either. The translator who represents himself as being in charge of the production of the Later Version composed two English prologues: a prologue to the Prophets (prefixed to the book of Isaiah) and a prologue to the Bible as a whole. However, the consensus attributes the latter Prologue to Purvey without evidence. Purvey's revision replaced many Latinate constructions by native English idiom. It also replaced the preface of Jerome by an extensive prologue written by Purvey.

According to David Daniell, "From 1401 and the Act of Parliament *De heretico comburendo* until the 1530s and Henry VIII's break with Rome, writing in England, and most especially that suggesting religious protest or an English Bible, was under the severest censorship in the country's history."[19]

---

16. Josiah Forshall and Frederic Madden, eds., *The Holy Bible, Containing the Old and New Testaments*, 4 vols. (Oxford: Clarendon Press, 1850).

17. Dove, *The First English Bible*, 3; Appendix 1, 199–209. Appendix 2 contains "Additions and select emendations to Forshall and Madden's edition of the Wycliffite Bible," 210–21.

18. Ibid., 4.

19. David Daniell, *The Bible in English* (New Haven: Conn., Yale Univ. Press, 2003), 108.

Hounding John Wycliffe and the Lollards, Thomas Arundel, archbishop of
Canterbury, summoned a synod at Oxford (1408) resulting in The Constitutions of Oxford (1409),[20] which forbade anyone to translate, or even read,
a vernacular version of the Bible in whole or in part without the approval of
his diocesan bishop or of a provincial council.[21] With the national disrup-
tion and political instability accompanying the Wars of the Roses, the net
result was a continued weakening of papal influence over the English people. In broader form, the first complete English Bible was published, revised,
and circulated prior to the work of John Hus (ca. 1369–1415) in Bohemia. It
was also published before the invention of Johann Gutenberg (ca. 1454), a
revolutionary development which had a dampening effect on the spread of
the Wycliffite translations.

SIXTEENTH-CENTURY BIBLE TRANSLATIONS:
THE AGE OF CONFESSIONAL BIBLES

The transformation of England, and all of Europe for that matter, followed the Renaissance and the feature accompanying it: the literary revival,
the rise of nationalism, and the spirit of exploration and discovery. The
resurgence of the classics followed the fall of Constantinople in 1453, the
invention of movable type printing by Johann Gutenberg (1396–1468), and
the introduction of cheaper paper into Europe. Gutenberg's Bible, commonly called the Mazarin Bible, was published (1452–1454) and sold at the
Frankfurt Book Fair (1455). Greek began to be studied publicly at the University of Paris in 1458, the first Greek grammar appeared in 1476, and a
Greek lexicon was published in 1492. In 1488 the Hebrew Bible was published, the first Hebrew grammar came out in 1503, and the earliest Hebrew
lexicon appeared in 1506.

Even prior to 1500 more than eighty editions of the Latin Bible had been
published in Europe, within a generation of the introduction of the new
printing method into England by William Claxton in 1476. "About 1500, the
Spanish scholar Cardinal Francesco Ximénes de Cisneros founded—and paid

---

20. This is reminiscent but distinct from and not to be confused with The Constitutions of Clarendon
    (1164), when Henry II (1159–1189) restored the lost efficiency of the Norman monarchy and regu-
    lated anew the troubled relations of church and state with Thomas Becket, Archbishop of Canter-
    bury (1154–1170).

21. F. F. Bruce, *History of the English Bible*, 3rd ed. (New York: Oxford, 1978), 20–21.

for—the first trilingual university in Spain, devoted to the three ancient biblical languages, Hebrew, Greek, and Latin. He assembled scholars at Alcalá de Henares (Complutum in Latin). By July 1517, they had made and set up in print a set of six remarkable large volumes"[22] (see discussion in chap. 12). Indeed, the setting was such that a scholarly man was needed to fashion the Hebrew and Greek originals into a fitting English idiom, for no mere rendering of the Latin text would suffice to meet the demands of the situation.

William Tyndale (ca. 1492–1536). William Tyndale was the man who could do what was needed, and he had the faith and courage to persist whatever the cost. Following unsuccessful attempts to complete his translation in England, and the firm attitude of Henry VIII (1509–1547) against any translation of Scriptures into English, Tyndale sailed to the European continent (1524) and visited Martin Luther (1525). After further difficulties he finally printed the New Testament at Cologne in late February 1526. It was followed by a translation of the Pentateuch at Marburg (1530) and of Jonah in a commentary at Antwerp (1531). The influences of Wycliffe and Luther were evident in Tyndale's work, and these kept him under constant threat. In addition, these threats were such that Tyndale's translations had to be smuggled into England. Once they arrived there, copies were purchased by Cuthbert Tunstall, bishop of London, who had them burned publicly at St. Paul's Cross. Even Sir Thomas More (1478–1535),[23] humanist Lord Chancellor of England under Henry VIII and author of the *Utopia,* attacked Tyndale's translation as belonging to the same "pestilent sect" as did Luther's German translation.[24]

Tyndale's translations were part of a wider reformation that has become known "by the opening of the records of sixteenth-century Eastern Europe." Understanding of religious events in the sixteenth century throughout Europe as far east as Transylvania has increased greatly.[25] The early sixteenth-century church across Europe was "a bureaucratic institution which was a massive, successful, complex, deeply rooted multiple organism at work,

---

22. Daniell, *The Bible in English,* 119.

23. Ibid., 69–70.

24. C. S. Lewis, *English Literature in the Sixteenth Century* (Oxford: Oxford Univ. Press, 1954), 187–91.

25. Janet Hamilton and Bernard Hamilton, *Christian Dualist Heresies in the Byzantine World, ca. 650– ca. 1450,* trans. assistance of Old Slavonic texts by Yuri Stoyanov (Manchester: Univ. Press, 1998).

centrally disturbed, locally various right across Europe."[26] Some Slavic groups, such as the Bogomils–Cathari, emigrated from the East into the West in the Piedmont, L'Occitane, and Spain, where they translated Latin Bibles. Their theological ideas were translated into vernacular prayer books and other vernacular works. These groups had contact with English Lollards and may have been known to Wycliffe, Tyndale, and Milton. Georgi Vasilev claims that Wycliffe, Tyndale, and Milton, among others, adopted their dualistic views.[27]

"Tyndale's gift, not only to English speaking New Testament Christians, but to language and literature, secular as well as religious, came from his unique ability as a translator," writes David Daniell. "He had the technical skills of fluent and accurate Greek, Hebrew, Latin and German (and other languages) and the machinery of recent dictionaries and grammars. He had a complete understanding of the complex art of rhetoric."[28] While in Germany in 1526, Tyndale translated the whole New Testament into English from the original Greek for the first time. His translation method has come to be known as "dynamic equivalence" rather than "formal equivalence."[29]

In 1534 Tyndale published his revision of Genesis and began work on a revision of the New Testament. Shortly after completing this revision, he was kidnapped in Antwerp and taken to the fortress at Vilvorde in Flanders. There the imprisoned Tyndale began translation of the Apocrypha and continued translating the Old Testament, but was unable to complete it. In August 1536, he was found guilty of heresy, degraded from his priestly office, and turned over to the secular authorities for execution. This was carried out on October 6, when he was strangled and burned alive at the stake.

26. Daniell, *The Bible in English*, 123–25.

27. See Ralph S. Werrell, *The Theology of William Tyndale* (Cambridge: James Clarke & Co. Ltd., 2006). Also see Werrell's insightful Review, which asserts that Georgi Vasilev projects his own dualistic views on these English counterparts, in *Reformation* 15 (2010): 214–16. Georgi Vasilev, "Bogomils and Lollards, Dualistic Motives in England During the Middle Ages" (1993); "Bogomils, Cathari, Lollards" (1998); "Dualistic Ideas in the Works of Tyndale" (2003); and "Dualist Philosophy and Imagery in John Milton Treatises: Speculation and Miltonian Self-Identification," paper presented at 8th International Milton Symposium, 7–11 June 2005, Grenoble, France. These online articles were published as *Heresy and the English Reformation: Bogomil-Cathar Influence on Wycliffe, Langland, Tyndale and Milton* (London: McFarland and Company, 2007).

28. Daniell, *The Bible in English*, 133.

29. Ibid., 133–34. See also Bruce M. Metzger, *The Bible in Translation* (Grand Rapids: Baker, 2001).

At the time of his execution, Tyndale cried out, "Lord, open the King of England's eyes." Indeed, events in England were working together to bring to pass the translator's last request. In 1534, Henry VIII became the head of the Church of England newly separated from the Church of Rome. During the next half century, England became the most Protestant country in Europe.

Miles Coverdale (1488–1569). Miles Coverdale, Tyndale's assistant and proofreader at Antwerp became the key individual in printing the first complete English Bible in 1535. He continued translating those portions of the Bible (including the Apocrypha) Tyndale was unable to complete. This work was barely a revision of Tyndale's translation, with added insights from the German and Latin translations. It was a handsome folio edition that included the Old and New Testaments and Apocrypha, as did all major English Bibles until the twentieth century (Plates 48–49).

Coverdale introduced chapter summaries and some new expressions into the text of his translation. He also set the precedent of separating the Old Testament from the Apocrypha in those Bibles translated after the Latin Vulgate came into its position of dominance in the Western church. Coverdale's translation was reprinted twice in 1537, again in 1550, and once again in 1553. The Coverdale Diglot (Latin and English) was published in Paris (1538). In its prologue Coverdale wrote of the value of differing translations of the Scriptures. He wrote:

> Now for thy part, most gentle reader, take in good worth that I here offer thee with good will, and let this present translation be no prejudice to the other that out of the Greek have been translated afore, or shall be hereafter. For if thou open thine eyes and consider well the gift of the Holy Ghost therein, thou shalt see that one translation declareth, openeth and illustrateth another, and that in many cases one is a plain commentary unto another.[30]

Nevertheless, the true successor to the 1535 edition was the Great Bible of 1539 (see next page).

---

30. Cited by Curtis Vaughan, gen. ed., *The New Testament in 26 Translations* (Grand Rapids: Zondervan, 1967), Introduction.

Thomas Matthew (ca. 1500–1555). Thomas Matthew was the pen name of John Rogers, who was burned alive as the first martyr of the persecutions under Mary Tudor (1553-1558). He too had been an assistant to Tyndale. In 1537 he published another English Bible by combining the Old Testament texts of Tyndale and Coverdale (including for the first time Tyndale's Old Testament historical books—Joshua through 2 Chronicles[31]—with the 1535 revision of Tyndale's New Testament.) This "Tyndale-Coverdale Bible" became the basis of all English Bible translations (revisions) to the present. Richard Grafton and Edward Whitchurche of London were the designated printers.[32] It was published as a slightly revised edition in 1549. In 1551 a Bible called "Matthew's" on the title page appeared containing Taverner's New Testament and the 1548 edition of Tyndale's New Testament (Plates 51–52).

Although John Rogers refused to attach his given name to work done by others, he added copious notes and references and published it using the pen name Thomas Matthew. In addition to the editions of Tyndale and Coverdale, he borrowed heavily from the French editions of Lefèvre (1534) and Olivétan (1535). When he published his 1537 edition, he was licensed to do so from Henry VIII. With its release, there were two licensed English Bibles in circulation within a year of Tyndale's execution. His assistants had carried on the work of their martyred associate, and others would follow in their train.

Richard Taverner (1505–1575). Taverner was a layman who knew Greek quite well. In 1539 he applied his talent to a revision of Matthew's Bible and produced a translation that made better use of the Greek article. Nevertheless, Taverner's work was soon to be eclipsed by still another revision of Matthew's Bible, the Great Bible of 1539.

The Great Bible (1539). The notes and prologues to the two major translations of the printed English Bible in circulation in 1539, Coverdale's and Matthew's, gave affront to so many groups in England that Henry VIII was frequently besought to provide a new translation free from interpretations. Thomas Cromwell (ca. 1485-1540), Protestant Lord Chancellor under Henry VIII, was authorized to proceed with such an undertaking. With further approval by Thomas Cranmer (1489-1556), first Protestant archbishop

---

31. Daniell, *The Bible in English*, 193–95.

32. Beriah Botfield, *Notes on the Cathedral* (Libraries of London, 1849), 194.

of Canterbury, Miles Coverdale was willing to prepare a new text for it and to use the work of others—Matthew's Bible (1537)—in preference to his own, published two years earlier.

Under the direction of Coverdale, the Great Bible was offered as a means of easing the tensions stemming from the Bible situation in England. It received its name because of its great size and format, for it was larger than any previous edition and was elaborately decorated. Its title page was a fine woodcut attributed to Hans Holbein that depicts Henry VIII, Cranmer, and Cromwell distributing Bibles to the people who in turn cry, "Vivat rex" ("Long live the king"), and "God save the king" (Plate 53). The Bible contained no dedication and had only simple prefaces.

In addition, the Apocrypha was removed from the remainder of the Old Testament text and placed in an appendix entitled "hagiographa" (holy writings). The situation was extremely awkward since most of the bishops of the church were still Roman Catholic. The Great Bible was "authorized to be read in the churches" in 1538. Nevertheless, its delicate position was threatened by the fact that it was neither a version nor a revision of a version; it was a revision of a revision.

Cranmer's Bible (1540). In April 1540, a second edition of the Great Bible was published. It contained a preface by Thomas Cranmer, then archbishop of Canterbury, and some further revisions based on Coverdale's earlier work. It was followed by five other editions before the end of 1541. These Bibles are called Cranmer's because of the preface he wrote for them. In that preface is the statement, "This is the Byble apoynted to the use of the churches." Coverdale's Bible of 1535 and Matthew's Bible of 1537 had been licensed, but this was definitely an authorized translation, which the "revision" of 1611 never was.

In the third and fifth of these six editions of Cranmer's Bible a notice was printed on the title page to the effect that bishops Tunstall and Heath had "overseen and perused" the edition. It is a curious irony that Tunstall as bishop of London had condemned Tyndale and his work. Now he officially authorized a Bible that largely contained Tyndale's translation and revisions of it. By 1547 Cranmer's Bible attained a predominate position in the churches. In 1549 and 1553 it was again reprinted, and Cranmer's order was not rescinded even during the brief and turbulent years of the reign of Mary Tudor (1553–1558).

The Geneva Bible (1557, 1560). During the persecutions under Mary Tudor many reformers fled to the Continent for safety. Among those who settled at Geneva were scholars and Bible lovers, like Miles Coverdale and John Knox (ca. 1513–1572). They produced a revision that was to have a great influence on the people of England. In 1557 one of their group, William Whittingham, a brother-in-law to John Calvin, produced a stopgap revision of the New Testament. This was the first time the English New Testament had been divided into verses, although it had been so divided in the 1551 Greek Testament of Stephanus as well as earlier editions in Latin and Hebrew. Long prologues were added to the translation, along with chapter summaries and copious marginal notes. Italics were introduced into the translation to indicate where English idiom required words that were not in the original text.

Shortly after the New Testament was published at Geneva, work was begun on a careful revision of the entire Bible. In 1560 the Old Testament and a revision of the New were completed that included the latest textual evidence, and the long and eventful history of the Geneva Bible began (Plate 54). In 1576 a revised edition of the Geneva Bible was published by Laurence Tomson, the secretary to Elizabeth I's secretary of state, Sir Francis Walsingham. It is noteworthy for introducing the demonstrative pronoun "that" for the Greek definite article ὁ (*ho*, "the" in Matt. 16:16). In 1598, Francis Junius, Huguenot divine, introduced annotations on the book of Revelation. By 1644 the Geneva Bible had gone through at least 144 editions.

The Geneva Bible was the Bible of William Shakespeare, John Milton, John Bunyan, the colonists at Jamestown (1606), the Pilgrims (1620), and the Puritans (1630s–1640s). Although its notations were milder than those of Tyndale, they were too Calvinistic and anti-Catholic for either Elizabeth I (1558–1603) or James I (1603–1625). Nevertheless, it was so popular that it withstood the Bishops' Bible (1568) and the first generation of the so-called Authorized Version (AV, 1611).

The Bishops' Bible (1568). The Geneva Bible was not sponsored by the established church, but it quickly became the household Bible of the realm. Its immediate success made this new revision of the Great Bible the authorized Bible of the churches. The work was given to a group of scholars including about eight bishops, hence the name the Bishops' Bible. They were to use the Great Bible as the basis of their revision and, while the intention was to make only slight alterations, some of the bishops went beyond their instructions. The revisers were better scholars in Greek than Hebrew, and their work in the New Testament is superior to that in the Old (Plates 55–56).

The Bishops' Bible was published in London "cum privilegio regiae majestatis," although the device does not appear on the title page of either the 1568 or 1569 Bishops' Bible. From the beginning of his reign the first Tudor, Henry VII (1485–1509), concerned himself with printing and the book trade. He granted "privileges" *(privilegio)* to protect the work of his royal printer. The Tudors were interested in and controlled the press by issuing licenses, or privileges, to the new printing class that moved into England in the late fifteenth century.[33] Each Tudor monarch named a royal printer at the beginning of his or her reign. With Henry VIII's break with Rome in 1538, and the rise to power of Thomas Cromwell, *cum privilegio ad imprimendum solum* (with exclusive license to imprint) became widespread by Henrician proclamation (16 November 1538) that called for licensing of all printed works. "The proclamation's clear end was to institute pre-print censorship of scripture, and other religious texts and to prevent the printing of objectionable texts . . . by sundry strange persons called Anabaptists and Sacramentaries."

The Bishops' Bible New Testament portion was published on thicker paper than the Old Testament in order to withstand greater wear. It contained two prefaces, Cranmer's and one by Matthew Parker, then archbishop of Canterbury. Following the Great Bible, it had few marginal notes. The Convocation of 1571 ordered that copies be placed throughout the land, in the houses of every bishop and archbishop, and in each cathedral and every church if possible. From 1568 to 1611 this compromise translation was generally found in the churches. Nevertheless, the Geneva Bible had already won over the households of the land. Its insurmountable disadvantage, however, did not keep the Bishops' Bible from being the basis for the famous 1611 revision.

---

33. Cyndia Susan Clegg, *Press Censorship in Elizabethan England* (Cambridge: Cambridge Univ. Press, 1997), 1–30, traces the development of the "cum privilegio" (with privilege) that appears in various forms: before 1538 when the Henrician proclamation made *cum privilegio ad imprimendum solum* ("with exclusive license to imprint") the only form to be used, *cum privilegio regis* ("with royal privilege"), and *cum privilegio regiae majestatis* ("with privilege by his royal majesty"). Sometimes the printer's renewable "license" or "copyright" notice does not appear on the title page.

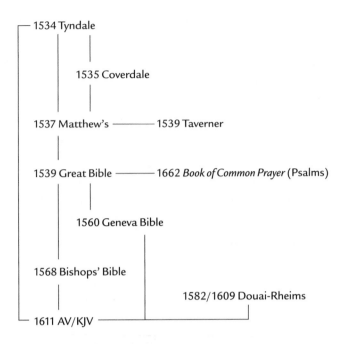

1534 Tyndale

1535 Coverdale

1537 Matthew's ————— 1539 Taverner

1539 Great Bible ————— 1662 *Book of Common Prayer* (Psalms)

1560 Geneva Bible

1568 Bishops' Bible

1582/1609 Douai-Rheims

1611 AV/KJV

SOURCE: David Dewey, *Which Bible?* (Leicester, England: InterVarsity, 2004), 111. Copyright © 2004 by David Dewey. This chart is reproduced from *Which Bible?* First published by InterVarsity Press, Nottingham, England, 2004. Used by permission.

STANDARD TRANSLATIONS OF THE BIBLE IN ENGLISH

While Protestants were busy making vernacular translations of the Bible for use in England, their Roman Catholic counterparts expressed a similar desire. After the death of Mary Tudor in 1558, Elizabeth I ascended to the throne and Roman Catholic exiles of her reign undertook a task similar to that of Protestant exiles at Geneva during Mary's reign. The multiplicity and diversity of translations was such that by the time James I ascended to the throne in 1603, a more unified translation was needed so the various groups within the church could appeal to a common authority in their theological discussions. As a result of the efforts then set into motion, the King James Bible, the most influential single revision of the English Protestants, was produced.

The Rheims-Douay (Douai-Rheims, Douay-Rheims) Bible (1582, 1609) Douay-Rheims-Challoner Bible (1749–1750)

In 1568 a group of Roman Catholic exiles from England founded the English

College at Douay in Flanders. They sought to train priests and others who would preserve their Catholic faith. William Allen (1532-1594), Oxford canon during Mary Tudor's reign, led in the founding of this college and in its move to Rheims, France, when political troubles arose in 1578. At Rheims the English College came under the direction of another Oxford scholar, Richard Bristow (1538-1581), who had gone to Douay in 1569. During this time Allen was called to Rome where he founded another English College and was later made cardinal. In 1593 the English College at Rheims returned to Douay.

The Roman hierarchy desired an English translation of the Latin Vulgate, and Allen expressed this wish in a letter to a professor at the college in Douay in 1578. Gregory Martin (d. 1582), still another Oxford scholar, undertook the task. Martin had received his M.A. in 1564. He then renounced his Protestantism and went to Douay to study. In 1570 he became lecturer in Hebrew and Holy Scripture, and proceeded with his translation of the Old Testament at the rate of about two chapters a day until his death in 1582. Just before his death, the New Testament was published with many notations. These notes were the work of Bristow and Allen. They were joined in their efforts by another Protestant turned Catholic, William Reynolds, although his role in the task is not fully known.

While the Rheims New Testament translation (1582) was designed to counteract the existing English translations of the Protestants (Plate 57), it had some serious limitations. It was a poor rendition of the text into English and was based on still another translation (the Latin Vulgate) rather than the original language of the New Testament. The translators guarded themselves "against the idea that the Scriptures should always be in our mother tongue, or that they ought, or were ordained by God, to be read indifferently by all." Not only that, the translators made no secret that they were making a polemic work, as their copious notes indicate. The New Testament was republished in 1600, 1621, and 1633.

In the meantime, the Old Testament, actually translated before the New, was delayed until 1609, as several new editions of the Vulgate text were published (Plate 58). A second edition was released in 1635. The actual translation was begun by Martin and probably completed by Allen and Bristow, with notes apparently furnished by Thomas Worthington, although the details are so obscure that these matters cannot be determined with certainty. It was based on the unofficial Louvain Vulgate text (1547), edited by Henten, but conformed to the Sixtene-Clementine text of 1592. The translation itself was uniform throughout, including the over-literal use of Latinisms. The annotations were basically designed to bring the interpretation of the text into harmony with the decrees of the Council of Trent (1546–1563). "The dogmatic intentions of the translators found expression in the preface and in the notes that accompany the text. Annotations in the form of marginalia and notes at the end of chapters rival those of the Geneva Bible in profuseness and exceed them in polemic nature."[34]

The Rheims New Testament was in circulation long enough to have an important influence on the English Bible translators of 1611. The Douay Old Testament translation, however, was not published in time to influence those translators. With a Protestant queen on the throne and a Protestant king as her successor, the Douay-Rheims Bible had little possibility of competing with or replacing the Protestant translations already available. The scarcity of reprints of the Douay-Rheims Bible indicates that Catholics had "no fear that the few available copies would be found in the hand of every husbandman." After 1635 several reprints were made, but the second revised edition did not appear until 1749–1750, and the third in 1752, when Richard Challoner, bishop of London, removed its literalistic Latinisms and united the Old and New Testaments and Apocrypha in five volumes (Plate 60).

The King James Bible (1611)

In January 1604 James I was summoned to the Hampton Court Conference in response to the Millenary Petition, which he received while on his way from Edinburgh to London following the death of Elizabeth I. Nearly one thousand Puritan leaders had signed a list of grievances against the church of England, and James desired to be peacemaker in his new realm and placed himself above all religious parties. He treated the Puritans with rudeness at the conference until John Reynolds, Puritan President of Corpus Christi College, Oxford, raised the question of having an authorized version of the Bible for all parties within the church. The king expressed his support for the translation because it would help him to be rid of the two most popular translations and raise his esteem in the eyes of his subjects. A committee

---

34. Metzger, *The Bible in Translation*, 69.

was named, following the example of the Geneva Bible, which King James regarded as the worst of all existing translations. It and the Bishops' Bible were the Bibles he hoped to replace in the church.

Six companies of translators were chosen: two at Cambridge to revise 1 Chronicles through Ecclesiastes and the Apocrypha; two at Oxford to revise Isaiah through Malachi, the Gospels, Acts, and the Apocalypse; and two at Westminster to revise Genesis through 2 Kings and Romans through Jude. Only forty-seven of the fifty-four men chosen actually worked on this revision of the Bishops' Bible. They were instructed to follow the text of the Bishops' Bible unless they found that the translations of Tyndale, Matthew, Coverdale, Whitchurche,[35] and Geneva more closely agreed with the original text. That original text was based on few if any of the superior texts of the twelfth to the fifteenth centuries, since it followed the 1516 and 1522 editions of Erasmus's Greek text, including his interpolation of 1 John 5:7. Using the Bishops' Bible as its basis meant that many old ecclesiastical words would be retained in the new revision. In an unofficial way, the recent publication of the Rheims Bible would influence the reintroduction of many Latinisms into the text. The Douay Old Testament was not published until 1609 (see previous discussion).

Few marginal notes were affixed to the new revision, and the so-called Authorized Version was never actually authorized, nor was it actually a version. It was a revision "Appointed to be read in Churches." In recent years it has come to be known as the King James Bible (KJB; see Plate 59 for title page).[36] It replaced the Bishops' Bible in the churches because no editions of it were published after 1606. Being cast in the same format as the Geneva Bible gave the 1611 publication added influence, as did its use of precise expression. In the long run the grandeur of its translation was able to successfully compete with and overpower the influence of the Geneva Bible of the Puritans, its chief rival. Three editions of the new translation appeared in 1611. Further editions were published in 1612, and its popularity continued to call forth new printings.

During the reign of Charles I (1625–1649), the Long Parliament

---

35. Richard Grafton and Edward Whitchurche of London were the first printers of English Bibles and Prayer Books with the support of Miles Coverdale.

36. Brian J. McMullin, "A Textual History of the King James Bible," *The Transactions of the Bibliographical Society*, vol. 7, no. 1 (March 2006): 99–100.

established a commission to consider either revising the Authorized Version or producing a new translation altogether. "Over the centuries the three most important publishers of the KJV (KJB)[37] have been the king's (or queen's) printer, Cambridge University Press, and Oxford University Press. ... The Cinderella Press is the king's printer."[38] Notable for careful editorial work were the Cambridge revisions of 1629 and 1638, with other minor revisions in 1653 and 1701. More comprehensive corrections were completed by F. S. Parris of Cambridge (1762).

In 1769 Dr. Benjamin Blayney of Oxford produced what has come to be the standard edition of the King James Bible. His revisions varied in about 75,000 details from the text of the 1611 edition.

Slight changes have continued to appear in the text. A revision edited for the Syndics of the [Cambridge] University Press by F. H. A. Scrivener, *The Cambridge Paragraph Bible* (1873), included the Apocrypha but failed to achieve popular appeal. It was republished and edited by David Norton to become *The New Cambridge Paragraph Bible: with the Apocrypha, King James Version* (2005). The current standard text of the Paragraph Bible departs from the 1611 text approximately 11,000 times, yet is still "the most faithful presentation of the King James Bible."[39] As with its counterparts, the Paragraph Bible title page says it is "translated out of the original tongues and with former translations diligently compared and revised by His Majesty's Special Commandment. Appointed to be read in Churches. Cum privilegio."

37. Cameron A. MacKenzie, "Theology and the Great Tradition of Engish Bibles," *Concordia Theological Quarterly* 64, no. 4 (October 1999): 281–91

38. Gordon Campbell, *BIBLE: The Story of the King James Version, 1611–2011* (Oxford: Oxford Univ. Press, 2010), xi.

39. James D. Price, "Review of David Norton, A Textual History of the King James Bible," dissertation, Tennessee Temple Seminary, 2006.

20

MODERN ENGLISH BIBLE TRANSLATIONS

ENGLISH BIBLE TRANSLATIONS during the late nineteenth and twentieth centuries would center on those translations growing out of the Douay-Rheims and the King James Bible traditions of the late fifteenth and early sixteenth centuries. The Douay-Rheims was reprinted several times after 1635; the second revised edition was published in 1749–1750, and the third in 1752, when Richard Challoner (1691–1781), bishop of London, removed its literalistic Latinisms and united the Old and New Testaments and Apocrypha in the five-volume Douay-Rheims-Challoner version. The traditional standard edition of the King James Version (KJV) by Dr. Benjamin Blayney of Oxford was published in 1769 and has been the standard KJB translation ever since. In tracing developments since the mid-eighteenth century, this chapter will follow a topical-chronological arrangement.

PROTESTANT TRANSLATIONS AND VERSIONS

In keeping with their Reformation principle of private interpretation, Protestants have produced a greater number of private translations of the Bible than have Roman Catholics. Some of the earlier translations grew out of the discoveries of new manuscript materials, since none of the great manuscripts had been discovered at the time of the King James translation (see chap. 14) except Codex Bezae (D), which was used very little. Before turning to those private translations, however, we should look at some of the official attempts to bring the King James Bible into alignment with the manuscript discoveries.

Revised Version, RV, English Revised Version, ERV (1881, 1885, 1895)

All revisions of the King James Bible (KJB) mentioned to this point were without official ecclesiastical or royal authorization. In fact, no official revision was forthcoming for over a century after the work of Dr. Blayney (1769), which became the standard text of the KJB. Some of the revisions made were ill-advised, such as additions like Bishop Ussher's chronology. Nevertheless, some were excellent revisions in an unofficial capacity, as in the case of an anonymous edition of *The Holy Bible Containing the Authorized Version of the Old and New Testaments, with Many Emendations* (1841). In the preface of this unofficial revision of the KJB, the author mentions that he used manuscripts not available in 1611.

A revision by F. H. A. Scrivener, *The Cambridge Paragraph Bible* (1879), placed the text in a single column, but it failed to achieve popular appeal. In commemoration of the KJB quatercentenary this text was re-edited by David Norton as *The New Cambridge Paragraph Bible* (2005), who states that "thousands of specks of dust have been blown away from the received text of *The New Cambridge Paragraph Bible*, leaving the KJB presented with a fidelity to the translators' own work never before achieved, and allowing the most read, heard and loved book in the English language to speak with new vigor to modern readers."

With advances in biblical scholarship during the nineteenth century, including the accumulation of earlier and better manuscripts, archaeological discoveries in the ancient world as a whole, and changes in English society and its language, the revision of the King James Bible on a more "official" basis was becoming mandatory. Before this could be accomplished, however, a group of outstanding scholars published *The Variorum Edition of the New Testament of Our Lord and Saviour Jesus Christ* (1880). The editors of this work, R. L. Clark, Alfred Goodwin, and W. Sanday, made this revision at "his majesty's special command." Their task was to revise the King James Bible in light of the various readings from the best textual authorities. As a result, The Variorum Bible followed the tradition of Tyndale, Coverdale, Great, Geneva, Bishops', and the various editions of the KJB. It also prepared the way for an English Revised Version (ERV), the Revised Version (RV).

The widespread desire for a full-fledged revision of the Authorized Bible (AV) resulted in a convocation of the Province of Canterbury in 1870. Samuel Wilberforce, bishop of Winchester, proposed to revise the New Testament where Greek texts revealed inaccurate or incorrect translations in the King James text. Bishop Ollivant enlarged the motion to include the Old Testament and Hebrew texts. As a result, two companies were appointed. Originally there were twenty-four members in each company, but they were later enlarged to include some sixty-five revisers from various denominations. They began their work in 1871, and in 1872 a group of American scholars joined the enterprise in an advisory capacity. Oxford and Cambridge University presses absorbed the costs of the project with the provision that they had exclusive copyright privileges to the finished product. Over three million copies of the revision were sold in the United States and Great Britain in less than a year. The Revised Version (RV) New Testament was released in 1881, the Old Testament in 1885, and the Apocrypha in 1895 (1898 in the United States without the Apocrypha), and the entire Revised Version Bible was published in 1898. While the text of the revision was much more accurate than the KJB, it would take several generations for acceptance of the altered words and rhythms. Oxford University Press published *The Interlinear Bible: The Authorized Version and The Revised Version*, together with the marginal notes of both versions and central references (1898).

American Standard Version, ASV (1901)

Some of the renderings of the English Revised Bible (ERV, RV) were not completely favored by the American revision committee, but they had agreed to give for fourteen years "no sanction to the publication of any other editions of the Revised Version than those issued by the University Presses of England." In 1901 the American Standard Edition of the Revised Version (ASV) was published, indicating there had been some unauthorized or nonstandard editions published previously. Further revisions were made by the American committee, such as changing the names *Lord* to *Jehovah* and *Holy Ghost* to *Holy Spirit*. Paragraph structures were revised and shortened, and short page headings were added. Slowly this ASV won acceptance in the United States and even began to be imported into Great Britain. Unlike the RV, the ASV omits the Apocrypha, and an appendix indicates differences between the RV and ASV translations at the end of the Old Testament.

According to the preface, the ASV incorporates a number of revisions originally adopted by the RV revisers but later rejected by them; they return numerous readings to agree with the AV; they sometimes returned their readings to the RV; and sometimes went beyond the literalness demanded by their appendix as a matter of consistency, English idiom, accuracy, marginal treatment of readings from ancient sources, marginal parallel and illustrative passages, as well as paragraph division and punctuation. Yet another appendix at the close of the New Testament presents a "list of Readings and Renderings which appear in the Revised Version New Testament of 1881 in place of those preferred by the American New Testament Revision Company."

The ASV committee proposed it work under four heads: Text, Translation, Language, and Marginal Notes. For the text, the ASV was served by members from different schools of criticism, who finally adopted a rule that differences between the text underlying the AV and the RV would retain the AV rendering unless a change was decided by two-thirds majority; translation was governed by "revision" not "re-translation"; language expression was governed, as far as possible, in the language of the AV or the versions preceding it; significant developments were introduced into marginal notes.

Like its English counterpart, the ASV lacks the beauty of the KJB, but its more accurate readings have made it quite acceptable to teachers and students of the Bible. In 1929 its copyright passed to the International Council of Religious Education and they revised the text again. Like the earlier translations building on the foundation laid by William Tyndale, the ASV was the work of many hands and several generations. "The RV and ASV, though appreciated for their scholarly improvements, lacked the rhythms and cadences of the AV/KJV and were deemed too excessively literal. And all the others were basically private or personal translations intended for personal use." (See chap. 20 discussion of eighteenth- to twentieth-century translations.)

REFERENCE BIBLES

Following the publication of the ERV (1885) and the ASV (1901), an old tradition was renewed with significant ramifications for Bible publication. This new emphasis and format is reflected in the appearance of reference (or study) Bibles. Three of these (discussed here), published in the first decade of the twentieth century, remain a force in English Bible publications.

Nave's Topical Bible, Nave (1897, 1905)
The Student's Bible (1907)

Orville J. Nave was an American Methodist theologian and chaplain in the

U.S. Army, best known for compiling *Nave's Topical Bible: A Digest of the Holy Scriptures* (1896, 1897), an index of topics addressed in the Christian Bible. Nave spent fourteen years studying the KJB with his wife, and created this concordance of over 20,000 topics in 1896 and 1897). Each topic has multiple Scripture references to give readers a complete sense of the word or phrase. This volume is more helpful for beginners than a traditional concordance. Users are also able to search for all the verses related to a topic or all the topics related to a verse. Topics range from the broad (concepts like salvation or repentance) to the minute (references to rope or doves in Scripture); it also includes listings for names and places in the Bible.

In the preface of the seventh edition (1905), Nave writes that his work is based on the King James Version (KJV), but the increasing demand for the readings of the Revised Version (RV) introduces these readings more liberally than seemed to be required when the work was first published. "A true cornerstone of Biblical knowledge, Nave's Topical Bible is endorsed and used by Christians of all backgrounds. Though it was first completed over a century ago, it is still sure to suit any need."[1] Following publication of the ASV (1901), Orville Nave and his wife Anna Semans Nave published *The Student's Bible*[2] (1907). The subtitle indicates its scope and purpose. Unlike Nave's Topical Bible, developed from the RV, The Student's Bible followed the ASV. The Student's Bible included the complete text of the KJB and copious notes from the ASV. This last feature is more akin to the *Thompson Chain Reference Bible*, and the *Scofield Reference Bible* discussed below. Later, S. Maxwell Coder published a revised edition of *Nave's Topical Bible* (Moody, 1974), without the indices of earlier printings.

PIONEERING STUDY AND REFERENCE BIBLES

Dr. Frank C. Thompson was a young preacher who became dissatisfied with the reference Bibles then available to preachers. Believing the Bible

---

1. Available at Abby Zwart, "Nave's Topical Bible," Christian Classics Ethereal Library (www.ccel.org/ ccel/nave/bible.html).

2. Orville J. Nave and Anna Seman Nave, *The Student's Bible (King James Version, with Copious Readings from the American Revised Version)*, published by Oxford and Cambridge Universities with marginal notes and an exhaustive topical analysis of all passages, citing explanatory footnotes with numerous subheadings and with references to all related scriptures (Lincoln, Neb.: Topical Bible Publishing Company, 1907).

should be presented in a simple but scholarly way, he saw the need for a well-organized reference Bible that would be of practical use to the layman as well as the minister. In 1890, Dr. Thompson entered "thought suggestions" opposite verses throughout the Bible. These became the "chain-links" that are the heart of the Thompson system. Some of the men in his church helped him to have his Bible published with marginal references.

The first version of Thompson's study Bible was published in 1908 by the Methodists Book Concern of Dobbs Ferry, New York. Five years later, in 1913, Dr. Thompson was joined by B. B. Kirkbride, of Indianapolis, Indiana. The two men formed the Kirkbride Bible Company, in order to further improve and distribute Thompson's work. The original *Thompson Chain-Reference Bible*, as well as several subsequent versions, was based on the KJB. Currently, available editions are based on the KJB, NKJV, NIV, and NAS (1977 version) as well as electronic versions that incorporate other features. As of 2006, over four million *Thompson Chain-Reference Bibles* have been sold.

Before the close of the twentieth century, annotated, reference, and study Bibles had became a dominant feature of Bible publication. Most included the King James Bible, which had grand commemorations of its 300th and 400th anniversaries. On the occasion of the KJB's 300th anniversary in 1911, Oxford University Press held its tercentenary celebration on both sides of the Atlantic. In England Alfred Pollard was commissioned to write a book-length introduction to two editions of the 1611 Bible, one a facsimile edition and the other a version set in Roman type. In America the Press published *The 1911 Tercentenary Commemoration Bible* "with a new system of references prepared by C. I. Scofield," who had already published the first edition of his annotated Bible[3] (1909) as the *Scofield Reference Bible* (1911). Further changes have been made in the text of the Authorized Version accompanying the *New Scofield Reference Edition* (1967). In the meantime, extensive alterations and corrections occurred in English translations as a result of the new textual discoveries and the changing character of the language itself.

In anticipation of the 400th anniversary of the King James Bible, Oxford University Press published a special *Oxford Anniversary Edition 1611*

---

3. Gordon Campbell, *BIBLE: The Story of the King James Version, 1611–2011* (Oxford: Oxford Univ. Press, 2010), vi–vii.

King James Bible (2011). In the *Oxford World Classics* series, Robert Carroll and Stephen Pricket edited, with notes, *The Bible: Authorized King James Version, with Apocrypha* (Oxford University Press, 1988, reissued 2008). In addition to many special editions of the KJV, Gordon Campbell was commissioned to write *The Bible: The Story of the King James Version, 1611–2011* (Oxford University Press, 2010). In the meantime, David Horton wrote *The King James Bible: A Short History from Tyndale to Today* (Cambridge University Press, 2011). Norton also edited *The New Cambridge Paragraph Bible, with the Apocrypha; King James Version* (Cambridge University Press, 2005).

Roman Catholic Translations and Versions

The major English Bible translation for Roman Catholics during the Reformation era was the Douay-Rheims Bible of 1582, 1609 (see chap. 19). Sales began slowly but the translation came to dominate the scene by 1635 and was published several times after that date. Nevertheless, it was not the only Roman Catholic translation of the Bible into English.

The Douay-Rheims-Challoner Bible

Although several printings of the Douay-Rheims Bible were made after 1635, it was not until 1749–1750 that Richard Challoner, bishop of London, published the second revised edition. It was little more than a new translation of the Bible into English, for it took advantage of several developments in Bible translation made during the eighteenth century. In 1718, for instance, a new translation of the Vulgate New Testament was published by Cornelius Nary. In 1730 Robert Witham, president of the English College at Douay, published a revision of the Rheims New Testament. It had some revisions that are attributed to Challoner, who had been an associate with Witham at Douay following his conversion from Protestantism. A fifth edition of the Rheims New Testament was published in 1738. It contained some revisions generally attributed to Challoner and was the first revised edition of this New Testament published in over a century (the fourth revised edition being published in 1633). In 1749 Challoner published his Revised Rheims New Testament, as he did again in 1750, 1752, 1763, and 1772. His revision of the Douay Old Testament was published in 1750 and 1763.

Since that time, further editions of the Douay-Rheims Bible have been made, but they are practically all based on the 1749–1750 revision. As a result, Father Hugh Pope has correctly observed that "English-speaking Catholics the world over owe Dr. Challoner an immense debt of gratitude, for he provided them for the first time with a portable, cheap, and readable version which in spite of a few inevitable defects has stood the test of two hundred years of use."[4]

The Confraternity of Christian Doctrine Bible

The first Roman Catholic Bible published in the United States (1790) was a large quarto edition of the Douay Old Testament and a mixture of several of the Challoner revisions combined with the 1752 edition of the Rheims-Challoner New Testament text. This Bible was actually the first quarto Bible of any kind in English to be published in North America. In 1849–1860, Francis Patrick Kenrick made a new revision of the Challoner Bible in six volumes, although he claimed that he had made his translation from the Latin Vulgate after it had been diligently compared with the Hebrew and Greek texts. From this time onward, other editions appeared on both sides of the Atlantic.

In 1936 a new revision of the Rheims-Challoner New Testament was begun under the sponsorship of the Episcopal Committee of the Confraternity of Christian Doctrine. They named a committee of twenty-eight scholars to work on the revision under the direction of Edward P. Arbez. It used the Latin Vulgate text as its basis, but made use of recent developments in biblical scholarship. Many of the archaic expressions of the earlier revisions were removed, as were many of the copious notes. The text was arranged in paragraphs and American spelling was employed. The St. Anthony Guild Press published the Confraternity New Testament in 1941, and it was quickly used by English-speaking Catholics around the world.

Modern Speech Translations for Roman Catholics

The initial attitude of the Roman Catholic Church toward publishing the Scriptures for laymen was far from enthusiastic. Pope Pius IX (1846–1878) condemned Bible societies as pestilent sects in his famous Syllabus of Errors (1864), some sixty years after the founding of the British and Foreign

---

4. There have been so many revisions and editions of this Challoner's Bible, which differs very much from the original Douay-Rheims Bible, that it is no longer accurate to identify his work by its predecessor's name. It is indeed Challoner's Bible translation.

Bible Society in 1804. He reflected the attitude of the Roman Catholic hierarchy at large, but others felt that the Bible should be placed into the hands of Catholic laymen. As early as 1813, for instance, a group of enthusiastic churchmen founded the Roman Catholic Bible Society and published the Douay-Rheims Bible without notes. In 1815 the same group published another improved edition of the same translation.

Meanwhile, a host of editions of the *Bible for Roman Catholics* appeared, including *Coyne's Bible* (1811), *Haydock's Bible* (1811–1814), the *Newcastle New Testament* (1812), *Syer's Bible* (1813–1814), *MacNamara's Bible* (1813–1814), *Bregan's New Testament* (1814), and *Gibson's Bible* (1816–1817). Other Bibles were published throughout the nineteenth century in both England and the United States. In 1901 the Dominican Father Francis Spencer published a remarkable version of the Gospels. He completed the rest of what would become the *Laymen's New Testament* just prior to his death in 1913. First printed in London in 1927, the *Laymen's New Testament* was not published in America until 1937. In the meantime, James A. Kliest and Joseph L. Lilly published still another translation entitled *The New Testament Rendered from the Original Greek with Explanatory Notes* (1956).

The Jerusalem Bible (1966); The New Jerusalem Bible (1985)
New Catholic Bible (2007)
The Bible in Its Traditions (2008+)

Probably the most significant twentieth-century translation in this category produced by Roman Catholic scholars is the Jerusalem Bible (JB, TJB, 1966). These Bibles are the projects of the École Biblique et Archéologique in Jerusalem.[5] Although it is translated from the original texts, it owes a great debt to *La Bible de Jerusalem* (1961), whose introduction and notes were translated without substantial variation directly into the English text. In 1985 a revision of the Jerusalem Bible (JB, TJB) was published as the New Jerusalem Bible (NJB, 1985). The translation and notes represent the work of the "liberal" wing of Catholic biblical scholarship, although the translation itself is basically literal and contemporary in style. The JB and NJB have become the most widely used English Bibles for Catholics outside the United States. The original English draft of the Old Testament was a literal translation of

---

5. The website for the École Biblique et Archéologique in Jerusalem is http://www.ebaf.edu.

the French *La Bible de Jerusalem*, although the published text was compared to Hebrew and Aramaic originals. These English translations were especially good at rendering Hebrew poetry into English. J. R. R. Tolkein added stylistic and literary critiques and translated the book of Jonah before other responsibilities caused him to withdraw from the team.

Criticism of the JB and NJB has been largely confined to the notes and commentaries. One significant change in the JB, TJB was its introduction of "Yahweh"[6] (personal name) for "Lord" (title) in the Old Testament. This followed the lead of the ASV (1901) which had adopted the term "Jehovah" to translate the Tetragrammaton יהוה, YHWH, although the RSV and NRSV reverted to more familiar KJB rendering of the vowels added by the Masoretes. This was quite unpopular in light of the Jewish tradition against using the personal name for the Hebrew tetragrammaton יהוה, YHWH. The Mosaic authorship of the Pentateuch and Solomonic authorship of the Book of Wisdom are rejected. The NJB uses more inclusive language than does the JB. Both translations include the deuterocanonical books.

A third edition of *La Bible de Jerusalem* (1998) was translated into English by the Catholic Truth Society (CTS)[7] as the New Catholic Bible (NCB, 2007). As the most widely used Bible text used in Catholic Church service books, its literary and phonetic qualities deserve serious consideration. In 2007, in view of its liturgical role and ecumenical appeal, Pope Benedict XVI requested that "Yahweh" should not be used in future English translations. Thus the New Catholic Bible (NCB) returned to the traditional rendering of "LORD" instead of "Yahweh" for the Hebrew tetragrammaton יהוה, YHWH. Although the Masoretic Text remains the basis for the Old Testament, the translators placed more emphasis on the Septuagint (LXX). The New Catholic Bible is currently being updated as *The Bible in Its Traditions* (2008+) as an ongoing project of the École Biblique et Archéologique in Jerusalem. The French edition portions are currently available for viewing as PDF documents in "The Demonstration Volume," with English portions being listed as they become available. For English materials not completed, a default English text is shown from public domain KJV texts.

---

6. See discussion in chapter 11.

7. The website of the CTS is http://www.cts-online.org.uk.

The Knox Translation of the Bible

Just as the New American Bible published by the Confraternity of Christian Doctrine is the official Roman Catholic Bible in the United States, the Knox translation is the official Roman Catholic Bible in Great Britain. It had been requested by Ronald A. Knox in 1939 when he, as a new convert to Roman Catholicism, approached the English hierarchy about making a new translation. In 1935 an excellent new version of the New Testament had been published under the general editorship of Cuthbert Lattey. This *Westminster Version of the Sacred Scriptures* (1935) was based on the original languages of the New Testament, but it did not receive the official sanction of the Roman Catholic hierarchy. Following the same principles, the first installment of the Old Testament was published. Work continued, but was delayed slightly because of the death of Lattey in 1954.

Although the *Westminster Version of the Sacred Scriptures* had been published in 1935, and a new Latin Vulgate text appeared in 1945 following the encyclical of Pope Pius XII of 1943, Monsignor Knox did not incorporate these materials in his New Testament (1945) or Old Testament translations (1949). Instead, he based his translations on the Sixto-Clementine Vulgate text of 1592. Still, in 1955 the Roman hierarchy gave its official sanction to Knox's translation for English-speaking Catholics.

From the outset, Knox's translation rests on a much weaker foundation than does the American Confraternity Version, and its sequel, the New American Bible (NAB). These are based on more recent manuscript evidence as well as the texts of the original languages. In addition, the Knox translation is weaker textually and inferior as a translation than the *Westminster Version of the Sacred Scriptures*, which remains an unofficial work. Yet, because of its unofficial status, it is difficult to imagine that the Westminster Version will overtake Knox's translation.

New American Bible (1970)
The Catholic Study Bible: New American Bible (1990)
New American Bible, Revised Edition, NABRE (2011)

A fully Americanized edition of *The New Testament of Our Lord and Saviour Jesus Christ* (1941) appeared as the first installment of the Confraternity of Christian Doctrine Version (see previous discussion). Until Pope Pius XII (1939–1958) issued his encyclical *Divino Afflante Spiritu* (1943), Catholic scholars had been prohibited from direct translation of the Greek and Hebrew texts. American Catholics began to translate the sacred Scriptures from the original languages in 1944. The Old Testament was translated in a series of volumes between 1952 and 1969. "In January 1959, Pope John XXIII (1958–1963) proposed three major projects: a diocesan synod for Rome, an ecumenical council, and the revision of the canon law."[8] The Second Vatican Council (1962–1965) was the greatest achievement of Pope John XXIII, which was continued after his death by Pope Paul VI (1963–1978). One outcome of Vatican II was the revision of the Old Testament and a completely new translation of the Greek New Testament which was released as the New American Bible (NAB, 1970).

Pope Pius XII's *Divino Afflante Spiritu* (1943) stated that translations of the Bible could be based on the original Hebrew and Greek texts rather than merely on the Latin Vulgate. This was a sharp reversal of the position taken by the translators of the Douay-Rheims Bible (see chap. 19). After wartime restrictions were lifted, the Confraternity began to publish a completely new version of the Old Testament. The underlying text of the NAB Old Testament supposes the Received Text—Masoretic Text (MT)—but corrected by the more ancient manuscripts of the Qumran community and important evidence from the Septuagint (LXX), both in its oldest form and its Lucianic recension (see chaps. 12 and 17). Unlike any translation by Catholics in over a millennium and a half, this would be based on the original languages rather than some earlier Latin translation.

By 1967 the four Old Testament volumes had been completed and published. Work was then begun, under the direction of Louis F. Hartman, on a new version of the New Testament. In 1970 the New American Bible was published, based on the most recent developments in textual criticism and translated directly from Hebrew, Aramaic, and Greek texts. The Revised New Testament of the NAB was released in 1986, and combined as the biblical text of the Catholic Study Bible: New American Bible (1990). Spellings of proper names in the NAB follow customary forms found in most English Bibles since the KJB (1611). The Psalter of the NAB was revised in 1991.

Authorized by the Board of Trustees of the Confraternity of Christian Doctrine and approved by the Administrative Committee of the United

---

8. J. N. D. Kelly, *The Oxford Dictionary of Popes* (Oxford: Oxford Univ. Press, 1986), 321.

States Conference of Catholic Bishops, the New American Bible, Revised Version (NABRV) was published in 2011. Like its predecessors, the NABRV is translated from the original languages, with critical use of all the ancient sources. In the preliminary pages the NABRV lists collaborators to all the releases and revisions (as previously indicated), with its most recent revision of the New Testament (1986), the Old Testament (2010), and the Psalms (2010). According to the preface, this is an ecumenical approach to Bible translation that brings to bear "advances in linguistics of the biblical languages which make possible a better understanding and more accurate translation of the original languages." They also "incorporate changes and developments in vocabulary and cultural development of the receptor language."

The translators reflect the "three pillars" of good biblical translation spoken of by Pope John Paul II (1978-2005). First, there must be a deep knowledge of the language and the cultural world at the point of origin. Next, there must be a good familiarity with the language and cultural context at the point where the work will arrive. Lastly, to crown the work with success, there must be an adequate mastery of the contents and meaning of what one is translating—and he praises the translation that "utilizes the vocabulary and idioms of everyday speech."[9]

The NABRV follows the earlier Old Testament textual tradition in its modifications. As for the Psalms, the NABRV Psalter follows the Hebrew numbering, which differs from the NAB text that observed the Septuagint numbering system. This brings it into conformity with other translations of the Psalter. Two special features of the Psalms are (1) they were composed originally for liturgical worship, and (2) they follow certain distinct patterns of liturgical worship. Another type of psalm is similar to the hymn: the thanksgiving psalm. There are more psalms of lament than of any other type.

The NABRV New Testament (1986) is a fresh translation of the Greek text first published in complete form in 1970. One primary aim is to produce an accurate translation of the Greek text. A second is to reflect contemporary American usage understandable to ordinary educated people, on a

---

9. The NABRV preface indicates these statements are from an address by John Paul II to the United Bible Societies (UBS) on 26 November 2003.

formal rather than a colloquial level. A particular effort has been made to ensure consistent vocabulary. One especially sensitive area is the problem of discrimination in language, where there is little consensus. The underlying Greek text used follows the UBS3 text (see previous discussions). While the NAB is a Roman Catholic translation, it has received collaboration from the broader Christian community. One example may be seen in the generally accepted translation of μονογενής (monogenēs) as "only son" instead of "only begotten son" (e.g., John 1:14; 3:16) as it had been translated in the Douay-Rheims-Challoner editions.

Jewish Translations and Versions

Although Jews have sought to preserve the study of Old Testament Scripture in its original language (Hebrew), they have not always been able to do so. They have run into the same problems faced by Roman Catholics and the Latin Bible, as indicated by the very existence of the Septuagint. As early as the third century BCE, Jews found it necessary to translate their Bible into the vernacular language of Alexandria, Greek. Their translation of portions of the Old Testament into Aramaic further attests to the fact that they were not always able to study the Scriptures in the Hebrew language (see chap. 12).

Throughout the Middle Ages, the conditions under which Jews lived were not conducive for scholarship of any kind, and the attitude of the church about their role in the crucifixion of Christ made it even more difficult for them to openly participate in biblical scholarship. Nevertheless, about 1400 they began to make new and fresh translations of the Old Testament into various languages. It was not for about four hundred years after these early vernacular translations, however, that Jews began to translate the Old Testament into English. In 1789, the year of the French Revolution, a Jewish version of the Pentateuch appeared, claiming to be an emendation of the King James Bible (KJB). A similar work was published by Salid Neuman (1839). Between 1851 and 1856 Rabbi Benisch produced a complete Bible for English-speaking Jewry. A final attempt at amending the KJB for use by Jews was made by Michael Friedländer in 1884. Isaac Leeser made a marked departure from tradition when he produced his version of *The Hebrew Bible* (1853), a longtime favorite in British and American synagogues.

Before the turn of the century, however, English Bible translation entered into what may be called the "Age of Scientific Bibles,"[10] beginning with the publication of the Revised Version (RV, 1881, 1885, 1895) in England and of the American Standard Version (ASV, 1901) in America. A new age of English Bible translations emerged (see discussion in the following section). The Jewish Bible Society felt the inadequacy of Leeser's translation and decided to revise *The Hebrew Bible* during its second biennial convention (1892). As the work of revision proceeded, it became apparent that it would have to be a little short of an entirely new translation. Considerable time was spent reorganizing the project before the Jewish Publication Society finally released its new version of *The Hebrew Bible* (1917), which closely paralleled the ASV (1901).

The Jewish Publication Society did not stop its work with the 1917 publication. Following the release of the RSV (1952) and activity toward the publication of the NEB (1970), they began to publish a new translation of the Old Testament, *The Torah: A New Translation of the Holy Scriptures According to the Masoretic Text* (1962). The preface states its purpose is "to improve substantially on earlier versions in rendering both the shades of meaning of words and expressions and the force of grammatical forms and constructions." To accomplish its task, translators utilized neglected insights from ancient and medieval Jewish scholarship as well as new knowledge from the Near East. Also based on the Masoretic Text is the Megilloth (1969). The Jewish Publication Society (JPS, NJPS) published the entire Old Testament as *TANAKH, A New Translation of The Holy Scriptures According to the Traditional Hebrew Text* (NJV, NJPS, 1985), and the bilingual revision, entitled *JPS Hebrew-English TANAKH* (NJV, NJPS, 2001).

The first Bible published in modern Israel was *The Koren Jerusalem Bible* (1962) which Harold Fisch said was a "thoroughly corrected, modernized, and revised" edition based on Michael Friedländer's *Hebrew-English Jewish Family Bible* (1881).[11] Perhaps the first Orthodox translation into contemporary English was by Arvch Kaplan as *The Living Torah* (1981). Since Kaplan's death in 1983, his Orthodox translation with commentaries has been published by various organizations as well as on the Internet. It is notable for

---

10. Cameron A. MacKenzie, "Theology and the Great Tradition of English Bibles," *Concordia Theological Quarterly* 64, no. 4 (October 1999): 292–300.

11. See http://www.innvista.com/culture/religion/bible/versions/jbk.htm.

its use of contemporary colloquial English, and it reverses the distinction between "God" and "Lord," noting that in modern English "God" is more appropriate for a proper name. Kaplan's translation was influenced by traditional rabbinic interpretation, religious law, and Jewish mysticism.

Many later Orthodox translators follow Kaplan's approach.[12] David E. S. Stein addresses the gender question in his review of three recent translations of the Torah into English as "gender accurate" or "gender sensitive" renditions because of how they treat language related to the Torah's human characters: *The Torah: A Modern Commentary* (TAMC), revised edition, for the Union of American Hebrew Congregations (UAHC), currently known as the Union of Reformed Judaism (URJ, 2005); *The Contemporary Torah: A Gender-Sensitive Adaptation of the JPS Translation* (CJPS, 2006); and *The Torah: A Woman's Commentary* (TAWC, 2008).[13] His central aim is to demonstrate the plausibility that the composer(s) of the complete Torah had good reason to believe that the ancient audience would construe its deity as a God beyond gender (p. 109). This is done by encountering the biblical God as a persona who is "beyond" human gender classification, thus referring to God in a non-gender (or social gender) term by default (p. 108).

David H. Stern, an Israel-based theologian trained at Fuller Theological Seminary, graduate study at the University of Judaism (American Jewish University), taught the first course in "Judaism and Christianity" at Fuller Seminary and at UCLA. He lives in Jerusalem and is active in Israel's messianic Jewish community. Stern published the *Jewish New Testament: a translation of the New Testament that expresses its Jewishness* (1989). His translation brings out the Jewishness of the New Testament in three ways: (1) cosmetically by replacing "church language" with neutral terminology to encourage the reader to think; (2) culturally and religiously to strengthen the reader's awareness of the Jewish cultural or religious context in which New Testament events took place; and (3) theologically in contrast to most Gentile-Christian theologies which deemphasize the Jews as still being God's people

---

12. For the Torah and commentary, see, bible.ort.org/books/pentd2.asp. Also see *Complete Torah with Rashi* (Judaica Press), a five-volume bilingual Hebrew–English translation with commentary in both Hebrew and English.

13. See David E. S. Stein, "On Beyond Gender: Representation of God in the Torah and in Three Recent Renditions into English," *Nashim: A Journal of Jewish Women's Studies & Gender Issues* 15 (spring 2008): 108-37.

(Introduction). He draws on "Jewish English" (Hebrew and Yiddish expressions that English-speaking Jews incorporate into their everyday speech). The translation tends toward a dynamic equivalence of United Bible Societies' *The Greek New Testament* (UBS3), although he does not translate words consistently. See, for example, translations of μονογενής, monogenēs ("only-begotten," "born of the same mother"); "the Father's only Son" (John 1:14); "No one has ever seen God; but the only and unique Son, who is identical with God and is at the Father's side" (1:18); "For God so loved the world that he gave his only and unique Son" (3:16); etc.

Next, Stern paraphrased the JPS *TANAKH* (1917) to publish the Complete Jewish Bible, (CJB, 1998). In this, Stern's "purpose is to restore God's Word to its original context and culture as well as be in easily read modern English" (Introduction). Books of the *TANAKH* follow the order of Jewish (not Christian) Bibles. It also intends to be fully functional for Messianic synagogues where the B'rit Chadashah (New Testament) is read as well as the Torah and Prophets.

PROTESTANT TRANSLATIONS AND VERSIONS

In keeping with their Reformation principle of private interpretation, Protestants have produced a greater number of private translations of the Bible than have Roman Catholics. Some of the earlier translations grew out of the discoveries of new manuscript materials, since none of the great manuscripts had been discovered at the time of the King James translation (see chap. 14) except Codex Bezae (D), which was used very little. Before turning to those private translations, we should look at some of the official attempts to bring the King James Bible (KJB) into alignment with the manuscript discoveries.

Revised Standard Version (RSV, 1952, 1957, 1977)

Half a century after the English Revision (ERV, RV) of the KJB was published, a new era in the history of English Bible translation began with the RSV, a Bible produced "with widespread denominational support and not just by keen individuals."[14] The International Council of Religious Education obtained the copyright for the ASV and expressed its desire to utilize

---

14. David Dewey, *Which Bible?* (Leicester, England: InterVarsity, 2004), 124.

the great advances in recent biblical scholarship (see chaps. 12 and 13). The Westcott-Hort text of the New Testament (see chap. 14) had been sharply modified as a result of the papyrus and new manuscript discoveries. In addition, ongoing changes in English literary style and taste made a new revision necessary. In 1937 the International Council authorized a committee to proceed with such a revision. The revision committee consisted of twenty-two outstanding scholars who were to follow the meaning of the American Standard Version unless two-thirds of the committee agreed to change the reading. Among the guidelines were to use simpler and more current forms of pronouns except in reference to God and a more direct word order.

Delayed by World War II (1939–1945), the New Testament did not appear until 1946; the Old Testament was published in 1952 and the Apocrypha in 1957. Oxford University Press also published an Annotated Apocrypha (1965, 1977). The Third and Fourth Books of the Maccabees, as well as Psalm 151, were added to the Apocrypha (1977). These publications followed a tremendous publicity campaign which set into motion almost predictable reactions.

In contrast to the ASV, the RSV was accused of blurring traditional messianic passages, such as the substitution of "young woman" for "virgin" in Isaiah 7:14. Criticism of the New Testament was not so sharp, although it was sharp enough. All the criticism notwithstanding, the RSV provided the English-speaking church with an up-to-date revision of the Bible based on the "critical text" (see chap. 14). All that was changed, however, with the discovery of the Dead Sea Scrolls (DSS) in the caves at Qumran (1947) and Documents in the Judean Desert (DJD) in the 1950s (see chaps. 12 and 13). Among other things, these discoveries opened the door to reevaluation of the underlying texts of Scripture and divergent translations of those texts illustrated in the following discussion.

The New English Bible (NEB, 1970)
The Revised English Bible (REB, 1989)

Not satisfied that the Revised Standard Version was a continuation of the long-established tradition of earlier English Bible translations, the General Assembly of the Church of Scotland met in 1946 to consider a completely new translation. A joint committee was appointed in 1947, and three companies were chosen: one each for the Old Testament, the New, and the Apocrypha. C. H. Dodd was appointed chairman of the New Testament panel and became the director of the entire translation team in 1949. The New Testament of the New English Bible (NEB) released in 1961; the Old Testament and the Apocrypha followed in 1970. The NEB was later published in a "corrected impression" (1972). Principles of translation for NEB were aimed at presenting a genuinely English idiom that would be "timeless," avoiding both anachronisms and transient modernisms. The translators sought to make their version plain enough to convey its meaning without being bald or pedestrian, for they hoped to produce a translation that would be a second authoritative version alongside the KJB.

Over four million copies of the NEB were sold during its first year of publication. It differed greatly from both the English Revised and the Revised Standard editions that preceded it; its translators frequently departed from literal renderings of the text, especially when they felt the text permitted two possible interpretations. In addition, the NEB has been criticized for its Anglicisms and its concentration on intelligibility over literalness of meaning, as well as its critical rearrangement of some sections of the Old Testament. This undoubtedly reflects the influence of contemporary theology on the translation through the translators. All things being considered, however, this translation has continued the tradition of its English forebears and is a valuable work in its own right. Oxford University Press published *The New English Bible with the Apocrypha: Oxford Study Edition* (1976), which inscribed this statement following its preface: "Since publication of The New English Bible the Roman Catholic Church in England and Wales, The Roman Catholic Church in Ireland, and The Roman Catholic Church in Scotland joined as sponsors. In addition, since the above Preface was written The Congregational Church in England and Wales and The Presbyterian Church of England have united under the name of The United Reformed Church."

The Revised English Bible with the Apocrypha (REB, 1989) was served by an even broader coalition of representatives. Due to its widespread reception, unanticipated by its translators, it became desirable to review the translation and set in motion a major revision of the text. The substantial revision of the REB expresses the mind and conviction of biblical scholars and translators of the 1980s, as the NEB had a generation earlier. According to its preface, "Care was taken to ensure the style of English used is fluent and of appropriate dignity for liturgical use, while maintaining intelligibility for worshipers of a wide range of ages and backgrounds." The REB made more extensive use than the NEB of textual subheadings, printed in italics, "to mark broad structural divisions or substantial changes of direction or theme." Designed for liturgical use and public reading, it has no central column cross-references, and very few footnotes. R. Kittel's *Biblia Hebraica* (1937) and its thoroughly revised edition *Biblia Hebraica Stuttgartensia* (1967/77) have been supplemented by materials from the DSS, SamP, and other resources (discussed at length in chap. 12). The guiding principle adopted in the REB "has been to seek a fluent idiomatic way of expressing biblical writing in contemporary English."

For the New Testament of the REB, "the complete text eventually followed was edited by R. V. G. Tasker and published by Oxford and Cambridge university presses (1964), with the Nestle-Aland (NA26) text (1979) being a major point of reference." Following KJB translators, the REB recognized no obligation to render the same Greek word everywhere by the same English word. This version claims to be a translation rather than a paraphrase, observing faithfulness to the meaning of the text without necessarily reproducing grammatical structure or translating word for word" ("Introduction to the New Testament").

The New American Standard Bible (NASB, 1963–1977, UPDATE 1995)

Beginning in 1959, still another revision of the ASV was undertaken by the Lockman Foundation in an attempt to revive as well as revise the ASV. Its translation committee set forth its fourfold purpose in the preface accompanying the New Testament (1963). The entire New American Standard Bible (NASB, 1971) was published using the same twofold purpose: "to adhere as closely as possible to the original languages of the Holy Scriptures, and to make the translation in a fluent and readable style according to current English usage." Their fourfold aim sought to be true to the original Hebrew and Greek texts, be grammatically correct, be understandable to the masses, and give proper place to the Lord Jesus Christ. The NASB retained the ASV paragraph structure but reintroduced a single-column format used by F. H. A. Scrivener, *The Cambridge Paragraph Bible* (1879), and David Norton, *The New Cambridge Paragraph Bible* (2005).

Although NASB translators attempted to renew the American Standard Version, their translation does not equal the literary work of other standard versions. It is, however, an accurate and faithful heir of the ASV. The Old

MAJOR ENGLISH BIBLE TRANSLATIONS 1610–PRESENT

King James Bible [KJV]   Douay OT (1610)
(1611)   *Textus Receptus* (1624)

Important Manuscripts Discovered (1840)

English Revised NT (1881)
English Revised OT (1885)

Papyri Discovered (1897)

American Standard Version [ASV] (1901)
    Weymouth New Testament (1902)
    Centenary New Testament (1904)   English Old Testament
                                            Jewish Publication Society [JPS] (1917)

Papyri Discovered (1930)

    Moffatt Bible (1924-1926, 1935)
    Smith-Goodspeed Bible (1927, 1935)

Revised Standard Version   Confraternity New Testament
New Testament (1946, 1952)   Roman Catholic (1946)

Dead Sea Scrolls Discovered (1947)

Old Testament Apocrypha (1952)   The Holy Bible
    NT in Plain English, Williams (1952)   Knox (1944-1955)
    NT in Modern English, Phillips (1958)   Confraternity Bible
    Revised Standard Version (1957, 1977)   (1952, 1955)
    The Modern Language Bible   The Authentic New Testament
        Berkeley (1959)   Schonfield (1955)
    The Amplified Bible (1958-1965)   The New World Translation
                                               Jehovah's Witnesses (1953-1960, 1961)
Anchor Bible (1964)   The New Jewish Version
New American Standard Bible [NASB] (1966)   JPS (1962-1982)
New English Bible [NEB] (1970)
The Living Bible (1971)   Jerusalem Bible (1966)
Good News Bible [TEV] (1976)   New American Bible [NAB] (1970)

New International Version [NIV] (1979)   Reader's Digest Bible (1982)
New King James Version [NKJV] (1982)
                                                      JPS Tanakh [OT] (1985)
English Standard Bible [ESV] (2000)   New Jerusalem Bible (1985)
Orthodox Study Bible [OSB] (2008)
                                              Holman Christian Standard Bible
                                                      [HCSB] (2004)

SOURCE: Norman L. Geisler and William E. Nix, *A General Introduction to the Bible*, rev. ed. (Chicago: Moody, 1986), 285.

Testament translation utilizes Rudolf Kittel's *Biblia Hebraica*, as well as cognate languages and the Dead Sea Scrolls (see chap. 12). Recent developments in New Testament textual criticism enabled the translation committee to employ the latest Nestle–Aland (NA26) Greek text (see chap. 12). The editorial board continued to function after the NASB was published. Reviews and evaluations were sought and carefully considered to improve renderings of contemporary English grammar and terminology in the "update" edition (1995).

King James II, KJII (1971)
Literal Translation of the Holy Bible, LITV (1977–2000)
KJ21; KJ2000; AND KJ3 (2006)

Before embarking on his major work, Jay P. Green published *The Children's "King James" New Testament* (1960), *The Teen-Age Version of the Holy Bible* (1962), and *The Living Scriptures: A New Translation in the King James Tradition, New Testament* (1966). The prodigious translator then produced a series of translations as a reaction against such modern English Bible translations as the ERV (1885), ASV (1901), RSV (1952), and NEB (1970) as discussed previously. Green regarded those translations as "slanted and dangerous" because their underlying Hebrew and Greek texts differed from the AV (1611). He also charged that they paraphrased, interpreted, deleted, and added to God's words without regard to the facts of the texts. His King James II Version (KJII, 1971) was later renamed *Literal Translation of the Holy Bible*, (LITV, 1977–2000); *King James for the 21st Century* (KJ21); *King James 2000* (KJ2000); and finally KJ3 (2006).

One key feature of KJII is its parallel Hebrew-Greek Interlinear Bible. Green states that his is "a word-for-word attempt to give the literal rendition of each and every one of God's words. . . . None of God's words are left out."[15] He does not attempt to update the AV text, nor does he always accept its rendering. In fact, he frequently changes AV readings, such as "hell" to "sheol" (Old Testament) and to "hades" (New Testament). He modifies the AV, "Behold, a virgin shall conceive, and bear a son, and shall call his name Immanuel" (Isa. 7:14) to "So the Lord himself will give you this sign: A virgin will become pregnant and give birth to a son, and she will name him Immanuel [God Is With Us]." The change from "shall conceive" to "become pregnant" diminishes the import of the gospel of Matthew (1:18–25), which says Mary "was found to be with child by the Holy Ghost (Spirit) . . . for that which is conceived in her is of the Holy Ghost(Spirit)" and gives no indication of her "becoming pregnant." Although a prodigious translator who purported to make literal translations of the

---

15. See Robert G. Bratcher, "Old Wine in New Wineskins," *Christianity Today*, 8 October 1971, 16.

Bible, Green falls prey to his subjectivism and lack of a broader accountability.

New International Version, NIV (1973, 1978, 1984)
The NIV Study Bible, NIVSB (1985)
New International Version Inclusive, NIVI (1997)
Today's New International Version, TNIV (2002, 2005, 2011)

Another independent translation, The Holy Bible: New International Version (NIV), was made under the sponsorship of the New York Bible Society. The New Testament portion was released in 1973, and the Old Testament in 1976. The third and final edition was published in 1979. For a generation this was the most popular English Bible.

As early as 1953, two committees had formed to consider how an evangelical edition of the RSV might be suited for evangelistic work. Soon inquiries were made about the proposed project, one by the Christian Reformed Church (1956) and the other by the National Association of Evangelicals (1957). A joint committee of the two groups formed in 1961. In 1966 the RSV Committee denied an evangelical edition of the RSV, although a Catholic edition appeared that same year.[16] The Berkeley Version (see below) and the still incomplete NASB were deemed unsuitable. When the New York Bible Society moved to Colorado Springs and was renamed the International Bible Society (IBS), it chose to begin its own translation (1965). The result was the NIV New Testament, published in 1973. The complete NIV appeared in 1978 and was revised in 1983.

The NIV reverted to the two-column paragraph format with a center column of cross-references. According to the preface, the NIV "is a completely new translation of the Holy Bible made by over a hundred scholars working directly from the best available Hebrew, Aramaic and Greek texts. . . . International and trans denominational scholars . . . safeguard the translation from sectarian bias. . . . Translators were united in their commitment to the authority and infallibility of the Bible as God's Word in written form." Concern for clear and natural English—that the NIV should be idiomatic but not idiosyncratic, contemporary but not dated—motivated translators and consultants. Although not in the Tyndale/KJV style, the NIV is not far removed from it as its contemporary, the God News Bible (GNB), the NIV

---

16. Dewey, *Which Bible?*, 142.

translators have declared it to be a translation that strives for a balance between "Accuracy, Beauty, Clarity and Dignity."[17]

The NIV Study Bible: New International Version (NIVSB, 1985) following the precedent of the *Scofield Reference Bible* and the *New Scofield Reference Bible* (see discussion in chap. 19) is a groundbreaking work in English Bible translations. Like the NIV, it is the work of a trans-denominational team of biblical scholars who confess to the authority of the Bible as God's infallible Word to humanity and seek to clarify understanding of, develop appreciation for, and provide insight into that Word. The interrelationship of the Scriptures is a major theme of the *NIV Study Bible*. Doctrinally it reflects traditional evangelical theology. Where editors are aware of significant doctrinal differences of opinion on key passages or doctrines, they try to handle them with an evenhanded approach by indicating those differences (e.g., Rev. 20:2). Introductions to individual books of the Bible are provided. Where problems arise in those introductions, solutions are offered as far as biblical and nonbiblical evidence provides.

A smaller fifteen-member Committee on Bible Translation (CBT) was formed from a wide variety of denominations. This CBT is responsible for the translation of both the NIV and Today's New International Version (TNIV, 2002, 2005, 2011). The CBT "subjected the UBS text to a critical review, and, somewhat unsurprisingly, their independent scholarship led them to favor different readings in the case of selected variants" (differing from the UBS in 285 places). The NIV was based on the variant readings selected by the CBT from the possibilities offered by the UBS text (see chap. 14). Because no accessible records were kept for these decisions, Edward Goodrich and John Kohlenberger III decided to compile the Hebrew and Greek texts that underlie the NIV translation. In the mid-1980s they compiled an eclectic text representing "an alternate view of the original text of the New Testament.... When the Committee on Biblical Translation worked on the TNIV in the mid-1990s, ... Gordon Fee adjusted and authenticated the Greek textual decisions made by the TNIV committee. This is the text used in A Reader's Greek New Testament."[18]

---

17. Dewey, *Which Bible?*, 143.

18. Richard J. Goodrich and Albert L. Lukaszewski, *A Reader's Greek New Testament*, 2nd ed. (Grand Rapids: Zondervan, 2007), 9–10.

Since the 1980s there has been a backlash against the principles used in the NIV and TNIV translations, and this development of a limited eclectic Greek text based on the English translation appears to be reminiscent of Erasmus (see chap. 14) and has the proverbial cart before the horse. In late 1996, the International Bible Society (IBS) and CBT announced an "inclusive language" or "gender neutral" translation, the NIVI (1997). Opposition was quick and broadly based, especially from Focus on the Family and the Council on Biblical Manhood and Womanhood, and on May 27, 1997, the NIVI ceased production and the recently released NIV for children was revised by the IBS. The IBS continued publication of the NIV (1984) without further revision.

In 2002 the IBS announced publication of Today's New International Version, TNIV, complete with "gender-accurate" language. The New Testament was released in 2002, and the first edition of *A Reader's Greek New Testament* (2002) was published to support its eclectically reconstructed text (see previous discussion). Three specific changes in terminology illustrate sensitive issues causing difficulties for the TNIV. One is the frequent substitution of "Messiah" for "Christ" in the Gospels and Acts, although "Christ" is retained in the Epistles. Another is the variety of terms used as substitutions for the word "saints" in the New Testament. The third issue is the removal of nearly all vocative O's and the elimination of most instances of the generic use of masculine nouns and pronouns; the so-called singular "they/their/them" and "anyone" or "everyone" or some other equivalent is generally used as well.[19] "In places, the TNIV seems to move slightly to the direction of a form-driven philosophy: the translation is often tighter. But elsewhere, when compared to the NIV, it moves in a meaning-driven direction," notes Dewey.[20]

The TNIV added the Old Testament in 2005 and used *A Reader's Greek New Testament*, 2nd ed. (2005) to support its New Testament update. In 2009, IBS changed its name to Biblica before publishing still another revision of The New International Version (NIV, 2011). *A Reader's Greek New Testament*, 2nd ed. (2005) may be used to compare some additional issues with the revision of the NIV. Since on average the NIV 2011 retains over 70 percent of the

---

19. "A Word to the Reader," The Holy Bible, Today's International Version, TNIV (Grand Rapids: Zondervan, 2005), 11–12.

20. Dewey, *Which Bible?*, 172.

readings in previous editions, critiques mentioned earlier still apply.

Here, however, attention needs to turn to theological issues, and particularly to the question of the translation of μονογενής in John's Gospel (1:14, 18; 3:16, 18) and in 1 John 4:9. The NIV renders this word as "one and only." Traditionally, the word is understood to mean "only begotten," and in the history of Christian doctrine this form of words has some importance. The Nicene Creed, which continues to be used as a confession of faith in many churches, declares that Christ is "the only-begotten Son of God, begotten of His Father before all worlds . . . begotten, not made, being of one substance with the Father." It expresses the ontological equality between the Father and the Son, and prevents the Arian teaching that the Son is a heavenly subordinate "made" by the Father. He who is "begotten" shares the natural qualities of his begetter. The CBT translators do not follow *A Reader's Greek New Testament*, claiming to follow the Septuagint text of Genesis 22:2, 12, 16 and Jubilees 18:2, 11, 15 (and possibly Josephus Antiquities 1:222) incorrectly identifies the passages as "your son, your only son," asserting that the LXX uses μονογενής, or *monogenēs* ("only-begotten") *lábe ton huion sou ton agapēton* ("take your son, the beloved one"); but the LXX reads, λάβε τὸν υἱόν σου τὸν ἀγαπητὸν ("take your son, the beloved one"), not μονογενής (*monogenēs*) ("only–begotten"). In point of fact, *A New English Translation of the Septuagint* (NETS, 2007) translates the Genesis passages in question as "your beloved son," since the word *monogenhv* does not occur in LXX versions of the Pentateuch at all.[21] A Hebrew-English interlinear text reads אהב אשר (*'šr 'hb*, "whom you love") אות יחיד אתה (*'wt yhyd*, "your only child") אות בז אתה (*'wt yhyd 'th*, "your son") לקח נא (*lqh n'*, "take").[22] This translation agrees with the NJPS Hebrew text which Sarna translates "Take your son, your favored one, Isaac, whom you love . . ." (Gen. 22:2).[23] Other recent translations make the same translation, probably based on the Hebrew

---

21. Michael Marlowe, "Review of The New International Version" at www.conservapedia.com/New_International_Version, who provides an extensive critique of Richard Longnecker's defense of the NIV rendering, which must have been based on the MT Hebrew rather than the LXX Greek text. The issue involved may be the result of an unintentional rather than an intentional textual critical error.

22. See Genesis 22:2 here—broken into word units that read from right to left in The Lexham Hebrew-English Interlinear Bible.

23. See Nahum M. Sarna, *Genesis: The Traditional Hebrew Test with the New JPS Translation*, The JPS Torah Commentary (Philadelphia: The Jewish Publication Society, 1989), 151.

Masoretic Text (MT) rather than the Greek Septuagint (LXX).

New King James New Testament (1979) and Psalms (1980)
New King James Version (NKJV, 1982)
NKJV Study Bible (NKJVSB, 1997, 2007)

The New King James New Testament (1979) and Psalms (1980) were completed and renamed The Holy Bible, New King James Version, NKJV (1982). The translators and editors have attempted to continue in the tradition of the earlier translators of the KJV. The Anglicized edition was originally called the Revised Authorized Version, but the NKJV title is now used universally. The Gideons International place the NKJV in hotels, hospitals, and schools.

In the mid-1970s, Thomas Nelson Publishers, successor to the firm that had first published the ASV (1901) and the RSV (1952), had summoned leading clergymen and lay Christians who discussed and decided to revise sensitively the KJV. From the outset their purpose was "to apply the best knowledge—of ancient Hebrew and Greek, 17th-century English, and contemporary English—to polish with sensitivity the archaisms and vocabulary of the 1611 (King James) Version, so as to preserve and enhance its originally intended beauty and content." Over 130 scholars from a broad spectrum of the Christian church were commissioned to work on the revision. Their efforts were directed toward several specific goals: to preserve the true meaning of the words of the KJV in view of changes in word meanings since 1611; to protect the theological terminology of the KJV; to improve the understanding of verb forms and verb endings by bringing them into conformity with twentieth-century usage; and to update punctuation and grammar to help in the understanding of the text. In addition, they capitalized pronouns that refer to God and added quotation marks, common features in the twentieth century not practiced in 1611.

The NKJV translation project was conceived by Arthur L. Farstad, co-editor with Zane C. Hodges of *The Greek New Testament According to the Majority Text* (1982, 1985), which differs from the Textus Receptus (TR). The underlying text of the Old Testament was the *Biblia Hebraica Stuttgartensia* (1967/1977), frequently compared with the Bomberg edition (1524–1525), in consultation with the Septuagint (Greek) and Latin Vulgate, as has been the case with most twentieth-century translators (see discussion in chap. 12). With the New Testament, however, they pursued an altogether different course. Convinced that New Testament textual criticism has followed a wrong path over the past century, they prefer a different textual basis from nearly all translations made since the ERV (1881). As a result, the NKJV, unlike its classic predecessor, is based on the Majority Text (𝔐), not the TR (see chap. 14). This is a critical matter, as may be seen from the introduction to the new revision, even though the revisers are not necessarily convinced that the TR is the best Greek text available. To buttress their position, the revisers identify their textual basis as the "Traditional Text" or "Majority Text" (𝔐) or Byzantine text type (see chap. 15). They identify the TR and the 𝔐 as coming from the same textual tradition, but indicate that the TR is a somewhat late and corrupted form of the 𝔐, or Traditional Text. Their principle of deriving the 𝔐 reading is the persuasion that the "best guide to a precise Greek text is the close consensus of the majority of Greek manuscripts."

In order to show where the 𝔐 differs from the Critical Text, which is identified as the Nestle-Aland/United Bible Societies' Text (NU-Text), they have presented textual information "in a unique provision in the history of the English Bible." They have identified the Critical Text variations as "NU-Text" and points of variation in the 𝔐 from the Traditional Text as "𝔐." That is a most significant and helpful contribution. The preference for the TR over the 𝔐 reading in many instances is a matter of accommodation, bringing clarity to the TR that hardly delights advocates of the 𝔐 or the NU-Text, while inclusion of the NU-Text readings in the footnotes may not bring joy to the proponents of the TR or the 𝔐.

Linguistically, the NKJV is in the formal equivalence category. The language is on the seventh grade level. Supporters of the NKJV will rejoice that it has preserved, to a large extent, an eloquence of style that is not apparent in other twentieth-century translations. Others will be distressed that the NKJV has not gone far enough in modernizing the KJB, especially if they are convinced that a version is no better than the original text on which it is based and that a modern critical Greek text based on the ancient manuscripts is preferred to the TR. The editorial decision to follow the KJB in making every verse a separate paragraph is not as helpful to the modern reader. Nevertheless, the diligent efforts by the revisers of the NKJV to a great degree achieved their goal to produce an English Bible that retains as much of the classic KJB as possible while at the same time bringing its English up-to-date. Several groups that published more objective "Reference Bible" editions (e.g., *The Student's Bible and Thompson Chain–Reference Bible*) have issued edition using the NKJV translation. More interpretive "Study Bible" editions (e.g., *The Orthodox Study Bible: New Testament and Psalms*[24] (1993) also have used the NKJV text, as has the NKJV Study Bible (1997, 2007). The *Scofield Study Bible* has appeared in several editions since departing from the KJV text of the *New Scofield Reference Bible*.

24. The *Orthodox Study Bible* will receive close attention in chapter 21.

21

ENGLISH BIBLE TRANSLATIONS
and the NEW MILLENNIUM

THE BIBLE IS THE MOST PUBLICIZED BOOK IN THE WORLD. One of the strongest evidences of this is its multitude of translations and the variety of languages.

The United Bible Societies reported that in 2011 Bibles had become available in ten more languages and New Testaments in twenty-seven additional languages than in 2010. The latest Scripture Language Report, the authoritative guide to the annual progress of worldwide Bible translation, published annually by United Bible Societies (UBS), . . . showed that by 2010, the complete Bible had been translated into 469 languages and the New Testament into 1,231. This report is slightly higher than that of the Wycliffe Bible Translators, who stated that 1,211 language communities have access to the New Testament in their heart language. The entire Bible had been translated into 457 languages, and Wycliffe was involved in over 1,500 translation programs, with portions of the Bible in more than two thousand languages and dialects.[1] The distinctions between UBS and Wycliffe may center on the question of dialects.

These translations provide ample illustration of the final link in the chain from God to us, but our primary concern and attention will be

---

1. According to http://www.unitedbiblesocieties.org/news/ and http://www.wycliffe.org/about/statis tics.aspx; as of October 2011. Also see http://en.wikipedia.org/wiki/Bible_translations.

directed to the translation of the Bible into English.[2] Our survey will center on those translations growing out of the Douay-Rheims and King James Bibles of the late fifteenth and early sixteenth centuries.

New Revised Standard Version (NRSV, 1989)

According to the preface, and for the translation committee, Bruce M. Metzger writes that the New Revised Standard Version (NRSV, 1989) "is yet another step in the long, continual process of making the Bible available in the form of the English language most widely current in our day. To summarize in a single sentence: the New Revised Standard Version of the Bible is an authorized revision of the Revised Standard Version, published in 1952, which was a revision of the American Standard Version, published in 1901, which, in turn, embodied earlier revisions of the King James Version, published in 1611." The RSV New Testament (1946) was followed by the RSV Old and New Testaments (1952) and the Apocryphal/Deuterocanonical Books of the Old Testament (1957). In 1977 an expanded edition containing three additional texts (3 and 4 Maccabees and Psalm 151) was received by Eastern Orthodox communions.[3] Thereafter the NRSV gained the distinction of being officially authorized for use by all major Christian churches: Protestant, Anglican, Roman Catholic, and Eastern Orthodox. Following the RSV Old Testament (1952) a second edition of the RSV New Testament was published (1971), and significant advances were made in the discovery and interpretation of documents in Semitic languages related to Hebrew. In 1974 the Policies Committee of the Revised Standard Version authorized the preparation of the entire RSV Bible.

For the Old Testament, the Committee made use of the *Biblia Hebraica Stuttgartensia* (1977, ed. Sec. emendata 1983). Occasionally it was evident that the text suffered in its transmission and that none of the versions provides a satisfactory restoration. Committee members entered reconstructions, marked with the abbreviation Cn ("Correction"), and added a translation of

---

2. See opening discussion in chapter 19 about the role of English in the modern world and why our discussion focuses on English Bible translations. For the necessary role of the Bible in establishing authority for Christian doctrine and practice, see Millard J. Erickson, Paul Kjoss Helseth, and Justin Taylor, eds., *Reclaiming the Center: Confronting Evangelical Accommodation in Postmodern Times* (Wheaton, Ill.: Crossway, 2004). Also see discussions of various theories of inspiration in chapter 2.

3. See previous discussion of the English Standard Version with Apocrypha, ESVAP (2009).

the Masoretic Text. For the Apocryphal/Deuterocanonical Books of the Old Testament, the committee used a number of texts. Mostly the Septuaginta of Alfred Rahlfs (1937) was supplemented by individual books of the Göttingen Septuagint project (see chaps. 12 and 13). For the New Testament, they used the Greek New Testament text prepared by an interconfessional and international committee (UBS3, 1966; corrected, 1983).

As for the style of English adopted, a directive instructed members to continue in the tradition of the KJB, but to introduce such changes as were warranted on the basis of accuracy, clarity, euphony, and current English usage. The translation followed the maxim, "As literal as possible, as free as necessary." As a result, the NRSV remains essentially a literal translation, but less so than the RSV. Another mandate specified that "in references to men and women, masculine-oriented language should be eliminated as far as this can be done without altering passages that reflect the historical situation of ancient patriarchal culture. The committee often found differing mandates to be in tension and frequently in conflict. Although the ASV had adopted the term "Jehovah" to translate the, Tetragrammaton YHWH, יהוה (see previous discussion and chap. 11), the RSV and NRSV reverted to more familiar KJB rendering of the vowels added by the Masoretes. The NRSV seeks to preserve all that is best in the English Bible as it has been known and used through the years. It is intended for public reading and congregational worship, as well as for private study, instruction, and meditation.

The New Revised Standard Version, Catholic Edition (NRSV-CE 1991) is a translation of the Bible adapted, with the approval of the Catholic Church, for the use of Catholics in the United States and Canada. It contains all the canonical books of Scripture accepted by the Catholic Church arranged in the traditional Catholic order. Thus, all the deuterocanonical books of the Old Testament are returned to their traditional Catholic order. The books of Tobit and Judith are placed between Nehemiah and Esther; the books of 1 Maccabees and 2 Maccabees are placed immediately after Esther; the books of Wisdom and Ecclesiasticus (Sirach) are placed after the Song of Songs; and the Book of Baruch (including the Letter of Jeremiah as Baruch chapter 6) is placed after Lamentations. The deuterocanonical additions to the Hebrew books of Esther and Daniel are included at their proper places in these protocanonical books: the Greek additions to Esther are interspersed in the Hebrew form of Esther according to the Septuagint, while the additions to Daniel are placed within chapter 3 and as chapters 13 and 14 of Daniel. The Apocryphal books (that is, 1 Esdras, 2 Esdras, the Prayer of Manasseh, 3 Maccabees, 4 Maccabees, and Psalm 151) are not included in the NRSV-CE.

There are no other significant changes in the text. An Anglicized Text form of the NRSV-CE, embodying the preferences of users of British English, is also available from various publishers. Excerpts are taken from the New Revised Standard Version, Catholic Edition, to form the approved *English Lectionary for Mass* by the Canadian Conference of Catholic Bishops. The NRSV-CE is also one of the versions of the Bible used in English editions of the Catechism of the Catholic Church.

The Anchor and the Common Bibles

The first attempt by a joint ecumenical committee to produce a common Bible is the *Anchor Bible* (1964). Under the general editorship of William F. Albright and David Noel Freedman, it claims to be international and interfaith in its scope. Specifically, it claims to encompass Protestant, Catholic, and Jewish scholars from many countries among the translators. Their effort is to make available to all English-speaking peoples all of the significant historical and linguistic knowledge that bears on the interpretation of the biblical record. It is being produced in separate volumes, each of which is to be accompanied by a complete introduction and notes.

A revision of the RSV was published as the *Common Bible* (1973). The *Common Bible* ordered the books in a way to please the Eastern Orthodox, Roman Catholics, and Protestants based on acceptance of the Ecumenical Creeds of the Christian Church. It was divided into four sections: (1) the Old Testament (thirty-nine books); (2) the Catholic deuterocanonical books (twelve Books); (3) the additional Eastern Orthodox deuterocanonical books (three books; six books after 1977); and (4) the New Testament (twenty-seven books). The extra deuterocanonicals gave the *Common Bible* a total of eighty-one books. It included 1 Esdras (also known as 3 Ezra), 2 Esdras (4 Ezra), and the Prayer of Manasseh, books that have appeared in the Vulgate's appendix since Jerome's time "lest they perish entirely," but are not considered canonical by Catholics and are thus not included in most modern Catholic Bibles. In 1977, the RSV Apocrypha was expanded to include 3 Maccabees, 4 Maccabees, and Psalm 151, three additional sections accepted in the Eastern Orthodox canon (4 Maccabees again forming an appendix in that tradition), although it still does not include additional books in the Syriac and Ethiopian canons. This action increased the *Common Bible* to eighty-four books, making it the most comprehensive English Bible translation to date in its inclusion of books not accepted by all communions. The goal of the *Common Bible* was to help ecumenical relations among the churches.

BIBLE REVISIONS IN THE TYNDALE/KJV TRADITION

Holman Christian Standard Bible, HCSB (1999–2004)

The Holman Christian Standard Bible, HCSB, originated in 1984 as an independent project of Arthur Farstad, who had formerly served as general editor for the NKJV. Farstad's original concept was to produce a modern English translation of the New Testament based on *The Greek New Testament According to the Majority Text* (1982), which he had edited with Zane Hodges (see chap. 12). Edwin A. Blum joined Farstad to produce translations of some portions of the New Testament.

In 1998 Broadman & Holman Publishers took notice of the project, as they were seeking to buy the copyright of some already existing Bible version for their publishing projects. For many years they had been using the NIV, but this was not convenient because the copyright holder (the IBS) had sold exclusive North American publishing rights to the Zondervan Corporation, and Zondervan would allow other publishers to use the NIV only under expensive and restrictive license agreements. In addition, at the time no small concern arose about a planned revision of the NIV. In 1997 it had become public knowledge that the IBS was preparing a politically correct "inclusive language" revision to make the NIV less accurate but more acceptable to feminists (see previous discussion).

The answer of B & H Publishing Group (formerly Broadman & Holman), operated by the Southern Baptist Convention, to the NIV plan for an inclusive language update was the Holman Christian Standard Bible. The Bible is basically a conservative Baptist/Presbyterian production, although some other denominations are represented.

The HCSB states that formal equivalence and dynamic equivalence are meaningful but inadequate translation philosophies. Instead, HCSB translators use an optimal equivalence approach, which means that "form cannot be neatly separated from meaning and should not be changed . . . unless comprehension demands it." They use literal translation unless "clarity and readability demand idiomatic translation." Changes are introduced into the text and the original reading is placed into footnotes.

The textual base of the New Testament is the *Nestle-Aland Novum Testamentum Graece*, 27th edition, and the United Bible Societies' Greek New Testament, 4th corrected edition. The Old Testament uses the *Biblia Hebraica Stuttgartensia*, 5th edition. After the death of Arthur Farstad (1998), the HCSB was directed away from its original objective. At times, however, translators follow an alternative manuscript tradition, disagreeing with the editors of these texts about the original reading (see discussion in chaps. 12 and 14). In that regard, the approach seems similar to that used by translators of the TNIV (2002, 2005) and NIV 2011. (See the chart "Versions in the Tyndale/KJV Tradition" to see its place among more recent translations.) The HCSB is somewhat "churchy" in serving Southern Baptist churches, other institutions, and their vast array of LifeWay Bookstores.[4]

VERSIONS IN THE TYNDALE/KJV TRADITION

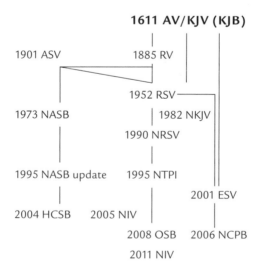

Adapted from David Dewey, *Which Bible?* (Leicester, England: InterVarsity, 2004), 178.

---

4. Publishing the HCSB also seems to be a "market driven" and "control" decision, since B & H Publishing's nearby out-of-house publisher, Thomas Nelson, already had produced the NKJV.

The Orthodox Study Bible, New Testament and Psalms (1993)
The Orthodox Study Bible, OSB (2008)

The *Orthodox Study Bible* began as *The Orthodox Study Bible: New Testament and Psalms, OSBNT* (1993), under the direction of the Academic Community of St. Athanasius Orthodox Academy (Santa Barbara, California). With father Peter Gilquist as project director, they used the NKJV text for the New Testament and Psalms, with added notes reflecting Orthodox theology. The choice of the NKJV text was based on their view that "the translators and editors, while sensitive to English idiom, believe in the divine inspiration of Scripture and have adhered faithfully to the Hebrew, Aramaic, and Greek texts." OSBNT uses a "red letter" edition of the NKJV text. "Discovering Orthodox Christianity in the Pages of the New Testament" is accomplished by study aids and articles written from an Orthodox Christian perspective "working within a tradition of biblical tradition which goes back to the apostles themselves."

The St. Athanasius Orthodox Academy also produced *The Orthodox Study Bible*, OSB in 2008. It is a milestone marker because, "Though the Orthodox Church has never officially commited itself to a single text and list of Old Testament books, it has traditionally used the Greek Old Testament of the Septuagint (LXX). However, in Orthodoxy's 200-year history in North America, no English translation of the LXX has ever been produced by the Church."[5] The OSB is an eclectic text, combining elements of the Greek Septuagint (see discussions in chapters 12 and 17) with the Hebrew Masoretic Text (MT), which differs in several places. Contributors used the Alfred Rahlfs Septuaginta translated by Sir Lancelot C. L. Brenton (1851), and the English text of the NKJV Old Testament where the Greek Old Testament text agreed with the Hebrew of the Masoretic Text and other documents. The English style of the OSB follows the NKJV, which served as the template for translators. Utilizing the NKJV template allowed translators to include exact quotations of the Old Testament in the New Testament.

The OSB has a comparative list of its Orthodox canon, side by side with the Orthodox, Roman Catholic, and Protestant canons of the Old

---

5. See "Introduction to the Orthodox Study," *The Old Testament According to the Seventy* (published with the approval of the Holy Synod of the Church of Greece, 1928), xi.

Testament.[6] The OSB arranges the Old Testament and Apocryphal books after the canonical order of The Old Testament According to the Seventy.[7] In the OSB where LXX numbers of Psalms differs from the NKJV and NRSV, the LXX psalm number appears first, followed by the alternate number in parentheses. Different chapter numbers also occur in Jeremiah and Malachi, where the Septuagint differs from the Masoretic Text. Unlike other standard translations, the OSB "Introduction" asserts that "the Old Testament text in this volume does not claim to be a new or superior translation. The goal was to produce a text to meet the Bible reading needs of English-speaking Orthodox Christians." A comparison of the Old Testament books in the Orthodox Bible with the books of the Roman Catholic, Protestant, and Hebrew Scriptures concludes this chapter.

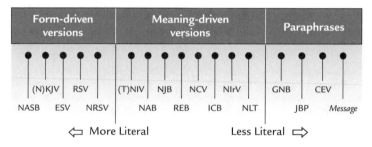

SOURCE: Adapted from David Dewey, *Which Bible? A Guide to English Translations* (Leicester, England: InterVarsity, 2004), 47.

LITERAL TO FREE SPECTRUM OF BIBLE TRANSLATIONS

Bible translations range from form-driven through meaning-driven to paraphrase. Each can be placed somewhere on the spectrum of literal to free (see chart above). Making an assessment as to where on that spectrum a particular translation lies is, of course, somewhat subjective. If the translation is a broad-based or cooperative enterprise, placement tends to be somewhat more objective. Individual, personal, small group, denominational, or theologically directed translations (e.g., Darby, NWT, NET Bible) tend to raise

6. Nestorian Christians who moved to the East following the ecumenical councils addressed such issues as "Why is the Mother of God essential to the Faith?" This remains problematic in the contemporary church. For these and other comments see *The Orthodox Study Bible: Ancient Christianity Speaks to Today's World* (Nashville: Nelson, 2008); http://orthodoxwiki.org/Orthodox_Study_Bible as well as http://en.wikipedia.org/wiki/Orthodox_Study_Bible.

7. "Introduction to the Orthodox Study Bible," *The Old Testament According to the Seventy*, xi.

other questions about objectivity and/or reliability.

English Standard Version (ESV, 2001, 2003)
ESV Study Bible, English Standard Version (ESVB, 2008)
English Standard Version with Apocrypha (ESVAP, 2009)

The Holy Bible, English Standard Version, ESV (2001, 2003) had its roots in discussions that took place before the May 1997 meeting called by James Dobson at the ministry headquarters of Focus on the Family to resolve the inclusive NIV issue. Some months later, Trinity Evangelical Divinity School professor Wayne Grudem and Crossway President Lane Dennis entered into negotiations with the National Council of Churches to use the 1971 revision of the RSV as the basis for a new translation. An agreement was reached in September 1998 allowing translators freedom to modify the original text of the RSV as necessary to rid it of de-Christianing translation choices.

An agreement signed by all the participants (the Colorado Springs Guidelines) set forth principles of translation that would rule out the use of gender-neutral language. Clearly the ESV was projected as a version that would deliberately adhere to these guidelines, and this is confirmed in the preface to the version, which gives three paragraphs in defense of generic masculine terms. The preface states:

> The ESV publishing team includes more than a hundred people. The fourteen-member Translation Oversight Committee has benefited from the work of fifty biblical experts serving as Translation Review Scholars and from the comments of the more than fifty members of the Advisory Council, all of which has been carried out under the auspices of the Good News Publishers Board of Directors. This hundred-member team, which shares a common commitment to the truth of God's Word and to historic Christian orthodoxy, is international in scope and includes leaders in many denominations.

The first edition of the ESV became available in late September 2001 as the *ESV Classic Reference Bible*, which featured brief introductions to each of the books, section headings within the text, and a center column very full of cross-references. The introductions briefly and simply present traditional views of the authorship and purpose of the books. In 2007 a slightly revised edition appeared, in which about 360 changes were made. In order to give an idea of the frequency and types of changes in the revision, J. I. Packer provides a full collation of the first three chapters of the epistle to the Romans in the RSV and the first edition of the ESV.

In these chapters there are as many changes as there are verses, and the great majority of them serve to make the version more literal. There are six instances in which the ESV seems less literal than the RSV, and four of these have to do with gender language. Two (at 3.4 and 3.28) involve the elimination of the word "man" as a translation of *anthropos*, one (2.29) involves the replacement of "men" with "man," and one (2.28) involves the elimination of the word "he." There is also in the margin at 1.13 a long note explaining that *adelphoi* ("brothers") may be translated "brothers and sisters." The ESV revisers have normally left unchanged the RSV's generic use of "man" and "men" (see the translation of *anthropos* in 1.18, 1.23, 2.1, 2.3, 2.16, 2.29) and also "his" (see 2.6, 2.29), and so it is hard to see on what principle they have changed or qualified "men," "man," "brothers," and "he" in these places. But apart from these few places, the changes of the ESV are a distinct improvement upon the RSV.

In the Old Testament ESV, revisers tend to be more conservative than the RSV in handling of text-critical questions. In many places where the RSV rendering was based upon an emended text, the ESV revision represents a return to the Masoretic Text. The deliberateness of this tendency is especially noticeable in the book of Job. The RSV had made sixty-three emendations in this book (often by somewhat hazardous conjectures), but in the ESV revision all but six of them have been eliminated. In these examples ESV revisers preferred to translate the existing Hebrew text, without speculative text-critical alterations. But the ESV does not always follow the traditional Hebrew text. Sometimes it lets the emendations of the RSV stand.

More significant than any of the changes listed above are the following examples from the Old Testament. These passages of the RSV are representative of many that were found to be highly objectionable to evangelicals, and prevented the RSV from ever gaining acceptance outside of liberal circles—Genesis 22:15–18; Psalm 2:11–12; Psalm 16:10; and Isaiah 7:14. Although the ESV is in general more literal and reliable than most English versions published in recent years, critics argue the translation would benefit from emendations.

In Genesis 3:6 the ESV follows the example of the NIV instead of the more literal KJB, ASV, and NASB. The sentence should be interpreted "she gave some to her husband as well, or also." This is the interpretation of the Vulgate, RSV, Berkeley, NEB, REB, TEV, and TANAKH translations, and of most commentators. In Genesis 41:8 the ESV translators were less careful than the RSV to indicate a departure from the Masoretic Text. In Genesis 41:56 the RSV is more informative than the ESV. In their revision of the RSV, the ESV editors tend to substitute numerals for words expressing quantities. In Deuteronomy 15:4–5 the RSV punctuation is much better than the ESV's. The ESV has obscured the meaning of the sentence with its revised punctuation.

In John's gospel the ESV (following most other modern versions) translates the word μονογενής, *monogenēs* as "only" rather than "only-begotten." in describing Jesus as God's Son. Although most commentators of the present day have argued that "only" is an adequate translation of this word, others maintain that this is an undertranslation of an important theological term. The ESV revisers would do well to include a footnote informing readers of the traditional rendering, "only begotten."[8] The ESV's use of "wife" as a translation of γυνή, *gunē* in 1 Corinthians 11 is questionable. This passage is about the status and behavior suitable to womankind, not just of wives. And there is no indication here that Paul viewed head coverings as a symbol of the married state. There is a tendency in the ESV to substitute the singular "man" for the plural "men" in various places.

As modern versions go, the ESV should be counted as one of the best for use in a teaching ministry. The ESV is most frequently compared with the NRSV and the NIV. It is more literal than the NIV; and so it is largely free of the problems that come with the use of so-called dynamic equivalence versions; but it is not so severely literal that ordinary readers will struggle to understand it. Its English recalls the classic diction of the KJV, and so it has some literary power (this is not unimportant in a Bible version). Its handling of the Old Testament is agreeable to conservative principles of interpretation. As a revision of the RSV, it is much better than the NRSV in several ways. However, there are some weaknesses in it, such as the negative

---

8. For a full discussion of this matter see the previous discussion on the NIV translation and Michael Marlowe's article, "The Only Begotten Son" at www.bibleresearcher.com as discussed in chapter 20.

COMBINING READING EASE WITH DEGREE OF LITERALNESS

Form-driven versions	Meaning-driven versions	Paraphrases

Grade 8 — KJV

Grade 6

Grade 4

(N)KJV   RSV   (T)NIV   NJB   NCV   NIrV NLT   JBP

NASB   ESV NRSV   NAB   REB   ICB   GNB   CEV *Message*

⇦ More Literal   Less Literal ⇨

SOURCE: Adapted from David Dewey, *Which Bible? A Guide to English Translations* (Leicester, England: InterVarsity, 2004), 52.

influence of the NIV in several places.[9]

For close study, the ESV is less suitable than the NASB or NKJV, and the latter two versions were dominant until publication of the *ESV Study Bible, English Standard Bible* (ESVSB, 2008). Like the *NIV Study Bible* (see above), the purpose of the ESVSB is to help people understand the Bible in a deeper way. It benefits from a team of ninety-five scholars and teachers from nine countries and nearly twenty denominations, including academics from fifty seminaries, colleges, and universities. The translators assert that it is an extraordinary resource, equivalent to a twenty-volume Bible study library, and it is enhanced by the ESV with Apocrypha (ESVAP, 2009). The ESVSB, also available on the Internet (see www.esvstudybible.org), is a broader, more inclusive, more objective, and more consistent with the doctrinal tradition of the Christian church than the NET Bible (NET), 1999–2007 (see below).

The English Standard Version with Apocrypha is an attempt to project the ESV into a broader context of English-speaking readers. It contains the ESV 2007 text combined with the Oxford Apocrypha, Deuteronomicals (2009). According to Oxford University Press (OUP), the translation

---

9. This treatment follows and summarizes Michael Marlowe's review of the ESV at www. bible-researcher.com.

of the Apocryphal books is based on the RSV Apocrypha (1971) as well as the expanded Apocrypha (1977; see discussion below), following the Latin Vulgate except 2 Esdras, which appears as part of the Greek Septuagint (LXX), with the additional books of 3 and 4 Maccabees and Psalm 151. The Expanded RSV Apocrypha of the OUP Apocrypha also included books from the Septuagint in use among Orthodox Christians. The textual base for all books except 4 Maccabees and 2 Esdras is the Göttengin Septuagint (see chaps. 12 and 17 discussion); 4 Maccabees is translated from Rahlfs's Septuaginta, while 2 Esdras is from the Latin Vulgate (1983) edition published by the German Bible Society. Since both the NRSV and ESV are used in the United Kingdom, a few comparisons are warranted:

ESV	NRSV	ESV	NRSV
Overseer— 1 Tim. 3; Titus 1	Bishop	Propitiation Rom. 3:25	Sacrifice of atonement
Hell— Matt. 16:18	Hades	Born again John 3:3	Born from above
Brothers—	Brothers and sisters	Son of Man OT / Heb. 2:6	Mortals/ Human Beings
A pillar 1 Tim. 3:15	The pillar	Grasped Phil 2:6	Exploited
Made himself nothing Phil 2:7	Emptied himself	Virgin Isa. 7:14	Young woman
Behold	Look or See	Husband of one wife 1 Tim. 3:2	Married only once
Rage Ps. 2:1	Conspire	the Christ Matt. 16:16	the Messiah

EIGHTEENTH- AND NINETEENTH-CENTURY TRANSLATIONS

All these current translations derive from the Douay-Rheims and King James Bibles of the late fifteenth and early sixteenth centuries. Yet many other notable translations appeared during the interval of the eighteenth and nineteenth centuries. Alongside the official translations discussed above, there were a host of unofficial translations and versions published. In 1703, for example, Daniel Whitby edited a *Paraphrase and Commentary on the New Testament*. Edward Wells followed with a revised text of the King James Bible called *The Common Translations Corrected* (1718–1724). In 1745 William Whiston, known for his translation of *The Life and Works of Flavius Josephus*, published a *Primitive New Testament*; and John Wesley made some 12,000 changes in the KJB New Testament text. Edward Horwood made a *Liberal Translation of the New Testament* in 1768 to round out the translations of the eighteenth century.

During the nineteenth century, efforts to translate the Old Testament began to appear more frequently. The first of these was *The Septuagint Bible* published by Charles Thompson in 1808. In 1844 Lancelot Brenton followed it up by publishing his Septuagint Version of the Old Testament. The Unitarian scholar Samuel Sharpe published his New Testament in 1840 and his Old Testament in 1865. In the meantime, Robert Young produced his *Literal Translation of the Bible* (1862), and Dean Alford published his Greek New Testament and a revision of the Authorized Bible in 1869. John Nelson Darby, a leader of the Plymouth Brethren, published a *New Translation of the Bible* (1871, 1890), while Joseph Bryant Rotherham was publishing *The Emphasized Bible* (1872, 1902). Thomas Newberry edited *The Englishman's Bible* during the 1890s. One of the best-known examples of translations of portions of the Bible appears in W. J. Conybeare and J. S. Howson, *The Life and Epistles of St. Paul* (1964), where the translation is embedded in a commentary.

A Parade of Twentieth-Century Translations

The great profusion of English Bible translations did not occur until the mid-twentieth century after: (1) the great manuscripts had been published and more were discovered (at Qumran and in the caves in the Judean Desert), (2) public sentiment sought colloquial translations, (3) attempts were being made to make official translations, and (4) additional textual evidence was discovered. From that time there has been a virtual parade of scholars and their translations.

Arthur S. Way, a classical scholar, led the parade with his translation of *The Letters of St. Paul* (1901). The very next year witnessed the publication of *The Twentieth Century New Testament* based on the text of Westcott and Hort. A consultee for this translation, Richard Francis Weymouth, translated *The Resultant Greek Testament*, which was published posthumously in 1903 and thoroughly revised by James A. Robertson in 1924.

Perhaps the most ambitious enterprise by one man was *The Holy Bible in Modern English* (1895, 1903) by Ferrar Fenton. It was based on Hebrew, Chaldee, and Greek manuscripts. James Moffat, an Oxford scholar, published

The New Testament (1913) and The Old Testament (1924), which he later combined into *A New Translation of the Bible* (1928). Moffat's work is characterized by its Scottish tone, freedom of style and idiom, and his modernistic theological bias. The American counterpart to Moffat appears in Edgar J. Goodspeed, *The Complete Bible: An American Translation* (1927), although Goodspeed's contribution was the Apocrypha and the New Testament. G. W. Wade presented a fresh translation arranged in what he believed were the chronological order of books in *The Documents of the New Testament* (1934). *The Concordant Version of the Sacred Scriptures* (1926+) was based on the principle that every word in the original should have an English equivalent.

In 1937 Charles B. Williams issued *The New Testament in the Language of the People*, in which he tried to convey the exact meaning of the Greek verb tenses into English. During that same year Gerald Warre Cornish's *St. Paul from the Trenches* was published posthumously. W. C. Wand produced *The New Testament Letters* in 1943 in the format of a bishop writing a monthly letter to his diocese. In another attempt to get the Bible into the hands of laymen, J. H. Hooks served as chairman of a committee that translated *The Basic English Bible* (1940–1949) using only one thousand "basic" English words. Charles Kingsley Williams attempted a similar work in *The New Testament: A Translation in Plain English* (1952).

A conservative attempt to produce a counterpart to the Revised Standard Bible was led by Gerrit Verkuyl of Berkeley, California. The Bible translation was entitled *The Berkeley Version in Modern English* (1945, 1959). The New Testament portion of this work was revised and published as *The Modern Language Bible* (1969). The aim of this version was to achieve a plain, up-to-date expression that reflects as directly as possible the meaning of the Hebrew, Aramaic, and Greek. It is not a paraphrase, but a very extensive revision without being a retranslation. Explanatory notes were revised as well as added. Topical headings were rephrased.

After releasing several components, John Bertram Phillips, often referred to as just J. B. Phillips, published *The New Testament in Modern English* (1958). It was subsequently revised and republished in 1961 and then again in 1972. His work translating the New Testament made him one of Britain's most famous Bible communicators. He also translated parts of the Old Testament before his death in 1982. He talked of the revelation received as he translated the New Testament, describing it as "extraordinarily alive" unlike any experience he had had with nonscriptural ancient texts. He referred to the Scriptures speaking to his condition in an "uncanny way." As a masterful apologist and defender of the Christian faith, Phillips upheld the basic tenets of the faith, and was able to present them fresh to the modern reader and hearer, much as he had done with his translation of the New Testament. *The New Testament in Modern English* has been adapted for use on the Internet for a new generation of believers.

Emphatic Diaglott (1864)
The New World Translation, NWT (1984)

Quite different from Phillips are the Jehovah's Witnesses publications, beginning with Benjamin Wilson's *Emphatic Diaglott* (1864)[10] by Zion's Watch Tower. The second edition was published under that name by the Watchtower Bible and Tract Society. In 1950 The New Testament was entitled *The New World Translation of the Christian Greek Scriptures*, and the Old Testament, entitled *The New World Translation of the Hebrew Scriptures*, was published in 1953.

Today the Jehovah's Witnesses read and distribute the entire Bible as *The New World Translation of the Holy Scriptures* (NWT, 1961). Though the NWT is not the first Bible published by the group, it is their first original translation of ancient classical Hebrew, koine Greek, and Old Aramaic biblical texts. As of 2011, the Watchtower Bible and Tract Society has published 168 million copies of the New World Translation in ninety-eight languages.

Benjamin Wilson's Emphatic Bible translates John 1:1: "In a beginning was the word, and the word was with the God, and a god was the Word." This translation is virtually the same as that of the New World Translation (NWT), which has been criticized by Bruce M. Metzger and others for its rendering of John 1:1. Most English translations render this verse: "In the beginning was the Word, and the Word was with God, and the Word was God." By contrast, the NWT renders the verse: "In [the] beginning the Word was, and the Word was with God, and the Word was a god." Metzger made a definitive critique regarding the erroneous translation of John 1:1 and other favorite

---

10. The full title of the New Testament is *The Emphatic Diaglott Containing the Original Greek Text of What Is Commonly Styled the New Testament (According to the Recension of Dr. J. J. Griesbach) with an Interlineary Word for Word English Translation, a New Emphatic Version Based on the Interlineary Translation, on the Renderings of Eminent Critics, and on the Various Readings of the Vatican Manuscript*, no. 1209 in the Vatican Library by Benjamin Wilson, 1864, repr. 1902.

mistranslations used in various Jehovah's Witnesses publications including the NWT.[11] Other critiques of the NWT by Robert Countess, Raymond Franz, Jack Lewis, and Sakae Kubo[12] are poignant evaluations of additional erroneous renderings in Wilson's *Emphatic Diaglott* (1864), Goodspeed's *An American Translation* (1927), and the New World Translation.

An early copy at hand of the *Emphatic Diaglott*, which was presented in 1903 to a "Br. Silas Arnold of Dayton, Ohio, by Br. Russell," includes an editor's page not reproduced in later editions. The text of this item is reprinted here:

"A Friendly Criticism."

This work we regard as a very valuable help to all Bible students, whether conversant with the Greek language or not. We esteem it (as a whole) the most valuable translation of the New Testament extant. We call special attention to the 'word for word' translation, found immediately under the Greek text, in the left hand column. It will be found valuable, especially for a critical examination of any particular text. A little study will enable you to appreciate it. Like all things made and done by imperfect mortals, we think this valuable work is not without its faults. It would seem to us that the author must have held the view that Jesus had no prehuman existence, and that there is no personal devil; i.e., that when the word 'devil' is used evil principle is meant; also that Jesus is still a man and flesh, in glory. In commending this work to you as a whole so highly as we have done, we deem it but a duty to draw your attention to a very slight bias which we think pervades the work in the direction named. As some pointed illustrations of what we have remarked, we suggest an examination and comparison between the right and left columns of the work, in the following scriptures, viz: John 1:10; Rev. 13:8; Jude 9; Heb. 10:20.

Editor of Zion's Watch Tower.

11. Bruce M. Metzger, "Jehovah's Witnesses and Jesus Christ," *Theology Today*, April 1953, 65–85; and "The New World Translation of the Christian Greek Scriptures," *The Bible Translator* 15, no. 3 (July 1964): 150–53.

12. Robert H. Countess, *The Jehovah's Witnesses' New Testament*, 2nd ed. (Phillipsburg, N.J.: Presbyterian and Reformed Publishing, 1987); Raymond V. Franz, *Crisis of Conscience* (Atlanta: Commentary Press, 1983). Both contain numerous evaluations and critiques of the NWT historically, grammatically, and theologically; Jack P. Lewis, *The English Bible from the KJV to the NIV* (Grand Rapids: Baker, 1981), 229–36, passim; and Sakae Kubo & Walter F. Specht, *So Many Versions?*, rev. ed. (Grand Rapids: Zondervan, 1983), 98–116, passim.

Although "A Friendly Criticism" was not published in later printings, Wilson's views were subsequently adopted by the Watchtower Bible and Tract Society and incorporated into the NWT. Among other translation issues running contrary to generally accepted practices, Jehovah's Witnesses have introduced the name "Jehovah" to their New Testament text. This is totally without textual justification, since the term does not appear in any recognized Greek text of the New Testament. Frequently the term "Jehovah" or "Jehovah's" is used for the Greek word *Kurios* (Lord). Sometimes the Greek word *Kurie* (Lord), *Kurion* (Lord), or *Kurio* (Lord) is replaced by "Jehovah." The Greek word *Kuriou* (of Lord, or Lord's) is replaced most frequently by "Jehovah" or "Jehovah's." The NWT translators even translate the Greek word *Theo* (God), *Theos* (God), or *Theon* (God) to "Jehovah," and *Theou* (of God, or God's) is changed to "Jehovah's." Three examples from NWT (1996) underscore this violation of the principles of textual criticism and sound translation—Acts 16:32, Rom. 10:13, and Rev. 21:22—and flies in the face of the position of Catholic translators and their response to Pope Benedict XVI's request in 2007 that the word "Yahweh" should not be used in future English translations (see above and in chap. 11).

Modern Translations from Lamsa, Schonfield, Wuest, and Others

In the meantime, others attempted to modernize their personal translations of the Bible into English. George M. Lamsa, for instance, translated *The Holy Bible from Ancient Eastern Manuscripts* (1933–1957) using the Syriac Peshitta (see chap. 16) instead of Greek manuscripts. A distinguished Jewish scholar, Hugh J. Schonfield, attempted to reconstruct the "authentic" New Testament Jewish atmosphere for Gentile readers in *The Authentic New Testament* (1955).

Kenneth S. Wuest followed the tradition of J. B. Phillips (see previous discussion) in publishing his *Expanded Translation of the New Testament* in a series of installments before they were combined in 1959. Wuest's translation, like the Amplified Bible (see below), was not as useful for public reading as was the "Free Translation" of Phillips. Olaf M. Norlis published *The Simplified New Testament in Plain English* (1961), and R. K. Harrison translated *The Psalms for Today* to accompany it.

Amplified Bible (1965, 1987)

In 1958 the Lockman Foundation and Zondervan Publishing House issued the first edition of the Amplified New Testament after 20,000 hours of research and prayerful study. The Old Testament came out in a series of releases before the Amplified Bible (1965) was published in a single volume. Zondervan Bible Publishers and the Lockman Foundation, with its aim to communicate the Word of God and to exalt Jesus Christ, published *The Amplified Bible, Expanded Edition* (1987). Amplified Bibles are like short commentaries as they faithfully present the Scriptures in contemporary language. They are designed for individuals who have little or no background in Hebrew, Aramaic, or Greek languages, and are more readily useful for Bible study than for public liturgy.

The New Testament from 26 Translations (1967)

In the prologue of the Paris edition of the 1538 Coverdale Diglot (Latin and English), Miles Coverdale wrote of the value of differing translations of the Scriptures (see chap. 19). He concluded his remarks saying, "For if thou open thine eyes and consider well the gift of the Holy Ghost therein, thou shalt see that one translation declareth, openeth and illustrateth another, and that in many cases one is a plain commentary unto another." *The New Testament from 26 Translations* was published in the firm belief that this is true. General editor Curtis Vaughan states that the Bible that has enjoyed the most widespread and lasting acceptance in the English speaking world is the KJB. It is marked by simplicity, dignity, and power of statement that for centuries has nurtured God's people. The KJB is the basis for this work. Its aim is to clarify the meaning of the KJB by the use of more recent translations of the biblical text. These serve somewhat as a commentary on the text of the older translation.

In *26 Translations*, only the KJB is quoted in its entirety (in boldface type), and other translations are cited (in Roman type) only when they differ significantly from the KJB. In this sense *The New Testament from 26 Translations* is akin the Amplified New Testament (1965) also published by Zondervan (see above).

The Living Bible (1971)
Holy Bible, New Living Translation (NLT, 1996, 2004)

In 1962 Kenneth Taylor began publishing portions of The Living Bible as a paraphrase of the ASV, with comparisons of other translations, including the KJB and some Greek texts (see following discussion of paraphrase Bibles). The completed translation of The Living Bible (1971) and The Catholic Living Bible (1976) enjoyed amazingly wide circulation. The Catholic Living Bible does not use the word "paraphrased" on the front cover but uses it on the title page and adds "A Thought-For-Thought Translation" (also used in some later Protestant printings), and contains the deuterocanonical books. It received the imprimatur of the Catholic Church as well as an introduction entitled, "Why Read the Bible?" by Pope John Paul II. From the very beginning, Taylor had assigned the copyright to Tyndale House Foundation, so all royalties were given to charity.

In the late 1980s, Tyndale House Publishers invited a team of ninety Greek and Hebrew scholars to participate in a project of revising the text of The Living Bible. The result was Holy Bible: New Living Translation (NLT 1996, 2004). The text for the Old Testament is basically the MT (*Biblia Hebraica Stuttgartensia*) as further compared with other sources, such as the Dead Sea Scrolls, Septuagint, Greek manuscripts, Samaritan Pentateuch, Syriac Peshitta, and Latin Vulgate. The New Testament text is based on two standard Greek editions from the Westcott-Hort tradition, UBS4 and NA27 (but not the M or TR).

Using translators from "a broad spectrum of denominations, theological perspectives, and backgrounds within the worldwide Evangelical community," its focus was to create a text to be read publicly. Translations are generally governed by one of two general theories: (1) "formal-equivalence," "literal," or "word–for–word" translation, or (2) "dynamic-equivalence," "functional-equivalence," or thought-for-thought" translation. The NLT attempted to translate the original texts simply and literally with a "dynamic equivalence synergy" approach. While making the NLT easier to understand, it may limit its suitability for those wishing to undertake detailed study of the Bible. By design, the NLT (1996) was soon revised (2004), and slight revisions were added in 2007.

New Century Version (NCV, 1978, 1988, 1991, 2005)
Holy Bible, Easy-to-Read Version (ERV, 1980, 2005)
English Version for the Deaf (EVD, 1978)
The Holy Bible: Children's Version (1986, 1987)

The Holy Bible, New Century Version (NCV) is a dynamic equivalence version actually begun in 1978 as the *English Version for the Deaf* (EVD) by Baker Book House. Baker published it as a new easy-to-read version (1980). The New Testament was revised and published as the *International Children's New Testament* (1983), slightly revised; the complete Bible was published as *The Holy Bible: Children's Version* (1986, 1987), the New Century Bible (NCV 1987), and a special edition, *The Everyday Bible* (1988). Another more extensive revision was published by Word Publishing (1991) and by Thomas Nelson (1992) under the name New Century Version, NCV. The Translation Center of Fort Worth, Texas, published a revised edition of The Holy Bible: Easy-to-Read Version (2005).

Originally published and adapted to the needs of deaf people who were "unfamiliar with many idioms of English as it is commonly spoken," the EVD "is perhaps the simplest English version ever written, being done with a third-grade level vocabulary and with very short sentences." The preface continues:

> *The English Version for the Deaf* is not a revision of any English version designed for the hearing. It is an original translation based on the Hebrew and Greek Biblical texts. The wording will often strike the reader as different from other English translations, but it accurately expresses the full meaning of the original text in a style that is clear and easy to understand.... The result might appear to be just a simple English version of the Bible, but is much more than that. It is a carefully constructed translation, designed to communicate to those who are deaf. Although the language used will not be familiar to those accustomed to standard English versions, it does convey to the deaf the meaning that was originally intended. It is the purpose of this translation to provide the deaf with their own Bible for personal reading and study and to aid the vital ministry of those who teach the deaf, giving them relief from the need to "translate" existing English versions as they teach.[13]

13. Ervin Bishop, et al. "Preface," Holy Bible: English Version for the Deaf (Ft. Worth, Tex.: World Bible Translation Center, 2003).

The Old Testament translation is based on *Biblia Hebraica Stuttgarten-sia*, BHS (1984), while referring occasionally to some earlier readings in the Dead Sea Scrolls (DSS). In some cases, they also followed the *Septuagint* (LXX), the Greek translation of the Old Testament, where it has readings that are actually earlier than any known Hebrew manuscript. For the New Testament, the source text was that which is found in both the United Bible Societies' *Greek New Testament* UBS3 (1975) and UBS4 (1993), and the Nestle-Aland *Novum Testamentum Graece* (twenty-seventh edition, 1993). Occasional variation from these printed editions was guided by reference to the findings of more recent scholarship (see discussions in chap. 12).

God's Word to the Nations (GWN, 1988–1990; NET, 1992)

William F. Beck began translating *The New Testament: God's Word to the Nations* (GWN) in 1966. First published in 1988, it was slightly revised in 1989 and 1990, before being renamed *God's Word to the Nations: New Testament, New Evangelical Translation* (NET) and published by NET Publishing of Cleveland (1992). It claims to be the "first literal translation that's also easy to read." The Old Testament translation project is the work of a single individual, who died before his project was completed. One feature of his work is that the book of Revelation is set entirely in poetic form.

The Five Gospels (1993)

Westar Institute, a scholarly think tank of mostly liberal gospel critics headquartered in Sonoma, California, sponsored The Jesus Seminar. The result was *The Five Gospels: The Search for the Authentic Words of Jesus New Translation and Commentary* (Macmillan Publishing) by Robert W. Funk, Roy W. Hoover, and The Jesus Seminar gathering in 1993. These gospel critics worked closely together for six years on a common question: What did Jesus really say? They produced a translation of all the gospels, known as the Scholars Version (SV). The gospels involved were Matthew, Mark, Luke, John, and Thomas, and the accumulated sayings of Jesus. A total of 1,500 sayings were cataloged and each one was voted upon before being included in the color-coded collection.

Comments in the so–called *Sayings Gospel Q* (Q) were incorporated into the narratives of Matthew and Luke). The English text of *The Five Gospels* is a translation of the Scholars Version, although no Greek or Coptic text of the SV was provided for verification of the translation. A very elaborate and intricate process was involved to bring forth *The Five Gospels* text, whose novel translation is designed to bring about variety instead of sounding like one another as do traditional English translations. The scholars insisted that the Gospel of Thomas must be given equal footing and recognition as Matthew, Mark, Luke, and John.

The SV is based on the ancient languages in which the gospels were written or into which they were translated at an early date: Greek, Coptic, Latin, and other exotic tongues. In some cases only secondary translations are available. The Gospel of Thomas, for example, was written in Greek but survives only in Coptic. The SV is free of ecclesiastical and religious control, unlike other major translations into English, including the King James Bible and its descendants (Protestant), Douay–Rheims Version and its progeny (Catholic), and the New International Version (evangelical). The SV is not bound by the dictates of church councils, and its contents and organization vary from traditional Bibles. Because scholars believe Mark was written first, they have placed it first among the five gospels. The SV is authorized by scholars (see preface of "Introductory Remarks"), but is having diminished impact.

TWENTY-FIRST-CENTURY TRANSLATIONS

NET Bible (NET, 1999, 2007)

The New English Translation, or NET Bible (NET, 1999, 2007), is not to be confused with the New English Bible (NEB, 1970), the *New Evangelical Translation* (NET, 1992), or *A New English Translation of the Septuagint* (NETS, 2007).[14] Similar to the HCSB (1999–2003), the NET Bible was a reaction against the publisher of the updated NIV and the TNIV (see previous discussion), and aimed at a narrower constituency. The HCSB aimed at Southern Baptists, and the NET Bible focused on the Dallas Theological Seminary community. Initially NET was conceived at an annual meeting of the Society of Biblical Literature (SBL) in November 1995 to provide a digital version of a modern English Bible over the Internet and on CD-ROM without cost to the user. "This vision was shared by a group of evangelical scholars and adopted by Bible.org—World's Largest Bible Study Site" for online pub-

---

14. See previous and subsequent discussions as well as chapter 12.

lication." The adoption by Bible.org brought a change in scope and purpose for the project. "The NET BIBLE project was thus commissioned to create a faithful Bible translation that could be placed on the Internet, downloaded for free, and used around the world for ministry."[15] Composition of the twenty-plus members of the translation team became dominated by faculty, staff, and students from Dallas Theological Seminary. The only woman on the team, Dorian G. Coover-Cox, is a graduate of the seminary, adjunct teacher of Old Testament studies, and associate editor of *Bibliotheca Sacra*. Wycliffe Bible Translators provided outside assistance.

The NET Bible is published in three presentations on the Internet as a free download at www.bible.org: (1) The NET Bible (1999–2007); (2) *The NET Bible, Readers Edition* (1996–2006); and (3) *The NET Bible First Edition: A New Approach to Translation* (2005). The translation is most notable for its immense number of footnotes, some of which are quite lengthy. Here are four common ones:

NET BIBLE Translators' Note Types

tn Translators' Note	**sn** Study Note
tc Text-critical Note	**map** Map Note

Since there were no official representatives of any denomination, and input was requested from lay people who had no expertise in Hebrew, Aramaic, or Greek, some of the translator's notes (tn) and study notes (sn) lack in adequate scholarship, having been written by students and/or staff members instead of professors from a broader scope of the scholarly community. For a text-critical (tc) note, Old Testament translators did not rely on the traditional *Biblia Hebraica Septuaginta* (BHS), or even the Leningrad Codex, and added materials from the Dead Sea Scrolls and other sources (see chap. 12). Each translator submitted a preliminary draft for consideration by an Old Testament Editorial Committee. Translations were then reviewed by the editors and a textual consultant, and in some instances revised. Conjectural emendations were employed only where necessary to make sense of the Hebrew text in order to translate it. Significant textual variations and

---

15. The preface of the NET Bible, first edition (2005), states that the idea came from its current home, www.bible.org.

emendations are noted in the text-critical notes. The result is that The NET Bible Old Testament does not represent a critical or reconstructed text.

The *NET Bible New Testament* has an eclectic text differing in several hundred places from the standard critical text as represented by the Nestle–Aland 27th edition/UBS4 (see chap. 12). These differences are indicated in text-critical notes. Individual books were translated, then submitted to the Editorial Committee to be evaluated by editors and a textual consultant. Where there are significant variant readings, these are normally indicated in a text-critical note. Although the SBL has published its own Greek text (see chap. 12), and the CBT has published it as *A Reader's Greek New Testament* (see previous discussion), the New Testament textual consultant appears to be in the process of developing still another Greek text.[16] A critical review of the translations and notes has been published online as "The NET Bible" by Michael Marlowe at www.bible-researcher.com, which seems fitting in view of Daniel Wallace's negative reviews of other translations.

The following extract is from its "Introduction to the First Edition":

> In addition to format and content, the broad framework of the project is unique among translations. The NET Bible is not funded by any particular denomination, church, or special interest group. . . . Translators and editors were left free to follow where the text leads and translate as they thought best. There was never any pressure to make sure the text reads a certain way or conforms to a particular doctrinal statement. The NET Bible is responsible and accountable to the universal body of Christ, the church worldwide. This seems to be an "undefined responsibility and accountability" factor, since everything comes under the aegis of personal approval and/or acceptance. Nevertheless, The NET Bible (with all the translators' notes) has also been provided to Wycliffe Bible Translators to assist their field translators. The NET Bible Society is working with other groups and Bible Societies to provide the NET Bible translators' notes to complement fresh translations in other languages.

---

16. See Daniel Wallace, various articles, papers, and reviews published at www.bible.org, www.sbl-site. org, *Bibliotheca Sacra*, and his own website.

The Message (2003)

Eugene H. Peterson published a paraphrase of the epistle to the Galatians after discovering that his congregation had become bored with the familiar text of Scripture. An editor at NavPress noticed his translation as part of a devotional book and asked him to publish an entire New Testament (1993). Upon its release, this New Testament version became a bestseller. During the next nine years Peterson gradually completed a new version of the entire Bible in contemporary English. NavPress published *The Message* (2003), advertising it as a "translation from the original languages" that "accurately communicates the original Hebrew and Greek" and brings out "the subtleties and nuances of the Hebrew and Greek languages," being the work of a respected "exegetical scholar." Actually, it is a free paraphrase of the text, often very eccentric, with many unlikely renderings, lengthy insertions, and omissions. Peterson's purpose is to present something new and provocative at every turn, something vivid and unusual, in order to stir up the minds of people bored with their familiar Bibles.

His method is comparable to that of a preacher in the pulpit, who dwells on one thing for a while and then rushes over another, alternatingly serious and jocular, doing whatever it takes to retain the attention of his audience. The version incorporates a number of interesting but peculiar interpretations that can be best described as homiletic. Long and formal-sounding sentences in the original are often replaced with punchy phrases. In many places the translation is extremely colloquial, and often the version portrays things in a more colorful way than the original. Sometimes Peterson obscures the main point of a passage by distracting attention from it with a homiletic flourish or breezy slang.

Peterson defends his paraphrase, while indicating that it is not really the Word of God and not suitable for use in the church. "For most of my adult life I have been given a primary responsibility for getting the message of the Bible into the lives of the men and women with whom I work. . . . *The Message* is a reading Bible. It is not intended to replace the excellent study Bibles that are available" (Preface, 7, 8). It is a paraphrase not suitable for Bible study, but it is a way to understand the message of the Bible.

Nevertheless, by mid 2010 sixteen million copies had been sold. Some critics say *The Message* has found a ready audience among evangelicals who are bored with the Bible and want a jazzy and fun paraphrase to take its place, and that its popularity is just one more example of levity in the contemporary church and its unhealthy taste for novelties and fads. Peterson responds that American church leaders have been "transformed into a company of shopkeepers with shopkeepers concerns—how to keep the customers happy, how to lure customers away from the competitors down the street, how to package the goods so that the customers will lay out more money."[17] Speaking of entertainment-driven ministry, he says, "There are others who do not desert the place of worship, but in staying, they do something worse: they subvert it. They turn it into a place of entertainment that will refresh bored and tired consumers and pump some zest into them."[18]

While we concur with Peterson's critique of contemporary church culture, it is not necessary to use his solution. One must use *The Message* with discernment, recognizing its conversational style frequently obscures the full meaning of the text. It began as a stimulating paraphrase of the epistle to the Galatians included in a popular devotional book, and it remains a piece of stimulating devotional literature. But it is not the Word of God. As Craig Blomberg of Denver Seminary has put it, "It is freer even than a paraphrase. I think of it more as devotional literature than as a version of the Bible and wouldn't recommend it for any other role."[19]

A New English Translation of the Septuagint (NETS, 2007)

Before drawing this discussion to a close, readers should be made aware of *A New English Translation of the Septuagint*, NETS (2007). This translation of the Septuagint is an important contribution to biblical readers and scholars (see the discussion in chap. 17). The basic text underlying this translation is the NRSV. The translation itself seems a bit awkward for individuals who are unfamiliar with the Septuagint (LXX) text. Names of individuals, places, and things may seem strange to the unskilled reader. The Greek text behind the NETS is based on texts written between 1931 and 2006. The readings

---

17. Eugene Peterson, *Working the Angles: The Shape of Pastor Integrity* (Grand Rapids: Eerdmans, 1987), also cited in www.bible-researcher.com/themessage.html.

18. Eugene Peterson, *Reversed Thunder* (San Francisco: Harper and Row, 1988), 141; also see www.bible-researcher.com/themessage.html.

19. Craig Blomberg, quoted in "Review of The Word of God in English, by Leland Ryken," *Denver Journal: An Online Review of Current Biblical and Theological Studies* 6 (July 2003); also cited in www.bible-researcher.com/themessage.html.

differ from those found in the *Biblia Hebraica Stuttgartensia*, which has been found to be wanting in terms of its critical apparatus. Due to its expense, individual readers might wish to obtain the collection in electronic format available at Logos Bible Software (www.logos.com).

The Lexham English Bible (LEB, 2010)

The online edition of Michael Holmes (ed.), *The Greek New Testament: SBL Edition* (2010) by the Society of Biblical Literature (SBL) and Logos Bible Software, reflects the ongoing enterprise of biblical study in its original languages. W. Hall Harris III is general editor of The Lexham English Bible (LEB 2010).[20] The LEB is an English translation of the SBL text of the New Testament by various scholars from the broad evangelical community, reflecting the SBL constituency. The LEB is an addition to a larger series of interlinear online diglot Bibles: *The Lexham Greek-English Interlinear New Testament*; *The Lexham Greek-English Interlinear New Testament: SBL edition*; *The Lexham Greek-English Interlinear Septuagint*; *The Lexham Greek-English Interlinear Septuagint: Alternate Text*; and *The Lexham Hebrew-English Interlinear Bible*, the MCWT collated with Dotan's Hebrew Bible and using the WM (4.2) database.[21]

These advances in digital publication of the LEB with the most recent developments in textual retrieval make it a first step in developing an entire "Lexham English Bible," not just the New Testament. Contact with Logos Bible Software has indicated no current plans to include the Apocrypha in future publications. With *A New English Translation of the Septuagint* (NETS)[22] and the broader range of users, including the ESV with Apocrypha (ESVAP, 2009), *The Bible in Its Traditions* (2008+), the Orthodox Study Bible (OSB, 2008), and the New American Bible, Revised Edition (NABRV, 2011), it seems to be only a matter of time before the Apocrypha are added.

---

20. See http://www.LexhamEnglishBible.com. This program is installed in Logos Bible programs as are the various research tools.

21. See http://www.logos.com. The Greek text for the interlinear Septuagint is Alfred Rahlfs, ed., *Septuaginta* (see chap. 12), while *Biblia Hebraica Stuttgartensia* (BHS Hebrew) with Westminster 4.2 Morphology (WM) is utilized for the Hebrew interlinear text (see chap. 12).

22. See chapters 12 and 17 of Albert Pietersma and Benjamin G. Wright, eds., *A New English Translation of the Septuagint* (NETS) and the other Greek translations traditionally included under that title (New York: Oxford Univ. Press, 2007).

SUMMARY

Even at a glance the seemingly endless procession of modern English translations indicates that the late twentieth and early twenty-first centuries, as like no previous time in human history, includes the greatest proliferation of translations of the Bible in both an official and an unofficial venues. Manuscripts never before available to biblical and textual scholars (or the general public) have resulted in an abundance of English Bibles, reference Bibles, study Bibles, and specialty Bibles. Commercial, denominational, sectarian, and individual interests have produced their own biblical texts and canons, with translations based on them.

In the new millennium, many English Bible translations are market-driven and reflect cultural and theological influence. Reference and study Bibles often emphasize positions covering sectarian theology rather than historic Christian belief. Some translations appeal to an invisible "universal" church as opposed to visible "historic" churches. Some translations present or introduce dangerous aberrant teaching, doctrinal distortion, or theological heresies that may be, and indeed have been, introduced into the translation itself.

With the great opportunity comes an equally great responsibility to know the background of the translators as well as their source documents in making their translation.

THE OLD TESTAMENT BOOKS LISTED AND COMPARED

Orthodox (Eastern) Old Testament	Roman Catholic Old Testament	Hebrew* and Protestant Old Testament
Genesis	Genesis	Genesis
Exodus	Exodus	Exodus
Leviticus	Leviticus	Leviticus
Numbers	Numbers	Numbers
Deuteronomy	Deuteronomy	Deuteronomy
Joshua	Joshua	Joshua
Judges	Judges	Judges
Ruth	Ruth	Ruth
1 Kingdoms (1 Samuel)	1 Kings	1 Samuel
2 Kingdoms (2 Samuel)	2 Kings	2 Samuel
3 Kingdoms (1 Kings)	3 Kings	1 Kings
4 Kingdoms (2 Kings)	4 Kings	2 Kings
1 Chronicles (1 Paraleipomenon)	1 Chronicles (1 Paraleipomenon)	1 Chronicles
2 Chronicles (2 Paraleipomenon)*	2 Chronicles (2 Paraleipomenon)	2 Chronicles
1 Ezra**	1 Esdras	Ezra
2 Ezra** (Ezra)	2 Esdras (Nehemiah)	Nehemiah
Nehemiah	Tobit	Esther*
Tobit	Judith	Job
Judith	Esther	Psalms (150 in number)
Esther	1 Maccabees	Proverbs
1 Maccabees	2 Maccabees	Ecclesiastes
2 Maccabees	Psalms (150 in number)	Song of Solomon
3 Maccabees	Job	Isaiah
Psalms (151 in number)	Proverbs of Solomon	Jeremiah
Job	Ecclesiastes	Lamentations
Proverbs of Solomon	Canticle of Canticles	Ezekiel
Ecclesiastes	Wisdom of Solomon	Daniel**
Song of Songs	Ecclesiasticus (Sirach)	Hosea
Wisdom of Solomon	Hosea	Joel
Wisdom of Sirach	Amos	Amos
Hosea	Micah	Obadiah
Amos	Joel	Jonah
Micah	Obadiah	Micah
Joel	Jonah	Nahum
Obadiah	Nahum	Habakkuk
Jonah	Habakkuk	Zephaniah
Nahum	Zephaniah	Haggai
Habakkuk	Haggai	Zechariah
Zephaniah	Zechariah	Malachi
Zechariah	Isaiah	
Malachi	Jeremiah	
Isaiah	Baruch*	
Jeremiah	Lamentations	
Baruch	Ezekiel	
Lamentation of Jeremiah	Daniel	
Epistle of Jeremiah		
Ezekiel		
Daniel***		

* Includes the Prayer of Manasseh
** Also known as 1&2 Esdras
*** "Susanna" is at the beginning of Daniel, "Bel and the Serpent" at the end. Also includes the "Hymn of the Three Young Men."

*Includes Epistle of Jeremiah

* Hebrew Old Testament is identical. See *TANAKH, a new translation of the Old Testament according to the traditional Hebrew text* (Philadelphia: JPS, 1985).
*Esther does not include those sections called "Additions to Esther."
**Daniel here does not include those sections separately labeled as the "Hymn of the Three Young Men," "Susanna," "Bel and the Serpent."

SOURCE: Adapted from Orthodox Study Bible (Nashville: Nelson 2008) xiii.

In Conclusion

THROUGHOUT HISTORY God has given to us an inspired and inerrant Word, revealed by His prophets and written in the languages of humanity that we might know Him. The Bible is the collection of that record of "God–breathed" Scripture. Old and New Testament claims for inspiration are confirmed by a review of historical affirmations in the face of various conflicting theories of inspiration.

When the question is raised about the books to be contained within the catalogue of inspired writings, the historical record affirms the traditional canon of the Hebrew Scriptures. The Hebrew canon, as followed by the historic Protestant view, is compared and contrasted with Roman Catholic, Eastern Orthodox, and secular views. Again the traditional canon of the Hebrew Bible, the Masoretic Text, and the canon of the Greek New Testament, without the Apocrypha and pseudepigrapha, are confirmed.

Attention to the writing of biblical texts, the languages, and materials of writing is an important development. Once written, the great Hebrew, Greek, Aramaic, and Latin manuscripts were preserved, discovered, and translated into various languages. Publication of these textual materials has moved well beyond a single or dual source. The "basic" Hebrew, the Masoretic Text, is now available from many different sources (see chap. 12). The Greek text of the Old Testament, the Septuagint (LXX), is available in several venues, along with critical commentaries (see chaps. 12 and 17). The Greek New Testament text currently has several different traditions, including the Textus Receptus (TR), the Majority Text (Ï), Critical text of the West-cott-Hort (W–H) tradition, the Nestle-Aland and UBS texts (NA27/UBS4), the Society of Biblical Literature (SBL) text, and several individual texts. The Latin text of the Old Latin, Vulgate, and other translations are available, as well as the Dead Sea Scrolls, Discoveries in the Judean Desert, the Nag Hammadi texts, and other Coptic discoveries. There are also the new emphases on lectionaries.

All these materials, and more, provide the serious student of Scripture with an awesome responsibility in translating the Bible texts into English and other languages. Some translations present or introduce dangerous aberrant teaching, doctrinal distortion, or theological heresies that may be, and indeed have been, introduced into the translation itself. The great diversity and multiplication of translations brings an even greater responsibility for the reader to understand the background of the translators and to know the translators' source documents. The translators' goal should always be to communicate the whole counsel of God contained in His inspired and inerrant Book.

For the sincere, seeking student of the Bible, receiving such communication from personal reading holds the promise of renewal, transformation, and hope of unending life with God (see Isa. 55:10–12).

Acknowledgments

Several individuals have contributed to this work. It is our pleasure to acknowledge Dr. Joseph Holden, president of Veritas Evangelical Seminary, Murrieta, California, whose research contribution, consultation, and the securing of rare photographs for publication has enhanced the value of this book in many ways. We also wish to thank Veritas Evangelical Seminary for its strong stance on biblical inerrancy and assistance in making this work a reality.

A word of appreciation is also due to Zev Radovan of BibleLandPictures.com, who has graciously made available his quality archaeological photographs. They are used by permission. We are grateful as well to John C. Tyler, Ph.D., who supplied a valuable photograph of the Isaiah A Scroll, to Donald L. Brake Sr., Dean Emeritus of Multnomah Biblical Seminary, Portland, Oregon, and to Jim Bolton of Dallas, Texas.

A special thanks goes to W. Harold Rawlings of the Rawlings Foundation for permission to photograph Bibles from its rare Bible collection on display at the Dead Sea Scrolls exhibit at Southwestern Biblical Theological Seminary, Fort Worth, Texas, and to Dr. C. Berry Driver Jr., the dean of libraries, and archives secretary Christina Hoeffner Floyd for their gracious assistance.

Finally, we acknowledge the Archdiocese of Chicago for their assistance with this book.

SUBJECT INDEX

PERSON INDEX

SCRIPTURE INDEX

(Order of Book Based on Orthodox [Eastern] Old Testament)

A General Introduction to the Bible

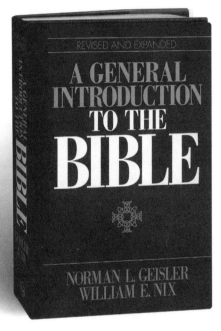

978-0-8024-2916-2

The most important book in the world must be handled with precision and understanding. The revised and expanded *A General Introduction to the Bible* provides the resources and tools to understand God's Word in a comprehensive manner. Giving special emphasis to conservative scholarship, the authors discuss the doctrine of inspiration, recent trends in textual criticism, canonization, and modern English translations, among many other topics. Photographs and charts illustrate important details. *A General Introduction to the Bible* is an indispensable tool for any student of Scripture.

Also available as an eBook

MOODY
PUBLISHERS

www.MoodyPublishers.com